☑ P9-CDA-362

# WINDOWS
# SERVER
# HACKS™

WITHDRAWN
NORTHEASTERN ILLINOIS
UNIVERSITY LIBRARY

*Mitch Tulloch*

## O'REILLY®

Beijing · Cambridge · Farnham · Köln · Paris · Sebastopol · Taipei · Tokyo

**Windows Server Hacks**™
by Mitch Tulloch

Copyright © 2004 O'Reilly Media, Inc. All rights reserved.
Printed in the United States of America.

Published by O'Reilly Media, Inc., 1005 Gravenstein Highway North, Sebastopol, CA 95472.

O'Reilly & Associates books may be purchased for educational, business, or sales promotional use. Online editions are also available for most titles (*safari.oreilly.com*). For more information, contact our corporate/institutional sales department: (800) 998-9938 or *corporate@oreilly.com*.

| | | | |
|---|---|---|---|
| **Editor:** | Rael Dornfest | **Production Editor:** | Philip Dangler |
| **Series Editor:** | Rael Dornfest | **Cover Designer:** | Hanna Dyer |
| **Executive Editor:** | Dale Dougherty | **Interior Designer:** | David Futato |

**Printing History:**

| | |
|---|---|
| March 2004: | First Edition. |

Nutshell Handbook, the Nutshell Handbook logo, and the O'Reilly logo are registered trademarks of O'Reilly Media, Inc. The *Hacks* series designations, *Windows Server Hacks*, the image of a squeegee, "Hacks 100 Industrial-Strength Tips and Tricks," and related trade dress are trademarks of O'Reilly Media, Inc.

Many of the designations used by manufacturers and sellers to distinguish their products are claimed as trademarks. Where those designations appear in this book, and O'Reilly Media, Inc. was aware of a trademark claim, the designations have been printed in caps or initial caps.

While every precaution has been taken in the preparation of this book, the publisher and author(s) assume no responsibility for errors or omissions, or for damages resulting from the use of the information contained herein.

Ronald Williams Library
Northeastern Illinois University

 This book uses RepKover™, a durable and flexible lay-flat binding.

ISBN: 0-596-00647-0
[C]

# Contents

Credits . . . . . . . . . . . . . . . . . . . . . . . . . . . . . . . . . . . . . . . . . . . . . . . . . . . . . . . . . . vii

Foreword . . . . . . . . . . . . . . . . . . . . . . . . . . . . . . . . . . . . . . . . . . . . . . . . . . . . . . . xvii

Preface . . . . . . . . . . . . . . . . . . . . . . . . . . . . . . . . . . . . . . . . . . . . . . . . . . . . . . . . . . xix

Chapter 1. General Administration . . . . . . . . . . . . . . . . . . . . . . . . . . . . . . . 1

   1. Use Run As to Perform Administrative Tasks         1

   2. Drag and Drop to the Run Menu         7

   3. Find and Replace Registry Keys from a Command line         9

   4. Automatically Log On After Booting         10

   5. Wait for and Optionally Terminate a Process         13

   6. Shut Down a Remote Computer         21

   7. Rename Mapped Drives         26

   8. Execute a Command on Each Computer in a Domain         27

   9. Add, Remove, or Retrieve Environment Variables         31

  10. Extend Group Policy         34

  11. Disable EFS         37

  12. Get Event Log Information         39

  13. Shortcut to Remote Assistance         42

  14. Desktop Checker         43

  15. Top Five Tools         56

  16. myITforum.com         58

Chapter 2. Active Directory . . . . . . . . . . . . . . . . . . . . . . . . . . . . . . . . . . . . . . 62

  17. Retrieve the List of Old Domain Computer Accounts         62

  18. Automate Creation of OU Structure         65

19. Modify All Objects in the OU      69

20. Delegate Control of an OU to a User      70

21. Send OU Information in Active Directory to an HTML Page      72

22. Display Active Directory Information      75

23. Store and Display Contact Information in Active Directory      77

24. Restore the Active Directory Icon in Windows XP      85

**Chapter 3. User Management** . . . . . . . . . . . . . . . . . . . . . . . . . . . . . . . . **88**

25. Search for Domain Users      88

26. Manage User Accounts in Active Directory      91

27. Get a List of Disabled Accounts      93

28. Get User Account Information      95

29. Check for Passwords that Never Expire      97

30. Enumerate Group Membership to a CSV File      99

31. Modify User Properties for All Users in a Particular OU      102

32. Check Group Membership and Map Drives in a Logon Script      103

33. Script Creation of a User's Home Directory and Permissions      106

34. Prevent Ordinary Users from Creating Local Accounts      108

35. Put a Logoff Icon on the Desktop      109

**Chapter 4. Networking Services** . . . . . . . . . . . . . . . . . . . . . . . . . . . . . . **111**

36. Manage Services on Remote Machines      111

37. Simplify DNS Aging and Scavenging      115

38. Troubleshoot DNS      120

39. Manually Recreate a Damaged WINS Database      123

40. Change WINS for All Enabled Adapters      124

41. Ensure DHCP Server Availability      126

42. Change a Network Adapter's IP Info      128

43. Change from Static IP to DHCP      129

44. Release and Renew IP Addresses      131

45. Use netsh to Change Configuration Settings      132

46. Remove Orphaned Network Cards      133

47. Implement Windows 2000 Network Load Balancing      135

**Chapter 5. File and Print** . . . . . . . . . . . . . . . . . . . . . . . . . . . . . . . . . . . **138**

48. Map Network Drives      138

49. Determine Who Has A Particular File Open on the Network      140

50. Display a Directory Tree .......................................... 142

51. Automate Printer Management ..................................... 144

52. Set the Default Printer Based on Location ........................ 146

53. Add Printers Based on Name of Computer ......................... 147

## Chapter 6. IIS ....................................................... 164

54. Back Up the Metabase ............................................ 164

55. Restore the Metabase ............................................ 171

56. Map the Metabase ............................................... 173

57. Metabase Hacks ................................................. 180

58. Hide the Metabase .............................................. 187

59. IIS Administration Scripts ...................................... 189

60. Run Other Web Servers .......................................... 199

61. IISFAQ ......................................................... 201

## Chapter 7. Deployment ............................................... 203

62. Get Started with RIS ........................................... 203

63. Customize RIS .................................................. 208

64. Tune RIS ....................................................... 214

65. Customize SysPrep .............................................. 216

66. Remove Windows Components from the Command Line ................. 222

67. Unattended Installation of Windows Components ................... 224

68. Easily Create a Network Boot Disk .............................. 225

## Chapter 8. Security ................................................. 227

69. Fundamentals of a Virus-Free Network ........................... 227

70. Antivirus FAQ .................................................. 237

71. Rename the Administrator and Guest Accounts .................... 239

72. Get a List of Local Administrators ............................. 241

73. Find All Computers that Are Running a Service .................. 242

74. Grant Administrative Access to a Domain Controller ............. 249

75. Secure Backups ................................................. 251

76. Find Computers with Automatic logon Enabled ................... 256

77. Security FAQ ................................................... 257

78. Microsoft Security Tools ....................................... 260

**Chapter 9. Patch Management** ................................... 264

    79. Best Practices for Patch Management      264

    80. Beginners Guide to Enterprise Patch Management      271

    81. Patch-Management FAQ      275

    82. Enumerate Installed Hotfixes      277

    83. Apply Patches in the Correct Order      279

    84. Windows Update FAQ      279

    85. Obtain Updates via the Windows Update Catalog      282

    86. Use Automatic Updates Effectively      284

    87. Use Group Policy to Configure Automatic Updates      290

    88. Automatic Updates FAQ      293

    89. Software Update Services FAQ      294

**Chapter 10. Backup and Recovery** ............................... 299

    90. Collect Disaster Recovery Files      299

    91. Back Up Individual Files from the Command Line      303

    92. Back Up System State on Remote Machines      306

    93. Back Up and Restore a Certificate Authority      309

    94. Back Up EFS      316

    95. Work with Shadow Copies      322

    96. Back Up and Clear the Event Logs      331

    97. Back Up the DFS Namespace      334

    98. Recover with Automated System Recovery      336

    99. Recovery Roadmap      342

   100. Data Recovery of Last Resort      348

**Index** ...................................................... 349

# Credits

## About the Author

Mitch Tulloch is the author of over a dozen computer books, including three Nutshells for O'Reilly & Associates, Inc. (*Microsoft Exchange Server in a Nutshell*, *Windows 2000 Administration in a Nutshell*, and *Windows Server 2003 in a Nutshell*), two encyclopedias for Microsoft Press (the *Microsoft Encyclopedia of Networking*, currently in its second edition, and the *Microsoft Encyclopedia of Security*), and a string of titles for system administrators from Osborne/McGraw-Hill. Mitch has also written feature articles for industry magazines such as *NetworkWorld* and *Microsoft Certified Professional Magazine*, has developed university-level courses in Windows system administration, and provides training and consulting in Microsoft platforms and products. Mitch is based in Winnipeg, Canada, and you can contact him through his web site (*http://www.mtit.com*).

## Contributors

The following people contributed their hacks, writing, and inspiration to this book:

- Dennis Abbott is a columnist on myITforum.com (*http://www.myitforum.com*) and has been working in the high tech industry for eight years. He has worked with Microsoft Systems Management Server since Version 1.1 and with Windows NT Server since Version 3.51. Dennis discovered the power of Microsoft scripting while building in-house solutions for software distribution that required industry-standard infrastructure and a minimum amount of code. He has coded numerous scripts that combine Windows Management Instrumentation, Active Directory Service Interfaces, and Windows Scripting Host to create simple solutions to complex problems. He currently works for Schneider National in Green Bay, WI, where he bicycles to work through rain, sleet, or snow. Previous employers include Dell Computers and Advanced Micro Devices. He can be reached at *speckled_trout@hotmail.com*.

- Sean Ademy is a columnist on myITforum.com (*http://www.myitforum.com*) and has been in the IT industry for eight years. He is thankful to be lucky enough to be able to turn a hobby into a career. He is a life-long resident of St. Petersburg, FL, where he currently resides with his wife, Wendy, and son, Kyle. In his spare time, you can usually find Sean cheering for his hometown Tampa Bay Buccaneers, playing one of his guitars, or fishing the waters of Tampa Bay with Wendy. You can reach Sean at *seanademy@yahoo.com*.

- Michael Brainard is a columnist on myITforum.com (*http://www.myitforum.com*) and has worked in the computer industry for the past 10 years. He has worked in Tennessee, Georgia, and Florida. During that time he has worked for companies such as Eastman Chemical Company, Cox Communications, MCI, and Motorola. He currently runs his own business, Computing Xperts (CX) (*http://www.computingxperts.com*), in the South Florida area. He has spent 6 of his 10 years in the computer industry administrating Systems Management Server (SMS), package automation, and scripting, and he spent the other 4 years offering automated solutions utilizing Active Directory and Group Policy. In his current assignment, he is working as a consultant for Mortgage Systems International to design an SMS 2003 hierarchy for an international mortgage company.

- Chris Crowe works as a Database Administrator for Trimble in Christchurch, New Zealand. He has a MCP, MCP+I, MCSA, and MCSE, and he has been a Microsoft MVP since 1997, specializing in Internet Information Server (IIS). In early 2000, Chris started a web site called IISFAQ (*http://www.IISFAQ.com*) as a resource to help him maintain a set of answers to frequently asked questions on the *microsoft.public.inetserver.iis* newsgroup on *msnews.microsoft.com*. IISFAQ has since grown to be the premier independent IIS resource on the Internet. Chris can be reached via IISFAQ or via email at *chris@iisfaq.com*.

- Matthew Goedtel is a columnist on myITforum.com (*http://www.myitforum.com*) and is President and CEO of IT Centric Inc. (*http://www.itcentric.biz*), an IT solutions and consulting company that offers professional services and technology solutions. Matthew founded IT Centric in 2002, with the vision of forming a leading-edge solutions firm, creating innovative solutions while ensuring cost effectiveness. Prior to IT Centric, he was Senior Systems Architect with National Life of Vermont, where he led the design and migration to Windows 2000, evaluated and redefined single vendor solution for data center server and storage solutions, assisted with the design and implementation of a SAN and enterprise backup solution, and much more. Prior to National Life, he held a Systems Engineer position at Merrill Lynch, developing change and configuration management solutions and assisting in the development and support of a global Windows NT 4.0 infrastructure. Matthew has also worked as a consultant for many leading financial and retail companies throughout his career, providing similar responsibilities.

- John Gormly is a columnist on myITforum com (*http://www.myitforum. com*) and has worked for a leading public accounting firm for the last 15 years. He earned his bachelor's degree in Accounting and Finance from the University of Cincinnati. He began his career as an auditor and made the transition in to IT nine years ago, when he was asked to head the IT department for the firm's Cincinnati location. He is now a Regional Technology Director and is responsible for all aspects of technology, including PC support, LAN/WAN infrastructure, telecommunications, project management, training, IT deployments, and personnel management. John has written many training courses for end users, technical articles for newsletters, and presentations specifically for the IT community. He specializes in all Microsoft operating systems and all versions of Microsoft Office. He also maintains certifications in Novell Netware (CNE3, 4, and 5) and is an A+ Certified Technician. John lives in Lebanon, OH, with his wife, Cynthia, and three young sons—John, Jacob, and Joshua. John can be reached at *jgormlyjr@yahoo.com*.

- Harvey Hendricks is a columnist on myITforum.com (*http://www. myitforum.com*) and started working with computers as a hobby that later became an occupation. He bought his first computer in 1982 and taught himself to write basic language programs. Writing programs soon went from being a hobby to an obsession, and when a career change became desirable he returned to college after an 18-year hiatus. There he became a member of a national honor society and earned a degree in Computer Science in 1993. He is employed at a great company in Houston, Texas, where his responsibilities include Microsoft Systems Management Server, Network Associates Inc. Total Virus Defense, IBM Tivoli Storage Manager, Microsoft Software Update Server, RSA SecurID, and SecurPBX. He holds the following certifications: TIAComp A+, Microsoft Certified Professional, and Microsoft Certified Systems Engineer. He is active in the martial arts, holding a second degree black belt in Tae Kwon Do and a first degree black belt in Torite-jutsu, and he is a member in good standing of Dragon Society International. He rides his Harley Davidson motorcycle every chance he gets and in his spare time also likes riding his dirt bikes, scuba diving, camping, hunting, fishing, and snow skiing.

- Don Hite is a columnist on myITforum.com (*http://www.myitforum.com*). The eldest of four children, he was born to American parents in the Army hospital at Wurzburg Germany in November 1957. After living in Bad Kissingen, Germany, for the first few years of his life, the Hite family moved back to the United States when Don was still in khaki army diapers. Educated by trade as a commercial maintenance electrician and holding a master electrician's license, Don made the career change from terminating copper conductor cable to terminating Ethernet cable in the early 1990s. Don lives in Raymore, MO, with his wife, Ginny. He has a son, Lee, a stepdaughter, Lisa, and a grandson named Blake.

- David Jaffe is a columnist on myITforum.com (*http://www.myitforum.com*) and has been in IT for over six years. He has worked with a wide variety of applications specializing in system management. Dave is the co-owner of SMSExpert.com (*http://www.smsexpert.com*), the largest provider of SMS third-party tools.

- Janis Keim is a columnist on myITforum.com (*http://www.myitforum.com*) and is the PC Technical Support Supervisor for State Street, a mutual funds company in Kansas City, MO, and has over 15 years of experience in computer technology. As the SMS administrator for approximately 1,700 workstations, her responsibilities include software packaging, testing, and deployment. She is also responsible for image build creation from start to finish, deployment of new PCs, ePO administration, security-related patch deployment for all workstations, maintenance of the company's entire fire call password process, and management of six support personnel. She is also cofounder of the Kansas City Regional SMS User Group (KCRSMSUG).

- Tim Kelly is a columnist on myITforum.com (*http://www.myitforum.com*) and is Technology Leader for TSYS (*http://www.tsys.com*), the world's largest credit card processing company. Tim leads the implementation of Microsoft.NET-based web services and applications. He worked for three years at Microsoft (1998–2001) during the time of the Windows 2000 rollout and assisted multiple enterprise customers with Active Directory implementations. He has worked extensively in e-commerce and the highly available web applications space during the last five years and counts as specialties IIS, MSCS, MS SQL high availability and management, Active Directory, and core network technologies. He is a graduate of the University of Idaho and received a Master's degree in Business from Auburn University. Tim enjoys his family— Lynn, Russell, and Jackson—when he's not jumping out of perfectly good airplanes. His web site is *http://www.skydiveopelika.net*.

- Thomas Lee (*http://www.psp.co.uk/tfl/tfl.htm*) is Chief Technologist at QA, the UK's largest independent training firm, and has worked with Windows since it was first released. He graduated from Carnegie Mellon University and subsequently worked on two successful operating system projects (Comshare's Commander II and ICL's VME) before joining Andersen Consulting in 1981, where he was a manager in the London office. He was an independent consultant from 1987 until he joined QA in 2003, where he now lectures, consults, and owns QA's technical portfolio. Thomas is a Microsoft Certified Systems Engineer (MCSE), Microsoft Certified Trainer (MCT), Microsoft Valued Professional (MVP) and Microsoft Regional Director (Europe). Thomas lives in a cottage in the English countryside with his wife, Susan, and daughter, Rebecca.

- Tim Mintner is a columnist on myITforum.com (*http://www.myitforum. com*) and is President and a Systems Architect Consultant for MMH Services (*http://www.mmhservices.com*). Tim has worked in the IT industry for over 10 years and has designed Microsoft networks for over 50 companies in the Midwest. Tim specializes in Microsoft Infrastructure technologies and has a deep background in Active Directory, SMS, SQL Server, MOM, Exchange, and ISA server. Tim is based in St. Louis, MO, where he runs the Microsoft Infrastructure Professional Users Group (*http://www.mipug.org*). Tim can often be found answering questions in the forums at myITforum.com. You can reach Tim by emailing him at *tmintner@mmhservices.com*.

- Chris Mosby is a columnist on myITforum.com (*http://www.myitforum. com*) and worked for three years at Bechtel Hanford Inc. (BHI) as a full-time SMS/Virus Protection Administrator. During his tenure at that company, Chris turned SMS into an essential management tool for BHI. His complete redesign of BHI's antivirus system and antivirus policy led to the elimination of 7,356 viruses and to zero network downtime due to virus infection from January 2000 until he left employment at BHI in June 2003. At last report, this antivirus system is still protecting the BHI network and was able to fend off thousands of additional virus infections during the global outbreaks of Blaster, Mimail, Welchia, and Swen viruses during the period of August and September 2003. His other accomplishments include beta-testing the current version of SMS Installer for Microsoft, designing and implementing the initial SMS 2.0 system of Bechtel National's Waste Treatment Plant Project, obtaining his Symantec Product Specialist Certification in Norton AntiVirus Corporate Edition 7.5/7.6, and coauthoring *Configuring Symantec AntiVirus Corporate Edition* (Syngress). Chris is also the creator of SMS Admin gear (*http://www.cafeshops.com/smsadmin*). Chris now works as the SMS Administrator for a large regional bank and lives in Tupelo, MS, with the love of his life, his wife Debbie. He can be contacted at *mozbe@yahoo.com*.

- Marcus Oh is a team leader for the Windows Core Technologies Group at Cox Communications, Inc. (*http://www.cox.com*), specializing in Systems Management. He lives happily with his wife, Joanna, in Alpharetta, GA. In his spare time, Marcus writes articles for myITforum.com (*http://www.myitforum.com*), maintains geek status by reading a mound of technical articles and white papers, and helps his wife with her web site (*http://www.webcritter.net*). He can be reached at *marcus@webcritter.net*.

- Rob Olson is a columnist on myITforum.com (*http://www.myitforum. com*) and is the founder of DudeWorks Software (*http://www. dudeworks.com*), which develops add-on solutions for SMS and many other Windows systems-management tools and solutions and provides custom systems-management programming solutions. Rob also serves as a senior software distribution engineer for a major financial company in the United States, supporting over 50,000 (and growing) SMS clients. He can be reached at *rob@dudeworks.com*.

- Marcin Policht has been contributing to a number of popular technology web sites, such as myITforum.com (*http://www.myitforum.com*), ServerWatch (*http://www.ServerWatch.com*), and Database Journal (*http://databasejournal.com*) for several years. While he focuses on engineering and administration of large Windows deployments (primarily in financial institutions) involving a variety of Windows-based products, such as SMS, SQL, IIS, Exchange, and Citrix, he is also interested in programming and scripting topics. This interest is best exemplified by his book *WMI Essentials for Automating Windows Management* (SAMS), published in 2001. He also cowrote *Windows 2003 Server Bible* (Wiley) and *Mastering Active Directory for Windows Server 2003* (Sybex). Marcin has also been actively involved as a technical trainer in the field of certifications. One of the first recipients of Windows 2000 and Windows 2003 MCSE and MCSA, he has also worked with Microsoft on setting criteria for Windows 2000 Clustering exam.

- Brian Rogers is a columnist on myITforum.com (*http://www.myitforum. com*) and is currently a consultant with Collective Technologies Inc. (*http://www.colltech.com*), providing SMS 2.0 and 2003 analysis, proof of concepts, implementations, and upgrades, with focus on patch management. His previous experience includes over five years with Systems Management Server, beginning with SMS 1.2 and continuing through to

SMS 2003, over two years as an MCT, teaching SMS 1.2 and 2.0; and over three years as an SMS 2.0 Administrator.

- Janet Ryding is a columnist on myITforum.com (*http://www.myitforum.com*), based in the UK, and has more than 10 years of experience in the IT industry. Working mainly with Windows NT/2000, Citrix, and the standard BackOffice products, she provides network consultation to a variety of large multinational organizations and has worked in the past for Ford Motor Company, the Ministry of Defense, and the National Health Service. Janet holds an MCSE in NT4 and 2000, the Citrix CCA and CCSP certifications, and Cisco's CCNA. Janet is currently working on a variety of projects and is looking to move into more project management roles. She can be reached at *pn1995@yahoo.co.uk*.

- Peter Rysavy is a columnist on myITforum.com (*http://www.myitforum.com*) and is currently the webmaster and network administrator at a small private business college. He spends his day taking care of the academic network and labs, administering an Exchange email system and the college intranet, supporting the campus-wide wireless network, and maintaining the college web site. In his spare time, Peter is actively involved in the Tablet PC community, evangelizing the platform, contributing news stories, interacting with users, and writing about Tablet PCs on his web site, Tabula PC (*http://www.kstati.com/tabula*).

- Hans Schefske is a columnist on myITforum.com (*http://www.myitforum.com*) and has over eight years experience engineering and designing the architecture and implementation of Microsoft client/server-based network solutions. Consulting and leading projects in the IT industry, he has provided technical expertise in the areas of designing and implementing infrastructures for large enterprise-level companies such as Nabisco, Prudential, AIG, Simpson, Thatcher and Bartlett, Novartis, and Hoffman LaRoche Pharmaceuticals. In 2003, Hans was awarded a Microsoft Most Valuable Professional (MVP) Award for SMS for his outstanding technical skills and willingness to share knowledge with his peers. As a technical author at myITforum.com, he provides technical information, tools, scripts, and utilities for IT professionals and administrators to better assist them in managing their Microsoft-based solutions. Hans is currently a Senior Active Directory and SMS consultant at a large telecommunications company based in Atlanta, GA.

- Pat Sklodowski is a contributor to myITforum.com.com (*http://www.myitforum.com*) and a Microsoft Certified Systems Engineer with over eight years of industry experience. His specialties include Windows NT/2000, Active Directory, SMS, Exchange, and scripting. Pat is currently working as a Senior Engineer with a global provider of engineering solutions and specialized staffing. He is responsible for developing new initiatives, architectural solutions, technical project-management, and ongoing support. Pat can be reached at *psklodow@yahoo.com*.

- Donnie Taylor is a columnist for several web sites, including myITforum.com (*http://www.myitforum.com*), and is currently the Systems Management Administrator for Central Technology Services. His duties include the installation, maintenance, and administration of SMS, MOM, SQL, and various management applications. He has been with Central Technology Services for four years. Donnie lives with his wife and two daughters in Jefferson City, MO. He met his wife while attending Southwest Missouri State University, where he pursued degrees in CIS/MIS, English, and Anthropology. Donnie enjoys PC and console gaming, exploring his Cherokee heritage, and spending time with his family.

- Dan Thomson is a columnist on myITforum.com (*http://www.myitforum.com*) and an influential member of the IT staff at a local college, where he assists with many aspects of supporting the computing systems. Some of Dan's responsibilities include maintaining antivirus software, OS imaging, group policies, software deployments, and SMS. Dan is always happy to share whenever he can and can be found participating in many online forums and newsgroups. Dan enjoys spending time with his wife and 10-month-old daughter.

- Richard Threlkeld is a columnist on myITforum.com (*http://www.myitforum.com*) and was employed as a contractor for Motorola, where he eventually worked his way up to manage the SMS infrastructure for all of Motorola's Boynton Beach facilities, including packaging, software deployments, site maintenance, client support, and reporting. Along with his local SMS responsibilities, Richard also helped develop packages for Motorola's Global Packaging Team which distributed software and security updates to workstations and servers worldwide. In late 2002, Richard moved to San Diego, CA, to work for QUALCOMM Inc. (*http://www.qualcomm.com*). Richard currently heads the SMS Infrastructure for the QUALCOMM CDMA Technologies division, which spans locations worldwide, and deals with other Active Directory and engineering issues. Outside of work, Richard takes part in different SMS forums and user communities, where he is regularly found assisting other administrators with issues in their environments. Richard is also a Microsoft MVP for SMS because of his community involvement.

- Rod Trent, manager of myITforum.com (*http://www.myitforum.com*), is the leading expert on Microsoft Systems Management Server. He has over 18 years of IT experience, 8 of which have been dedicated to SMS. He is the author of such books as *Microsoft SMS Installer, Admin911: SMS,* and *IIS 5.0: A Beginner's Guide* and has written thousands of articles on technology topics. myITforum.com is the central location for third-party SMS support, as well as the online gathering place for IT professionals and the IT community. Rod speaks at least three times a year at various conferences and is a principal in NetImpress, Inc. (*http://www.netimpress.com*).

- Chuck Young is a columnist on myITforum.com (*http://www. myitforum.com*) and began his IT career during his time in the Air National Guard, when he converted an old Banyan Vines network to an NT environment. After pursuing a degree in Computer Science and holding several jobs in the computer industry, Chuck now finds himself working almost exclusively with Microsoft Systems Management Server (SMS). Often mistaken for SMSMAN, Chuck is just a dedicated perfectionist that will not settle for less than 80%; his philosophy is "Why give 100% at anything? It doesn't leave anything for the fun stuff!" Chuck can be reached at *chuck.young@acs-inc.com*.

- Oren Zippori is a columnist on myITforum.com (*http://www.myitforum. com*) and is currently working for Team Computers, a gold-certified Support Center for Microsoft. Oren specializes in system-management products and has also been involved in Windows 2000 and Exchange 2000 migrations. Oren also manages an open forum for Microsoft in Israel that supports SMS and MOM products. Oren spends his free time scuba diving, mountain climbing, and playing snooker. He knows how to enjoy a good fiction book and likes to write short stories for fun. You can reach him at *orenzp@hotmail.com*

## Acknowledgments

Talk about a book being a cooperative venture; this one was definitely so, for without the time, expertise, and content contributed by so many other IT professionals—many of them columnists on myITforum.com (*http:// www.myitforum.com*)—this book wouldn't be the valuable resource to Windows system administrators that it is. So, a big thanks to everyone who contributed hacks to this book. You deserve it first, so *thanks*! And thanks especially to Rod Trent, CEO of myITforum.com, for his friendship and support—thanks, man!

Second comes my thanks to Rael Dornfest, my editor at O'Reilly, who has been great fun to work with and whose gentle prodding has helped keep me focused on the task at hand—making this book as good as possible. Thanks, Rael!

Third in line for thanks is my agent, Neil Salkind of Studio B (*http://www.studiob.com*), for his friendship and support in writing this, my 14th book. Thanks, Neil!

Fourth, thanks to MTS Communications Inc. (*http://www.mts.ca*) for providing Internet services and web hosting for my web site (*http://www.mtit.com*), with special thanks to Dinis Prazeres there at MTS. Thanks!

Last but not least, thanks to my wife and business partner, Ingrid, coauthor of the *Microsoft Encyclopedia of Networking, 2nd Edition* and consultant for our company MTIT Enterprises. (*http://www.mtit.com*). Thanks, Schatz!

# Foreword
## I'm a Sci-Fi freak

Just because I work in the computer technology field, you might automatically assume that I'm also an avid science fiction reader. And, while there are many IT professionals who have never spoken a single word of Klingon or adeptly wielded a light saber made of paper towel rolls, if you point your finger at me, you can rest assured that your accusation is spot on. To be fair, my love of Science Fiction began years before I had my hands on a computer keyboard. I was practicing the Vulcan hand greeting long before I was potty trained, and I was mind-melding with my favorite pet before I knew how to feed myself. You can imagine my parents' joy.

When Mitch Tulloch approached me about helping out with Windows Server Hacks, there was no hesitation in my response. Even though I've known Mitch for years and his work is always top-notch, Mitch has an unfair advantage when it comes to making Windows Server Hacks successful—he actually carried the nickname of "The Vulcan" during his university days. So, using a kind of mind-meld, Mitch pieced together a culmination of the most powerful solutions on Earth to load Windows Server Hacks with tricks, tips, scripts, tools, and workarounds to help systems administrators manage their Windows-based networks. We've all bought books and ended up skipping pages or chapters because the information provided simply does not apply to our specific situation. But because the information in Windows Server Hacks comes from real world experience based on tried-and-true solutions, you'll probably use more of this book than any other in your tech library.

In addition to working with Mitch, I was also excited that Windows Server Hacks would include many solutions from the myITforum.com community. Among the myITforum.com membership, you'll find some of the smartest individuals in the industry who are willing to share their solutions to help make the IT world a better place. This fact becomes clearly evident as you read and implement the solutions in this book. And, when you're ready to find more solutions like those represented in Windows Server Hacks, you can stop by myITforum.com and experience the community.

As many of you know, Vulcans show no emotion. So, I guess I may have ultimately tipped my hat when I was doubly excited that Windows Server Hacks was an O'Reilly project. O'Reilly is one of the top publishers in the world, spreading high-quality information to IT workers everywhere. For that, I am honored for the opportunity to introduce this book. I know you'll find it as useful as I do.

To all those that contributed to this book, I salute you. Of course, that salute comes in the form of a perfectly crafted Vulcan hand greeting—Mitch would know.

—Rod Trent

Live long and prosper, Rod
—Mitch :-)

# Preface

For some time now, Microsoft Windows (in all its incarnations) has been the dominant desktop operating system for businesses small and large. But in recent years, the platform has also made significant inroads into the server side of the equation. In the late 1990s, for example, the now-legacy Windows NT 4.0 Server platform became popular for running web servers using IIS and largely displaced Novell NetWare in the file/print server arena. Other server applications that ran on top of NT, such as Microsoft Exchange and Microsoft SQL Server, also made Windows a top platform for messaging/collaboration and database servers.

Windows 2000 Server built upon the success of NT by adding increased stability, reliability, and a new feature called Active Directory that quickly overtook Novell Directory Services (NDS) as the dominant enterprise-level directory service product. And Windows Server 2003, the latest incarnation of server-side Windows, is likely to further cement Microsoft's dominant position in the enterprise, despite the serious challenges arising from Linux and other open source software.

Why has Microsoft made such rapid gains in the server market? The answer is found in the simplicity of administering the platforms. An easy-to-use GUI, a consistent set of tools, wizards that walk you through performing complex tasks—such features make it possible to learn how to install, configure, and maintain Windows servers in weeks, without any knowledge of a programming or scripting language or learning a lot of complicated command-line syntax. In fact, you can probably accomplish about 90% of all Windows administration without ever opening a command prompt or running a script.

But it's that other 10% that can really matter sometimes, and that's what this book is mainly about.

# Why Windows Server Hacks?

While most common, day-to-day tasks of Windows administration can be performed from the GUI, it's not always the best way, especially with complex or repetitive tasks. Scripts and command-line tools often provide a faster and more flexible approach, and Windows has grown more powerful in this area with the progressive addition of VBScript, Active Directory Services Interface (ADSI), Windows Management Instrumentation (WMI), and dozens of new commands to each new version of the platform. Unfortunately, learning to leverage the power of these different features takes time—a precious commodity for today's busy system administrator.

That's why a large portion of this book consists of scripts and other tools that can make your life much easier as an administrator. These tools, or *hacks*—quick and dirty solutions to problems or clever ways of doing things—were created by other professionals who have had to struggle to find solutions to administering their own Windows environments, and you can benefit from their expertise in two important ways. First, you can use their scripts, tools, tips, and advice to save valuable time as you manage your own Windows-based network. Second, by studying the scripts and learning a little VB/ADSI/WMI, you can easily customize these scripts to create even more powerful tools that meet your own specific needs.

## Getting and Using the Scripts

To save you the time and effort of typing long scripts by hand, all the scripts (except those that are only a few lines long) are available for download from the O'Reilly web site at *http://www.oreilly.com/catalog/winsvrhks/*.

Before you use them in your own networking environment, however, make sure you have the latest scripting engines on the workstation from which you run the scripts. You can download the latest scripting engines from the Microsoft Scripting home page (*http://msdn.microsoft.com/scripting/*).

Also note that, when working with the Active Directory Services Interface (ADSI), you must have the same applicable rights you need to use the built-in administrative tools. See Microsoft's ADSI web page (*http://www.microsoft.com/windows2000/techinfo/howitworks/activedirectory/adsilinks.asp*) for more information.

Furthermore, for VB scripts that interact with WMI, apply the most current version of the WMI agents, which are downloadable from the MSDN WMI SDK (*http://msdn.microsoft.com/library/default.asp?url=/library/en-us/wmisdk/wmi/wmi_start_page.asp*). This information is important enough that we mention it again several times at the beginning of the first few chapters.

Finally, please note that while every all of the scripts, tools, procedures, and resources described and contained in this book have been tested, both the author and those experts who contributed them make no guarantee or warranty that they will work as intended in your own networking environment, nor do we assume any liability or responsibility for any loss or damage arising from their use. In other words, the information provided in this book is presented on an *as is* basis, and we strongly recommend that you try out a hack in a test environment first before using it in your company's production environment.

## How to Use This Book

Although this book is divided into chapters, as described in the following section, you can use it in a variety of different ways. One approach is to think of the book as a toolbox and start by becoming familiar with the tools in each chapter. Then, when a need arises or a problem occurs, you can simply use the right tool for the job. Or, you might decide to browse or read the book from cover to cover, studying the procedures and scripts to learn more about power administration of Windows systems. Some of the hacks are helpful in this area, because they contain tutorials about complex subjects or well-documented scripts. You might also pick one chapter and see what you find useful to your current situation or might find helpful in the future.

## How This Book Is Organized

Whichever way you choose to use this book, you will probably first want to familiarize yourself with the contents, so here's a brief synopsis of each chapter and what you'll find:

Chapter 1, *General Administration*
> Think of this chapter as the removable top drawer of your toolbox—usually cluttered, but containing your favorite, indispensable tools. The topics in this chapter include ways of hacking the Run As command, collecting event log information, running commands, extending your environment, shutting down processes, renaming mapped drives, and more. You'll also learn how to disable file encryption if you don't need or want it, collect configuration settings from remote machines, use automatic logon where it's safe to do so, and make it easier for users to access Remote Assistance when they need to. We'll also list some of our favorite third-party tools and a terrific online resource for Microsoft management technologies.

Chapter 2, *Active Directory*
> Most of the time, when you're administering Active Directory, you'll find the GUI tools are easy to use but ill suited for complex or repetitive

tasks. That's where scripts come in, and this chapter includes scripts that leverage ADSI and WMI to make your life easier. These scripts can be used to perform tasks such as searching for old computer accounts, creating organizational units (OUs), delegating authority over OUs, and displaying information about objects stored in Active Directory.

Chapter 3, *User Management*

A large part of day-to-day administration of an Active Directory environment is managing users and their accounts. The usual way of doing this is by using the GUI, but when it comes to organizations with hundreds or even thousands of users, this approach can be frustrating. This chapter is mostly about alternatives—ways of doing things faster using scripts. You'll find scripts for displaying information about users, finding specific users on your network, changing user passwords, unlocking user accounts, getting a list of disabled accounts, displaying which groups a user belongs to, and more. If you're familiar with VBScript, you can also customize these scripts further to meet the specific needs of your own networking environment.

Chapter 4, *Networking Services*

Under the hood of Windows are the core networking services and components that enable systems to communicate across a network. These components include services such as Dynamic Host Configuration Protocol (DHCP), Domain Name System (DNS), Windows Internet Name Service (WINS), and other services that run on top of TCP/IP. Configuring these services can be complex, and it can be hard to pinpoint the problem when things go wrong. This chapter is about managing such services and other networking components. You'll learn how to use a script to manage services on remote computers, how to ensure DHCP server availability so your clients can communicate, how DNS aging and scavenging work and can be configured, how to troubleshoot common DNS problems when Active Directory is deployed, how to perform complicated network configuration tasks using scripts and from the command line, and several other important tasks.

Chapter 5, *File and Print*

File and print is the traditional bread and butter of networking, and while it's gradually being overtaken by more advanced document-management solutions, not many companies are planning on retiring their file servers anytime soon. Managing shared folders and printers also makes up a major component of an administrator's daily routine, and a high proportion of calls to help desk as well. So it's worth examining some new ways of doing old tasks, such as mapping drives or configuring default printers, as well as some ways to perform tasks that are not easy using standard Windows tools, including mapping the structure of a directory or determining who has a certain file open on the network. That's what this chapter is about—doing old tasks in new ways and making complex tasks simple.

Chapter 6, *IIS*

Internet Information Services (IIS) is one of the more popular features of Windows server platforms. Whether you're running IIS 5 (Windows 2000 Server) or IIS 6 (Windows Server 2003), the ability to hack the metabase (the place where IIS stores its configuration settings) lets you do things that are impossible to do using the standard GUI tool for managing IIS—namely, Internet Services Manager. Before you start hacking the metabase, however, you better be sure you've backed it up properly and know your way around inside it. Several hacks in this chapter deal with these topics, including how to restore the metabase when you have no working backup. Also included are tips on hiding the metabase from attackers to make it more secure, managing different aspects of IIS by using scripts, and allowing other HTTP services, such as the Apache web server, to run on Windows and coexist with IIS.

Chapter 7, *Deployment*

Administering Windows-based networks begins with deployment, and the focus of this chapter is on how to manage the installation (and uninstallation) of Windows 2000/XP/2003 and its individual components. In particular, the first several articles deal with Remote Installation Services (RIS) and Sysprep, two powerful but complex tools for installing Windows images on large numbers of machines. Other articles deal with removing unneeded components manually from the command line and during unattended setup, and creating a network boot disk for unattended installation of Windows. These tips and tools are designed to make the job of deploying Windows easier, so you can get on with the day-to-day job of configuring, maintaining, and troubleshooting systems on your network.

Chapter 8, *Security*

Probably no aspect of the system administrator's job is more important these days than security, and this is especially so with systems running Windows. The ever-increasing threats of viruses, worms, Trojans, and other exploits means administrators have to spend time and energy learning how to protect their company's networks against the wiles of malicious hackers on the Internet. This chapter looks at some of the ways you can protect your network from these threats. It includes coverage of best practices in virus protection, protecting Administrator accounts, securing backups, protecting domain controllers, and finding machines with automatic logon enabled. A security FAQ and a review of security tools you can download from Microsoft's web site round out this chapter and help you build an arsenal of best practices and tools that can help keep your network secure.

Chapter 9, *Patch Management*

Patch management is a way of life for system administrators nowadays. With the proliferation of Internet worms and other threats, new patches are being released for Windows platforms on an almost weekly basis. It takes time and energy to test these patches and deploy them on production systems, and occasionally something goes wrong and a patch designed to correct one problem actually creates another. The first key to effective patch management is proper business practices: test, deploy, and verify. The second key is proper tools; Windows platforms come with several built-in tools, while others can be obtained from Microsoft's web site and third-party vendors. The third key is knowledge—knowing how patch-management tools work and how to troubleshoot them when things go wrong. The hacks in this chapter touch on all three keys to effective patch management and help enlarge your understanding and skills in this crucial area of a system administrator's job description.

Chapter 10, *Backup and Recovery*

Finally, this chapter looks at the backup process and examines how to back up specific entities, such as your System State, certificate authority (CA) information, Encrypting File System (EFS) keys, and Distributed File System (DFS) namespace. We also look at how to back up something as simple as an individual file from the command line, to something as complicated as an entire system using the new Automated System Recover (ASR) feature of Windows Server 2003. Also included is a script that can be used to collect disaster recovery files and event logs from remote Windows 2000 servers. We also map out procedures you can try to recover a failed system, short of restoring everything from backup, navigating through a maze of options like Safe Mode, Emergency Repair, Last Known Good Configuration, and the Recovery Console. Finally, we mention a few services you can call on when your worst nightmare happens and you need to recover your business data from a failed disk that has no backup.

## Conventions Used in This Book

The following typographical conventions are used in this book:

*Italic*

Indicates new terms, URLs, email addresses, filenames, file extensions, pathnames, directories, and Unix utilities.

Constant width

Indicates commands, options, switches, variables, attributes, keys, functions, types, classes, namespaces, methods, modules, properties, parameters, values, objects, events, event handlers, XML tags, HTML tags, macros, the contents of files, or the output from commands.

**Constant width bold**

Used in examples and tables to show commands or other text that should be typed literally by the user.

*Constant width italic*

Used in examples, tables, and commands to show text that should be replaced with user-supplied values.

Color

The second color is used to indicate a cross-reference within the text.

> This icon signifies a tip, suggestion, or general note.

> This icon indicates a warning or caution.

The thermometer icons, found next to each hack, indicate the relative complexity of the hack:

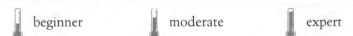

beginner          moderate          expert

## Using Code Examples

This book is here to help you get your job done. In general, you may use the code in this book in your programs and documentation. You do not need to contact us for permission unless you're reproducing a significant portion of the code. For example, writing a program that uses several chunks of code from this book does not require permission. Selling or distributing a CD-ROM of examples from O'Reilly books *does* require permission. Answering a question by citing this book and quoting example code does not require permission. Incorporating a significant amount of example code from this book into your product's documentation *does* require permission.

O'Reilly & Associates and the author both appreciate, but do not require, attribution. An attribution usually includes the title, author, publisher, and

ISBN. For example: "*Windows Server Hacks,* by Mitch Tulloch. Copyright 2004 O'Reilly & Associates, Inc., ISBN 0-596-00647-0."

If you feel your use of code examples falls outside fair use or the permission given above, feel free to contact us at *permissions@oreilly.com*.

## How to Contact Us

We have tested and verified the information in this book to the best of our ability, but you may find that features have changed (or even that we have made mistakes!). As a reader of this book, you can help us to improve future editions by sending us your feedback. Please let us know about any errors, inaccuracies, bugs, misleading or confusing statements, and typos that you find anywhere in this book.

Please also let us know what we can do to make this book more useful to you. We take your comments seriously and will try to incorporate reasonable suggestions into future editions. You can write to us at:

> O'Reilly & Associates, Inc.
> 1005 Gravenstein Hwy N.
> Sebastopol, CA 95472
> (800) 998-9938 (in the U.S. or Canada)
> (707) 829-0515 (international/local)
> (707) 829-0104 (fax)

To ask technical questions or to comment on the book, send email to:

> *bookquestions@oreilly.com*

For more information about this book and others, see the O'Reilly web site:

> *http://www.oreilly.com*

For details about *Windows Server Hacks*, including examples, errata, reviews, and plans for future editions, go to:

> *http://www.oreilly.com/catalog/winsvrhks/*

For code examples, additions and corrections, and other related miscellany:

> *http://www.oreilly.com/catalog/winsvrhks/*

## Got a Hack?

To explore Hacks books online or to contribute a hack for future titles, visit:

> *http://hacks.oreilly.com*

# CHAPTER ONE

# General Administration

## Hacks 1–16

We'll begin with a catchall chapter of tips and tools that cover a wide range of general Windows system administration topics. Think of this chapter as the removable top drawer of your toolbox—usually cluttered, but containing your favorite, indispensable tools. The topics in this chapter include ways of hacking the Run As command, collecting event log information, running commands, extending your environment, shutting down processes, renaming mapped drives, and more. You'll also learn how to disable file encryption if you don't need or want it, collect configuration settings from remote machines, use automatic logon where it's safe to do so, and make it easier for users to access Remote Assistance when they need it. We'll also list some of our favorite third-party tools and a terrific online resource for Microsoft management technologies.

A number of the hacks in this chapter include scripts. To ensure these scripts run properly on your systems, make sure you download the latest scripting engines on the workstation from which you run the scripts. You can get these scripting engines from the Microsoft Scripting home page at *http://msdn.microsoft.com/scripting/*. Also, when working with the Active Directory Services Interface (ADSI), you must have the same applicable rights you need to use the built-in administrative tools, which basically means that you need administrator credentials to run the scripts.

### HACK #1 Use Run As to Perform Administrative Tasks

Use Run As to protect your administrator workstation from Trojans and other nasties.

If you're lazy, like I am, you probably use the default administrator account on your desktop workstation for browsing the Web, checking your email, and managing the servers on your company's network.

Not a good idea.

What if you unknowingly visited a web page that executed a script that downloaded a Trojan to your machine? Your administrator account would be compromised, and the attacker would have total access to your workstation and possibly to your whole network! To avoid such dangers, administrators should always have two user accounts: a regular (user-level) account for ordinary activities, such as web browsing and messaging, and an administrator-level account, used only for performing administrative tasks. This way, when you are reading your email and suddenly remember you have to reschedule a backup, you can simply log off, log back on using your administrator account, perform the task, log off again, and log on again as a regular user.

Who am I kidding? That's too much to expect of a lazy system administrator.

## How Run As Works

The Run As service (called Secondary Logon service in Windows Server 2003 and Windows XP) is a hack designed to enable you to run programs by using alternate credentials while you're logged on using another account. For example, if you are an administrator and are logged on to your desktop using your regular user account, you won't be able to run administrative tools such as Computer Management, because they require administrator credentials to run properly. (Actually, you *can* open Computer Management as an ordinary user; you just can't do much with it.) Using Run As, however, you can run Computer Management as an administrator while remaining logged on as an ordinary user.

There are two ways to use Run As: using the GUI or from the command line. To use the GUI method, first find the program you want to run in Windows Explorer or My Computer. Then, for executables (*.exe* files), hold down the Shift key, right-click the program's icon, and select Run to open the Run As Other User dialog box shown in Figure 1-1. For MMC consoles (*.msc* files) and Control Panel utilities (*.cpl* files), you do the same thing but don't need to hold down the Shift key.

Once you specify the appropriate alternate credentials and click OK, the program you selected runs in the security context of those alternate credentials until you close or terminate the program. If you prefer, the alternative credentials can also be entered as *domain\user* or *user@domain*, which in Figure 1-1 would be *MTIT\Administrator* or *Administrator@mtit.com* for an example domain named *mtit.com* (replace these credentials with the name of your own domain). The advantage of doing it the way shown in Figure 1-1 is that, if your computer is a member server, you can specify a local user account by entering the name of the computer in the Domain field.

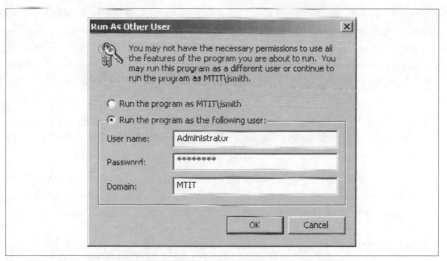

*Figure 1-1. Using Run As to run a program using administrator credentials*

Using Run As from the command line is just as easy, but you need to know the path to the program (unless the program file is located within the system path). For example, the Computer Management console file *compmgmt.msc* is located in the *\system32* directory. To run it as Administrator in the MTIT domain, simply type the following at a command prompt:

```
runas /user:MTIT\Administrator "mmc %windir\system32\compmgmt.msc"
```

You'll be prompted for a password for the account, after which Computer Management will open. Note that you can also type this command directly into the Run box (accessed by Start → Run).

## Limitations of Run As

While Run As is useful, it has some limitations. First, the alternate credentials you specify must have the Log On Locally user right on the computer. Since Run As is usually used with administrator credentials (which have that right by default), this is usually an issue only in certain circumstances. For example, say you grant a few knowledgeable users a second user account that belongs to the Power Users group, to allow them to update device drivers and perform other minor maintenance on their desktop computers. If you try to reduce the attack surface of your network by removing the right to Log On Locally from the Power Users group using Group Policy, then these users won't be able to perform such tasks.

Also, there are certain tasks you can't perform directly using Run As, such as opening the Printers folder to administer a printer that is connected to your machine. The reason for this is that the special folders such as Printers and

Network and Dial-up Connections are opened indirectly by the operating system, not by a command. You also can't use Run As to open Windows Explorer and access the filesystem on your computer as administrator, because the Windows shell *explorer.exe* is already running as your current desktop environment and Windows allows only one GUI shell to run at a time.

Finally, Run As also might not work if the program you are trying to run is located on a network share, because the credentials used to access the share might be different than the credentials used to run the program.

Most limitations have workarounds of some sort, if you try hard enough to find them. So, let's see if we can figure out ways to get around these limitations (except for the Log On Locally limitation, which is absolute).

**Running programs without an executable.** Say you want to change some settings for the Local Area Connection in the Network and Dial-up Connections folder. If you try doing this as an ordinary user, you'll get a message saying "The controls on this properties sheet are disabled because you do not have sufficient privileges to access them." Here's how to access these settings as an administrator without logging out of your regular account. Right-click on the task bar and open Task Manager. Then, switch to the Processes tab, select *explorer.exe*, and click End Process to kill the desktop but leave Task Manager running. Now, switch to the Applications tab, click New Task, type runas /user:MTIT\Administrator explorer.exe to run the Windows Explorer shell in an administrator context, and click OK. Finally, move Task Manager out of the way and type your password into the command-prompt window.

A new desktop will now appear, running in the security context of your administrator account. You can now change the settings of your Local Area Connection, modify the properties of a printer in the Printers folder, browse the filesystem, or do anything you want to do as administrator. But be sure to *leave Task Manager running*, because it is your only connection to your original desktop! You can minimize it so it won't be in the way.

Once you're finished performing your administrative tasks, you can return to your original desktop (the one running under the security context of your regular account) as follows. Maximize Task Manager so that you'll have access to it when your desktop disappears again. Then, to log off of your administrator session, click Start → Shut Down and select Log Off.

Do *not* try to log off by pressing Ctrl-Alt-Del and clicking Log Off, because this will log off the session for your regular user account.

Your administrator desktop has now disappeared, but Task Manager is still running (in the security context of your regular account), so switch to the Applications tab, click New Task, type runas /user:MTIT\Administrator explorer.exe, and click OK. Your desktop has returned.

At this point, you might ask, "Why should I go to all that trouble? It would be faster just to log off as a regular user and log on as an administrator." True, but any applications you have running as a regular user would then have to be terminated. Doing it the way shown here, however, leaves all your desktop applications running in the background.

**Running programs from network shares.** Here's how to get around the limitation of running programs from network shares with appropriate credentials. To run a program named *test.exe* found in the *TOOLS* share on server *SRV230*, use Start → Run to open a command-prompt window as administrator, type runas /user:MTIT\Administrator cmd to open a command shell in administrator context, and then map a drive to the shared folder by typing net use Z:\\SRV230\TOOLS. Now, switch to the Z: drive and run the program as desired. This lets you connect to the shared folder using domain administrator credentials and run the program under the same credentials. This approach is also useful for installing applications from a network distribution point.

## Run As Shortcuts

To make your life easier, instead of having to type stuff at the command line, you can use Run As to create a shortcut that will run a program under alternate credentials. For example, to run the Computer Management console from a Run As shortcut, right-click on your desktop, select New → Shortcut, and type %windir%\system32\compmgmt.msc as the command string. Name your shortcut Computer Management and click OK. Then, right-click on the shortcut, select Properties to open its properties sheet, and on the Shortcut tab select the checkbox labeled "Run program as other user" (on Windows Server 2003, click the Advanced button on the Shortcut tab to configure this). Now, whenever you double-click on the shortcut to run Computer Management, the Run As Other User dialog box (see Figure 1-1) will appear. Just type in your administrator password to run Computer Management in administrator context.

There's another way to create Run As shortcuts that you might find even easier to use. Just right-click on your desktop, select New → Shortcut, and type the following command string:

```
%windir%\system32\runas.exe /user:MTIT\Administrator "mmc %windir%\system32\
compmgmt.msc"
```

Save the shortcut with the name Computer Management. Now, when you double-click the shortcut, a command-prompt window opens, prompting you for the password for the *MTIT\Administrator* account. Type the password, press Enter, and Computer Management starts in administrator context.

What if you get tired of typing your administrator password each time you want to run a Run As shortcut? On Windows Server 2003, there's a way to get around that. Just create a new shortcut with this command string:

```
%windir%\system32\runas.exe /user:MTIT\Administrator /savecred "mmc
%windir%\system32\compmgmt.msc"
```

Notice the /savecred switch in this string. This option first appeared in Windows XP. The first time you double-click on the shortcut, a command-prompt window opens to prompt you for the password for the alternate credentials, just like before. The next time you double-click on the shortcut, however, you are not prompted for the password; it was stored on your machine the first time you ran the shortcut. Now you no longer have to type a password each time you use your Run As shortcut. Time-saver, right? Yes, but it's also a possible security hole: once the credentials for your administrator account are stored locally on the machine, they can be used to run *any* command-line program using administrator credentials.

Here's a scenario to illustrate what I mean. Let's say you need to run an administrative tool on a user's desktop machine without logging the user off the machine. You ask the user to take a coffee break. Then, you open a command-prompt window and use runas with /savecred to start the tool (you use /savecred because you might have to run several administrative tools and you don't want to have to type your complex 24-character password repeatedly). When you're finished, you close all the tools you started and walk away. When the user returns to her desktop, she opens a command prompt and types runas /user:MTIT\Administrator /savecred cmd. A command-prompt window opens, displaying administrator credentials in the title bar. The user now knows that she can use this approach to run any program on her machine using administrator credentials.

What did you do wrong as administrator in this scenario? Two things: you used /savecred on a user's desktop machine, which saved your administrator password locally on the machine, and you haven't renamed the default administrator account. If you had changed the name of this account to something complex and unknown to ordinary users, the runas /user:MTIT\ Administrator /savecred cmd command the user typed wouldn't work.

What do you do if you have used /savecred on an unsecured machine without thinking about the consequences? Just delete your stored credentials on the machine by opening Stored User Names and Passwords in the Control Panel.

# Drag and Drop to the Run Menu

**If you're tired of having to drop out to a command prompt and navigate through folders to run an executable that requires switches, try this.**

The following easy-to-use steps can be used to run the program of your choice from the Run menu with any command-line switches you need to include. This is much handier than opening a command prompt and changing to the directory where the executable is located, especially if long filenames are involved, which requires you to enclose your path in double quotes.

First, navigate in Windows Explorer to the executable you want to launch (Figure 1-2).

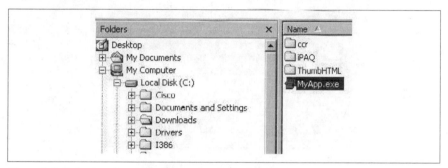

*Figure 1-2. Selecting the executable to run in Explorer*

Next, use Start → Run to invoke the Run menu (Figure 1-3).

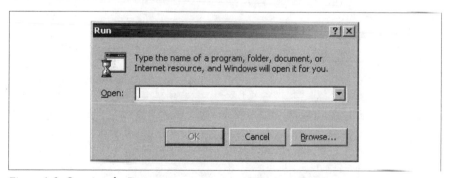

*Figure 1-3. Opening the Run menu*

Then, drag and drop your executable to the Run menu (Figure 1-4). Make sure the Open box is empty before you perform this step, or unexpected results might occur.

Now, simply add your switches and click OK to launch your application (Figure 1-5).

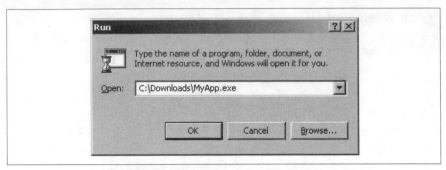

Figure 1-4. Dragging and dropping the executable into the Run menu

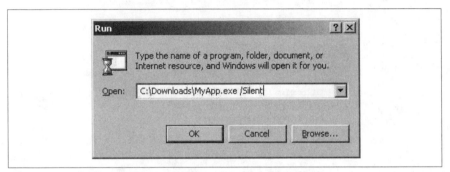

Figure 1-5. Adding switches as needed

You'll want to keep in mind that any filenames or paths that don't follow the old 8.3 naming convention should be within quotation marks to run properly (Figure 1-6).

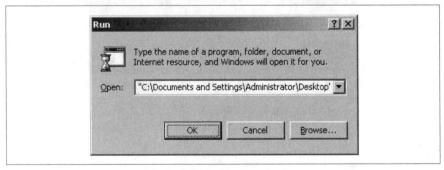

Figure 1-6. Using quotation marks for long filenames/paths

Note that your switches and arguments can reside outside of the quotation marks.

—*Sean Ademy*

# Find and Replace Registry Keys from a Command Line

Using the Regfind utility, you can easily search the Registry for a value, regardless of the key, and replace it.

Regfind (from the Windows 2000 Server Resource Kit) can be an invaluable tool when you need change a Registry key that you know the value for but when do not necessarily know the full path. Recently tasked with changing the hardcoded DNS server IP on all the servers in our organization, I was pleasantly surprised when I located this gem. The problem with trying to change the DNS server entry in the Registry is that all the IP parameters are broken up by a hashed ID. The ID references several things, but most of them have to do with the network card. Regfind allows you to search a set of subkeys in the Registry for a specific value and, when found, replace it. Another real beauty of this program is that it will work remotely; all you need to do is supply it with a list of machines and let it go. Using a list of computer names (generated from SMS, Server Manager, or AD Users and Computers), combined with two batch files, you can make sweeping changes in a dynamic environment.

## The Code

Here's an example of how to change the DNS server entry on all servers in your organization. First, create a batch file called *Regchange2.bat* with the following syntax:

```
regfind -m \\%1 -p HKEY_LOCAL_MACHINE\SYSTEM\CurrentControlSet\Services\
Tcpip\parameters "OLDIP" -r "NEWIP"
```

You will obviously want to replace *OLDIP* with the old DNS server IP and replace *NEWIP* with the new DNS server IP.

Now, create a second batch file called *regchange1.bat* with the following syntax:

```
for /F %%A in (servers.txt) do (call regchange2.bat %%A)
```

This searches the *servers.txt* file for computer names and passes them to the *regchange2.bat* file as a command-line argument.

Now you need to create a list file for your batch files to use. Create a listing of servers that need to have their DNS IP's changed and save that list as *servers.txt*. An SMS report or a copy/paste from the server manager will suffice, or you can create the file manually if you like.

## Running the Hack

Now, simply run the *regchange1.bat* batch file by calling it from a logon script and watch all your servers have their IP settings changed!

This is just one simple example of how to use Regfind. There are many command-line arguments, so please examine those to meet your needs.

—*Donnie Taylor*

## H A C K
## #4
# Automatically Log On After Booting
It's sometimes convenient to configure machines to log on automatically when booted. Here are three ways to do this.

In all versions of Windows that are based on Windows NT (including Windows 2000, Windows XP, and Windows Server 2003), a user is required to log on before he can use the system interactively. This is usually done by pressing Ctrl-Alt-Del and typing the user's credentials. Automatic logon is an option you can set to enable Windows to log on automatically using credentials that are stored in the Registry. To invoke automatic logon, you set Registry entries that define the user ID, the password, and the domain to be used to log on. Why use this feature? There are a number of reasons. As an IT professional, I have several of my home systems set up to do this, and it makes life simpler. Test systems in a lab might be another place to use this feature. I also use it all the time on virtual machine images I have running on my laptop.

Automatic login makes things simpler, but it creates a security hole. First, the credentials are stored in clear text in the Registry. Thus, anyone with remote Registry privileges can see the clear text user ID and password. Also, if you have automatic logon set on a laptop, anyone who turns on the laptop is automatically logged in as you. So use this feature carefully!

### Manual Configuration

You can configure automatic logon manually by adding the following four key Registry entries: AutoAdminLogon, DefaultDomainName, DefaultUserName, and DefaultPassword. These entries inform Windows whether to attempt automatic logon and provide the credentials (username, password, and domain).

Start Registry Editor (Start → Run → regedit) and find the Registry key HKLM\SOFTWARE\Microsoft\Windows NT\CurrentVersion\Winlogon, which is where the Registry values you set to control automatic logon are located. Two of these values, DefaultDomainName and DefaultUserName, already exist.

DefaultDomainName is a string that holds the domain (or workstation) name where the user ID exists, and DefaultUserName is the user ID that Winlogon will attempt to use to log on. This username is authenticated against the domain (or workstation) name set in the DefaultDomainName setting.

Now, create two new values by right-clicking on Winlogon and selecting New → String Value, which will create new values of type REG_SZ. Name the first value AutoAdminLogon, and specify a value data of 1 to instruct Winlogon to attempt to use automatic logon. Name the second value DefaultPassword; this value specifies the password for the user set in the DefaultUserName setting.

The result will looking like Figure 1-7.

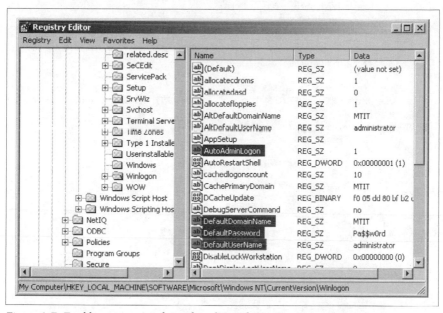

*Figure 1-7. Enabling automatic logon by editing the Registry*

## Script Method

An easier way to configure automatic logon on your machines is to use two VBScript scripts, one to enable automatic logon and the other to disable it. Here's the script for enabling it:

```
' Script to turn on automatic logon
' (c) Thomas Lee 2002
' Freely distributed!
Dim Prompt, oWSH,UserName, UserPass, UserDomain
set oWSH = WScript.CreateObject("WScript.Shell")

' get user name
```

```
Prompt = "Enter the autologon user name"
UserName = InputBox(Prompt, Title, "")

' get password
Prompt = "Enter the autologon user password for " & UserName
UserPass = InputBox(Prompt, Title, "")

' get domain
Prompt = "Enter the autologon user domain for " & UserName
Userdomain = InputBox(Prompt, Title, "")

' now set these in the Registry
oWSH.RegWrite "HKLM\SOFTWARE\Microsoft\Windows NT\CurrentVersion\Winlogon\
AutoAdminLogon","1","REG_SZ"
oWSH.RegWrite "HKLM\SOFTWARE\Microsoft\Windows NT\CurrentVersion\Winlogon\
DefaultDomainName", UserDomain, "REG_SZ"
oWSH.RegWrite "HKLM\SOFTWARE\Microsoft\Windows NT\CurrentVersion\Winlogon\
DefaultUserName", UserName, "REG_SZ"
oWSH.RegWrite "HKLM\SOFTWARE\Microsoft\Windows NT\CurrentVersion\Winlogon\
DefaultPassword", UserPass, "REG_SZ"

' ensure the change is persistent!
oWSH.RegWrite "HKLM\SOFTWARE\Microsoft\WindowsNT\CurrentVersion\Winlogon\
ForceAutoLogon", "1", "REG_SZ"

' All done
```

And here's the script for disabling automatic logon:

```
' Script to remove autoadmin logon
' (c) Thomas Lee 2002
' Freely distributed!
Option Explicit
On Error Resume Next

'Declare variables
Dim Prompt, oWSH

'Set the Windows Script Host Shell
set oWSH = WScript.CreateObject("WScript.Shell")

' delete the relevant keys
oWSH.RegDelete "HKLM\SOFTWARE\Microsoft\Windows NT\CurrentVersion\Winlogon\
AutoAdminLogon"
oWSH.RegDelete "HKLM\SOFTWARE\Microsoft\Windows NT\CurrentVersion\Winlogon\
DefaultDomainName"
oWSH.RegDelete "HKLM\SOFTWARE\Microsoft\Windows NT\CurrentVersion\Winlogon\
DefaultUserName"
oWSH.RegDelete "HKLM\SOFTWARE\Microsoft\Windows NT\CurrentVersion\Winlogon\
DefaultPassword"

' All done - say goodbye!
Legend = "Autoadmin removed - have a nice day!"
MyBox = MsgBox (legend, 4096, "We're Done")
```

You can use Notepad to type these scripts and save them with a *.vbs* file extension, or download *autoadminlogon.vbs* and *noautoadminlogon.vbs* from *http://www.oreilly.com/catalog/winsvrhks/*.

## Sysinternals Tool

Finally, here's one more way to configure automatic logon on machines. Mark Russinovich, of Sysinternals fame, also wrote a simple program to do this. You can download the program and the source from *http://www.sysinternals.com/ntw2k/source/misc.shtml#AutoLogon*, where you can find lots of other great tools.

*—Thomas Lee*

# Wait for and Optionally Terminate a Process

If you've wondered how to write code that waits for a process to finish before terminating it, here's the answer.

I have seen a number of discussions regarding the need for a VB script that waits for a process to finish. The script in this hack does this and more: it waits for a process to finish and optionally terminates the process if it has not finished within a specified amount of time.

This code is a modified form of what I use to control my software deployments, and it has two purposes. First, the code is designed to be certain that the deployment script waits until the initiated software setup executable is fully finished before proceeding. Even though the majority of recent software releases do not require this functionality when being deployed, it is still required for some legacy installations. Second, the code can perform a forceful termination of an application if this functionality is required.

This script accepts three arguments: the name of the executable to wait for or terminate, the amount of time to wait before terminating the specified executable, and (optionally) a switch specifying that the script should run silently. Note that the script uses Windows Management Instrumentation (WMI) for the process-management tasks, so make sure you're running the latest WMI version on your machine.

## The Code

The script consists of several sections, which are described inline in the following sections.

**Main routine.** First, command-line switches are read in the main body area:

```
Option Explicit
'.............................................................................
'
'
' File:     vbsWaitForProcess.vbs
' Updated:  Nov 2002
' Version:  1.0
' Author:   Dan Thomson, myITforum.com columnist
'           I can be contacted at dethomson@hotmail.com
'
' Usage:    The command processor version must be run using cscript
'           cscript vbsWaitForProcess.vbs notepad.exe 60 S
'           or
'           The IE and Popup versions can be run with cscript or wscript
'           wscript vbsWaitForProcess.vbs notepad.exe -1
'
' Input:    Name of executable  (ex: notepad.exe)
'           Time to wait in seconds before terminating the executable
'               -1 waits indefinitely for the process to finish
'               0 terminates the process imediately
'               Any value > 0 will cause the script to wait the specified
'               amount of time in seconds before terminating the process
'           Silent mode  (S)
'
' Notes:
'
'.............................................................................


On Error Resume Next

'Define some variables
Dim strProcess
Dim intWaitTime
Dim strSilent

'Get the command line arguments
strProcess = Wscript.Arguments.Item(0)
intWaitTime = CInt(Wscript.Arguments.Item(1))
strSilent = Wscript.Arguments.Item(2)

Call WaitForProcess (strProcess, intWaitTime, strSilent)
```

**Check if process is running.** Next, the ProcessIsRunning function determines if a process is running:

```
'.............................................................................
'
'
' Function: ProcessIsRunning
'
' Purpose:  Determine if a process is running
```

```
'
' Input:    Name of process
'
' Output:   True or False depending on if the process is running
'
'.........................................................................
Private Function ProcessIsRunning( strProcess )
    Dim colProcessList

    Set colProcessList = Getobject("Winmgmts:").Execquery _
        ("Select * from Win32_Process Where Name ='" & strProcess & "'")
    If colProcessList.Count > 0 Then
        ProcessIsRunning = True
    Else
        ProcessIsRunning = False
    End If

    Set colProcessList = Nothing
End Function
```

**Terminate the process.** In the next section, the ProcessTerminate function terminates a process:

```
'.........................................................................
'
'
' Function: TerminateProcess
'
' Purpose:  Terminates a process
'
' Input:    Name of process
'
'.........................................................................
Private Function ProcessTerminate( strProcess )
    Dim colProcessList, objProcess

    Set colProcessList = GetObject("Winmgmts:").ExecQuery _
        ("Select * from Win32_Process Where Name ='" & strProcess & "'")
    For Each objProcess in colProcessList
        objProcess.Terminate( )
    Next

    Set colProcessList = Nothing
End Function
```

**Wait for process to terminate.** Finally, in the WaitForProcess subroutine, the user interface is set up, the script waits while the process is active, and the process termination is initiated. I created three versions of the subroutine in

an effort to demonstrate a few methods for displaying status messages. For
example, here's how to display these messages using the command console:

```
'''''''''''''''''''''''''''''''''''''''''''''''''''''''''''''''''''''''''
'
'
' Sub: WaitForProcess
'
' Purpose:  Waits for a process
'
' Input:    Name of process
'           Wait time in seconds before termination.
'             -1 will cause the script to wait indefinitely
'             0 terminates the process imediately
'             Any value > 0 will cause the script to wait the specified
'             amount of time in seconds before terminating the process
'           Display mode.
'             Passing S will run the script silent and not show any prompts
'
' Output:   On screen status
'
' Notes:    The version echos user messages in the command window via StdOut
'
'''''''''''''''''''''''''''''''''''''''''''''''''''''''''''''''''''''''''
Private Sub WaitForProcess( strProcess, intWaitTime, strMode )

    If ProcessIsRunning(strProcess) Then
      Dim StdOut
      Dim w : w = 0
      Dim strPrompt
      Dim intPause : intPause = 1

      If UCase(strMode) <> "S" Then
        strPrompt = "Waiting for " & strProcess & " to finish."
        Set StdOut = WScript.StdOut
        StdOut.WriteLine ""
        StdOut.Write strPrompt
      End If
      'Loop while the process is running
      Do While ProcessIsRunning(strProcess)
        'Check to see if specified # of seconds have passed before terminating
        'the process. If yes, then terminate the process
        If w >= intWaitTime AND intWaitTime >= 0 Then
          Call ProcessTerminate(strProcess)
          Exit Do
        End If
        'If not running silent, post user messages
        If UCase(strMode) <> "S" Then _
          StdOut.Write "."
        'Increment the seconds counter
        w = w + intPause
        'Pause
        Wscript.Sleep(intPause * 1000)
```

```
      Loop
      If UCase(strMode) <> "S" Then
        StdOut.WriteLine ""
        Set StdOut = Nothing
      End If
   End If
End Sub
```

The result is shown in Figure 1-8.

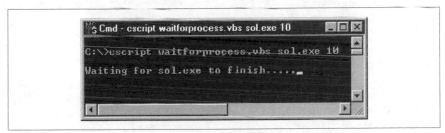

*Figure 1-8. Status message displayed in command console*

Alternatively, here's some code for displaying status messages in Internet Explorer:

```
'.................................................................
'
'
' Sub: WaitForProcess
'
' Purpose:  Waits for a process
'
' Input:    Name of process
'           Wait time in seconds before termination.
'             -1 will cause the script to wait indefinitely
'             0 terminates the process imediately
'             Any value > 0 will cause the script to wait the specified
'             amount of time in seconds before terminating the process
'             Display mode.
'             Passing S will run the script silent and not show any prompts
'
' Output:   On screen status
'
' Notes:    This version uses Internet Explorer for user messages
'
'.................................................................
Private Sub WaitForProcess( strProcess, intWaitTime, strMode )

   If ProcessIsRunning(strProcess) Then
     Dim objIntExplorer
     Dim c : c = 0
     Dim w : w = 0
     Dim strPrompt
     Dim intPause : intPause = 1
```

```
    strPrompt = "Waiting for " & strProcess & " to finish."

    'If not running silent, create reference to objIntExplorer
    'This will be used for the user messages. Also set IE display attributes
    If UCase(strMode) <> "S" Then
      Set objIntExplorer = Wscript._
      CreateObject("InternetExplorer.Application")
      With objIntExplorer
        .Navigate "about:blank"
        .ToolBar = 0
        .Menubar = 0            ' no menu
        .StatusBar = 0
        .Width=400
        .Height = 80
        .Left = 100
        .Top = 100
        .Document.Title = "WaitForProcess"
      End With
      'Wait for IE to finish
      Do While (objIntExplorer.Busy)
          Wscript.Sleep 200
      Loop
      'Show IE
      objIntExplorer.Visible = 1
    End If
    Do While ProcessIsRunning(strProcess)
      'Check to see if specified # of seconds have passed before terminating
      'the process. If yes, then terminate the process
      If w >= intWaitTime AND intWaitTime >= 0 Then
        Call ProcessTerminate(strProcess)
        Exit Do
      End If
      If UCase(strMode) <> "S" Then
        objIntExplorer.Document.Body.InnerHTML = strPrompt & String(c, ".")
        'Increment the counter.
        'Reset the counter indicator if it's > 25 because
        'we don't want it taking up a lot of screen space.
        If c > 25 Then c = 1 Else c = c + 1
        'Increment the seconds counter
        w = w + intPause
      End If
      'Pause
      Wscript.Sleep(intPause * 1000)
    Loop
    objIntExplorer.Quit( )             ' close Internet Explorer
    Set objIntExplorer = Nothing       ' release object reference

  End If
End Sub
```

The resulting status message is shown in Figure 1-9.

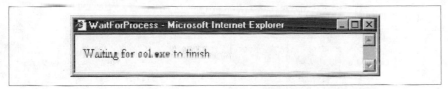

Figure 1-9. Displaying status messages in Internet Explorer

Finally, here's code that uses the Popup method of Windows Scripting Host for displaying status messages:

```
'..........................................................................
'
' Sub: WaitForProcess
'
' Purpose:  Waits for a process
'
' Input:    Name of process
'           Wait time in seconds before termination.
'             -1 will cause the script to wait indefinitely
'             0 terminates the process imediately
'             Any value > 0 will cause the script to wait the specified '
'             amount of time in seconds before terminating the process
'           Display mode.
'             Passing S will run the script silent and not show any prompts
'
' Output:   On screen status
'
' Notes:    This version uses WshShell.Popup for user messages
'
'..........................................................................
Private Sub WaitForProcess( strProcess, intWaitTime, strMode )

   If ProcessIsRunning(strProcess) Then
      Dim objWshShell
      Dim c : c = 0
      Dim w : w = 0
      Dim strPrompt
      Dim intPopupTimer : intPopupTimer = 2
      Dim intPause : intPause = 1

      strPrompt = "Waiting for " & strProcess & " to finish."

      'If not running silent, create reference to objWshShell
      'This will be used for the user messages
      If UCase(strMode) <> "S" Then _
        Set objWshShell = CreateObject("WScript.Shell")
      'Loop while the process is running
      Do While ProcessIsRunning(strProcess)
        'Check to see if specified # of seconds have passed before terminating
```

```
        'the process. If yes, then terminate the process
        If w >= intWaitTime AND intWaitTime >= 0 Then
          Call ProcessTerminate(strProcess)
          Exit Do
        End If
        'If not running silent, post user prompt
        If UCase(strMode) <> "S" Then
          objWshShell.Popup strPrompt & String(c, "."), intPopupTimer, _
          "WaitForProcess", 64
          'Increment the counter.
          'Reset the counter indicator if it's > 25 because
          'we don't want it taking up a lot of screen space.
          If c > 25 Then c = 1 Else c = c + 1
        End If
        'Increment the seconds counter
        w = w + intPause + intPopupTimer
        'Pause
        Wscript.Sleep(intPause * 1000)
      Loop
      Set objWshShell = Nothing
    End If
  End Sub
```

The resulting dialog box is shown in Figure 1-10.

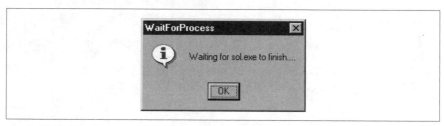

*Figure 1-10. Displaying status messages in a dialog box*

Note that if you are assembling a standalone script, it should contain sections 1, 2, 3, and one option from section 4. If you would rather incorporate this code into your existing script, you need only sections 2, 3, and one option from section 4. You'll also need to add the call statement that is at the end of the main routine section. All the code sections are self-contained, which makes them easy to import into existing scripts.

## Running the Hack

To use this hack, type the code into Notepad (with Word Wrap disabled) and save it with a *.vbs* extension as *WaitForProcess.vbs*. Or, if you don't want to tire your fingers out, download it from the O'Reilly web site instead.

Here are a few sample command-line examples. This will wait indefinitely until Notepad is closed:

```
cscript WaitForProcess.vbs notepad.exe -1
```

This will wait silently and indefinitely until Notepad is closed:

```
cscript WaitForProcess.vbs notepad.exe -1 S
```

And this will wait 10 seconds before Notepad is forcefully closed:

```
cscript WaitForProcess.vbs notepad.exe 10
```

—*Dan Thomson*

## HACK #6 Shut Down a Remote Computer

Here's a nifty way to use a script to shut down remote machines.

Sometimes, you need to be able to shut down a server remotely. This script pings the computer in question prior to sending the Win32Shutdown method. It operates on remote PCs and has been tested on systems running Windows 2000. It will probably work on NT4 systems with the proper WHS/WMI/VB scripting, though it has not been tested on such systems.

Using the Win32Shutdown method, the script provides you with the option of logging off the current user of the machine, powering the machine down, or rebooting it. In addition, each of these options can be *forced* so that the action occurs even if applications are running. Use this option carefully, though, because it might cause the logged-on user to lose his work if he has open files. Note that forced log off/power down/reboot will not work if the screen saver is password-protected and is currently active.

### The Code

Make sure you have the latest scripting engines on the workstation you run this script from. You can download the latest scripting engines at the Microsoft Scripting home page (*http://msdn.microsoft.com/library/default. asp?url=/nhp/default.asp?contentid=28001169*). Note that, when working with the Active Directory Services Interface (ADSI), you must have the same applicable rights as you need to use the built-in administrative tools. Also, for VB scripts that interact with Windows Management Instrumentation (WMI), apply the most current version of the WMI agents.

Type the following code into a text editor such as Notepad (making sure to have Word Wrap disabled) and save it with a *.vbs* extension. Alternatively, you can download the *RemoteShutdown.vbs* script from the O'Reilly web site at *http://www.oreilly.com/catalog/winsvrhks/*.

```
'/'|| RemoteShutdown.vbs
'||
'|| Created by Harvey Hendricks, MCP, MCSE, A+
'|| March 2001
'|| email: Harvey.Hendricks@aramcoservices.com
'||
'||
'|| Based on techniques and ideas from:
'|| SMS admin, SMS Installer, & WMI forums ->
'|| http://www.myITforum.com/forums
'|| Win32 Scripting -> http://cwashington.netreach.net/
'|| Microsoft Windows Script Technologies ->
'|| http://msdn.microsoft.com/scripting
'|| Microsoft Online Library ->
'|| http://msdn.microsoft.com/library/default.asp
'|| Microsoft VBScript 5.5 documentation and Microsoft WMI SDK
'||
'||~~~~~~~~~~~~~~~~~~~~~~~~~~~~~~~~~~~~~~~~~~~~~~~~~~~~~~~~~~~~~~~~~~~~~
'|| SCRIPT LOGIC FLOW:
'|| Collects computername from user, calls function to ping the computername
'|| to determine if it is accessible, if not then display message and exit
'|| otherwise continue.
'|| Collects desired action to perform from the user, does error checking on
'|| the input to determine if it is acceptable, if not then display message
'|| and exit otherwise continue.
'|| Set variables and output messages based on the action chosen. Calls
'|| Win32Shutdown with the appropriate variable. Displays success message
'|| and exits
'||
'|| Uses WMI Win32Shutdown method from the Win32_OperatingSystem class
'|| to perform different logoff / powerdown / reboot functions
'||
'|| Testing found the following values to be effective on Win32Shutdown:
'|| Action decimal binary
'|| Logoff 0 0000
'|| Force Logoff 4 0100
'|| Reboot 2 0010
'|| Force Reboot 6 0110
'|| Powerdown 8 1000
'|| Force Powerdown 12 1100
'||
'|| Notice that the third bit from the right appears to be the "FORCE" bit.
'||
'|| A value of 1 will do a shutdown, ending at the "It is safe to turn
'|| off your computer" screen. I have no use for this and did not test it.
'||
'||
'||NOTES: - tested under Windows 2000 Pro. with ACPI compliant systems -
'|| SHOULD work under Windows NT4 without modification IF the
'|| system has compatible versions of WSH / WMI / VBscripting
'||
'||Logoff / Powerdown / Reboot:
'|| Does not work if a password protected screen saver is active or
```

```
'|| there is data to save. Either way the system waits for user input.
'||
'||Force logoff / Force Powerdown / Force Reboot:
'|| Does not work if a password protected screen saver is active, will wait
'|| for user input. Otherwise will close open applications without saving
'|| data.
'||
'\/
~~~~~~~~~~~~~~~~~~~~~~~~~~~~~~~~~~~~~~~~~~~~~~~~~~~~~~~~~~~~~~~~~~~~~~~~~~~~


'/\/\/\/\/\/\/\/\/\/\/\/\/\ start function
function Ping(byval strName)
dim objFSO, objShell, objTempFile, objTS
dim sCommand, sReadLine
dim bReturn

set objShell = WScript.CreateObject("Wscript.Shell")
set objFSO = CreateObject("Scripting.FileSystemObject")

'Set default return value
bReturn = false

'Create command line to ping and save results to a temp file
sCommand = "cmd /c ping.exe -n 3 -w 1000 " & strName & " > C:\temp.txt"

'Execute the command
objShell.run sCommand, 0, true

'Get the temp file
set objTempFile = objFSO.GetFile("C:\temp.txt")
set objTS = objTempFile.OpenAsTextStream(1)

'Loop through the temp file to see if "reply from" is found,
'if it is then the ping was successful
do while objTs.AtEndOfStream <> true
sReadLine = objTs.ReadLine
if instr(lcase(sReadLine), "reply from") > 0 then
bReturn = true
exit do
end if
loop

'Close temp file and release objects
objTS.close
objTempFile.delete
set objTS = nothing
set objTempFile = nothing
set objShell - nothing
set objFSO = nothing

'Return value
Ping = bReturn
end function
```

```
'/\/\/\/\/\/\/\/\/\/\/\/\/\ end function

'/\/\/\/\/\/\/\/\/\/\/\/\/\ Start Main body of script
'Get computer name to operate on
ComputerName=InputBox("Enter the Machine name of the computer" & vbCRLF _
& "you wish to Shutdown / Reboot / Logoff", _
"Remote Shutdown / Reboot / Logoff", _
"ComputerName")

'if Cancel selected - exit
If (ComputerName = "") Then Wscript.Quit

'change the name to uppercase
ComputerName=UCase(ComputerName)

'ping the computername to see if it is accessible
bPingtest = ping(Computername)

If bPingtest = FALSE Then
y = msgbox ("'" & ComputerName & "' is not accessible!" & vbCRLF _
& "It may be offline or turned off." & vbCRLF _
& "Check the name for a typo." & vbCRLF, _
vbCritical, ComputerName & " NOT RESPONDING")
Wscript.Quit
end IF

'Get the action desired
Action=InputBox( _
"Select Action to perform on " & ComputerName & vbCRLF & vbCRLF _
& " 1 - Logoff" & vbCRLF _
& " 2 - Force Logoff ( NO SAVE )" & vbCRLF _
& " 3 - Powerdown" & vbCRLF _
& " 4 - Force Powerdown ( NO SAVE )" & vbCRLF _
& " 5 - Reboot" & vbCRLF _
& " 6 - Force Reboot ( NO SAVE )" & vbCRLF & vbCRLF _
& "NOTE:" & vbCRLF _
& " Using Force will close windows" & vbCRLF _
& " without saving changes!", _
"Select action to perform on " & ComputerName, "")

'if Cancel selected - exit
If (Action = "") Then Wscript.Quit

'error check input
If (INSTR("1234567",Action)=0) OR (Len(Action)>1) then
y = msgbox("Unacceptable input passed -- '" & Action & "'", _
vbOKOnly + vbCritical, "That was SOME bad input!")
Wscript.Quit
end if

'set flag to disallow action unless proper input achieved, 1 => go 0 => nogo
flag = 0
```

```
'set variables according to computername and action
Select Case Action
Case 1 'Logoff
x = 0
strAction = "Logoff sent to " & ComputerName
flag = 1
Case 2 'Force Logoff
x = 4
strAction = "Force Logoff sent to " & ComputerName
flag = 1
Case 3 'Powerdown
x = 8
strAction = "Powerdown sent to " & ComputerName
flag = 1
Case 4 'Force Powerdown
x = 12
strAction = "Force Powerdown sent to " & ComputerName
flag = 1
Case 5 'Reboot
x = 2
strAction = "Reboot sent to " & ComputerName
flag = 1
Case 6 'Force Reboot
x = 6
strAction = "Force Reboot sent to " & ComputerName
flag = 1
Case 7 'Test dialog boxes
y = msgbox("Test complete", vbOKOnly + vbInformation, "Dialog Box Test
Complete")
flag = 0
Case Else 'Default -- should never happen
y = msgbox("Error occurred in passing parameters." _
& vbCRLF & " Passed '" & Action & "'", _
vbOKOnly + vbCritical, "PARAMETER ERROR")
flag = 0
End Select

'check flag
' if equal 1 (TRUE) then perform Win32Shutdown action on remote PC
' and display a confirmation message
' if not equal 1 (FALSE) then skip the action and script ends
if flag then
Set OpSysSet=GetObject("winmgmts:{(Debug,RemoteShutdown)}//" _
& ComputerName & "/root/cimv2").ExecQuery( _
"Select * from Win32_OperatingSystem where Primary=true")
for each OpSys in OpSysSet
OpSys.Win32Shutdown(x)
y = msgbox(strAction,vbOKOnly + vbInformation,"Mission Accomplished")
next
end If

'Release objects
set OpSys = nothing
set OpSysSet = nothing
```

## Running the Hack

To run the hack, simply double-click on the *RemoteShutdown.vbs* file in Windows Explorer (or a shortcut to this file on your desktop) and type the name of the remote computer you want to log off from, power down, or reboot. This name can be the NetBIOS name, DNS name, or IP address of the remote machine. You will then be presented with an input box that displays a menu of options:

1 - Logoff
2 - Force Logoff
3 - Powerdown
4 - Force Powerdown
5 - Reboot
6 - Force Reboot

Simply type the number for the action you want to perform and press Enter.

—*Harvey Hendricks*

# HACK #7   Rename Mapped Drives

Renaming drive mappings can be done in several ways, but automating the process is most efficient using a script.

Occasionally, an administrator might need to change drive-mapping names to hide share paths or to make the drive name user-friendly. This is an easy operation when done manually through a console, but when you try to automate this task, it becomes a little more difficult. Because mapped drives are not partitions on the local hard disk, common DOS commands, such as `label`, can't be used. Most drive-mapping commands, such as `net use`, don't have a way to customize the name of the mapped drive either.

One common way to perform this task is to hack the following Registry key and add the `_LabelFromReg` string value:

    HKCU\Software\Microsoft\Windows\CurrentVersion\Explorer\MountPoints2\%key%

Here, the `%key%` variable is the drive letter to be changed.

There is a whole host of ways to make this method work, either by editing the Registry directly, via script, or by importing a *.reg* file using `regedit /c`. All of these methods require many steps and some require external files, so they might not fit into every administrative scheme. But there's an easier approach.

## The Code

As it turns out, our old friend VBScript can be used to make this task a little more seamless. This simple script can be used on mapped drives as well as local partitions:

```
mDrive = "drive letter"
Set oShell = CreateObject("Shell.Application")
oShell.NameSpace(mDrive).Self.Name = "AnyName"
```

## Running the Hack

To use this hack, simply edit the script to change the drive letter and drive name as desired. For example, if E: is a mapped drive that has the label Budgets on 172.16.33.14, and you want to change the label on the mapped drive to simply Budgets, change this line:

```
mDrive = "drive letter"
```

to this:

```
mDrive = "e:\"
```

Then, change this line:

```
oShell.NameSpace(mDrive).Self.Name = "AnyName"
```

to this:

```
oShell.NameSpace(mDrive).Self.Name = "Budgets"
```

Finally, run the script by creating a shortcut to it and double-clicking on the shortcut, by calling it from a logon script, or by any other method suitable for your environment.

—*Michael Brainard*

# Execute a Command on Each Computer in a Domain

HACK
#8

This handy script lets you easily run any command on a specified subset of computers in your domain.

Running the same command on multiple computers in your domain can be tedious indeed, but such a scenario is common in an administrator's life. I've written this hack to make this chore easier. The script traverses member systems of a domain, executing a command against each system that has a name that matches a particular specification you specify in the command line. Note that regular expressions are legal in this script, which makes it a powerful and flexible addition to the administrator's toolkit.

## The Code

To use this script, type it into a text editor such as Notepad (make sure Word Wrap is disabled) and save it with a *.vbs* extension as *ExecuteAll.vbs*. Alternatively, if you don't want to wear your fingers out, you can download the script from the O'Reilly web site.

```
'Script Name: ExecuteAll.vbs

Option Explicit

Dim oDomain, oService, oItem, oShell
Dim strDomain, strSpec, strCommand, intButton
Dim oArgs, strFinalCommand, oRegEx, boolConfirm

' Prepare to execute commands & do popups
Set oShell = CreateObject("WScript.Shell")

GetArguments

' Access the domain so we can traverse objects
WScript.Echo "Accessing NT Domain " & strDomain
Set oDomain = GetObject("WinNT://" & strDomain)

' Initiate our regular expression support
Set oRegEx = New RegExp
oRegEx.Pattern = strSpec
oRegEx.IgnoreCase = True

' Traverse each computer (WinNT) object in the domain
WScript.Echo "Searching for " & strSpec
oDomain.Filter = Array("Computer") ' only look at computers
For Each oItem In oDomain
If oRegEx.Test(oItem.Name) Then
WScript.Echo " Matched " & oItem.Name
strFinalCommand = Replace(strCommand, "$n", oItem.Name)

intButton = vbNo
If boolConfirm Then
intButton = oShell.Popup("Execute " & strFinalCommand & "?",,_
"System " & oItem.Name, vbYesno + vbQuestion)
End If
If (boolConfirm = False) Or (intButton = vbYes) Then
WScript.Echo " Executing: " & strFinalCommand
execute strFinalCommand
End If
End If
Next

' All done; clean up
Set oItem = Nothing
Set oRegEx = Nothing
```

```
Set oDomain = Nothing
Set oShell = Nothing
Set oArgs = Nothing

'

' Glean the arguments for our run from the command line, if provided.
' If any are missing, prompt for input. A blank input signals an abort.
'

' /Y is an optional last argument
Sub GetArguments
Dim i, strConfirm, intButton
Set oArgs = WScript.Arguments

boolConfirm = True ' assume always confirm
strDomain = "" ' domain to be traversed
strSpec = "" ' name specification to be matched
strCommand = "" ' command to be executed on each match
strConfirm = "" ' track prompting for confirmation setting

' Look for our optional 4th argument
If oArgs.Length = 4 Then
If UCase(oArgs.Item(3)) = "/Y" Then
boolConfirm = False
strConfirm = "/Y" ' don't prompt below
End If
End If

' Look for any specified arguments, in order
If oArgs.Length >= 1 Then strDomain = oArgs(0)
If oArgs.Length >= 2 Then strSpec = oArgs(1)
If oArgs.Length >= 3 Then strCommand = oArgs(2)

' Prompt for any arguments not specified on the command line
If strDomain = "" Then
strDomain = InputBox _
("Enter the name of the NT Domain to be traversed", _
"NT Domain")
End If
If strDomain = "" Then WScript.Quit
strDomain = UCase(strDomain)

If strSpec = "" Then
strSpec = InputBox _
("Enter your name specification for the computer(s) " & _
"that will be matched within the " & strDomain & " Domain." & _
vbCrlf & "Regular Expressions are acceptable.", _
"Name Specification")
End If
If strSpec = "" Then WScript.Quit

If strCommand = "" Then
strCommand = InputBox _
("Enter the command to be executed on each computer matching " & _
```

```
      strSpec & " within the " & strDomain & " Domain." & _
      vbCrlf & "$n will be substituted for the computer name.", _
      "Command to Execute")
   End If
   If strCommand = "" Then WScript.Quit

   If strConfirm = "" Then
   intButton = oShell.Popup("Confirm each command prior to execution?",,_
   "Confirm?", vbYesNo + vbQuestion)
   If intButton = vbNo Then
   boolConfirm = False
   End If
   End If
   End Sub


   ' Execute a command. Each is always run under a new instance of the command
   ' processor. This allows the use of built-in commands and I/O redirection.
   '
   ' We won't wait for command completion.
   Sub Execute(strCommand)
   Dim RetVal

   strCommand = "%COMSPEC% /c " & strCommand

   RetVal = oShell.Run(strCommand, 1, False)
   End Sub
```

## Running the Hack

Here is the syntax for running the script:

```
ExexcuteAll.vbs <DomainToTraverse> <ComputerSpecification> <Command> [/Y]
```

When the script runs, the matched system's name will be substituted for the occurrence of $n in the command to be performed. By default, each command instance is confirmed before it is executed, but you can specify /Y to always answer Yes instead.

Here's an example of how to run the script:

```
ExexcuteAll.vbs MYDOMAIN WKSATL* "del \\$n\admin$\activitylog.txt"
```

This example traverses the MYDOMAIN domain, looking for computer names that start with WKSATL* (note the wildcard) and deletes the *activitylog.txt* file from the *C:\Winnt* folder.

*—Hans Schefske*

# HACK #9 Add, Remove, or Retrieve Environment Variables

Environment variables can easily be added, removed, or retrieved using the script in this hack.

Using VBScript to work with the Windows system environment can be pretty simple. This hack shows how to use a script to read variables, add new variables, remove variables, and recurse through all of them. Just take a look through the script and read the comments to see how to perform each task. Note that there are four types of values in the Windows Script Host (WSH) environment—System, User, Volatile, and Process—and the script uses all of them.

By the way, this script is provided by Dudeworks (*http://www.dudeworks. net*). For additional resources on Windows scripting and working with the environment, see *http://msdn.microsoft.com/library/default.asp?url=/library/ en-us/script56/html/wsProEnvironment.asp*.

## The Code

Type the following script into Notepad (with Word Wrap disabled) and save it with a *.vbs* extension as *GetEnvVars.vbs*:

```
'~~~~~~~~~~~~~~~~~~~~~~~~~~~~~~~~~~~~~~~~~~~~~~~~~~~~~~~~~~~~~~~~~~~~~~~~
'Created by: Rob Olson - Dudeworks
'Created on: 10/17/2001
'Purpose: Get Environment Variables.
'~~~~~~~~~~~~~~~~~~~~~~~~~~~~~~~~~~~~~~~~~~~~~~~~~~~~~~~~~~~~~~~~~~~~~~~~

wscript.echo "Working with the Environment: Provided by www.dudeworks.
net"&vbcrlf&vbcrlf&strval

'// Create an instance of the wshShell object
set WshShell = CreateObject("WScript.Shell")
'Use the methods of the object
wscript.echo "Environment.item: "& WshShell.Environment.item("WINDIR")
wscript.echo "ExpandEnvironmentStrings: "& WshShell.
ExpandEnvironmentStrings("%windir%")

'// add and remove environment variables
'// Specify the environment type ( System, User, Volatile, or Process )
set oEnv=WshShell.Environment("System")

wscript.echo "Adding ( TestVar=Windows Script Host ) to the System " _
& "type environment"
' add a var
oEnv("TestVar") = "Windows Script Host"

wscript.echo "removing ( TestVar=Windows Script Host ) from the System " _
& "type environment"
```

```
' remove a var
oEnv.Remove "TestVar"


'// List all vars in all environment types

'//System Type
set oEnv=WshShell.Environment("System")
for each sitem in oEnv
strval=strval & sItem &vbcrlf
next
wscript.echo "System Environment:"&vbcrlf&vbcrlf&strval
strval=""

'//Process Type
set oEnv=WshShell.Environment("Process")
for each sitem in oEnv
strval=strval & sItem &vbcrlf
next
wscript.echo "Process Environment:"&vbcrlf&vbcrlf&strval
strval=""

'//User Type
set oEnv=WshShell.Environment("User")
for each sitem in oEnv
strval=strval & sItem &vbcrlf
next
wscript.echo "User Environment:"&vbcrlf&vbcrlf&strval
strval=""

'//Volatile Type
set oEnv=WshShell.Environment("Volatile")
for each sitem in oEnv
strval=strval & sItem &vbcrlf
next

wscript.echo "Volatile Environment:"&vbcrlf&vbcrlf&strval
strval=""
```

## Running the Hack

To run the script, open a command prompt, change to the directory where the script is saved, and type cscript.exe  GetEnvVars.vbs. Here is an example of typical output from the script on a Windows 2000 machine:

```
Microsoft (R) Windows Script Host Version 5.6
Copyright (C) Microsoft Corporation 1996-2001. All rights reserved.

Working with the Environment: Provided by www.dudeworks.net

Environment.item: %SystemRoot%
ExpandEnvironmentStrings: C:\WINNT
```

Adding ( TestVar=Windows Script Host ) to the System type environment
removing ( TestVar=Windows Script Host ) from the System type environment
System Environment:

```
ComSpec=%SystemRoot%\system32\cmd.exe
Os2LibPath=%SystemRoot%\system32\os2\dll;
Path=%SystemRoot%\system32;%SystemRoot%;%SystemRoot%\system32\Wbem
windir=%SystemRoot%
OS=Windows_NT
PROCESSOR_ARCHITECTURE=x86
PROCESSOR_LEVEL=6
PROCESSOR_IDENTIFIER=x86 Family 6 Model 5 Stepping 2, GenuineIntel
PROCESSOR_REVISION=0502
NUMBER_OF_PROCESSORS=1
PATHEXT=.COM;.EXE;.BAT;.CMD;.VBS;.VBE;.JS;.JSE;.WSF;.WSH
TEMP=%SystemRoot%\TEMP
TMP=%SystemRoot%\TEMP
```

Process Environment:

```
=C:=C:\
=ExitCode=00000000
ALLUSERSPROFILE=C:\Documents and Settings\All Users
APPDATA=C:\Documents and Settings\Administrator\Application Data
CommonProgramFiles=C:\Program Files\Common Files
COMPUTERNAME=SNOOPY
ComSpec=C:\WINNT\system32\cmd.exe
HOMEDRIVE=C:
HOMEPATH=\Documents and Settings\Administrator
LOGONSERVER=\\SNOOPY
NUMBER_OF_PROCESSORS=1
OS=Windows_NT
Os2LibPath=C:\WINNT\system32\os2\dll;
Path=C:\WINNT\system32;C:\WINNT;C:\WINNT\System32\Wbem
PATHEXT=.COM;.EXE;.BAT;.CMD;.VBS;.VBE;.JS;.JSE;.WSF;.WSH
PROCESSOR_ARCHITECTURE=x86
PROCESSOR_IDENTIFIER=x86 Family 6 Model 5 Stepping 2, GenuineIntel
PROCESSOR_LEVEL=6
PROCESSOR_REVISION=0502
ProgramFiles=C:\Program Files
PROMPT=$P$G
SystemDrive=C:
SystemRoot=C:\WINNT
TEMP=C:\DOCUME~1\ADMINI~1\LOCALS~1\Temp
TMP=C:\DOCUME~1\ADMINI~1\LOCALS~1\Temp
USERDOMAIN=SNOOPY
USERNAME=Administrator
USERPROFILE=C:\Documents and Settings\Administrator
windir=C:\WINNT
```

User Environment:

```
TEMP=%USERPROFILE%\Local Settings\Temp
```

```
TMP=%USERPROFILE%\Local Settings\Temp

Volatile Environment:

LOGONSERVER=\\SNOOPY
APPDATA=C:\Documents and Settings\Administrator\Application Data
```

By the way, if you add a new variable via the command prompt, you will not see it when you try to read it via the script. You can read only the new values created via the same scripting type you used to create them. Although I've tested this only to a limited extent, it seems to be true. Try it for yourself; just open a command prompt, type Set DUDE=Dudeworks, and press Enter to set the new environment variable. Now, when you execute *GetEnvVars.vbs*, and you'll notice that it does *not* list that new variable. However, if you type SET at the command prompt, you will see it.

—*Rob Olson*

## Extend Group Policy

Group Policy is a powerful tool for managing Windows systems, but by configuring ADM files you can extend its capabilities even further.

One day, one of my customers gave me a phone call to say that "the Group Policy Plan we made was pretty nice, but there's something missing, and if we had this we could really impress our boss." From that day on, my life wasn't the same, because this comment led to me discover the true power of Group Policy through customizing ADM files.

But first you need to understand the basics of ADM files.

### ADM Files

An ADM file is an ASCII file that defines the Group Policy settings; every checkbox, drop-down menu, and folder in the Group Policy window is defined in this file. The ADM file can also be hacked with any text editor to extend the built-in settings of Group Policy, or you could even build a custom ADM to import to your own Group Policies files. This customization feature makes Group Policy a more powerful tool to manage computers.

The default Group Policy Object (GPO) created in Active Directory is composed of three ADM files: *conf.adm*, *inetres.adm,* and *system.adm*. The *conf.adm* file holds all the policy settings for Microsoft NetMeeting. The *inetres.adm* file holds some of the settings for the Windows Components section under both Computer and User Configuration portions of Group Policy. Finally, the *system.adm* file has additional settings for the Windows Components and System sections under Administrative Template in both the Computer and User Configuration portions of the Group Policy.

These ADM files are located in the *%winnt%\inf* folder, and every other ADM file that is installed on your machine will be put into that location as well. Also, many products that Microsoft has released for Windows 2000/ XP have their own ADM files. For example, the Microsoft Office XP Resource Kit has a corresponding ADM file for each product of the Office suite. For instance, an ADM file called *word10.adm* adds policy settings that affect Word XP on clients computers.

## Hacking ADM Files

How do you to find the policy you want to edit? And how do you change it? In the following example, I want to find and edit the "Save Word files as" policy in the *word10.adm* file. This policy defines the way a file is saved by default in Word XP. I usually add the option to save the Word file in a format that appears in a local version of Word but doesn't appear in the ADM.

Figure 1-11 shows what the policy looks like.

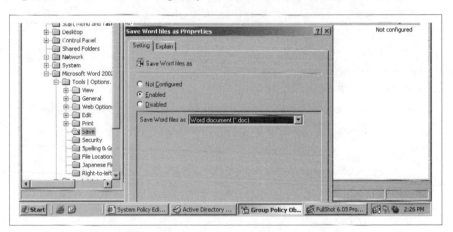

*Figure 1-11. Editing a policy setting*

As you can see, the policy setting is found in the Save folder and its name is "Save Word files as." Now, if I want to find this policy in the appropriate ADM file, I simply need to look for "Save Word files as." To do this, just open the correct ADM file (which in this case is *word10.adm*) and do a text search for the string "Save Word files as". You'll find the following section of the ADM file:

```
POLICY "Save Word files as"
KEYNAME Software\Policies\Microsoft\Office\10.0\Word\Options
PART "Save Word files as" DROPDOWNLIST
VALUENAME DefaultFormat
ITEMLIST
NAME "Word document (*.doc)" VALUE "DEFAULT"
```

```
NAME "Web Page (*.htm; *.html)" VALUE "HTML"
NAME "Word 6.0/95 (*.doc)" VALUE "MSWord6Exp"
NAME "Word 6.0/95 - Japanese (*.doc)" VALUE"MSWord6JExp"
NAME "Word 6.0/95 - Korean (*.doc)" VALUE "MSWord95KExp"
NAME "Word 97-2002 & 6.0/95 - RTF" VALUE "MSWord6RTFExp"
NAME "Works 4.0 for Windows (*.wps)" VALUE "MSWorksWin4"
NAME "Works 3.0 for Windows (*.wps)" VALUE "MSWorksWin3"
END ITEMLIST
NOSORT
END PART
END POLICY
```

As you can see, the first line, `Policy "Save Word files as"`, defines the name of the policy as it appears in Figure 1-11, while everything under that line defines the policy settings until the last line, `END POLICY`, closes the policy. Looking at this further, `KEYNAME` defines the path to the affected key in the Registry, `PART` defines the way the policy box will appear in the GUI (in this case, a drop-down menu list), `VALUENAME` defines the name of the affected value in the Registry, `NAME` defines the name of each option as it appears in the drop-down list, and `VALUE` specifies the actual data that will be inserted into the affected value that is defined by `VALUENAME`.

So, if I want to add another option to be displayed in the drop-down list of this policy, all I need to do is add the following line wherever I want (within the section bounded by `ITEMLIST` and `END ITEMLIST`):

```
NAME "Word 97-2002 & 6.0/95 Hebrew Converter\doc" VALUE "MSWord6HBRExp"
```

Figure 1-12 shows the result of what will be added to the policy drop-down list in the GUI.

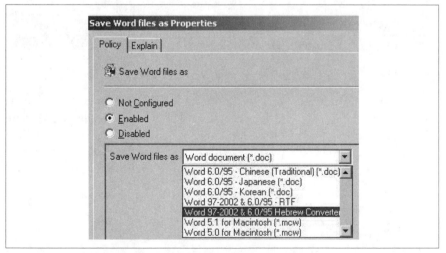

*Figure 1-12. Adding an option to a drop-down list*

Easy, isn't it? With this method, you can manipulate virtually any Registry key that is in the HKEY_LOCAL_MACHINE and HKEY_CURRENT_USER hives to extend Group Policy.

If you'd like to learn more about hacking ADM files, see *http://www. microsoft.com/windows2000/en/server/help/sag_spconcepts 34.htm* from the Windows 2000 Server online documentation. Note that occasionally you might not see the results of your hack; see article 228723 in the Knowledge Base on TechNet for more information (*http://support.microsoft.com/default. aspx?scid=kb;en-us;228723*).

—*Oren Zippori*

## Disable EFS
## #11
While the Encrypted File System of Windows 2000/XP can be useful for protecting data, your best approach might actually be to disable it.

The Encrypted File System (EFS) feature was first introduced in Windows 2000 and is also available in Windows XP Professional. EFS provides a much higher level of security than the one offered by NTFS alone, which can be circumvented without much effort as long as physical access to the computer is allowed. EFS is extremely easy to use and is available without any special configuration because it is enabled by default. Even though it seems that with all these advantages EFS should quickly find its place in everyone's environment, implementating it properly is a fairly complex task.

### The Problem

Your two primary concerns are the ability to recover encrypted files and the protection of private keys used for encryption, which are associated with each user's account and the recovery agent's account. Recovery of encrypted files might be a fairly common occurrence. Because the private keys necessary for decryption are stored in the user's profile, if the profile gets deleted or corrupted, the user can no longer access their encrypted files. The process of recovery involves simply logging on as an account that is designated as a data recovery agent. By default, this account is a local administrator on a standalone computer and a domain administrator in a domain environment. Because the private keys for data recovery agents are also stored as part of their profiles, it is recommended that private keys for data recovery agents should be exported from the computer that contains them and stored in a secure place until a recovery needs to be performed.

Currently, without using any custom solution, backup and storage of a user's private keys (without backing up the entire profile) tends to be a time-consuming process. In addition, using nondefault recovery agents (which is the recommended procedure) requires installation of the Certificate Authority feature, which also needs to be managed properly. If you are not ready to handle all these additional tasks, your best bet might simply be to temporarily disable EFS on users' machines.

## The Solution

In the Windows 2000 domain environment, launch the Group Policy MMC snap-in and select the Group Policy Object (GPO) linked to your domain. Then, drill down to Computer Configuration → Windows Settings → Security Settings → Public Key Policies → Encrypted Data Recovery Agents, right-click on the folder labeled Encrypted Data Recovery Agents, and select Delete Policy to delete the default recovery policy. Then, right-click on Encrypted Data Recovery Agents again and select Initialize Empty Policy. This will remove users' ability to use EFS on any Windows 2000 system that belongs to the domain. In absence of EFS recovery agent, Windows 2000 clients will refuse to encrypt any files or folders.

However, you might be in for a surprise if you try to use the same approach in Windows XP, because Microsoft changed the default EFS behavior to allow a Windows XP client to use encryption even if no Data Recovery Agent is available (the same is true for Windows Server 2003). Fortunately, there are several new ways of preventing this, which we'll look at now.

**Disabling EFS for a file.** Windows XP offers greater flexibility in configuring the scope of reach of EFS. If your intention is to disable EFS for a single file, you can simply assign the system attribute to the file. Although this is not the most elegant solution, it does provide a quick workaround. In order to apply the system attribute to a file, use the attrib command with +s parameter. For example, to apply the system attribute to the *info1.txt* file, type the following at the command prompt:

```
attrib +s info1.txt
```

**Disabling EFS for a folder.** If you instead want to prevent EFS on the folder level, you can create a *desktop.ini* file in the folder. The *desktop.ini* file should contain the following two lines:

```
[Encryption]
Disable=1
```

This will affect the folder itself and all of its files. However, it does not have any impact on its subfolders and their content.

**Disabling EFS for a system.** Finally, if you prefer, you can disable EFS on the system level. This can be accomplished by editing the Registry. Set the following entry of DWORD type to the value 1:

```
HKLM\SOFTWARE\Microsoft\Windows NT\CurrentVersion\EFS\EfsConfiguration
```

It is easier, however, to use Group Policy for this purpose. Start by launching Local Security Policy from the Administrative Tools menu. Next, double-click on the Public Key Policies folder. You will see a subfolder named Encrypting File System. Right-click on it and select Properties from the context-sensitive menu. You will notice a checkbox labeled "Allow users to encrypt files using Encrypting File System (EFS)," as shown in Figure 1-13.

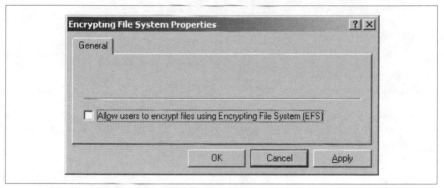

*Figure 1-13. Disabling EFS in Windows XP/2003*

Unchecking this box will disable EFS altogether on the system. Note that this setting can be also used to together with Group Policy to disable EFS for all computers residing in any of Active Directory containers—sites, domains, or organizational units.

—*Marcin Policht*

# Get Event Log Information

Need to check on the size and configuration settings of your event logs? Use this script instead of the GUI; it's faster!

Monitoring event logs is an essential part of an administrator's job. Unfortunately, viewing event log settings and log file sizes from the GUI is cumbersome, and it would be useful to have an easier way to obtain this information.

That's exactly what this hack is all about. You can run the script on Windows NT/2000 and later to obtain the current file size, maximum file size, and number of records, and you can overwrite settings on the Application, System, and Security logs.

## The Code

Type the following script into Notepad (make sure Word Wrap is disabled) and save it with a *.vbs* extension as *loginfo.vbs*. Or, if you like, you can download the script from the O'Reilly web site.

```
Option Explicit
On Error Resume Next
Dim strMoniker
Dim refWMI
Dim colEventLogs
Dim refEventLog
Dim strSource

'moniker string stub - security privilege needed to get
'numrecords for Security log
strMoniker = "winMgmts:{(Security)}!"

'append to moniker string if a machine name has been given
If WScript.Arguments.Count = 1 Then _
strMoniker = strMoniker & "\\" & WScript.Arguments(0) & ":"

'attempt to connect to WMI
Set refWMI = GetObject(strMoniker)
If Err <> 0 Then
WScript.Echo "Could not connect to the WMI service."
WScript.Quit
End If

'get a collection of Win32_NTEventLogFile objects
Set colEventLogs = refWMI.InstancesOf("Win32_NTEventLogFile")
If Err <> 0 Then
WScript.Echo "Could not retrieve Event Log objects"
WScript.Quit
End If

'iterate through each log and output information
For Each refEventLog In colEventLogs
WScript.Echo "Information for the " & _
refEventLog.LogfileName & _
" log:"
WScript.Echo " Current file size: " & refEventLog.FileSize
WScript.Echo " Maximum file size: " & refEventLog.MaxFileSize
WScript.Echo " The Log currently contains " & _
refEventLog.NumberOfRecords & " records"

'output policy info in a friendly format using OverwriteOutDated,
'as OverWritePolicy is utterly pointless.
'note "-1" is the signed interpretation of 4294967295
Select Case refEventLog.OverwriteOutDated
Case 0 WScript.Echo _
" Log entries may be overwritten as required"
```

```
Case -1 WScript.Echo _
" Log entries may NEVER be overwritten"
Case Else WScript.Echo _
" Log entries may be overwritten after " & _
refEventLog.OverwriteOutDated & " days"
WScript.Echo
End Select
Next

Set refEventLog = Nothing
Set colEventLogs = Nothing
Set refWMI = Nothing
```

## Running the Hack

To run the script, use *Cscript.exe*, the command-line version of the Windows Script Host (WSH). Simply type cscript loginfo.vbs at a command prompt from the directory in which the script resides. Here is a sample of typical output when the script runs on a Windows 2000 machine:

```
C:\>cscript loginfo.vbs
Microsoft (R) Windows Script Host Version 5.6
Copyright (C) Microsoft Corporation 1996-2001. All rights reserved.

Information for the Security log:
 Current file size: 65536
 Maximum file size: 524288
 The Log currently contains 166 records
 Log entries may be overwritten after 7 days

Information for the Application log:
 Current file size: 524288
 Maximum file size: 524288
 The Log currently contains 2648 records
 Log entries may be overwritten as required

Information for the System log:
 Current file size: 524288
 Maximum file size: 524288
 The Log currently contains 2648 records
 Log entries may be overwritten after 7 days
```

Note that when you run this script on a domain controller it displays information concerning the Directory Service, File Replication Service, and DNS logs as well.

*—Rod Trent*

# Shortcut to Remote Assistance

#13

Remote Assistance is a helpful feature for troubleshooting Windows XP
systems, but it's a pain for ordinary users to use. This hack creates a helpful
shortcut to this feature.

Windows XP provides a Remote Assistance feature, but you have to walk
through several screens to get to it. This can be a problem for users who are
not technically savvy, and you might find yourself spending a lot of time
explaining to them how to use the feature. However, there's a really cool
workaround. Place a shortcut to this feature on users' desktops. This will
provide them with quicker access to the screen where they can type in the
remote computer's IP address to ask for remote assistance. This approach
will make life easier for both you and your users.

First, right-click on the desktop and choose New → Shortcut. Then, in the
Create Shortcut box, type the following URL into the Location Box:

```
hcp://CN=Microsoft%20Corporation,L=Redmond,S=Washington,C=US/
Remote%20Assistance/Escalation/Unsolicited/unsolicitedrcui.htm
```

as shown in Figure 1-14.

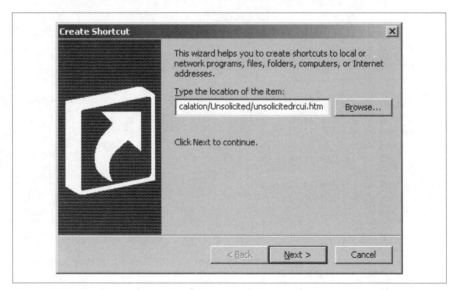

*Figure 1-14. Creating a shortcut to the Remote Assistance feature*

Click Next and name the shortcut something descriptive, like "Remote
Assistance" (Figure 1-15).

When the shortcut creation is finished, you'll have an icon on your desktop
for Remote Assistance (Figure 1-16).

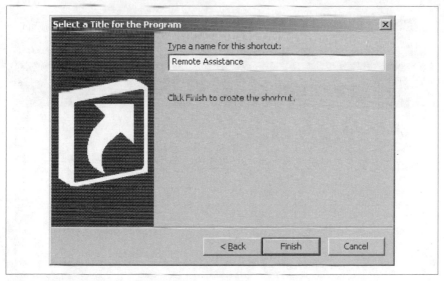

Figure 1-15. Naming the shortcut

Figure 1-16. Desktop icon for Remote Assistance

When you double-click on this icon, you'll be whisked away to the Remote Assistance feature, as shown in Figure 1-17. Simply type the computer name or IP address of the computer you want to connect to for remote assistance.

Pretty handy, eh?

—Rod Trent

### HACK    Desktop Checker
### #14

Here's a useful script to quickly display the configuration of a remote system for troubleshooting or inventory purposes.

This handy script will attempt to gather various Windows NT/2000/XP/2003 operating-system attributes and display them in a coherent way to assist in troubleshooting. I highly suggest modifying the customization variables located within the script. To edit this text file, just open it with Notepad (leave Word Wrap turned off). Even if you have no experience with VBScript,

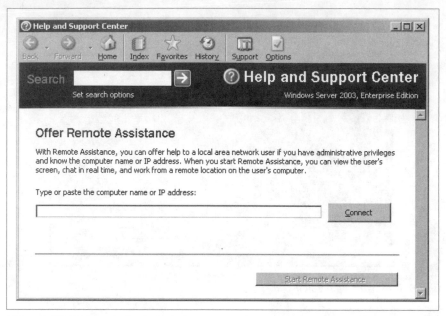

*Figure 1-17. Remote Assistance window*

you should find the changes quite easy to make. Please read the comments for different sections to make the tool viable for your organization.

This tool was intended to use only standard API calls and nothing from third-party COM objects. This keeps the tool lightweight and portable as only a text file. I suggest putting the tool into a local directory by itself so that the HTML pages it creates don't get out of hand. If a machine does not have WMI 1.5, then a lot of info might be missing. You will get similar results if you don't have administrator rights on the remote box. This script will not work on any Windows 9x operating systems.

## The Code

You can download this script as *DesktopChecker.vbs* from the O'Reilly web site at *http://www.oreilly.com/catalog/winsvrhks/*:

```
'************************************************************
'*                                                          *
'*  Desktop Checker - This script will ATTEMPT to gather    *
'*  various OS attributes and diplay them in a coherent     *
'*  way to assist in troubleshooting.  I highly suggest     *
'*  modifying the customization variables located 2 sections*
'*  below.  Please read the comments for different sections *
'*  to make the tool viable for your organization.  This    *
'*  tool was intended to use only standard API calls and    *
'*  nothing from 3rd party COM objects.  This keeps the     *
```

```
'*   tool lightwieght and portable as only a text file.        *
'*   I suggest putting the tool into a directory by itself      *
'*   so that the HTML pages it creates don't get out of hand    *
'*   If a machine does not have WMI 1.5 then lots of info may   *
'*   be missing.                                                *
'*                                                              *
'*   Dennis Abbott                                              *
'*   speckled_trout@hotmail.com                                 *
'*                                                              *
'**************************************************************
On Error Resume Next
Dim WshShell,WshFso,WshNet,WshSysEnv,IE,wmi,ADSIobj,OutPutFile,DumpFile
Dim PathToScript,ComSpec,Cnt,CompName,Company,Title,LogoLink,SelectServices, _
Domain,Progress,Instance,CurLine
Set WshShell = CreateObject("Wscript.Shell")
Set WshFso = CreateObject("Scripting.FileSystemObject")
Set WshNet = CreateObject("Wscript.Network")
Set WshSysEnv = WshShell.Environment("SYSTEM")
PathToScript = Left(WScript.ScriptFullName,(Len(WScript.ScriptFullName) - _
(Len(WScript.ScriptName) + 1)))
ComSpec = WshSysEnv("COMSPEC")
Cnt = 0


' grab contents of clipboard
' This allows you to work a LIST of boxes by cut-n-paste
Set IE = CreateObject("InternetExplorer.Application")
IE.Navigate("about:<script language=" & Chr(34) & "vbscr" & "ipt" & Chr(34)
& ">function go():document.all.it2.select" & "():document.execCommand " &
Chr(34) & "Paste" & Chr(34) & ":en" & "d function</script><body onload=go()>
<input type=t" & "ext value=" & Chr(34) & "start" & Chr(34) & " id=it2></
body>")
While IE.ReadyState <> 4:Wend
CompName = IE.document.all.it2.value
IE.quit()
Set IE = Nothing

' SET CUSTOMIZATION VARIABLES
Company = "myITforum"
Title = Company & " - Helpdesk Diagnostic Tool"
LogoLink = "http://www.myitforum.com/img/logo_final.gif"
' The next line allows you to query a variety of NT services of your choosing
' Make sure you enter the service NAME not the DISPLAY NAME, they can be
  different names
SelectServices = Array("WinMgmt","Norton Antivirus
Server","DefWatch","clisvc","Dhcp")
Domain = "amd"   'Your NT domain
Progress = True
'causes pop-up boxes when set to True it is silent when set to False

CompName = InputBox("Enter the name of the remote computer",Title,CompName)
If CompName = "" Then MsgBox "No machine name was entered.....goodbye" ; _
Wscript.Quit(0)
```

```
      Set wmi = GetObject("winmgmts:{impersonationLevel=impersonate}!//" & _
      CompName)
      Set ADSIobj = GetObject("WinNT://" & CompName & ",Computer")

      Call PrepHTML(CompName)   'create an HTML file

      If Progress Then
          WshShell.Popup "Getting OS information",2,Title, vbokonly + _
          vbsystemmodal
      End If
      Call GetOS(CompName)
      If Progress Then
          WshShell.Popup "Getting NT administrators",2,Title, vbokonly + _
          vbsystemmodal
      End If
      Call GetAdmins(CompName)
      If Progress Then
          WshShell.Popup "Checking Vital Services",2,Title, vbokonly + _
          vbsystemmodal
      End If
      Call Services(CompName,SelectServices)
      If Progress Then
          WshShell.Popup "Checking Admin shares",2,Title, vbokonly + vbsystemmodal
      End If
      Call AdminShares(CompName)
      If Progress Then
          WshShell.Popup "Getting date/time stamp",2,Title, vbokonly + _
          vbsystemmodal
      End If
      Call GetTime(CompName)
      If Progress Then
          WshShell.Popup "Getting NetBIOS information",2,Title, vbokonly + _
          vbsystemmodal
      End If
      Call GetNBTstat(CompName)
      If Progress Then
          WshShell.Popup "Pinging computer",2,Title, vbokonly + vbsystemmodal
      End If
      Call Ping(CompName)
      If Progress Then
          WshShell.Popup "Getting Registry Quota",2,Title, vbokonly + _
          vbsystemmodal
      End If
      Call GetRegQuota(CompName)
      If Progress Then
          WshShell.Popup "Getting Hardware information",2,Title, vbokonly + _
          vbsystemmodal
      End If
      Call GetHW(CompName)
      If Progress Then
          WshShell.Popup "Getting Network Card information",2,Title, vbokonly + _
          vbsystemmodal
      End If
```

```
Call GetNIC(CompName)
If Progress Then
    WshShell.Popup "Getting Software information",2,Title, vbokonly + _
    vbsystemmodal
End If
Call GetSW(CompName)
If Progress Then
    WshShell.Popup "Getting Critical NT Events",2,Title, vbokonly + _
    vbsystemmodal
End If
Call GetEvents(CompName)
Call ExitScript

Function PrepHTML(CompName)
    Set OutPutFile = WshFso.CreateTextFile(PathToScript & "\" & CompName _
    & ".html")
    OutPutFile.WriteLine "<body>"
    OutPutFile.WriteLine "<h1><center>" & Title & "</center></h1>"
    OutPutFile.WriteLine "<p><IMG SRC=" & Chr(34) & LogoLink & Chr(34) _
    & "</img></p>"
    OutPutFile.WriteLine "</p><p>" & "Account running this script is " _
    & WshNet.UserDomain & "\" & WshNet.UserName & " @ " _
    & Now & " from workstation " & WshNet.ComputerName & "</p>"
    OutPutFile.WriteLine "<p>Information on remote machine <b>\\" _
    & UCase(CompName) & "</b></p>"
    OutPutFile.WriteLine "<p><font color=red>To see information as it " _
    loads hit the REFRESH button on your web browser.</font></p>"
    OutPutFile.WriteLine "<hr>"
    WshShell.Run PathToScript & "\" & CompName & ".html"
End Function

Function GetOS(CompName)
    OutPutFile.WriteLine "<h3>1 - Operating System</h3>"
    OutPutFile.WriteLine "Operating System Version = " _
    & ADSIobj.OperatingSystem & " " & ADSIobj.OperatingSystemVersion & "<br>"
    For Each Instance in wmi.ExecQuery("Select * From Win32_OperatingSystem")
        OutPutFile.WriteLine "Operating System Caption = " _
        & Instance.Caption & "<br>"
        OutPutFile.WriteLine "Operating System Service Pack = " _
        & Instance.CSDVersion & "<br>"
        OutPutFile.WriteLine "Operating System LastBootUpTime = " _
        & StrDateTime(Instance.LastBootUpTime) & "<br>"
        OutPutFile.WriteLine "Operating System Directory = " _
        & Instance.WindowsDirectory & "<br>"
    Next
    OutPutFile.WriteLine "<hr>"
End Function

Function GetAdmins(CompName)
    Dim Admins,Admin
    Dim AdsInfo
    Set Admins = GetObject("WinNT://" & CompName & "/Administrators")
```

```
        OutPutFile.WriteLine "<h3>2 - Members of the local " _
        & "administrators group</h3>"
        OutPutFile.WriteLine "<table border=1><tr><td><b>Name</b></td><td><b>
Type</b></td><td><b>Description</b></td></tr>"
    For Each Admin in Admins.Members
        Set AdsInfo = GetObject(Admin.adspath)
        OutPutFile.WriteLine "<tr><td>" & AdsInfo.Name & "</td><td>" _
        & AdsInfo.Class & "</td><td>" & AdsInfo.Description & "</td></tr>"
    Next
    OutPutFile.WriteLine "</table>"
    OutPutFile.WriteLine "<hr>"
End Function

Function Services(CompName,SelectServices)
    Dim Service,srvc,State,Strg
    OutPutFile.WriteLine "<h3>3 - Status of vital services</h3>"
    OutPutFile.WriteLine "<table border=1><tr><td><b>Service Name</b></td>
<td><b>Display Name</b></td><td><b>Status</b></td></tr>"
    For Each Service in SelectServices
        Strg = "<tr><td>" & Service & "</td><td></td><td><b><font
color=FF0000>NOT PRESENT</font></b></td></tr>"
        ADSIobj.Filter = Array("Service")
        For Each srvc in ADSIobj
            Select Case srvc.Status
            Case 1 State = "<font color=FF0000>STOPPED</font>"
            Case 2 State = "<font color=FF0000>START_PENDING</font>"
            Case 3 State = "<font color=FF0000>STOP_PENDING</font>"
            Case 4 State = "RUNNING"
            Case 5 State = "<font color=FF0000>CONTINUE_PENDING</font>"
            Case 6 State = "<font color=FF0000>PAUSE_PENDING</font>"
            Case 7 State = "<font color=FF0000>PAUSED</font>"
            Case Else State = "<font color=FF0000>ERROR</font>"
            End Select
                If LCase(srvc.Name) = LCase(Service) Then Strg = _
                "<tr><td>" & srvc.Name & "</td><td>" & srvc.DisplayName _
                & "</td><td>" & State & "</td></tr></td>"
        Next
    OutPutFile.WriteLine Strg
    Next
    OutPutFile.WriteLine "</table>"
    OutPutFile.WriteLine "<hr>"
End Function

Function AdminShares(CompName)
    Dim Shares
    OutPutFile.WriteLine "<h3>4 - Status of administrative shares</h3>"
    Shares = True
    If WshFso.FolderExists("\\" & CompName & "\c$") = True Then
        OutPutFile.WriteLine "C$ share exists<br>"
    Else
        Shares = False
        OutPutFile.WriteLine "<font color=red>C$ share is not " _
        & "accessible</font><br>"
```

```
        End If
        If WshFso.FolderExists("\\" & CompName & "\admin$") = True Then
            OutPutFile.WriteLine "admin$ share exists<br>"
        Else
            Shares = False
            OutPutFile.WriteLine "<font color=red>admin$ share is not " _
            & "accessible</font><hr>"
        End If
        If Shares = False Then
            OutPutFile.WriteLine "<br>"
            OutPutFile.WriteLine "<font color=red>Shares made not be " _
            & "accessible due to the folowing reasons:</font><br>"
            OutPutFile.WriteLine "<font color=red>a - You do not have " _
            & "admin rights on this box</font><br>"
            OutPutFile.WriteLine "<font color=red>b - box is offline</font><br>"
            OutPutFile.WriteLine "<font color=red>c - Server service is not " _
            & "running</font><br>"
            OutPutFile.WriteLine "<font color=red>d - Shares have been " _
            & "disabled</font><br>"
            OutPutFile.WriteLine "<font color=red>e - remote machine's " _
            & "operating system is not NT-based</font><br>"
        End If
        OutPutFile.WriteLine "<hr>"
End Function


Function GetTime(CompName)
    OutPutFile.WriteLine "<h3>5 - Current date and time</h3>"
    OutPutFile.WriteLine "Current date and time of a domain controller<br>"
    WshShell.Run ComSpec & " /c net time /DOMAIN:" & Domain & " >" _
    & PathToScript & "\time.txt",6,True
    Set DumpFile = WshFso.OpenTextFile(PathToScript & "\time.txt", 1, True)
    Do While DumpFile.AtEndOfStream <> True
        CurLine = DumpFile.ReadLine
        If InStr(CurLine,"Current") <> 0 Then
            OutPutFile.WriteLine CurLine & "<br>"
        End If
    Loop
    DumpFile.Close
    OutPutFile.WriteLine "Current date and time of computer you are " _
    & "troubleshooting<br>"
    WshShell.Run ComSpec & " /c net time \\" & CompName " _
    & " >" & PathToScript & "\time.txt",6,True
    Set DumpFile = WshFso.OpenTextFile(PathToScript & "\time.txt", 1, True)
    Do While DumpFile.AtEndOfStream <> True
        CurLine = DumpFile.ReadLine
        If InStr(CurLine,"Current") <> 0 Then
            OutPutFile.WriteLine CurLine & "<br>"
        End If
    Loop
    DumpFile.Close
    OutPutFile.WriteLine "<hr>"
End Function
```

```
Function Ping(CompName)
    OutPutFile.WriteLine "<h3>7 - Ping test (DNS name resolution)</h3>"
    OutPutFile.WriteLine "<h4>If you get no reply on the ping yet other data
is retrieved on this page then there is most likely a problem with a static
DNS entry.  This needs to be fixed before anything else.  You MUST VERIFY
the machine is running DHCP before you modify the static DNS entry!!!!</h4>"
    WshShell.Run ComSpec & " /c ping " & CompName & " >" & PathToScript & _
    "\ping.txt",6,True
    Set DumpFile = WshFso.OpenTextFile(PathToScript & "\ping.txt", 1, True)
    Do While DumpFile.AtEndOfStream <> True
        OutPutFile.WriteLine DumpFile.ReadLine & "<br>"
    Loop
    Set DumpFile = Nothing
    OutPutFile.WriteLine "<hr>"
End Function

Function GetNBTstat(CompName)
    Dim User
    User = "Nobody Logged On"
    WshShell.Run ComSpec & " /c nbtstat -a " & CompName & " >" &
PathToScript & "\nbt.txt",6,True
    Set DumpFile = WshFso.OpenTextFile(PathToScript & "\nbt.txt", 1, True)
    Do While DumpFile.AtEndOfStream <> True
        CurLine = DumpFile.ReadLine
        If InStr(CurLine,"---") <> 0 Then
            CurLine = DumpFile.ReadLine
            CompName = Trim(Left(CurLine,InStr(CurLine,"<")-1))
        End If
        If InStr(CurLine,"<03>") <> 0 Then
            If Trim(Left(CurLine,InStr(CurLine,"<03>")-1)) <> _
            UCase(CompName) and _
            Trim(Left(CurLine,InStr(CurLine,"<03>")-1)) <> _
            UCase(CompName) & "$" Then
                User = Trim(Left(CurLine,InStr(CurLine,"<03>")-1))
            End If
        End If
        If InStr(CurLine,"<1E>") <> 0 Then
            If Trim(Left(CurLine,InStr(CurLine,"<1E>")-1)) <>
UCase(CompName) and Trim(Left(CurLine,InStr(CurLine,"<1E>")-1)) <>
UCase(CompName) & "$" Then
                Domain = Trim(Left(CurLine,InStr(CurLine,"<1E>")-1))
            End If
        End If
    Loop
    OutPutFile.WriteLine "<h3>6 - NetBIOS Info</h3>"
    OutPutFile.WriteLine "Current User Logged on = " & User & " (this value
may not be accurate, it depends on the box's messenger service)<br>"
    OutPutFile.WriteLine "Domain machine is joined to = " & Domain & "<br>"
    DumpFile.Close
        OutPutFile.WriteLine "<hr>"
End Function
```

```
Function GetNIC(CompName)
    OutPutFile.WriteLine "<h3>9 - Network Card Configurations</h3>"
    For Each Instance in wmi.ExecQuery("Select * From Win32_" & _
    "NetworkAdapterConfiguration Where IPenabled = 'True'")
        OutPutFile.WriteLine "<table border=1><tr><td><b>" & _
        "Attribute</b></td><td><b>Value</b></td></tr>"
        OutPutFile.WriteLine "<tr><td>Name of card</td><td>" _
        & Instance.Caption & "</td></tr>"
        OutPutFile.WriteLine "<tr><td>DHCP Enabled</td><td>" _
        & Instance.DhcpEnabled & "</td></tr>"
        OutPutFile.WriteLine "<tr><td>IP address</td><td>" _
        & Instance.IPAddress(0) & "</td></tr>"
        OutPutFile.WriteLine "<tr><td>Subnet Mask</td><td>" _
        & Instance.IPSubnet(0) & "</td></tr>"
        OutPutFile.WriteLine "<tr><td>MAC Address</td><td>" _
        & Instance.MACAddress & "</td></tr>"
        OutPutFile.WriteLine "<tr><td>DNS HostName</td><td>" _
        & Instance.DNSHostname & "</td></tr>"
        OutPutFile.WriteLine "<tr><td>DNS Servers(in order)</td><td>" _
        & Instance.DNSServerSearchOrder(0) & " : " _
        & Instance.DNSServerSearchOrder(1) & "</td></tr>"
        OutPutFile.WriteLine "<tr><td>Primary WINS</td><td>" _
        & Instance.WINSPrimaryServer & "</td></tr>"
        OutPutFile.WriteLine "<tr><td>Secondary WINS</td><td>" _
        & Instance.WINSSecondaryServer & "</td></tr>"
        OutPutFile.WriteLine "</table>"
    Next
    OutPutFile.WriteLine "<hr>"
End Function

Function GetRegQuota(CompName)
    OutPutFile.WriteLine "<h3>8 - Registry size information</h3>"
    For each Instance in wmi.InstancesOf("Win32_Registry")
        OutPutFile.WriteLine "Current Registry size is " _
        & Instance.CurrentSize & " MB's.<br>"
        OutPutFile.WriteLine "Maximum Registry size is " _
        & Instance.MaximumSize & " MB's.<br>"
        If Instance.MaximumSize - Instance.CurrentSize < 8 Then
            OutPutFile.WriteLine "<font color=red><b>The Registry quota on " _
            & CompName & " may need to be increased!!!</font></b><br>"
        End If
    Next
    OutPutFile.WriteLine "<hr>"
End Function

Function GetHW(CompName)
    Dim stuff
    OutPutFile.WriteLine "<h3>10 - Hardware Information</h3>"
    For Each Instance in wmi.ExecQuery("Select * From Win32_" & _
    "LogicalDisk Where DeviceID = 'C:'")
        OutPutFile.WriteLine "Total Drive space available on C: is " &
Left(Instance.FreeSpace/1000000,InStr(Instance.FreeSpace/1000000, ".")-1) &
" Megabytes.<br>"
```

```
                stuff = ((Instance.Size - Instance.FreeSpace)/Instance.Size)*100
                OutPutFile.WriteLine "The C: drive is " _
                & Left(stuff,InStr(stuff, ".")-1) & "% full.<br>"
        Next
        For Each Instance in wmi.ExecQuery("Select * From Win32_ComputerSystem")
                OutPutFile.WriteLine "Computer Manufacturer = " _
                & Instance.Manufacturer & "<br>"
                OutPutFile.WriteLine "Computer Model = " & Instance.Model & "<br>"
                OutPutFile.WriteLine "Total Physical Memory = " & Left(Instance.
TotalPhysicalMemory/1000000,InStr(Instance.TotalPhysicalMemory/1000000,".")-
1) & " MB's" & "<br>"
        Next
        For Each Instance in wmi.ExecQuery("Select * From Win32_" & _
        "SystemEnclosure")
                OutPutFile.WriteLine "Asset Tag = " & Instance.SMBIOSassettag " _
                & "<br>"
                OutPutFile.WriteLine "Serial Number = " & Instance.serialnumber " _
                & "<br>"
        Next
        For Each Instance in wmi.ExecQuery("Select * From Win32_Processor")
                OutPutFile.WriteLine "Processor Name = " & Instance.Name & "<br>"
                OutPutFile.WriteLine "Processor Clock Speed = " _
                & Instance.CurrentClockSpeed & " MHz<br>"
                OutPutFile.WriteLine "Processor Voltage = " _
                & Instance.CurrentVoltage & " Volts<br>"
                OutPutFile.WriteLine "Current Processor Load = " _
                & Instance.LoadPercentage & "%<br>"
        Next
        OutPutFile.WriteLine "<hr>"
End Function

Function GetSW(CompName)
        Dim oReg
        Dim NavParent,PatternDate,NavDir,NavVer,IEVersion,program,installed,
        Version,ProgramName
        OutPutFile.WriteLine "<h3>11 - Software Information</h3>"
        Set oReg=GetObject("winmgmts:{impersonationLevel=impersonate}!//" _
        & CompName & "/root/default:StdRegProv")
        oReg.getstringvalue 2147483650,"SOFTWARE\INTEL\LANDesk\VirusProtect6\
CurrentVersion\","Parent",NavParent
        oReg.getstringvalue 2147483650,"SOFTWARE\Symantec\SharedDefs\", _
        & "NAVCORP_70",PatternDate
        oReg.getstringvalue 2147483650,"SOFTWARE\Symantec\InstalledApps\" & _
        ","NAV",NavDir
        If UCase(Left(NavDir,1)) = "C" Then
                NavVer = WshFso.GetFileVersion("\\" & CompName & "\c$\" _
                & Right(NavDir,Len(NavDir)-3) & "\vpc32.exe")
                OutPutFile.WriteLine "Norton Antivirus Version = " &  NavVer _
                & "<br>"
        End If
        PatternDate = Right(PatternDate,12)
        OutPutFile.WriteLine "Norton Antivirus Parent Server = " & NavParent _
        & "<br>"
```

```
    OutPutFile.WriteLine "Norton Antivirus Definition Date = " _
    & Mid(PatternDate,5,2) & "/" & Mid(PatternDate,7,2) & "/" &
Mid(PatternDate,1,4) & " Revision " & Right(PatternDate,3) & "<br>"
    oReg.getstringvalue 2147483650,"SOFTWARE\Microsoft\Internet Explorer\" & _
    ","Version",IEVersion
    OutPutFile.WriteLine "<p>Internet Explorer Version = " & IEVersion
    OutPutFile.WriteLine "<p>Installed Programs (from Add/Remove Programs
applet)</p>"
    OutPutFile.WriteLine "<table border=1><tr><td><b>Program Name</b></td>
<td><b>Version(if available)</b></td></tr>"
    oReg.EnumKey 2147483650, "SOFTWARE\Microsoft\Windows\CurrentVersion\" & _
    "Uninstall", installed
    For each program in installed
        oReg.getstringvalue 2147483650,"SOFTWARE\Microsoft\Windows\" & _
        "CurrentVersion\Uninstall\" & program & "\","DisplayName",ProgramName
        oReg.getstringvalue 2147483650,"SOFTWARE\Microsoft\Windows\" & _
        "CurrentVersion\Uninstall\" & program & "\","DisplayVersion",Version
        If ProgramName <> "" Then
            OutPutFile.WriteLine "<tr><td>" & ProgramName & "</td><td>" &
Version & "</td></tr>"
        End If
    Next
    OutPutFile.WriteLine "</table>"
    OutPutFile.WriteLine "<hr>"
End Function

Function GetEvents(CompName)
    OutPutFile.WriteLine "<h3>12 - First 25 Errors from the system event
log</h3>"
    OutPutFile.WriteLine "<table border=1><tr><td><b>DateTimeStamp</b></td>
<td><b>EventSource</b></td><td><b>Message</b></td></tr>"
    For Each Instance in wmi.ExecQuery("Select * From Win32_NTLogEvent Where
Type = 'Error' and LogFile = 'System'")
        Cnt = Cnt + 1
        If Cnt = 25 Then Exit For
        OutPutFile.WriteLine "<tr><td>" & Mid(Instance.TimeGenerated,5,2) " _
        & "-" & Mid(Instance.TimeGenerated,7,2) & "-" _
        & Left(Instance.TimeGenerated,4) & "</td><td>" _
        & Instance.SourceName & "</td><td>" & Instance.Message & "</td></tr>"
    Next
    OutPutFile.WriteLine "</table>"
End Function
Function StrDateTime(d)
    Dim strVal,strDate,strTime
    strVal = CStr(d)
    strDate = DateSerial(Left(strVal, 4), _
    Mid(strVal, 5, 2), _
    Mid(strVal, 7, 2))
    strTime = TimeSerial(Mid(strVal, 9, 2), _
    Mid(strVal, 11, 2), _
    Mid(strVal, 13, 2))
    StrDateTime = strDate + strTime
End Function
```

```
Function ExitScript
    OutPutFile.WriteLine "</body>"
    OutPutFile.Close
    WshShell.Run PathToScript & "\" & CompName & ".html"
    If Progress Then
        MsgBox "The " & Title & " script is done.",vbokonly + _
        vbsystemmodal,Title
    End If
    Set WshShell = Nothing
    Set WshFso = Nothing
    Set WshNet = Nothing
    Set OutPutFile = Nothing
    Wscript.Quit(0)
End Function
```

## Running the Hack

To run this hack, simply double-click on the *DesktopChecker.vbs* file in Windows Explorer (or on a shortcut to the file on your desktop). Then, type the name of the remote computer you want to query using either its Net-BIOS name, DNS name, or IP address. At this point, Internet Explorer will open and display a page titled "myITforum Helpdesk Diagnostic Tool," followed by a series of dialog boxes that show the progress of the script (you don't need to click OK to close these dialog boxes, because they close automatically). Once the final dialog box appears—"The myITforum Helpdesk Diagnostic Tool script is done"—click OK and refresh the web page to view the information.

Here's some sample output generated when the script was run on a workstation using Domain Admin credentials. The target machine is a Windows Server 2003 machine named *SRV230*. The output of the script is in the form of an HTML page named *srv230.htm*, which is created in the same directory where the script itself resides, but the output has been reformatted here as text to make it easier to include in this book.

```
myITforum - Helpdesk Diagnostic Tool
Account running this script is MTIT2\administrator @ 12/3/2003 11:40:37 AM
from workstation SRV235
Information on remote machine \\SRV230
To see information as it loads hit the REFRESH button on your web browser.
-----------------------------------------------------------------------
1 - Operating System
Operating System Version = Windows NT 5.2
Operating System Caption = Microsoft(R) Windows(R) Server 2003, Enterprise
Edition
Operating System Service Pack =
Operating System LastBootUpTime = 12/3/2003 11:26:42 AM
Operating System Directory = C:\WINDOWS
-----------------------------------------------------------------------
```

2 - Members of the local administrators group
Name            Type    Description
Administrator   User    Built-in account for administering the computer/
domain
Enterprise Admins  Group  Designated administrators of the enterprise
Domain Admins      Group  Designated administrators of the domain
--------------------------------------------------------------------
3 - Status of vital services
Service Name           Display Name                          Status
winmgmt                Windows Management Instrumentation     RUNNING
Norton Antivirus Server                                      NOT PRESENT
DefWatch                                                     NOT PRESENT
clisvc                                                       NOT PRESENT
Dhcp                   DHCP Client                           RUNNING
--------------------------------------------------------------------
4 - Status of administrative shares
C$ share exists
admin$ share exists
--------------------------------------------------------------------
5 - Current date and time
Current date and time of a domain controller
Current date and time of computer you are troubleshooting
--------------------------------------------------------------------
6 - NetBIOS Info
Current User Logged on = Nobody Logged On (this value may not be accurate,
it depends on the box's messenger service)
Domain machine is joined to = amd
--------------------------------------------------------------------
7 - Ping test (DNS name resolution)
If you get no reply on the ping yet other data is retrieved on this page
then there is most likely a problem with a static DNS entry. This needs to
be fixed before anything else. You MUST VERIFY the machine is running DHCP
before you modify the static DNS entry!!!!
--------------------------------------------------------------------
8 - Registry size information
Current Registry size is 1 MB's.
Maximum Registry size is 88 MB's.
--------------------------------------------------------------------
10 - Hardware Information
Total Drive space available on C: is 1776 Megabytes.
The C: drive is 58% full.
Computer Manufacturer = System Manufacturer
Computer Model - System Name
Total Physical Memory = 536 MB's
Asset Tag - Asset-1234567890
Serial Number = Chassis Serial Number
Processor Name = Intel(R) Pentium(R) III processor
Processor Clock Speed = 501 MHz
Processor Voltage - 29 Volts
Current Processor Load = 2%
--------------------------------------------------------------------
9 - Network Card Configuration
Attribute              Value

```
Name of card            [00000001] 3Com EtherLink XL 10/100 PCI For Complete
PC Management NIC (3C905C-TX)
DHCP Enabled            False
IP address              172.16.11.230
Subnet Mask             255.255.255.0
MAC Address             00:01:02:FC:92:FC
DNS HostName            srv230
DNS Servers(in order)   172.16.11.230 :
Primary WINS
Secondary WINS
-----------------------------------------------------------------------------
11 - Software Information
Norton Antivirus Parent Server =
Norton Antivirus Definition Date = // Revision
Internet Explorer Version = 6.0.3790.0
Installed Programs(from Add/Remove Programs applet)

Program Name                                            Version(if
available)
FullShot V6
Windows Media Player Hotfix [See wm819639 for more information]
Remote Administration Tools                             5.2.3790.0
-----------------------------------------------------------------------------
12 - First 25 Errors from the system event log
DateTimeStamp  EventSource  Message
11-21-2003     W32Time      The time provider NtpClient is configured to
acquire time from one or more time sources, however none of the sources are
currently accessible. No attempt to contact a source will be made for 15
minutes. NtpClient has no source of accurate time.
11-13-2003     DCOM         The server {A9E69610-B80D-11D0-B9B9-
00A0C922E750} did not register with DCOM within the required timeout.
etc...
```

—*Dennis Abbott*

## Top Five Tools

HACK #15

Here's one IT professional's take on five third-party tools for Windows 2000 every system administrator should have.

There can be no doubt that with every release of Microsoft's operating system the need for third-party utilities becomes less and less. One major complaint about NT was its lack of disk quotas, something Unix has included since day one. A number of companies noticed this oversight and produced a product that did the trick. The release of Windows 2000 saw disk quotas become part of the OS, thus making the need to purchase this type of software an irrelevance for the majority of companies.

Whether you agree with Microsoft's policy of continually adding features to its products that were once available only from other sources is one for debate. But in my role as a network administrator, I still find a need to seek out additional software to help make my job a lot easier. I'm sure everyone has their favorite must-have utilities, but these are my top five must-have add-on products for Windows 2000.

## Server Monitor Lite

Server Monitor Lite is an invaluable monitoring product that allows you to monitor your servers centrally and get notified if a problem occurs. I use this utility to ping all my servers periodically, watch for low disk space, keep an eye on critical services, and make sure the company intranet is still accessible for my users. For more information, see *http://www.purenetworking.net/ Products/ServerMonitor/ServerMonitor.htm*.

## Lost Password Recovery

Have you inherited systems for which nobody knows the local administrator password, or do you have users that need access to Word, Excel, or Access documents that are password-protected and nobody knows the password? Well, this handy little product will save the day. It lets you reset the password on a huge array of systems. For more information, see *http://www. lostpassword.com*.

## Data Replicator

Do you need to copy files from one system to another on a regular basis? Data Replicator makes this job much easier—it allows you to watch files or folders for changes, and then replicate them to another location. You can copy files across a LAN, WAN, or via FTP, which makes Data Replicator a great alternative to traditional backup software. For more information, see *http://www.purenetworking.net/Products/DataReplicator/DataReplicator.htm*.

## Virtual Network Computing (VNC)

Take control of your remote servers from the comfort of your desk. VNC lets you control Windows, Unix, and Mac machines. For more information, see *http://www.realvnc.com*.

## Network View

With this handy tool, you'll never need to draw out your network. It automatically generates a network diagram for you within minutes. For more information, see *http://www.networkview.com*.

—*Janet Ryding*

# myITforum.com

One of the best resources around for administrators who deploy and manage Windows-based networks, myITforum.com is best described by its CEO and founder, Rod Trent.

myITforum.com (*http://www.myitforum.com*) is the leading systems administration web site and community. It was created to be the Internet's premiere knowledge and information forum for IT professionals. The web site provides IT administrators the opportunity to gain better insight about what they do by learning/sharing from other IT experts throughout the world. Through the web site, myITforum.com users give tips, share insight, and download utilities and tools to assist them in managing their IT enterprises. Whether you oversee 10 nodes or 100,000 nodes, myITforum.com can help you manage your environment.

myITforum.com is managed by Rod Trent (myself!), a Microsoft MVP and author of the best-selling books *Microsoft SMS Installer, Admin911: SMS*, and *IIS 5.0: A Beginner's Guide*. Rod Trent is the leading authority on Microsoft SMS and an annual presenter and keynote presenter at the annual Microsoft Management Summit (*http://www.microsoft.com/management/ training/mms.mspx*). He has over 18 years of IT experience, 8 of which have been dedicated to SMS. In addition to his best-selling books, Rod has written thousands of articles on technology topics in many publications, on the Web, and in the form of Microsoft white papers, case studies, and technical guides. Rod is also a principal in NetImpress, Inc. (*http://www.netimpress. com*), a technology publishing company.

## History

myITforum.com's roots lead back to the now defunct Swynk.com web site. Swynk.com was founded and operated by Stephen Wynkoop until 1999. Stephen had developed a web site that allowed administrators all over the world to gain support for their everyday IT tasks. myITforum.com was built on the success of the Systems Management Server (SMS) section of Swynk. com. The success of the SMS section led to an urgency to keep the ever-growing community alive when it was evident that the parent company of Swynk.com was not going to support it. Swynk.com had become much more than simply content and articles, and it became evident that the web site had outgrown its electronic boundaries. It had become a live community that was represented both on the Web and in the real IT world. So, the SMS community from Swynk.com migrated to its web site location: *http:// www.myitforum.com*.

Since the move, myITforum.com has grown by leaps and bounds, primarily due to the opportunities it presents to administrators all over the world to interact with their fellow administrators and peers. The members of the myITforum.com community are the most caring folks found in any corner of the Internet. They give their time, experience, and knowledge selflessly to help create a brain trust of smarter administrators who become efficient and proficient IT professionals.

## Scope

While myITforum.com was based on Microsoft Systems Management Server, it has grown far beyond this one topic. To be an SMS administrator, an IT professional must be proficient in far more than just SMS. SMS administrators are required to support many different applications, operating systems, and technologies. Because of this requirement and myITforum.com's ability to grow quickly with the community needs, myITforum.com expanded its topic base to include many more areas in the IT world. myITforum.com supports Altiris products, Microsoft Operations Manager (MOM), VBScript, SMS 1.2/2.0/2003, Windows, SQL Server, Networking, Active Directory, security and patch management, antivirus technologies, Windows Mobile technologies, web technologies, and deployment technologies such as Windows Installer.

MyITforum.com supports these many topics through articles, email discussion lists, and web-based forums Figure 1-18 shows the myITforum.com home page. The articles posted to the web site are quite a bit different than the articles you find in other publications. Instead of information from individuals you can't be sure have ever worked in IT, the myITforum.com articles are from real IT workers from real IT experiences. The premise is that if you are faced with a real-world situation, someone out there has probably already been through it and has the solution all wrapped up. By sharing their experiences through articles, the myITforum.com columnists provide a central location for IT administrators all of the world to get solutions to problems they might be facing, without having to spend days or weeks working through a tough situation. If it's a problem, someone has already faced it and succeeded, and the solution is probably outlined on myITforum.com.

In addition to providing these web resources for the myITforum.com community, myITforum.com has transcended the confines of the Internet. Because real IT professionals make up the myITforum.com community, myITforum.com has reached beyond the Web to aid real people in setting up real-world local communities. myITforum.com has been instrumental in setting up over 17 user groups all over the world. From the U.S. to Canada

*Figure 1-18. Home page of myITforum.com*

to Israel to Australia, myITforum.com has provided valuable time and resources to set up and manage some of the most successful user group communities in the real world. myITforum.com provides many things to the user groups, including a free web site for the group's web presence, contacts with vendors for speaking services, and an intermediary link between Microsoft and the user group for planning, support, and meeting facilities.

Over time, myITforum.com has also become a successful liaison between employers and prospective employees. Offered as a free service, myITforum.com has helped place hundreds of qualified employees into IT jobs. During the last few years, when the economy has caused layoffs and outsourcing, myITforum.com has stood as a central beacon for employers and employees to connect with each other. So, in addition to providing a central repository for connecting with peers, myITforum.com has become an informal meeting place, where workers find employment and employers locate the top candidates for open positions.

It has been noted that if you attend any IT event, anywhere in the world, you will find at least one myITforum.com community member. myITforum.com's influence reaches into almost every nook of the IT world, primarily because it provides what IT professionals need to advance to a higher level in their profession, but also because it provides a level of sharing that can't be experienced anywhere else. myITforum.com is a real community comprised of real people with real personalities. Participating in myITforum.com is like meeting with friends. myITforum.com is an ever-evolving, ever-growing community meeting place that extends experience and knowledge that is more valuable than sitting through a weeklong training class. At the end of the day, myITforum.com is the one location for everything IT.

—*Rod Trent*

# CHAPTER TWO

# Active Directory
## Hacks 17–24

Most of the time you're administering Active Directory, you're probably using the Active Directory Users and Computers console. Like most GUI tools, this console is easy to use but ill-suited for complex or repetitive tasks. That's where scripts come in, and this chapter includes a handful of VB scripts that leverage the Active Directory Services Interface (ADSI) and Windows Management Instrumentation (WMI) to make your life simple. These scripts can be used to perform tasks such as searching for old computer accounts, creating organizational units (OUs), delegating authority over OUs, and displaying information about objects stored in Active Directory. See Chapter 3 for additional scripts targeted mainly to administering users and groups with Active Directory.

As with any custom scripts, be sure to try them in a test environment before using them on your production network. Also make sure that you have the latest scripting engines on the workstation or server from which you run these scripts. You can download the latest scripting engines from the Microsoft Scripting Home Page (*http://msdn.microsoft.com/scripting/*). Finally, note that when you work with ADSI you must have the same applicable rights you use for running the built-in administrative tools. Typically, what this means is that you need to be a member of either the Administrators group on the machine being targeted or the Domain Admins group in an Active Directory environment.

### HACK #17 Retrieve the List of Old Domain Computer Accounts

Finding inactive computer accounts in Active Directory is a chore—unless, of course, you script it.

If you need to quickly retrieve a list of old (inactive) computer accounts in the domain, VBScript is your utility of choice. The script in this hack first asks for the domain name (Figure 2-1), then prompts for the number of days for active computer accounts (Figure 2-2), and then, finally, displays the old computer accounts that are found in the domain.

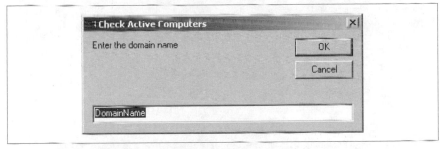

Figure 2-1. Specifying the name of your domain

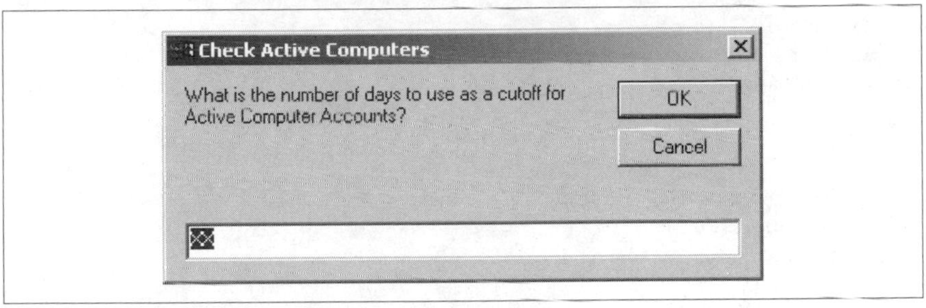

Figure 2-2. Specifying number of days for cutoff

The computer accounts shown have not been active during the days you specified. For example, when we run the script we can see that the computer account for the machine named SRV111 has a password whose age is beyond the cutoff, so the script recommends that you delete this account to be safe (Figure 2-3).

Figure 2-3. Recommending an account that should be deleted

This is a great, quick way to find those computers that could be having trouble authenticating, or those that have been brought down but remain in the domain's list.

## The Code

Type the following code into Notepad (make sure Word Wrap is turned off), and save it with a *.vbs* extension as *DeleteOldComputers.vbs*:

```
On Error Resume Next

DomainString=Inputbox("Enter the domain name","Check Active
Computers","DomainName")

if DomainString="" then
wscript.echo "No domain specified or script cancelled."
wscript.quit
end if

numDays=InputBox("What is the number of days to use as a cutoff for" & _
"Active Computer Accounts?","Check Active Computers","XX")

if numDays="" then
wscript.echo "No cutoff date specified or script cancelled."
wscript.quit
end if

Set DomainObj = GetObject("WinNT://"&DomainString)

if err.number<>0 then
wscript.echo "Error connecting to " & DomainString
wscript.quit
end if

DomainObj.Filter = Array("computer")
Wscript.echo "Computer Accounts in " & DomainString & " older than " & _
numDays & " days."
For each Computer in DomainObj
Set Account = GetObject("WinNT://" & DomainString & "/" & Computer.Name & _
"$")
RefreshTime = FormatNumber((Account.get("PasswordAge"))/86400,0)
If CInt(RefreshTime) >= CInt(numDays) Then
wscript.echo "**DELETE** " & Computer.Name & " Password Age is " & _
RefreshTime & " days."
End If
Next

set DomainObj=Nothing
set Shell=Nothing
Wscript.quit
```

## Running the Hack

To run this script, use *Cscript.exe*, the command-line script engine for the Windows Script Host (WSH). Here's some sample output when the script is run to delete computer accounts older than 90 days in the MTIT domain:

```
C:\>cscript.exe DeleteOldComputers.vbs
Microsoft (R) Windows Script Host Version 5.6
Copyright (C) Microsoft Corporation 1996-2001. All rights reserved.

Computer Accounts in mtit older than 90 days.
**DELETE** NEWTEST1 Password Age is 151 days.
**DELETE** QWER Password Age is 151 days.
**DELETE** SRV211 Password Age is 97 days.
**DELETE** SRV212 Password Age is 154 days.
```

*—Rod Trent*

# Automate Creation of OU Structure

Here's a snappy method for creating a standard hierarchy of organizational units (OUs) for a domain.

If you manage deployment of Active Directory in a medium-sized or large organization, you probably are spending a significant amount of time trying to maintain consistency in the Active Directory hierarchy. Even within a single domain, it typically makes sense to keep your organizational units (OUs) structured according to some agreed-upon rules. Regardless of whether your top-tier OU design is based on functional, business, geographic, or some other criteria, you will likely benefit from keeping the lower tiers arranged in the same fashion. This way, for example, you can formulate standard operating procedures that will apply across the entire organization. You can also attempt to automate some of the common administrative tasks, such as user, group, or computer account creation; script delegations and permission assignments; and group policy object management on the OU level.

One of the ways to make sure that the structure will remain consistent throughout Active Directory deployment is to script the OU-creation process. The script in this hack creates a sample OU hierarchy. The assumption is that the top-level OUs are created manually, while the lower layers are always the same. The structure follows Microsoft best practices and includes two second-tier OUs: Accounts and Resources. The Accounts OU is further divided into Users, ServiceAccounts, Groups, and Admins. Resources consists of Workstations and Servers. It is fairly easy to extend this structure (for example, you could create separate OUs for different server types, such as File, Print, or TerminalServices, beneath the Servers OU). The script performs some error checking to verify that the respective organizational units haven't been created yet.

## The Code

The following VBScript is a Windows script (*.wsf) file, a text document that contains Extensible Markup Language (XML) code. Using a text editor such as Notepad (with Word Wrap turned off) type the following code and save it as *CreateOU.wsf*:

```
<?xml version="1.0"?>
<job id="CreateOUs">
<script language="VBscript">
<![CDATA[

'*****************************************************************
'*** The script creates OU structure underneath top level OU
'*** Second level: Accounts and Resources
'*** Third level:
'*** Accounts children OUs - Users, ServiceAccounts, Groups, Admins
'*** Resources children OUs - Workstations, Servers
'***
'*** To execute, run cscript.exe //nologo CreateOUs.wsf OUName
'*** where OUName is the name of the top level OU
Option Explicit

Dim strOU1 'the first level OU
Dim strOU2 'the second level OU
Dim strOU3 'the third level OU
Dim arrOUTier2 'array of the second level OUs
Dim arrOUTier3a 'first array of the third level OUs
Dim arrOUTier3b 'second array of the third level OUs

Dim strDomainDN 'name of the domain
Dim strADsPath 'ADsPath of the first level OU
Dim strADsSubPath 'ADsPath of the second level OU
Dim adsRootDSE 'aDSRootDSE object
Dim adsContainer, adsSubContainer, adsOU
'variables representing AD container objects

'*****************************************************************
'*** Connect to the current domain

Set adsRootDSE = GetObject("LDAP://rootDSE")
strDomainDN = adsRootDSE.Get("defaultNamingContext")

'*****************************************************************
'*** Connect to the top level OU

strOU1 = WScript.Arguments(0)
strADsPath = "LDAP://OU=" & strOU1 & "," & strDomainDN
Set adsContainer = GetObject(strADsPath)

On Error Resume Next
```

```
arrOUTier2 = Array("Accounts", "Resources")
arrOUTier3a = Array("Users", "ServiceAccounts", "Groups", "Admins")
arrOUTier3b = Array("Workstations", "Servers")

'***************************************************************
'*** Populate the OU structure

For Each strOU2 in arrOUTier2

Set adsOU = adsContainer.Create("OrganizationalUnit", "OU=" & strOU2)
adsOU.SetInfo
If ErrCheck(Err, strOU2) <> 2 Then

strADsSubPath = "LDAP://OU=" & strOU2 & ",OU=" & strOU1 & "," & strDomainDN
Set adsSubContainer = GetObject(strADsSubPath)

Select Case strOU2
Case "Accounts"
For Each strOU3 in arrOUTier3a
Set adsOU = adsSubContainer.Create("OrganizationalUnit", "OU=" & strOU3)
adsOU.SetInfo
Call ErrCheck(Err, strOU3)
Next
Case "Resources"
For Each strOU3 in arrOUTier3b
Set adsOU = adsSubContainer.Create("OrganizationalUnit", "OU=" & strOU3)
adsOU.SetInfo
Call ErrCheck(Err, strOU3)
Next
End Select

End If

Next

On Error GoTo 0

Set adsOU = Nothing
Set adsContainer = Nothing

'***************************************************************
'*** Error checking function

Function ErrCheck(objErr, strObj)

If objErr.Number <> 0 Then
'if the object already exists
If objErr.Number = &H80071392 Then
WScript.Echo "The OU " & strObj & " already exists"
ErrCheck = 1
Else
WScript.Echo "Unexpected error " & objErr.Description
ErrCheck = 2
End If
```

```
Else

    ErrCheck = 0

End If

objErr.Clear

End Function

]]>
</script>
</job>
```

## Running the Hack

To execute the script, open a command prompt, change to the directory in which *CreateOUs.wsf* resides, and type `cscript.exe //nologo CreateOUs.wsf "OUName"`, where *OUName* is the name of the top-level OU. If *OUName* does not already exist, you'll get an error. To illustrate how this script works, I first created an OU named `Boston` in the *mtit.com* domain and then ran `cscript.exe //nologo CreateOUs.wsf "Boston"` from the command line. Figure 2-4 shows the result in Active Directory Users and Computers.

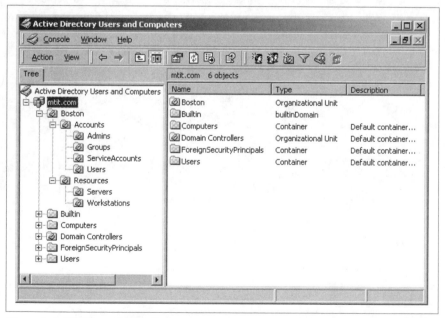

*Figure 2-4. OU hierarchy for Boston*

—*Marcin Policht*

# Modify All Objects in the OU

**HACK #19**

Use this script to quickly change specific properties of all objects within an organizational unit.

Using GUI tools such as Active Directory Users and Computers to modify the properties of objects stored in Active Directory is a slow process. In Windows 2000, you have to open the properties sheet for each object, switch to the appropriate tab, and make the change; then, you must do it over and over again for other objects. In Windows Server 2003, you can open the properties of multiple objects simultaneously, but not all tabs are available when you do this and only a small number of settings can be modified in this way. It would be nice if there were a faster way of doing this. Using VBScript, this is indeed possible.

The sample script in this hack shows how you can modify the properties of all objects in a specific OU. This particular script modifies the state, address, postal code, and city for all User objects in the Boston OU in the *mtit.com* domain, but it can easily be customized to modify other properties of objects. This script is particularly useful if you've planned your implementation of Active Directory so that users in the same OU have certain sets of similar properties, such as their business address information.

## The Code

Type the following script into Notepad (with Word Wrap disabled) and save it with a *.vbs* extension as *ModifyUsers.vbs*. Be sure to customize the second line to specify the OU and domain for your own environment, and customize the Put statements to use the address information appropriate for users in your OU.

```
Dim oContainer

Set oContainer=GetObject("LDAP://OU=Boston,DC=mtit,DC=com")

ModifyUsers oContainer

'cleanup
Set oContainer = Nothing

WScript.Echo "Finished"

Sub ModifyUsers(oObject)
Dim oUser
oObject.Filter = Array("user")
For Each oUser in oObject
oUser.Put "st","Your State"
oUser.Put "streetAddress","Your Address"
```

```
oUser.Put "postalCode","Your Zip"
oUser.Put "l","Your City"
oUser.SetInfo
Next
End Sub
```

## Running the Hack

To run the script, simply create a shortcut to it and double-click on the shortcut. A dialog box will appear, indicating that the script ran successfully. Figure 2-5 shows what the Address tab of the properties sheet for user Bob Smith (who is in the Boston OU) looks like after running the script.

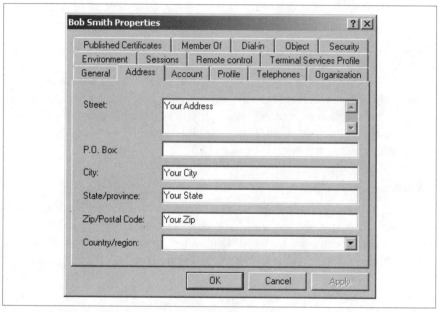

*Figure 2-5. Result of running the ModifyUsers.vbs script*

—*Rod Trent*

### HACK
### #20    Delegate Control of an OU to a User

Rather than use the Delegation of Control Wizard, use this script to delegate authority over an organizational unit (OU) to a particular user.

By delegating administrative responsibilities, you can eliminate the need for multiple administrative accounts that have broad authority (such as over an entire domain). Although you likely will still use the predefined Domain Admins group for administration of the entire domain, you can limit the accounts that are members of the Domain Admins group to highly trusted administrative users.

Administrative control can be granted to a user or group by using the Delegation of Control wizard. The Delegation of Control wizard allows you to select the user or group to which you want to delegate control, the organizational units and objects you want to grant those users the right to control, and the permissions to access and modify objects.

## The Code

While using the wizard to do this is straightforward, there is a quick and easy way to achieve the same effect through VBScript. Just open a text editor such as Notepad (making sure that Word Wrap is disabled), type the following script, and save it with a *.vbs* extension as *DelegateOU.vbs*:

```
Set ou = GetObject("LDAP://
OU=Test,OU=Users,OU=Services,OU=Network,DC=MY,DC=Domain,DC=com")
Set sec = ou.Get("ntSecurityDescriptor")
Set acl = sec.DiscretionaryAcl
Set ace = CreateObject("AccessControlEntry")
ace.AceType = ADS_ACETYPE_ACCESS_ALLOWED_OBJECT
ace.AccessMask = ADS_RIGHT_DS_CREATE_CHILD Or ADS_RIGHT_DS_DELETE_CHILD
ace.ObjectType = "{BF967ABA-0DE6-11D0-A285-00AA003049E2}"
'User's GUID (schemaIDGuid)
ace.AceFlags = ADS_ACEFLAG_INHERIT_ACE
ace.Flags = ADS_FLAG_OBJECT_TYPE_PRESENT
ace.Trustee = "MY\Jsmith" 'User to delegate to
acl.AddAce ace
sec.DiscretionaryAcl = acl
ou.Put "ntSecurityDescriptor", Array(sec)
ou.SetInfo
Set ace = Nothing
Set acl = Nothing
Set sec = Nothing
```

When you run this script, the result is to delegate to the user the ability to create and delete users in the MY.DOMAIN.COM/NETWORK/SERVICES/USERS/TEST organizational unit.

The first line you need to customize to make this work in your own environment is this one:

```
Set ou = GetObject("LDAP://OU=Test,OU=Users,OU=Services,OU=Network," & _
DC=MY,DC=Domain,DC=com")
```

You must insert the distinguished name (DN) of the OU to which you want to delegate this right in the LDAP URL section of the command line. For example, if you want the delegated user to be able to add and delete users in the OU called UR.DOMAINHERE.COM/HR/USERS, the line would need to look like this:

```
Set ou = GetObject("LDAP:// OU=Users,OU=HR,DC=Ur,DC=Domainhere,DC=com")
```

Here is another line you need to modify for your environment:

```
ace.Trustee = "MY\Jsmith" User to delegate to
```

In the section in double quotes ("MY\Jsmith"), you must insert the username for the user to whom you want to delegate the right to add and delete users. For example, if the user that you want to be able to ADD and DELETE users is called Janedoe, the line would look like this:

```
ace.Trustee = "UR\Janedoe" 'Who is the beneficiary of this ace
```

Make sure you have the latest scripting engines on the workstation you run this script from; you can download current scripting engines from the Microsoft Scripting home page (*http://msdn.microsoft.com/library/default. asp?url=/nhp/Default.asp?contentid=28001169*). When working with the Active Directory Services Interface (ADSI), you must have the same applicable rights you need to use the built-in administrative tools.

### Running the Hack

To run the script, simply create a shortcut to the script and double-click on the shortcut. The script itself does the rest.

*—Hans Schefske*

## Send OU Information in Active Directory to an HACK #21 HTML Page

Here's a terrific way to quickly display all the organizational units (OUs) in a domain.

If your Active Directory (AD) domains have a lot of OUs in them, it's easy to lose track of them, especially if you have OUs nested within OUs. This handy script generates an HTML page of all OUs in your current AD domain showing their path, description, and creation date. This information not only tells you which OUs you have in your domain, it also tells you which OUs contain other OUs, so you can easily create a map of the OU structure of your domain.

## The Code

Just open Notepad or some other text editor (with Word Wrap disabled), type the following script, and save it with a *.vbs* extension as *OU2HTML.vbs*:

```
On Error Resume Next

Dim Root,Domain,wshNetwork
Dim oFileSys,fh

Set Root = GetObject("LDAP://RootDSE")
DomainPath = Root.Get("DefaultNamingContext")
Set Domain = GetObject("LDAP://" & DomainPath)
set wshNetwork=CreateObject("Wscript.Network")

myDomain=wshNetwork.UserDomain

htmlfile=myDomain & "-OUs.htm"

Set oFileSys=CreateObject("Scripting.FileSystemObject")
Set fh=oFileSys.CreateTextFile(htmlfile)

fh.WriteLine "<HTML><Title>" & myDomain & " Organizational Units</Title>"
fh.WriteLine "<Body><Font Size=+1>" & myDomain & " " & _
"Organizational Units </Font><HR>"
fh.WriteLine "<Table Border=1 BorderColor=Blue CellSpacing=0><TR>"
fh.WriteLine "<TD BGColor=Blue><Font Color=White><P Align=Center> " & _
"<B>OU</B></TD>"
fh.WriteLine "<TD BGColor=Blue><Font Color=White><P Align=Center><B>
Description</B></TD>"
fh.WriteLine "<TD BGColor=Blue><Font Color=White><P Align=Center> " & _
"<B>Path</B></TD>"
fh.WriteLine "<TD BGColor=Blue><Font Color=White><P Align=Center> " & _
"<B>Created</B></TD></TR>"

wscript.echo "Getting OU information for " & mydomain & "..." & _
EnumOU Domain.ADSPath

fh.WriteLine "</Table><Font Size=-1><I>Page Generated " & Now & " _
"</I></Font>"
fh.WriteLine "</Body></HTML>"
fh.close

wscript.echo "Output has been sent to " & htmlfile

Set oFileSys=Nothing
Set fh=Nothing
Set domain=Nothing
Set Root=Nothing
Set wshNetwork=Nothing
```

```
wscript.quit

'*****************************************
Sub EnumOU(objPath)

'On Error Resume Next

Set objPath = GetObject(objPath)

objPath.Filter=Array("organizationalUnit")

For Each item in objPath
If item.Description="" Then
ouDescription="N/A"
Else
ouDescription=item.Description
End If

fh.writeLine "<TR><TD>" & MID(item.Name,4) & "</TD><TD>" & ouDescription & _
"</TD><TD>" & item.ADSPath & "</TD><TD>" & GetCreated(item.ADSPath) & "</TR>
"
'Uncomment next line for debugging purposes
' wscript.echo item.Name & vbTab & item.Description & vbTab & item.ADSPath

'Iterate through
EnumOU item.ADSPath

Next

Set objPath=Nothing

End Sub

'****************************
Function GetCreated(objPath)
On Error Resume Next

Set objDetail=GetObject(objPath)
Set objSchema=GetObject(objDetail.Schema)

For Each z in objSchema.OptionalProperties
Set adsProperty = GetObject("LDAP://Schema/" & z)
If z="whenCreated" Then
strCreated = objDetail.Get(z)
GetCreated=strCreated
'wscript.echo "Created " & strCreated
strValue=""
End If
Next

End Function
```

## Running the Hack

To run the script, simply create a shortcut to the script, double-click on the shortcut, and follow the prompts provided by the dialog boxes the script generates. When the script runs, it creates an HTML page in the same directory in which the script itself is located. The name of this HTML page is *domain-OUs.htm*, where *domain* is the name of your domain. Figure 2-6 shows a sample HTML page created for a test domain named *mtit.com*.

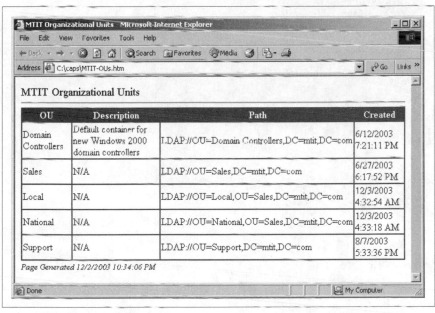

*Figure 2-6. OUs in the mtit.com domain*

It's easy to see from the Path column in Figure 2-6 that the Local and National OUs are contained within the Sales OU.

*—Hans Schefske*

## Display Active Directory Information

Here are five sample scripts that can be used to display information about computers, domains, sites, and trusts in Active Directory.

Scripts are a quick way to drill down into Active Directory to display information you'd otherwise have to hunt for using the GUI. These five sample scripts can be used by themselves or as starting points for developing more sophisticated scripts. Just type them into Notepad (with Word Wrap turned off) and save them with a *.vbs* extension. Then, type cscript.exe *scriptname*.vbs to run them from a command prompt. Enjoy!

## List All Computers in the Domain

The following VBScript retrieves a list of all computers in a given domain (or Active Directory container). Modify the *Domain* to your company's NT/2000 domain name or Active Directory container, and the list of registered computers will display:

```
Dim Container
Dim ContainerName
Dim Computer
ContainerName = "Domain"
Set Container = GetObject("WinNT://" & ContainerName)
Container.Filter = Array("Computer")
For Each Computer in Container
Response.Write Computer.Name & "<BR>"
Next
```

## Get a List of All Domains

This VBScript enumerates and lists all domains:

```
Dim NameSpace
Dim Domain
Set NameSpace = GetObject("WinNT:")
For Each Domain in NameSpace
Response.Write Domain.Name & "<BR>"
Next
```

## Get AD Site

This VBScript retrieves the name of the site to which the computer is assigned:

```
Set WshShell = Wscript.CreateObject("Wscript.Shell")
On Error Resume Next
Site = "Not Assigned"
Site = WshShell.RegRead( "HKEY_LOCAL_MACHINE\SYSTEM\CurrentControlSet\" & _
"Services\Netlogon\Parameters\SiteName" )
If Err.Number=-2147024894 Then
Site = WshShell.RegRead( "HKEY_LOCAL_MACHINE\SYSTEM\CurrentControlSet\" & _
"Services\Netlogon\Parameters\DynamicSiteName" )
End If

If Site = "Not Assigned" Then
WScript.Echo "This computer is not assigned to an Active Directory site."
Else
WScript.Echo "This computer is assigned to Active Directory site: " & site
End If
```

## Find a DC in a Site

Use this VBScript to verify that a specific domain controller (DC) exists in a site. Just replace the items in double quotes in the first two lines with your values:

```
strDcName = "DCName"
strSiteName = "SiteName"

Set objADSysInfo = CreateObject("ADSystemInfo")
strDcSiteName = objADSysInfo.GetDCSiteName(strDcName)

If UCase(strSiteName) = UCase(strDcSiteName) Then
WScript.Echo "TRUE: " & strDcName & " is in site " & strSiteName
Else
WScript.Echo "FALSE: " & strDcName & " is NOT in site " & strSiteName
End If
```

## List Trust Relationships

Use this script to enumerate the trust relationships for your domain and display the results:

```
strComputer = "."
Set objWMIService = GetObject("winmgmts:" _
& "{impersonationLevel=impersonate}!\\" & _
strComputer & "\root\MicrosoftActiveDirectory")
Set colTrustList = objWMIService.ExecQuery _
("Select * from Microsoft_DomainTrustStatus")
For each objTrust in colTrustList
Wscript.Echo objTrust.TrustedDomain
Wscript.Echo objTrust.TrustDirection
Wscript.Echo objTrust.TrustType
Wscript.Echo objTrust.TrustAttributes
Wscript.Echo objTrust.TrustedDCName
Wscript.Echo objTrust.TrustStatus
Wscript.Echo objTrust.TrustIsOK
Next
```

*—Rod Trent*

HACK
#23

# Store and Display Contact Information in Active Directory

Using a script and an Access database, you can store detailed contact information in Active Directory and display it as an HTML page.

Would you like to store all your employee contact information in Active Directory and then be able to display that information on an intranet page? Where I work, there are a number of individuals maintaining lists of user information. The telecom person maintains an Excel spreadsheet of employee names, phone numbers, and office locations. The Web person maintains a similar list for the Internet page. There's another list of sorts in a public folder on our Exchange server. I thought there must be a better way to get this information out that doesn't require quite so many people doing similar tasks.

Figure 2-7 shows my solution to this challenge.

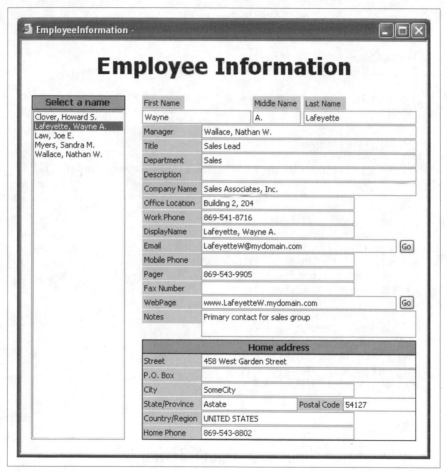

*Figure 2-7. HTML interface for Access database*

I created an Access database named *EmployeeInfo.mdb*, with fields for the information I'd like to make available. I then created a *.vbs* script named *ExportAdUsers.vbs*, which processes Active Directory user accounts that meet a specified criterion and exports the account information to the database. The information in the database is accessible via the Data Access Page shown in Figure 2-7.

While developing this solution, I found that I needed to be able to list information for employees who might not have an Active Directory user account. The database is open, so a designated person can maintain information for such employees.

Each time Active Directory account information is updated, the script should be run again to update the Access database. I added a field to the database that contains a value that differentiates records that were manually entered from records that were created by running the script. To be sure that no duplicates exist in the database, prior to performing each export, the script deletes all records that are indicated as being exported from Active Directory.

## The Code

Type the following VBScript into Notepad (with Word Wrap turned off) and save it with a *.vbs* extension as *ExportAdUsers.vbs*:

```
Option Explicit

'.........................................................................

' File:      ExportADUsers.vbs
' Updated:   Dec 2003
' Version:   1.0
' Author:    Dan Thomson, myITforum.com columnist
'            I can be contacted at dethomson@hotmail.com
'
' Usage:     This script should be run using cscript.
'            cscript ExportADUsers.vbs
'
' Input:     None
'
' Notes:     This script exports all users whose accounts are not disabled,
'            not expired, or do not have NoExport in their Notes section.
'            There is also a constant "Users2Skip" to which you should add
'            any names which should not be exported.
'
'.........................................................................


On Error Resume Next

' The name of the Access database to use
Const AccessDatabase = "EmployeeInfo.mdb"
' The name of the Access table to use
Const AccessTable    = "tblEmployeeInfo"

' List of users who should NOT be exported
' This list should contain the user's logon name
' Separate each name by a comma
Const Users2Skip     = "Guest"
```

```
' Constant for the account being disabled
Const ADS_UF_ACCOUNTDISABLE = 2
' Constant for the search to search subtrees
Const ADS_SCOPE_SUBTREE     = 2

Const adOpenStatic     = 3
Const adLockOptimistic = 3

' General variable declarations
Dim objConnectionDB, objRecordsetDB
Dim objConnectionAD, objCommandAD, objRecordsetAD
Dim dtStart
Dim strSQL
Dim objRootDSE, strDNSDomain
Dim strDN, intUAC, strSam, strDisplayName, strManagerDN, dtExpireDate
Dim blnProcessUser
Dim objUser, objManager

' Get the start time of the script
dtStart = TimeValue(Now( ))

'Create and open ADO connection to the Access database
Set objConnectionDB = CreateObject("ADODB.Connection")
Set objRecordsetDB  = CreateObject("ADODB.Recordset")

' Open the database
objConnectionDB.Open "Provider=Microsoft.Jet.OLEDB.4.0;" & _
                     "Data Source=" & AccessDatabase & ";"

' Open the recordset
objRecordsetDB.Open AccessTable, objConnectionDB, adOpenStatic,
adLockOptimistic

' Define the SQL statement used to clear out previous
' user info which was exported from AD
strSQL = "DELETE FROM " & AccessTable & " WHERE ImportedFromAD = 'True'"

Wscript.Echo "Removing previously exported records from the " & _
     AccessDatabase & " database."
objConnectionDB.Execute strSQL, , 129

' Determine the DNS domain from the RootDSE object.
Set objRootDSE = GetObject("LDAP://RootDSE")
strDNSDomain   = objRootDSE.Get("defaultNamingContext")

' Create and open an ADO connection to AD
Set objConnectionAD = CreateObject("ADODB.Connection")
Set objCommandAD    = CreateObject("ADODB.Command")

objConnectionAD.Provider = "ADsDSOObject"
objConnectionAD.Open "Active Directory Provider"
```

```
' Set connection properties
With objCommandAD
   .ActiveConnection = objConnectionAD

   ' Use SQL syntax for the query
   ' This retrieves all values named in the SELECT section for
   ' user accounts which do not have the Notes section = NoExport.
   ' The recordset is sorted ascending on the displayName value.
   .CommandText = _
             "Select userAccountControl, distinguishedName," & _
             " sAMAccountname, displayName" & _
             " FROM 'LDAP://" & strDNSDomain & "'" & _
             " WHERE objectCategory = 'person' AND" & _
             " objectClass = 'user' AND info <> 'NoExport'" & _
             " ORDER BY displayName"

   .Properties("Page Size")     = 1000
   .Properties("Timeout")       = 30
   .Properties("Searchscope")   = ADS_SCOPE_SUBTREE
   .Properties("Cache Results") = False
End With

Wscript.Echo "Running the query to find users."
Set objRecordSetAD = objCommandAD.Execute

' Move to the first record in the recordset
objRecordSetAD.MoveFirst

' Loop until we reach the end of the recordset
Do While NOT objRecordsetAD.EOF
   ' Blank out/reset a few variables..just in case.
   strDN  = ""
   intUAC = ""
   strSam = ""
   strDisplayName = ""
   strManagerDN   = ""
   dtExpireDate   = ""
   blnProcessUser = True

   ' Get the userAccountControl value. This lets us, among other things,
   ' determine if the account is disabled.
   intUAC = objRecordsetAD.Fields("userAccountControl")

   ' Process user if account is not disabled.
   If (NOT intUAC AND ADS_UF_ACCOUNTDISABLE) Then

      ' Get the user's logon name
      strSam        = objRecordsetAD.Fields("sAMAccountname")

      ' Determine if the user is included in the list of logon names to skip.
      If Instr(UCase(Users2Skip), UCase(strSam)) Then blnProcessUser = False
```

```
' Get the user's display name
strDisplayName = objRecordsetAD.Fields("displayName")

' Set boolean value to skip this user if the user's display name is
' blank.
If strDisplayName = "" Then blnProcessUser = False

' If our simple checks went ok, we can now process this user.
If blnProcessUser = True Then

    ' Get the distinguished name of this user
    ' The syntax is something like:
    '           CN=Joe E. Law,OU=Sales,OU=US,DC=mydomain,DC=local
    strDN = objRecordsetAD.Fields("distinguishedName")

    ' Bind to the user object
    Set objUser = GetObject("LDAP://" & strDN & "")

    ' Process the user
    With objUser
      Wscript.Echo "Processing user: " & strDisplayName

      ' Get the user's account expiration date
      dtExpireDate = CDate(.AccountExpirationDate)

      ' Process the user if the user's account expiration date is not
      '   passed
      If (dtExpireDate = "") OR _
        (dtExpireDate = CDate("01/01/1970")) OR _
        (dtExpireDate >= Date( )) Then

      'Add new record to the Access database
      objRecordsetDB.AddNew
        ' Get user data from AD and populate the new record in the
        ' Access database

        ' You can use the .Get("xxx") or .xxx formats to retrieve the data
        ' All fields on the left MUST exist in the Access table
        objRecordsetDB("FirstName")       = .Get("givenName")
        objRecordsetDB("MiddleName")      = .initials
        objRecordsetDB("LastName")        = .sn
        objRecordsetDB("DisplayName")     = .displayName
        objRecordsetDB("Description")     = .description
        objRecordsetDB("OfficeLocation")  = .physicalDeliveryOfficeName
        objRecordsetDB("WorkPhone")       = .telephoneNumber
        objRecordsetDB("Email")           = .mail
        objRecordsetDB("WebPage")         = .wwwHomePage
        objRecordsetDB("Street")          = .streetAddress
        objRecordsetDB("POBox")           = .postOfficeBox
        objRecordsetDB("City")            = .l
        objRecordsetDB("StateOrProvince") = .st
        objRecordsetDB("PostalCode")      = .postalCode
```

```
            objRecordsetDB("CountryOrRegion") = .co
            objRecordsetDB("HomePhone")       = .homePhone
            objRecordsetDB("Pager")           = .pager
            objRecordsetDB("MobilePhone")     = .mobile
            objRecordsetDB("FaxNumber")       = .facsimileTelephoneNumber
            objRecordsetDB("Notes")           = .info
            objRecordsetDB("Title")           = .title
            objRecordsetDB("Department")      = .department
            objRecordsetDB("CompanyName")     = .company


            ' Get the distiguished name of the manager
            strManagerDN = .manager
            ' If manager value is not blank then process
            If strManagerDN <> "" Then
              ' Bind to manager's account
              Set objManager = GetObject("LDAP://" & strManagerDN & "")
                ' Populate the Access database with the display name of the
                  manager
                objRecordsetDB("Manager")     = objManager.displayName
              ' Release this object reference
              Set objManager = Nothing
            End If


            ' Define that this record was exported from AD
            objRecordsetDB("ImportedFromAD")  = "True"


          ' Commit the record
          objRecordsetDB.Update


          ' Release this object reference
          Set objUser = Nothing
          End If
        End With
      End If
  End If


 ' Move to the next record in the AD recordset
   objRecordsetAD.MoveNext
Loop


' Close the Access database recordset
objRecordsetDB.Close
' Close the Access database connection
objConnectionDB.Close


' Release these object references
Set objRecordsetDB = Nothing
Set objConnectionDB = Nothing


' Close the AD recordset
objRecordsetAD.Close
' Close the AD connection
objConnectionAD.Close
```

```
' Release these object references
Set objRecordsetAD = Nothing
Set objConnectionAD = Nothing

' Let the user know how long this process took
WScript.Echo "The script completed in approximately " & _
             Second(TimeValue(now( )) - dtStart) & _
             " seconds."

' That's all folks!
Wscript.Quit
```

## Running the Hack

This database and script version has been tested on various versions of Windows (the minimum requirements tested were Windows 2000 Service Pack 2 running Internet Explorer 5 with Microsoft Windows Script v5.5 participating in a small Active Directory domain). Though this solution works for me, your results may vary due to environmental differences. I saved these items in a directory named *C:\EmployeeInfo*. If you save them somewhere else on your system, you will need to modify the Data Access Page connection string in the *EmployeeInfo.htm* file. This can be done from within Access or by editing the *.htm* file directly. Also, the script and database should be in the same directory. If they are in different directories, you should edit the AccessDatabase constant in the script to point to the proper location where the database is saved.

To run the script, simply type cscript ExportAdUsers.vbs from the command line from the current directory in which the script is found. The script, database, and HTML form page are all available from the O'Reilly web site.

Figure 2-8 shows a sample session on running the script.

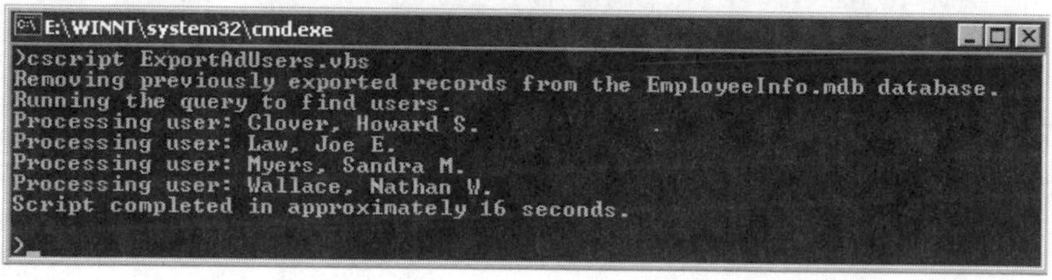

*Figure 2-8. Output of running the ExportAdUsers.vbs script*

—*Dan Thomson*

# Restore the Active Directory Icon in Windows XP

**#24**

A useful feature in Windows 2000 that enables users to browse Active Directory is missing in Windows XP; here's how to get it back.

In Windows 2000, when Active Directory is deployed, a user can easily browse Active Directory by double-clicking on My Network Places and then double-clicking on Entire Network. This displays the Directory icon (Figure 2-9), which represents Active Directory for the network.

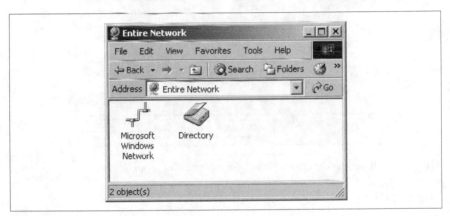

*Figure 2-9. The Directory icon in Windows 2000*

Successive double-clicking on this icon can then display information about which users, groups, printers, and other objects are listed for each domain. For each object selected, only a limited amount of information is displayed, but this can sometimes be handy for users who need to browse the directory for information. For example, a User object has a properties sheet with only three tabs on it: General, Address, and Business (see Figure 2-10), which is much less than the dozen or so tabs displayed when the properties sheet for the object is opened in Active Directory Users and Computers. Note that the user information is grayed out in the Figure 2-10; this is because the currently logged on user (James Brown) is an ordinary user and therefore can view selected information about other users but cannot change this information.

Unfortunately, in Windows XP the directory icon is now gone, but if you want your users to have access to it, you can use this hack to add it back. If you have Windows 2000 computers running on your network (hopefully, with the latest service pack), the steps are simple. If not, you'll need the full instructions.

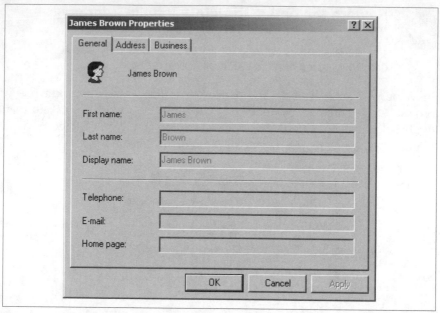

Figure 2-10. Browsing the Directory icon for information about a user

## The Easy Way

If you have a Windows 2000 computer handy, simply navigate to the *C:\ Windows\system32* directory of the Windows 2000 computer and find the *dsfolder.dll* file. Copy that file to the *system32* directory of your Windows XP computer. Now click Start, and then click Run. In the Open box, type regsvr32 dsfolder.dll and then click OK. When you receive the message "DllRegisterServer in dsfolder.dll succeeded," click OK.

## The Hard Way

If you don't have a Windows 2000 computer handy, do the following:

1. Download the latest Microsoft Windows 2000 service pack from *http:// www.microsoft.com/windows2000/downloads/servicepacks/*.

2. Use an extract program (e.g., WinZip) to extract the files to a new folder.

3. In the new folder, double-click *i386*.

4. In the *i386* folder, expand the compressed *Dsfolder.dl* file to *Dsfolder. dll*. To do so, first note the location of the folder where you extracted the files in step 2. For example, the *i386* folder path might be *C:\Documents and Settings\UserName\FolderName\i386* or something similar.

Click Start, and then click Run. In the Open box, type a command that is similar to this:

```
Expand "C:\Documents and Settings\UserName\FolderName\i386\Dsfolder.dl_"
"C:\Documents and Settings\UserName\FolderName\i386\Dsfolder.dll"
```

5. In Windows Explorer, copy *Dsfolder.dll* from the *i386* folder to the *C:\ Windows\System32* folder. Note that your Windows folder might be named something other than *Windows*, depending on whether you did a clean install or upgrade.

6. Finally, click Start, and then click Run. In the Open box, type `regsvr32 dsfolder.dll` and then click OK. When you receive the message "Dll-RegisterServer in dsfolder.dll succeeded," click OK.

The next time you view Network Neighborhood, you should have an Active Directory icon available.

*—John Gormly*

# CHAPTER THREE

# User Management
## Hacks 25–35

A large part of day-to-day administration of an Active Directory environment is managing users and their accounts. The usual way of doing this is with the Active Directory Users and Computers (ADUC) console, but when it comes to organizations with thousands of users, this tool can be frustrating to use.

This chapter is about alternatives to ADUC—ways of doing things faster using scripts. You'll find scripts to display information about users, find specific users on your network, change user passwords, unlock user accounts, get a list of disabled accounts, display which groups a user belongs to, and more. If you're familiar with VBScript, you can also customize these scripts further to meet the specific needs of your own networking environment.

For all these scripts, make sure you have the latest scripting engines on the workstation from which you run the script. You can download the latest scripting engines from the Microsoft Scripting home page (*http://msdn. microsoft.com/scripting/*). Also, when working with the Active Directory Services Interface (ADSI), you must have the same applicable rights you need to use the built-in administrative tools. For more information, see Microsoft's ADSI web page (*http://www.microsoft.com/windows2000/techinfo/howitworks/ activedirectory/adsilinks.asp*).

### HACK #25  Search for Domain Users

Programmatically search for a user in a mixed Windows NT/2000 environment.

If you are in the process of migrating from Windows NT to Windows 2000, you can certainly appreciate the search capabilities provided in Active Directory administrative tools. At the same time, more than ever, you suffer from its absence in the User Manager. This issue becomes especially acute in environments where there is no consistent naming convention or when the naming convention happened to change several times over years. The sorting feature might help, but only provided that a person responsible for creating accounts entered the full name correctly and in the same format. Misspellings or using diminutives and nicknames are other frequent causes of confusion. Your search becomes considerably more time consuming if you manage multiple domains with different naming conventions.

To resolve a problem, you can employ a couple of approaches. The first one involves exporting a user list, along with each user's properties, into a comma-delimited file or a database (e.g., Access or SQL). The main drawback of this solution is the need for regular updates of the exported list. The second drawback, which eliminates the need for maintenance, is using an ADSI-based script.

This approach is shown in the script that follows.

## The Code

The script allows searches against multiple domains. In order to accomplish this, you need to provide as the second input argument the list of domains (individual names need to be separated by semicolons). The first argument of the script is the part of the username (of any length) that you want to match against account names. Type the script into Notepad (with Word Wrap disabled) and save it with a .vbs extension as FindUser.vbs:

```
'*****************************************************************
'*** The script searches for a username in one on more domains by
'*** looking for a match on the string of characters you specify.
'***
'*** The syntax:
'*** cscript //nologo FindUser.vbs string dom1[;dom2]
'*** where string is used to match against the username
'*** dom1;dom2 is the semicolon separated list of one or
'*** more domains to search (no limit on number of entries)

'*****************************************************************
'*** variable declaration

Dim sName 'string to match against
Dim sDom 'string storing list of domains
Dim aDom 'array storing list of domains
Dim iCount 'counter variable
Dim oDomain 'object representing domain
Dim oUser 'object representing user account
Dim sLine 'string containing results of the search
```

```
'***************************************************************
'*** variable initialization

sName = Wscript.Arguments(0)
sDom = Wscript.Arguments(1)
aDom = Split(sDom, ";")

'***************************************************************
'*** search for matches in the loop

For iCount=0 To UBound(aDom)

Set oDomain = GetObject("WinNT://" & aDom(iCount))
oDomain.Filter = Array("user")
For Each oUser in oDomain
If InStr(1, oUser.name, sName, 1) > 0 Then
sLine = oDomain.Name & "\" & oUser.Name & ";"
SLine = sLine & oUser.Description & ";"
SLine = sLine & OUser.FullName & ";"
WScript.Echo sLine
End If
Next

Next
```

## Running the Hack

When you run *FindUser.vbs* using *Cscript.exe* in a command-prompt window, you can easily find the full name and domain for a user, given his username. For example, when I search to see if the username *bsmith* is present in the *MTIT* domain, I find that user Bob Smith is assigned that username (Figure 3-1).

*Figure 3-1. Using FindUser.vbs to check whether username bsmith is already used*

—Marcin Policht

# Manage User Accounts in Active Directory

### #26 Use these five handy scripts to easily manage domain user accounts.

While the usual way of managing user accounts in Active Directory is to use the Active Directory Users and Computers (ADUC) console, that GUI approach to managing accounts can be tedious if your organization is large and you have many accounts to manage. This hack provides examples of scripts you can use to simplify things and speed up common administrative tasks, and I think you'll find them quite useful. You can even use some of them to delegate certain tasks to nonadministrators to save you time and trouble.

To use one of these scripts, type it into Notepad (with Word Wrap turned off) and save it with a *.vbs* extension. Then, type cscript.exe *scriptname*.vbs from a command prompt, or create a shortcut to the script and double-click on the shortcut to run the script.

## Changing a User's Domain Password

This simple script allows you to give others the ability to change end users' passwords without having to install the administration tools. The script prompts for the domain, username, and new password, and notifies the user of whether the password change was successful:

```
Dim UserName
Dim UserDomain
UserDomain = InputBox("Enter the user's domain:")
UserName = InputBox("Enter the user's login name:")
Set User - GetObject("WinNT://" & UserDomain & "/"& UserName &"",user)

Dim NewPassword
NewPassword = InputBox("Enter new password")
Call User.SetPassword(NewPassword)

If err.number = 0 Then
Wscript.Echo "The password change was successful."
Else
Wscript.Echo "The password change failed!"
End if
```

## Changing User Account Names in Active Directory

Using VBScript, changing a user's account name in the Active Directory is a quick process:

```
Set oDomain - GetObject("WINNT:\\domainname")
Set oUser = oDomain.GetObject("originalusername")
oDomain.MoveHere oUser.AdsPath, "newusername"
```

You just need to connect to the specific domain (as indicated in the first line), set the original username (the second line), and then change the username using the MoveHere method (the third line). This is a much simpler process than opening up the MMC and either navigating to the username or searching the Active Directory for the account instances.

A script like this is extremely useful for occasions when names change due to things like marriage, or when the user just can't stand the name they were given for logging in.

Customize the script with the appropriate domain name (*domainname*), the user's old account name (*originalusername*), and the user's new account name (*newusername*).

## Unlocking a Windows 2000 Domain Account

Need a quick and easy way to unlock a Windows 2000 domain account? Use VBScript. The following script prompts for the username, then the user's domain, and unlocks the specified account:

```
UserName = InputBox("Enter the user's login name that you want to unlock:")

DomainName = InputBox("Enter the domain name in which the user account
exists:")

Set UserObj = GetObject("WinNT://"& DomainName &"/"& UserName &"")
If UserObj.IsAccountLocked = -1 then UserObj.IsAccountLocked = 0
UserObj.SetInfo

If err.number = 0 Then
Wscript.Echo "The Account Unlock Failed. Check that the account is, " & _
"in fact, locked-out."
Else
Wscript.Echo "The Account Unlock was Successful"
End if
```

## Disabling a Domain Account

Use this handy VBScript to quickly disable a user account in the specified domain. This script prompts for the username and domain and then disables the account you specify:

```
Dim Username
Dim UserDomain
UserDomain = InputBox("Enter the user's domain:")
UserName = InputBox("Enter the user's login name:")
Set UserObj = GetObject("WinNT://" & UserDomain & "/" & Username &)
UserObj.AccountDisabled = True
UserObj.SetInfo
Set UserObj = Nothing
```

## Setting the Account to Not Expire

This handy script configures a user account to not expire. The script works by setting the expiration date attribute to a past date:

```
Set objUser = GetObject _
("LDAP://cn=yourcontainer,ou=yourOU,dc=yourDC,dc=com")
objUser.AccountExpirationDate = "01/01/1970"
objUser.SetInfo
```

To use the script, customize the second line as desired. For example, if the user account for user Bob Smith resides in the Sales OU in the *mtit.com* domain, this line should be changed to:

```
("LDAP://cn=Bob Smith,ou=Sales,dc=mtit,dc=com")
```

Be judicious in deciding which accounts should be set to not expire, as such accounts could pose a security risk. See "Check for Passwords that Never Expire" [Hack #29] for a quick way to search for such accounts on your network.

*—Rod Trent*

## Get a List of Disabled Accounts

**#27** Here's a fast way to determine any disabled user accounts in your Active Directory forest.

Disabled accounts are accounts that still exist in Active Directory but cannot be used to log on to the network. For example, when an employee moves on to a different company, a common practice is to disable the individual's user account instead of deleting it. That way, the account can be reassigned to the individual's replacement, renamed, and used to access all the resources the previous employee had permission to access. Sometimes, though, you might forget which accounts have been disabled on your network, and it would be nice to have a way to find all disabled accounts.

You can use this VBScript to do just that—locate all of the disabled accounts in Active Directory. This is useful for inventory purpose but also for security—for example, to verify that the Guest account and other vulnerable accounts are in fact still disabled on your network.

## The Code

Simply type the script into Notepad (with Word Wrap turned off) and save it with a *.vbs* extension as *DisabledAccounts.vbs*:

```
Const ADS_UF_ACCOUNTDISABLE = 2

Set objConnection = CreateObject("ADODB.Connection")
objConnection.Open "Provider=ADsDSOObject;"
Set objCommand = CreateObject("ADODB.Command")
```

```
objCommand.ActiveConnection = objConnection
objCommand.CommandText = _
"<GC://dc=rootdomain,dc=com>;(objectCategory=User)" & _
";userAccountControl,distinguishedName;subtree"
Set objRecordSet = objCommand.Execute

intCounter = 0
While Not objRecordset.EOF
intUAC=objRecordset.Fields("userAccountControl")
If intUAC AND ADS_UF_ACCOUNTDISABLE Then
WScript.echo objRecordset.Fields("distinguishedName") & " is disabled"
intCounter = intCounter + 1
End If
objRecordset.MoveNext
Wend

WScript.Echo VbCrLf & "A total of " & intCounter & " accounts are disabled."

objConnection.Close
```

Make sure you have the latest scripting engines on the workstation you run this script from. You can download the latest scripting engines from the Microsoft Scripting home page (*http://msdn.microsoft.com/library/default. asp?url=/nhp/Default.asp?contentid=28001169*). Also, when working with the Active Directory Services Interface (ADSI), you must have the same applicable rights you need to use the built-in administrative tools.

## Running the Hack

To use the script, simply change this line to specify your own forest root domain:

```
"<GC://dc=fabrikam,dc=com>;(objectCategory=User)" & _
```

For example, if your forest root domain is *mtit.com*, then the line should read:

```
"<GC://dc=mtit,dc=com>;(objectCategory=User)" & _
```

Then, run the script by creating a shortcut to it and double-clicking on the shortcut. The output of the script is a series of dialog boxes, an example of which is shown in Figure 3-2.

*Figure 3-2. Displaying disabled domain user accounts*

—*Rod Trent*

## Get User Account Information

Need to find information about user accounts on a machine? Use this handy
script to do it fast.

This script lets you quickly query a Windows 2000 (or later) machine to
determine what user accounts are present, whether local accounts in the
SAM database or domain accounts in Active Directory. It will output a list of
accounts, giving the following information for each account:

- Username of user
- Full name of user
- Account lockout status
- Whether the user is allowed to change the password
- Whether the account is nonexpiring or not

### The Code

To use the script, simply type it into Notepad (with Word Wrap turned off)
and save it with a *.vbs* extension as *GetAccountInfo.vbs*:

```
ComputerName = localhost

winmgmt1 = "winmgmts:{impersonationLevel=impersonate}!//"& ComputerName &""

Set UserSet = GetObject( winmgmt1 ).InstancesOf ("Win32_UserAccount")

for each User in UserSet
WScript.Echo "==============================================="
WScript.Echo "Information for " & User.Name
WScript.Echo "The full username for the specified computer is: " & _
User.FullName
WScript.Echo "Account Locked? " & User.Lockout
WScript.Echo "Password can be changed?: " & User.PasswordChangeable
WScript.Echo "Password is expirable: " & User.PasswordExpires
WScript.Echo "==============================================="
Next
```

### Running the Hack

Here's some typical output when the script is run locally on a Windows
2000 domain controller. To avoid getting the series of dialog boxes that
would appear if you ran the script using *Wscript.exe*, use *Cscript.exe* to run it
from the command-line instead:

```
C:\>cscript.exe C:\MyScripts\GetAccountInfo.vbs
Microsoft (R) Windows Script Host Version 5.6
Copyright (C) Microsoft Corporation 1996-2001. All rights reserved.
```

```
=================================================
Information for Administrator
The full username for the specified computer is:
Account Locked? False
Password can be changed?: True
Password is expirable: False
=================================================
=================================================
Information for Guest
The full username for the specified computer is:
Account Locked? False
Password can be changed?: False
Password is expirable: False
=================================================
=================================================
Information for jsmith
The full username for the specified computer is: Jane Smith
Account Locked? False
Password can be changed?: True
Password is expirable: False
=================================================
=================================================
Information for bsmith
The full username for the specified computer is: Bob Smith
Account Locked? False
Password can be changed?: True
Password is expirable: True
=================================================
```

The output continues for the remaining accounts on the system.

## Hacking the Hack

You can easily modify the script to get user information from a remote computer instead of from the local computer on which the script is running. This is useful when you want to run the script from an administrator workstation instead of interactively on a domain controller.

Simply change this line:

```
ComputerName = localhost
```

to this:

```
ComputerName = InputBox("Enter the name of the computer you wish to query")
```

The script will prompt you with a dialog box (see Figure 3-3) for the name of the remote computer whose accounts you want to query. You can specify the NetBIOS name, DNS name, or IP address of the remote machine, as long as your currently logged-on account has administrative privileges on the remote machine.

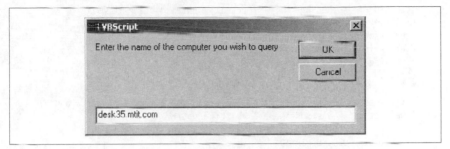

*Figure 3-3. Querying user account information on a remote computer*

—Rod Trent

# Check for Passwords that Never Expire

Here's a handy script that makes it simple to find user accounts with nonexpiring passwords.

User accounts set to never expire are sometimes used for permanent employees of a company, while temporary employees are assigned accounts that expire after a specified period of time. Ever wish you could quickly and simply find out which user accounts have their passwords set to never expire, along with the dates the flags were set? Here is a sample script that accomplishes this and more.

This script prompts for the desired domain, checks all user accounts in the domain to see if their passwords are set to never expire, and reports the date the flags were set. It then writes the output to a CSV file called *PWDNever-Expired.csv*, creating this file in the same directory where the script itself is located. If the password is *not* set to expire, the script instead records a No and the date the password will expire.

## The Code

To use the script, type it into Notepad (with Word Wrap turned off) and save it with a *vbs* extension as *PWDNeverExpired.vbs*:

```
' Set WshShell
Set WshShell = WScript.CreateObject("WScript.Shell")
strVer = "Ver 1.0 "
Set FileSystem = WScript.CreateObject("Scripting.FileSystemObject")
Set oFile = FileSystem.CreateTextFile("PWDNeverExpired.csv", true)

' Pull Environment variables for domain/user
strDomain = WshShell.ExpandEnvironmentStrings("%USERDOMAIN%")
strUserName = WshShell.ExpandEnvironmentStrings("%USERNAME%")
strOS = WshShell.ExpandEnvironmentStrings("%OS%")
```

```
strMessage = strMessage & "Hit Cancel or enter a blank to quit"
strTitle = "Domain to Search"
'get resource domain name, domain default
UserDomain = InputBox(strMessage, strTitle, strDomain)
strMessage = ""
strTitle = ""

'strMessage = "Please enter the USER Login ID" & vbCrLf & vbCrLf & _
'"Default is: " & strUserName & vbCrLf & vbCrLf
'strMessage = strMessage & "Hit Cancel or enter a blank to quit"
'strTitle = "USER Login ID"
'get resource domain name, domain default via input box
'objUserName = InputBox(strMessage, strTitle, strUserName)

' Display Just a minute!
strMessage = "This may take a few seconds. . ."
WshShell.Popup strMessage,2,"One moment please. . . "
strMessage = ""

Set ObjDomain = GetObject("WinNT://" & UserDomain)
ObjDomain.Filter = Array("User")
For Each ObjUser In ObjDomain

'Attempt to bind to the user
'Set objUser = GetObject("WinNT://"& UserDomain &"/"& objUser.Name, user)
Set UserName = GetObject("WinNT://" & UserDomain & "/" & ObjUser.Name & _
",User")

' Is password set to NEVER expire?
objPwdExpires = UserName.Get("UserFlags")
If (objPwdExpires And &H10000) <> 0 Then
objPwdExpiresTrue = "Yes"
strPwdExpires = "Date Set: "
msgPwdExpires = "Password Set to Never Expire: "
Else objPwdExpiresTrue = "No"
strPwdExpires = "Password Expires: "
msgPwdExpires = "Password Set to Never Expire: "
End If
oFile.WriteLine (UserName.fullname & "," & UserName.name & "," & _
msgPwdExpires & objPwdExpiresTrue & "," & strPwdExpires & _
objUser.PasswordExpirationDate)
'Wscript.Echo "Full Name: " & UserName.fullname & vbCrlf &_
'"Account Name: " & UserName.name & vbCrlf &_
'msgPwdExpires & objPwdExpiresTrue & vbCrlf &_
'strPwdExpires & objUser.PasswordExpirationDate & vbCrlf
Set UserName = Nothing
Next
Wscript.Echo "Done Cheking Accounts"
```

## Running the Hack

To run this hack, simply create a shortcut to the script and double-click on the shortcut. Figure 3-4 shows a sample CSV output file for the script, viewed in Excel.

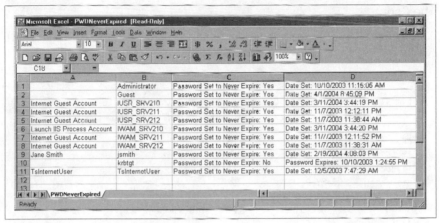

*Figure 3-4 Sample output from running PWDNeverExpired.vbs*

—*Hans Schefske*

## Enumerate Group Membership to a CSV File

Export a list of which users are in which groups to a comma-separated file that is suitable for opening In your favorite spreadsheet or database application.

Finding out which users belong to which groups is not a trivial task from the GUI. Using Active Directory Users and Computers (ADUC), you can view the Member Of tab of a user's properties sheet to see which groups the user belongs to but not which users belong to which group. The properties sheet of a group is more informative and has two tabs: Members, which shows which users belong to the group, and Member Of, which tells you if the group itself belongs to any other groups. Opening these properties sheets is a time-consuming process and doesn't always give you quick insight into users and the groups to which they belong.

But if you need a quick way of knowing what the members of different groups are, you can use VBScript. The script in this hack enumerates the groups in an Active Directory domain and places the information in a CSV file. The name of each group, the description of the group, the group's members (both full name and SAM account name), and whether that member is a user or group will all be placed into a CSV file called *GroupMembers.csv*, located in the directory in which the script is running. This script uses LDAP to query Active Directory. It won't run against an NT4 domain, although you should be able to run it from an NT4 workstation. If you are not running Windows 2000 Professional or later, this script requires ADSI 2.5.

## The Code

To use this script, type it into Notepad (with Word Wrap disabled) and save it with a *.vbs* extension as *GroupMembers.vbs*:

```
On Error Resume Next

Set FileSystem = WScript.CreateObject("Scripting.FileSystemObject")
Set oFile = FileSystem.CreateTextFile("GroupMemebrs.csv", True)

CRLF=CHR(13)+CHR(10)
strDC = "DC01GA.My.Domain.com" 'Substitute your AD domain server name
strRoot = "My.Domain.Com" 'Substitute your company/domain name
strDomain = "DC=MY,DC=DOMAIN,DC=COM"

Set DomainObj = GetObject("LDAP://" & strDC&"/CN=Users," & strDomain)
if Err.Number <0 then
wscript.echo "Failed to connect to " & strADName
wscript.quit
end if
DomainObj.Filter = Array("group")

For Each GroupObj In DomainObj

If GroupObj.Class = "group" Then
oFile.WriteLine ("Group Membership for: " & MID(GroupObj.Name & "," & _
"Description - " & GroupObj.Description,4))
wscript.echo ("Group Membership for: " & MID(GroupObj.Name & vbTab & _
CRLF & CRLF & _
' "Description - " & GroupObj.Description,4))
set memberlist=GroupObj.Members
For Each member In memberlist
oFile.WriteLine MID(member.Name & "," & member.SAMAccountName & "," & _
member.Class,4)
wscript.echo MID(Vbtab & member.Name & " (" & member.Class & ")",5)
next
end if
Next

set DomainObj = Nothing
set GroupObj = Nothing

if err.number<>0 then
wscript.echo CRLF
wscript.echo ("ERROR: "&err.number&" "&err.description & " from "&err.source)
```

```
wscript.echo CRLF
end if

Wscript.Echo "Done!!"
wscript.quit
```

## Running the Hack

Before you run the script, modify these three lines near the beginning:

```
strDC = "DC01GA.My.Domain.com" 'Substitute your AD domain server name
strRoot = "My.Domain.Com" 'Substitute your company/domain name
strDomain = "DC=MY,DC=DOMAIN,DC=COM"
```

For example, to query a domain controller named *srv210.mtit.com* in the *mtit.com* domain, change these lines to:

```
strDC = "srv210.mtit.com" 'Substitute your AD domain server name
strRoot = "mtit.com" 'Substitute your company/domain name
strDomain = "DC=MTIT,DC=COM"
```

Also note that the script lists only groups located in the Users container. To query other containers or organizational units, modify the following line accordingly:

```
Set DomainObj = GetObject("LDAP://" & strDC&"/CN=Users," & strDomain)
```

To run the hack, simply create a shortcut to it and double-click on the shortcut.

Figure 3-5 shows a sample of typical output for the script, with the CSV file imported into Excel to make it more readable. You can see that the Domain Admins group has members Bob Smith, Frank Jones, Jane Smith, and the default Administrator account.

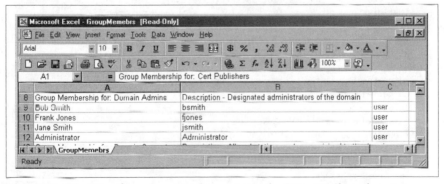

*Figure 3-5. A portion of sample output from running the GroupMembers.vbs script*

—*Hans Schefske*

# Modify User Properties for All Users in a Particular OU

Changing the logon script for all users in an organizational unit (OU) is a chore if you're working from the GUI, so try this script instead.

The ability to quickly change the logon script that members of a particular OU are running is quick and easy though VBScript. To change the properties of objects located in a specific OU, you must first bind to that OU using ADSI. To do this, you must list all the parent OUs of the OUs you are trying to bind to, as shown in the script in this hack. Then you must gather all the usernames in the OU you are modifying and check to make sure they are indeed just users and not some other object. If they are users, change the path of the logon script property in their account to *Network/NewLogon.cmd* and set the changes in place. Then notify the person running the script that the changes have been completed.

This script comes in handy when you need to modify common properties of many user accounts in a particular OU all at once in an Active Directory domain. In Windows 2000, unlike in NT4, you cannot just highlight the users you want to change, click on Properties and change a common property (e.g., Logon Script) for the users you have selected.

## The Code

To use this script, type it into Notepad (with Word Wrap disabled) and save it with a *.vbs* extension as *ModifyUsersOU.vbs*:

```
'~~Comment~~
'Modify all users in a specific OU in Active Directory at once. This script
'will change the logon script path For all users of the
'"Network/Services/Users/Test" OU To "Network/newlogon.cmd".
'~~Script~~
'This is the actual LDAP. If the OU is a sub-OU, you must enter ALL of them.
Set OU = GetObject("LDAP://DCServerName.MY.Domain.COM/
OU=Test,OU=Users,OU=Services,OU=Network,DC=MY,DC=Domain,DC=com")
'Setup to get all the users in the specified OU from above.
'Gather each username.
For Each oUser In OU
'Make sure they are only USER class.
If oUser.Class = "user" Then
'Set the name of the login script itself here.
oUser.Put "scriptpath", "Network\newlogon.cmd"
'Set these settings.
oUser.SetInfo
End If
Next
Wscript.echo "The Network/Services/Users/Test OU has been updated!"
Wscript.Quit
```

Change the following line to specify the appropriate OU in your own network environment:

```
Set OU = GetObject("LDAP://DCServerName.MY.Domain.COM/
OU=Test,OU=Users,OU=Services,OU=Network,DC=MY,DC=Domain,DC=com")
```

For example, if your OU is named Boston and your domain is *mtit.com*, then this line should be changed to:

```
Set OU = GetObject("LDAP://DCServerName.MY.Domain.COM/OU=Boston,
DC=mtit,DC=com")
```

Specify the new logon script, like so:

```
oUser.Put "scriptpath", "Network\newlogon.cmd"
```

Finally, specify the output for the ECHO by modifying this line as required:

```
Wscript.echo "The Network/Services/Users/Test OU has been updated!"
```

In our example, this line should be changed to:

```
Wscript.echo "The Boston OU has been updated!"
```

## Hacking the Hack

This script can easily be modified to change any of the User Object properties in a particular OU, such as:

Profile Path
Home Directory
Home Drive Letter
Email
Description

The script can of course be customized to modify virtually any other displayed properties of user objects.

*—Hans Schefske*

# HACK #32 Check Group Membership and Map Drives in a Logon Script

Find out which group a user referenced within a logon script belongs to.

Logon scripts are useful for mapping drives so that users can store their work files in standard locations on network file servers. It would be nice to be able to map drives based on a user's group membership, and that's what this hack is about. By placing a user's group membership information into a dictionary object, you can quickly find out if a user is a member of a group and then perform actions (such as mapping drives) if they are. The script in this hack allows you to accomplish this and more.

This script quickly checks to see if a user is a member of a particular group. It reads the Member Of tab information for the user account and places it into a dictionary object, because a dictionary object offers fast and easy access to group membership information. If the user is a member of the group specified, a dialog box will tell you so.

## The Code

To use this script, type it into Notepad (with Word Wrap disabled) and save it with a *.vbs* extension as *CheckMembership.vbs*.

```
Option Explicit ' Force explicit declarations
'
' Variables
'
Dim WSHNetwork
Dim FSO
Dim strUserName ' Current user
Dim strUserDomain ' Current User's domain name
Dim ObjGroupDict ' Dictionary of groups to which the user belongs

Set WSHNetwork = WScript.CreateObject("WScript.Network")
Set FSO = CreateObject("Scripting.FileSystemObject")
'
' Wait until the user is really logged in...
'
strUserName = ""
While strUserName = ""
WScript.Sleep 100 ' 1/10 th of a second
strUserName = WSHNetwork.UserName
Wend
strUserDomain = WSHNetwork.UserDomain

' Read the user's account "Member Of" tab info across the network
' once into a dictionary object.

Set ObjGroupDict = CreateMemberOfObject(strUserDomain, strUserName)
If MemberOf(ObjGroupDict, "Domain Admins") Then
wscript.echo "Is a member of Domain Admins."
'REM this line to Map Network Drives

'Map network Drives here, UNREM the below lines:
'WSHNetwork.MapNetworkDrive "O:", "\\server1\share"
'WSHNetwork.MapNetworkDrive "Q:", "\\server2\share"

Else
wscript.echo "Is NOT a member of Domain Admins"
End If

Function MemberOf(ObjDict, strKey)
' Given a Dictionary object containing groups to which the user
```

```
' is a member of and a group name, then returns True if the group
' is in the Dictionary else return False.
'
' Inputs:
' strDict - Input, Name of a Dictionary object
' strKey - Input, Value being searched for in
' the Dictionary object
' Sample Usage:
'
' If MemberOf(ObjGroupDict, "DOMAIN ADMINS") Then
' wscript.echo "Is a member of Domain Admins."
' End If
'
'

MemberOf = CBool(ObjGroupDict.Exists(strKey))

End Function


Function CreateMemberOfObject(strDomain, strUserName)
' Given a domain name and username, returns a Dictionary
' object of groups to which the user is a member of.
'
' Inputs:
'
' strDomain - Input, NT Domain name
' strUserName - Input, NT username
'
Dim objUser, objGroup

Set CreateMemberOfObject = CreateObject("Scripting.Dictionary")
CreateMemberOfObject.CompareMode = vbTextCompare
Set objUser = GetObject("WinNT://" _
& strDomain & "/" _
& strUserName & ",user")
For Each objGroup In objUser.Groups
CreateMemberOfObject.Add objGroup.Name, "-"
Next
Set objUser = Nothing

End Function
```

## Running the Hack

To map drives based on a different user group than Domain Admins modify this line as required:

```
If MemberOf(ObjGroupDict, "Domain Admins") Then
```

For example, if you want to map drives based on whether users are members of a global group named Sales use this line instead:

```
If MemberOf(ObjGroupDict, "Sales") Then
```

To map drives instead of displaying a message box, comment out the following line:

```
wscript.echo "Is a member of Domain Admins." 'REM this line to Map Network
Drives
```

and uncomment these lines:

```
'WSHNetwork.MapNetworkDrive "O:", "\\server1\share"
'WSHNetwork.MapNetworkDrive "Q:", "\\server2\share"
```

specifying drive letters and UNC paths as appropriate depending on your own networking environment. For example, to map the drive letter K: to a shared folder named Reports on file server fs3.mtit.com use this line instead of the above:

```
WSHNetwork.MapNetworkDrive "K:", "\\fs3.mtit.com\Reports"
```

*—Hans Schefske*

# HACK #33 Script Creation of a User's Home Directory and Permissions

Configuring home directories for users is a slow process using the GUI. Here's a script that does it faster.

Ever wish you could create a user and her home directory and set the necessary permissions on that directory all in one script? Here is a sample script that shows you how to accomplish this. If you know some VBScript, you can easily customize it further to meet your needs.

This script creates a user, adds additional properties such as telephone number and title, sets the password, and enables the user's account. Then the script creates the user's home folder and sets the Administrators group to have Full Control permission on the folder and the user's account to have Change permission on the folder. This script can easily be modified to set the permissions to fit the requirements of any environment. All you have to do is review the command-line switches for the cacls command and make the appropriate changes in the script.

## The Code

To use this script, type it into Notepad (with Word Wrap disabled) and save it with a *.vbs* extension as *CreateUserHomeDirectory.vbs*.

```
Option Explicit

Const WAIT_ON_RETURN = True
Const HIDE_WINDOW = 0
Const USER_ROOT_UNC = "\\dc1\users" 'Set Home Folder Location Here

Dim WshShell, WshNetwork, objFS, objServer, objShare
```

```
Set WshShell = Wscript.CreateObject("Wscript.Shell")
Set WshNetwork = Wscript.CreateObject("Wscript.Network")
Set objFS = CreateObject("Scripting.FileSystemObject")
Set ou = GetObject("LDAP://
OU=Users,OU-Billing,OU=Network,DC=my,DC=domain,DC=com")

'Create the User
Set usr = ou.Create("user", "CN=James Smith")
usr.Put "samAccountName", "jsmith"
usr.Put "sn", "Smith"
usr.Put "givenName", "James"
usr.Put "userPrincipalName", "jsmith@my.domain.com"
usr.Put "telephoneNumber", "(555) 555 0111"
usr.Put "title", "Network Billing Dept"
usr.SetInfo

'Now that the user is created, reset their password and enable the account.

usr.SetPassword "secret***!"
usr.AccountDisabled = False
usr.SetInfo

'Now create the User's Home Folder and set permissions.
strUser = usr.samAccountName
Call objFS.CreateFolder(USER_ROOT_UNC & "\" & strUser)
Call WshShell.Run("cacls " & USER_ROOT_UNC & "\" & strUser & _
" /e /g Administrators:F", HIDE_WINDOW, WAIT_ON_RETURN)
Call WshShell.Run("cacls " & USER_ROOT_UNC & "\" & strUser & _
" /e /g " & strUser & ":C", HIDE_WINDOW, WAIT_ON_RETURN)
```

## Running the Hack

To run the script, modify the following line to set the home folder location:

```
Const USER_ROOT_UNC = "\\dc1\users" 'Set Home Folder Location Here
```

Then modify the following line to specify the organizational unit (OU) in which you want to create the user:

```
Set ou = GetObject("LDAP://
OU=Users,OU=Billing,OU=Network,DC=my,DC=domain,DC=com")
```

Finally, modify the following lines to specify the personal information for the user, as desired:

```
Set usr = ou.Create("user", "CN=James Smith")
usr.Put "samAccountName", "jsmith"
usr.Put "sn", "Smith"
usr.Put "givenName", "James"
usr.Put "userPrincipalName", "jsmith@my.domain.com"
usr.Put "telephoneNumber", "(555) 555 0111"
usr.Put "title", "Network Billing Dept"
```

—*Hans Schefske*

# Prevent Ordinary Users from Creating Local Accounts

Here's a quick hack that will let you prevent users from creating new local user accounts on their desktop computers.

By default, ordinary users on Windows 2000 Professional workstations can use Computer Management to create new local user accounts on their machines. All they need to do is right-click on My Computer, select Manage to open Computer Management, locate Local Users and Groups under System Tools, right-click on Users, and select New User. This procedure lets them create ordinary user accounts only, not administrator accounts, but it still represents an undesirable loophole for most administrators. After all, it's usually not a desirable feature for users to create additional accounts for themselves on their desktop machines.

Here's a workaround to solve this problem. To disable a user's ability to create new local accounts on his machine, log on locally to his machine as a member of the Administrators group and open Computer Management. Select Groups under Local Users and Groups to display all local groups on the machine. Double-click on the Users group to display its members (see Figure 3-6), and you should see NT AUTHORITY\INTERACTIVE as a member of this group. Select this account and click Remove to remove it from the group (this doesn't delete the account; it only removes it from the group).

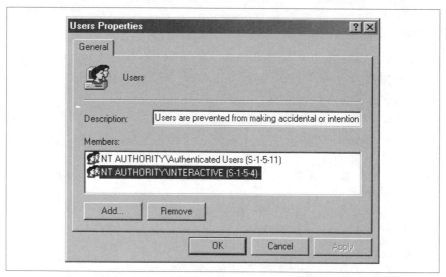

*Figure 3-6. Removing the INTERACTIVE special identity from the Users group*

This action removes the ability for logged-on users to create new local accounts on their systems.

If you don't want to log on interactively to user's machines using your Administrator account, you can use the runas command instead. While the user is logged on to her machine using her ordinary user account, open a command line and type:

```
runas /user:MyAdminAcct@MyDomain.com cmd
```

Type your password when prompted (make sure the user is not looking at the screen). This opens a new command-prompt window, running under your Administrator credentials. Now type the following command into the new window:

```
net localgroup users "NT AUTHORITY\INTERACTIVE" /DELETE
```

This removes the INTERACTIVE special identity from the Users group.

*—Rod Trent*

## Put a Logoff Icon on the Desktop

**Here's a script that will enable users to safely reboot their machines when necessary.**

Occasionally, users need a way to reboot their machines when applications hang or updates have been installed. Rather than give users instructions about how to do this properly, it would be nice if a user could instead simply click on an icon that would log them off properly and reboot their machine in a way that does not endanger their work.

That's what this script is about—allowing your users to *safely* reboot their machines from an icon on their desktops. This VBScript prompts the user to make sure he has saved his data, then logs the user off and automatically reboots. This is quite handy when you push updates via SMS but suppress the reboot.

### The Code

Just type the following script into Notepad (with Word Wrap disabled) and save it with a *.vbs* extension as *LogoffIcon.vbs*:

```
Set OpSysSet = GetObject("winmgmts:
{impersonationlevel=impersonate,(Shutdown)}" & _
"//./root/cimv2").ExecQuery("SELECT * FROM " & _
"Win32_OperatingSystem WHERE Primary = true")

ianswer = MsgBox("Did you save your data first?"+vbLf+vbLf+ " LOGOFF?",
vbCritical + vbYesNo, _
"Logoff?")
```

```
If ianswer = vbYes Then 'If OK, shut down

For Each OpSys In OpSysSet
outParam = OpSys.Reboot

If err.number <> 0 Then
WScript.echo "Error number: " & Err.Number & _
vbNewLine & _
"Description: " & Err.Description
End If

Next

Else ' user selected cancel
MsgBox "Logoff Aborted", , "Logoff Aborted"

End If
```

Copy the script to a folder on the user's machine and create a shortcut to the
folder on his desktop. Then, when the user needs to reboot his machine, he
can double-click on the shortcut and a dialog box (see Figure 3-7) will suggest that he save his work before logging off.

*Figure 3-7. Logging off and rebooting*

Once he saves his work and clicks OK, he is logged off and his computer
shuts down and restarts.

—*Chuck Young*

# CHAPTER FOUR

# Networking Services

## Hacks 36–47

Under the hood of Windows 2000 Server and Windows Server 2003 are the core networking services and components that enable systems to communicate across a network. This includes services such as Dynamic Host Configuration Protocol (DHCP), Domain Name System (DNS), Windows Internet Name Service (WINS), and other services that run on top of TCP/IP. Configuring these services can be complex, and it can be hard to pinpoint the problem when things go wrong.

This chapter is about managing key services and other networking components. You'll learn how to use a script to manage services on remote computers, how to ensure DHCP server availability so your clients can communicate, how DNS aging and scavenging work and can be configured, how to troubleshoot common DNS problems when Active Directory is deployed, how to perform complicated network configuration tasks using scripts and from the command line, and several other important tasks.

When running VB scripts for system administration, remember to ensure that you have the latest scripting engines on the workstation from which you run the scripts. Download the latest scripting engines from the Microsoft Scripting home page (*http://msdn.microsoft.com/scripting/*). Also, when working with the Active Directory Services Interface (ADSI), you must have the same applicable rights you need to use the built-in administrative tools. In other words, you should use an administrator account to run these scripts.

### HACK #36 Manage Services on Remote Machines

Here are three handy scripts for managing network services that run on remote machines.

While the Services node in Computer Management can be used to manage services on remote machines, using a script is easier if you have many systems to manage. This hack offers three VB scripts you can use to display the services that run on a remote computer, change the start mode for a service, and change the password for the account used by a service. Enjoy!

## Getting Remote Computer Service Information

If you want to check services on a remote computer, VBScript can help. Using the WMI repository and ADSI, you can easily retrieve information on stopped or started services.

The script prompts for the NetBIOS name of the remote computer. Alternatively, you can get the service information for the local computer by typing in the local name as localhost. The script responds by displaying complete information for the services that are registered on the specified computer.

**The code.** Type the following script into Notepad (with Word Wrap disabled) and save it with a *.vbs* extension:

```
ComputerName = InputBox("Enter the name of the computer for which you " & _
"want service information")

winmgmt1 = "winmgmts:{impersonationLevel=impersonate}!//"& ComputerName &""

Set ServSet = GetObject( winmgmt1 ).InstancesOf ("Win32_service")

for each Serv in ServSet
GetObject("winmgmts:").InstancesOf ("win32_service")
WScript.Echo ""
WScript.Echo Serv.Description
WScript.Echo " Executable: ", Serv.PathName
WScript.Echo " Status: ", Serv.Status
WScript.Echo " State: ", Serv.State
WScript.Echo " Start Mode: ", Serv.StartMode
Wscript.Echo " Start Name: ", Serv.StartName
next
```

**Running the hack.** To run the script, open a command prompt, switch to the directory where the script is located, and type the following:

```
cscript.exe GetRemoteServices.vbs > services.txt
```

The reason for redirecting output to a text file is because the script generates a lot of output. A dialog box appears (see Figure 4-1), requesting the name of the remote machine. The machine name can be a FQDN, NetBIOS name, or IP address, as desired.

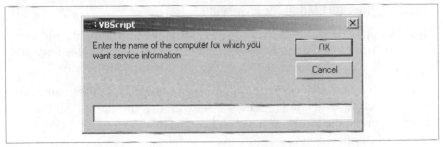

*Figure 4-1. Getting information about services running on a remote machine*

Here's a sample of what the output of the script might look like if the target machine is running Windows Server 2003:

```
Microsoft (R) Windows Script Host Version 5.6
Copyright (C) Microsoft Corporation 1996-2001. All rights reserved.

Notifies selected users and computers of administrative alerts. If the
service is stopped, programs that use administrative alerts will not receive
them. If this service is disabled, any services that explicitly depend on it
will fail to start.
 Executable:  C:\WINDOWS\system32\svchost.exe -k LocalService
 Status:  OK
 State:  Stopped
 Start Mode:  Disabled
 Start Name:  NT AUTHORITY\LocalService

Provides support for application level protocol plug-ins and enables
network/protocol connectivity. If this service is disabled, any services
that explicitly depend on it will fail to start.
 Executable:  C:\WINDOWS\System32\alg.exe
 Status:  OK
 State:  Stopped
 Start Mode:  Manual
 Start Name:  NT AUTHORITY\LocalService

Processes installation, removal, and enumeration requests for Active
Directory IntelliMirror group policy programs. If the service is disabled,
users will be unable to install, remove, or enumerate any IntelliMirror
programs. If this service is disabled, any services that explicitly depend
on it will fail to start.
 Executable:  C:\WINDOWS\system32\svchost.exe -k netsvcs
 Status:  OK
 State:  Stopped
 Start Mode:  Manual
 Start Name:  LocalSystem
```

Note that you can easily determine the start mode, service account, and state of each service from this output.

## Changing the Start Mode for a Service

This VBScript changes the Server service start mode to Automatic and works remotely. This can be a big help to sites where the security folks have gone nuts and disabled the Server service or set it to Manual start mode.

In its current form, the script prompts for a remote computer name, connects, and changes the Server service's start mode. The script could also be edited to run on the local computer and placed in a login script to hit a large number of computers at once.

**The code.** Type the following script into Notepad (with Word Wrap disabled) and save it with a *.vbs* extension:

```
strComputer = InputBox("Enter the name of the computer for which " & _
"you want to change the Start Mode for the Server service")
Set objWMIService = GetObject("winmgmts:" _
& "{impersonationLevel=impersonate}!\\" & strComputer & "\root\cimv2")
Set colService = objWMIService.ExecQuery _
("Select * from Win32_Service where DisplayName = 'Server'")
For Each objService in colService
errReturnCode = objService.Change( , , , , "Automatic")
Next
```

**Running the hack.** To run this script, simply create a shortcut to it and double-click on the shortcut.

To change the start mode of another service, simply change the DisplayName to the service you want to modify. For example, to change the start mode for the World Wide Web Publishing Service, you'd alter the select statement to read:

```
("Select * from Win32_Service where DisplayName = 'w3svc'").
```

And, of course, you can also use "Manual" or "Disabled" instead of "Automatic" in the second-to-last line.

## Changing a Service Password

Services always run within the context of some user account. Usually, this account is built in, such as LocalSystem or NetworkService, but some services, such as IIS and those for Exchange, use special accounts called *service accounts*. To ensure these accounts are secure, you can change the password used by these accounts, which this script will allow you to do.

The code. Type the following script into Notepad (with Word Wrap disabled) and save it with a *.vbs* extension:

```
Dim Computer
Dim ComputerName
Dim ComputerDomain
Dim Service
Dim TargetService
Dim NewPassword
TargetService = "YourServicename"
ComputerDomain = "YourDomain"
ComputerName = "YourComputerName"
NewPassword = "YourPassword"
Set Computer = GetObject("WinNT://" & ComputerDomain & "/" & ComputerName & _
",computer"
Set Service = Computer.GetObject("service", TargetService)
Service.SetPassword(NewPassword)
Service.SetInfo
```

Running the hack. Just replace the items in the following lines with your own information:

```
TargetService = "YourServicename"
ComputerDomain = "YourDomain"
ComputerName = "YourComputerName"
NewPassword = "YourPassword"
```

For example:

```
TargetService = "Network Agent"
ComputerDomain = "MTIT"
ComputerName = "SRV14"
NewPassword = "Pa$$w0rd"
```

*—Rod Trent*

## HACK #37 Simplify DNS Aging and Scavenging

Understanding the mysteries of how DNS aging/scavenging works can save you time and effort troubleshooting DNS name-resolution problems.

Dynamic DNS (DDNS, introduced in Windows 2000) brought with it a process called *DNS scavenging*, the automatic removal of stale DNS information. In a perfect world, DNS scavenging would not be necessary, but who lives in a perfect world? So, before you spend time reading the rest of this hack, let's see if it applies to you.

Have you pinged a machine before by name and gotten a reply, but when you attempt to connect to it, you connect to a different machine name or cannot connect at all? If you just shook your head in agreement, nodded, or mumbled something about this happening to you, then this hack might shed some light.

Still reading? Good. First, let me establish my bias: all of this information pertains to Active Directory Integrated Zones. That said, let's establish some definitions before we continue:

A
>    This record maps the name of the machine (host) to the IP address.

PTR
>    This record maps the IP address to the hostname.

## Why Scavenge?

There are two parts of DDNS that you need to understand before we answer the question of when scavenging is necessary: DNS and DHCP.

**DHCP process.** Wait a second. I thought we were talking about DNS? Before we go on about DNS, we first have to understand how DDNS works and why DHCP is important in this process.

Dynamic DNS registration happens at two places: either the DHCP client or the DHCP server. It all depends on configuration and client type. For the most part, Windows 2000 clients and above handle their own hostnameregistrations, while the DHCP server handles the PTR registration (except in the case of statically assigned IP addresses, in which case the client will handle both the hostnameand PTR registrations). In other configurations, the DHCP server can be made to handle the host and PTR registrations. Other, down-level clients (NT4, 9x, etc.), do not interact with the DDNS registration process. However, the DHCP server can be set to handle registration for these clients as well.

Okay, now we have an idea of how these records are getting in DDNS. Unfortunately, how the records go in is much more efficient than how the records come out.

> Read Larry Duncan's excellent article, "DNS for Active Directory: A 10 Minute Primer" (*http://www.myitforum.com/ articles/16/view.asp?id=3907*), to understand when clients likes to refresh their DNS records.

**DDNS process.** There's nothing to stop two records from holding the same IP address or the same host name. This scenario is problematic for image-based workstation/laptop deployments. During a portion of the image process, the client will register as WIN2KIMAGE in DNS (for example), before having the machine name changed later in the process. Another image is started and WIN2KIMAGE is added again with a different IP address. Sooner or later, you'll end up with 50 PTR records pointing to the same name, WIN2KIMAGE. This same process happens under different situations, in which a machine will establish a different dynamic IP address, but for some reason, the old reverse-lookup record is not removed. Generally, the DHCP client and server helps clean up these records. In some configurations, the DHCP server does it all. However, real-world experience might tell you that this is not getting done effectively. When this clean-up process does not occur properly, stale records reside in DNS.

This is where scavenging comes in. Scavenging deletes stale records if they're beyond a set age. All records have an age. However, the age of a record is not considered until scavenging is turned on. Once scavenging is turned on, DNS does not calculate how old the record was prior to when scavenging was enabled.

For more information on various triggers of the StartScavenging time frame, refer to the Microsoft DNS white paper at *http://www.microsoft.com/technet/treeview/default.asp?url=/ TechNet/prodtechnol/windows2000serv/plan/w2kdns2.asp.*

## How to Use Scavenging

There are three intervals you need to understand before you set up scavenging: Scavenging Period, No-refresh Interval, and Refresh Interval. These intervals are described in the DNS GUI. Just right-click on an Active Directory Integrated zone, select Properties, choose the General tab, and click the Aging button to see the screen shown in Figure 4-2.

If you're like me, your brain is twitching from the complex wording of the definitions. In order to understand this a little better (without needing the mental capacity to solve a Rubik's Cube in two minutes), let's break down what the definitions really mean:

*Scavenging Period*
>This is easy enough to understand. This interval simply tells your DNS server how often to check the zones for stale records. You can only get as granular as telling DNS to check every *x* number of hours or *x* number of days. By the way, this setting applies only to the DNS server, not the zones.

*No-refresh Interval*
>This a mechanism by which DDNS suppresses reregistration attempts. This helps keep replication of record information to a minimum. For example, using the default of seven days, after the DNS client registers with DDNS, all attempts to reregister for a period of seven days will be ignored.

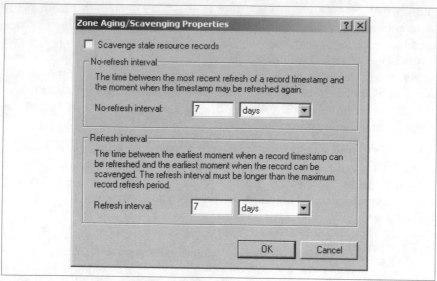

*Figure 4-2. Configuring DNS scavenging options*

*Refresh Interval*

This definition took awhile for me to grasp. It basically means the number of days after the No-refresh Interval expires that DDNS will wait for the client to refresh its record before the record becomes stale. Again, by default, this setting is also seven days.

Now, we'll put this all together in an example that makes sense. In this scenario, the DNS client does not reregister during the Refresh Interval period. Keep in mind, we are using the default of seven days:

1. DNS client registers with DDNS.

2. No-refresh Interval starts (seven days).

3. DDNS server will not accept reregistration attempts from this client for seven days.

4. No-refresh Interval expires.

5. Refresh Interval starts (seven days).

6. DNS client has seven days to refresh its records before the record is considered stale.

7. Refresh Interval expires.

8. Scavenging process removes record.

If the client had registered its record again, the No-refresh Interval would have started all over again. In the previous scenario, with the default settings of seven days, a record would have to be greater than 14 days old before DDNS would scavenge it. This might work if your DHCP lease times are eight days (the default). Otherwise, you might need to set the intervals closer to your DHCP lease times. Also, keep in mind the Scavenging Period runs only on the interval specified, which is also seven days by default.

Scavenging jobs *will* use processor time. However, the scavenging process is a low-priority thread of the DNS service. This ensures that scavenging does not use all the processing capacity, but it's horrible if your DNS servers are used heavily. As a low-priority thread on a highly used DNS server, there's a probability that the scavenging thread might never run. Also, if the server attempts to run the scavenging process during a time when the DNS server is highly used, it will miss the scheduled interval. It will not attempt to start running over and over but instead will wait until the next scheduled interval (remember the default of seven days). At the time of this writing, I haven't found a setting that can be adjusted to change which hour the scavenging process starts.

## For the Advanced Pack Rat

As I mentioned earlier, the Scavenging Period setting applies only to an individual DNS server. Unlike the other settings, which are replicated by Active Directory, this setting is specific to the DNS server in question. With this in mind, not enabling this setting means that no servers are scavenging records. Aging of records is taking place (No-refresh, Refresh), but nothing else is going on. This is good for a variety of reasons. First, you don't necessarily want *all* of your DNS servers to scavenge. You need only one server to scavenge. It'll replicate the record deletes to the other DNS servers. This also allows for some other configuration options:

*Small environment*
   Turn Scavenging Period on. This should be ample for you.

*Larger environment*
   Leave the Scavenging Period setting off. In other words, you don't want DNS servers scavenging records for you. Instead, use the dnscmd command (found in the *Support Tools* folder on your product CD) with the /StartScavenging option and schedule it on a recurring basis, at the time frame you're looking for. It's probably reasonable to suggest that nighttime hours have little DNS registrations or queries going on.

*Enterprise environment*
   Designate a DNS server to handle all scavenging and nothing else. This can be established by placing the DNS server in its own site so that clients do not refer to it for lookups or any Active Directory functions. If that sounds like too much work, the SRV records for this DNS server can be stripped from DNS to achieve the same effect.

## See Also

- DNS Scavenging on Windows 2000 Server (*http://www.microsoft.com/ windows2000/en/server/help/default.asp?url=/WINDOWS2000/en/server/ help/sag_DNS_imp_ManageAgingScavenging.htm*)

- Enable Aging and Scavenging for DNS (*http://www.microsoft.com/ technet/treeview/default.asp?url=/technet/prodtechnol/ windowsserver2003/proddocs/deployguide/dssbm_drd_dvwv.asp*)

- Scavenging Stale DNS Records (*http://www.winnetmag.com/Articles/ Index.cfm?ArticleID=19897*)

- Set Aging/Scavenging Properties for the DNS Server (*http://www. microsoft.com/technet/treeview/default.asp?url=/technet/prodtechnol/ windowsserver2003/proddocs/standard/sag_DNS_pro_ SetAgeScavengeServer.asp*)

- How to Optimize the Location of a Domain Controller or Global Catalog (*http://support.microsoft.com/?id=306602*)

*—Marcus Oh*

## HACK #38  Troubleshoot DNS

Here are some tips, tools, and resources to help you troubleshoot DNS problems on Windows 2000/2003-based networks.

DNS troubleshooting is usually straightforward, because most errors tend to be simple configuration or setup errors. To troubleshoot DNS, you must have details of the configuration of any DNS resolvers and/or DNS servers and be able to use common DNS troubleshooting tools. This hack provides some details and links to tools you can use to troubleshoot DNS, as well as tips on how to overcome common DNS errors.

## DNS Troubleshooting Tools

Here are a few useful web sites that offer tools for troubleshooting DNS:

*www.DNSreport.com (http://www.dnsreport.com)*
This site will check the DNS settings for an Internet zone and provide prescriptive guidance on optimizing the settings.

*www.DNSstuff.com (http://www.dnsstuff.com)*
This site has a number of DNS tools that you can use to diagnose DNS issues.

*SamSpade.org (http://www.samspade.org)*
> This site has some good tools for DNS troubleshooting. It promotes its tools and expertise as anti-spam utilities, as opposed to just DNS troubleshooting. The site's tools page (*http://www.samspade.org/t/*) provides tools similar to those at www.DNSstuff.com. I have the Sam Spade For Windows tool (*http://www.samspade.org/ssw/*) on my desktop and use it a great deal.

*AnalogX DNSDig (http://www.analogx.com/contents/dnsdig.htm)*
> This page provides an online version of DIG—a useful tool from the Unix world that is used to troubleshoot DNS issues. (Why can't Microsoft provide a port of DIG in Windows or the resource kit?)

*Squish.net DNS Checker (http://www.squish.net/dnscheck)*
> Given a record name and a record type, this page will return a report that details all possible answers.

*DNS Dump (http://www.reskit.net/DNS/dnsdump.cm_)*
> This is a truly awesome script by Dean Wells that exports/imports DNS server configurations. Read carefully before using it, and make sure you change the extension before you run it!

## Troubleshooting Common DNS Issues

Here is a list of common problems and solutions that have been discussed in online newsgroups:

*Running* nslookup *returns nonexistent domain*
> If you run nslookup, you might see an error that looks like this:

```
C:\>nslookup
*** Can't find server name for address 192.168.1.1: Non-existent domain
*** Default servers are not available
Default Server: UnKnown
Address: 192.168.1.1
```

> When nslookup starts, it attempts do a reverse lookup of the IP address of the DNS server. If the reverse lookup fails, nslookup returns the preceding error message, which is somewhat misleading. The solution is to either install a reverse lookup zone for your workstations or to ignore the message.

*Netlogon Error 5774 - DNS Operation Refused*
> This error is typically caused by the use of a DNS server that does not allow dynamic update or is set to refuse operations from your computer. Sometimes, this is due to a workstation that points to the ISP's DNS server instead of an internal DNS server. In general, all internal servers and workstations should point to one or more internal DNS servers that in turn point to a DNS server that forwards to the Internet.

*DNS Error 414 - The specified domain either does not exist or could not be contacted*

This error usually occurs when the computer is configured without a DNS domain name. If the computer is a DNS server that has only a single label name (e.g., *kona2* versus *kona2.reskit.net*), any zone created will have the default SOA and NS records created using just a single label. This in turn will lead to invalid or failed referrals for the zone used to provide lookups for this zone.

*DNS Error 5504 - The DNS Server encountered an invalid domain name in a packet from X.X.X.X*

This error indicates that the DNS server has received a packet with an invalid domain name and the packet has been rejected. The most common cause of this is DNS cache pollution, as described in Knowledge Base (KB) article 241352 (*http://support.microsoft.com/default. aspx?scid=kb;en-us;241352*).

*Troubleshooting dynamic update problems*

Dynamic update is a DNS feature that enables hosts to update their DNS details at the DNS server. Although easy to set up, there are some ways in which DNS dynamic update can fail. See the KB article 287156 for more details (*http://support.microsoft.com/default.aspx?scid=kb;en-us;287156*)

*Windows Server 2003 cannot resolve addresses that Windows 2000 can*

In some cases, it appears that server is just not functioning and not resolving some names. The cause is that Extension Mechanisms for DNS (EDNS0) requests from the 2003 DNS server are not recognized by all other DNS servers. To resolve this, you should disable EDNS0 requests, using the *DNScmd* program from the Windows Server 2003 Support Tools folder and type `dnscmd /config /enableednsprobes` at a command prompt.

## DNS Newsgroups

If the previous tips and tools do not help and you are using any version of Microsoft Windows (or DOS, for that matter), consider posting a query to the *microsoft.public.win2000.dns* newsgroup. This newsgroup can be obtained from *news://news.microsoft.com*. If you do post, you will need to provide some details of your particular issue, including most of all of the following:

- Is the problem a client problem or a DNS server problem?

- What operating system are you running and with which service packs or other fixes?

- What is the client configuration? (ipconfig /all provides this!)
- What specific error, if any, are you seeing?
- What zones are configured on your DNS server, and what properties are set for those zones?
- Are your DNS zones configured to be updated dynamically?
- What sort of Internet connection do you have? Does your ISP allow you to run servers on your connection? Does your provided IP address vary, or is it fixed?

## DNS Books

Finally, here are two books you can use to learn more about troubleshooting DNS issues:

*DNS and BIND*
By Cricket Liu and Paul Ablitz (O'Reilly). This book is possibly the best introduction to DNS in existence. It's Unix-based, but it's still a good book.

*Windows 2000 DNS*
By Herman Knief, Roger Abell, Jeffery Graham, and Andrew Daniels (O'Reilly). This is a pretty good Windows 2000 DNS book.

*—Thomas Lee*

## HACK #39 Manually Recreate a Damaged WINS Database

A corrupt WINS database can spell a host of problems and must be repaired if your network is to function properly. This hack shows you how to recreate a damaged WINS database.

If you're still using WINS on your network—typically in a mixed NT/2000 or NT/2003 environment while migration is underway—you might occasionally experience corruption of the Windows Internet Name Service (WINS) database. If your WINS database becomes corrupted, you can experience all manner of problems with your workstations and servers—most notably, name-resolution problems for legacy Windows clients. You'll need to fix your WINS database if these clients are to communicate on the network. This hack recreates a damaged Windows NT 4.0 or Windows 2000 WINS database.

## Windows NT 4.0

To recreate a damaged WINS database on Windows NT, first go to Control Panel → Services and stop the Windows Internet Name Service. Then, create a folder named *WINS_OLD* and move the contents of the *%SystemRoot%\System32\WINS* folder to *WINS_OLD*. Finally, restart the Windows Internet Name Service. When you are positive that the new WINS database is functioning properly, delete the *WINS_OLD* directory.

## Windows Server 2000/2003

To recreate a damaged WINS database on Windows Sever 2000/2003, first go to Control Panel → Administrative Tools → Services and stop the Windows Internet Name Service. Then, create a folder named *WINS_OLD* and move the contents of the *%SystemRoot%\System32\WINS* folder to *WINS_OLD*. Finally, restart the Windows Internet Name Service. When you are positive that the new WINS database is functioning properly, delete the *WINS_OLD* directory.

> The only difference between Windows NT 4.0 and Windows 2000 for recreating a WINS database is the location for accessing the services.

Again, when you are positive that the new WINS database is functioning properly, delete the *WINS_OLD* directory.

—*Rod Trent*

H A C K
# #40    Change WINS for All Enabled Adapters

Changing WINS settings on client machines can be a pain when you have to move your WINS servers. This hack makes it easier.

If you are using WINS as a name-resolution method (typically in a mixed NT/2000 environment) and have to change your WINS servers—for example, when you install a new WINS server—you have to reconfigure WINS settings on all your client computers. If you are using DHCP, you can configure the 044 WINS/NBNS Servers option on your DHCP servers to provide client computers with new WINS servers addresses, but this requires releasing and renewing DHCP leases on all your clients.

Here's another approach you can use. The following script changes the WINS server settings on client machines and is useful when you install new WINS servers and need to change your WINS server settings on workstations across the board. Note that the script also works on multihomed machines (machines that have two or more network adapters).

## The Code

Type the following code into Notepad (with Word Wrap disabled) and save it with a *.vbs* extension as *ChangeWINS.vbs*:

```
Option Explicit
On Error Resume Next

Dim objLocator, objService, NIC
Dim strComputer, strUsername, strPassword
Dim strWINS1, strWINS2
Dim intErr

strComputer = "."
strUsername = ""
strPassword = ""

strWINS1 = "172.16.1.122"
strWINS2 = "172.16.1.132"

Set objLocator = CreateObject("WbemScripting.SWbemLocator")
Set objService = objLocator.ConnectServer(strComputer, "root/cimv2", &
strUsername, strPassword)
objService.Security .impersonationlevel = 3

For Each NIC In objService.ExecQuery("Select * from Win32_
NetworkAdapterConfiguration Where IPEnabled=True")
WScript.Echo "Nic Index: " & NIC.index
WScript.Echo "Current Settings"
WScript.Echo "Primary Wins Server: " & NIC.WINSPrimaryServer
WScript.Echo "Secondary Wins Server: " & NIC.WINSSecondaryServer
intErr = NIC.SetWinsServer(strWINS1, strWINS2)
If intErr <> 0 Then Wscript.Echo "Error changing WINS"
Next
Set objService = Nothing
Set objLocator = Nothing
```

## Running the Hack

To run this hack, you first have to customize it. For example, if your primary WINS server is 10.0.0.15 and your secondary server is 10.0.0.16, change these lines:

```
strWINS1 = "172.16.1.122"
strWINS2 = "172.16.1.132"
```

to this:

```
strWINS1 = "10.0.0.15"
strWINS2 = "10.0.0.16"
```

Then, create a shortcut to the script and double-click on the shortcut to run the script. This will refresh your computer's WINS settings.

—*Rod Trent*

## HACK #41    Ensure DHCP Server Availability

Making sure a DHCP server is always available is critical if your network uses
dynamic TCP/IP addressing.

Microsoft DHCP server became much more popular in Windows 2000 environments, where it became part of the overall strategy for managing IP
addressing, host namespace, and name resolution (due to its close integra-
tion with Microsoft's implementation of DNS). Because of its significance, it
is imperative to have a solid plan that allows you to quickly recover from
DHCP server failures.

## Installing Redundant DHCP Servers

One approach to ensuring DHCP server availability is to install multiple
DHCP servers and divide the list of available IP addresses on each subnet
into multiple ranges, one per server. In the simplest case of two DHCP servers, configure each with the scopes that have matching start and end
address. Next, for each one create *mutually exclusive* exclusion lists. For
example, if your network is using class C nonsubnetted network 192.168.
168.0/24, then, on both servers, you should create the scope with the start
IP address 192.168.0.1 and the end IP address 192.168.168.254. Your
choice of exclusion lists depends on whether you want both servers to share
the load equally or whether one of them will be a *primary* choice for your
DHCP clients. For example, to balance the load, you would configure the
range 192.168.168.1–192.168.168.127 on the first server and 192.168.168.
128–192.16.168.254 on the second.

In order for this configuration to work, you have to ensure that broadcasts
from DHCP clients will reach both servers. Typically, this is done either by
installing DHCP relay agents on the servers that reside on clients subnet or
by configuring routers as BOOTP Relay Agents.

## Backing Up the DHCP Database

In addition to providing redundancy, you should also ensure regular backups of the DHCP database. Fortunately, the backup takes place automatically by default. Its behavior is determined by Registry entries that reside in
the following key:

    HKEY_LOCAL_MACHINE\SYSTEM\CurrentControlSet\Services\DHCPServer\Parameters

The Registry entries contain the following values:

BackupDatabasePath
    Determines the location of the backup (set initially to *%SystemRoot%\
    System32\DHCP\Backup*).

BackupInterval
    Determines the frequency of the automatic backup, in minutes (the default is 60).

RestoreFlag
    Can be used to force the restore by using the existing backup (by setting RestoreFlag to 1). Typically, the operating system does this automatically if it detects the DHCP database corruption.

Windows also automatically backs up the content of the Registry key HKLM\ SOFTWARE\Microsoft\DHCPServer\Configuration to the *DHCPCFG* file, which resides in the *Backup* folder.

## Recovering the Database

Recovering the database involves restoring both the database files and the Registry settings. You should first stop the DHCP server and then copy the files and load the Registry hive (using *REGEDT32.EXE*) to their target location by overwriting the existing HKLM\SOFTWARE\Microsoft\DHCPServer\ Configuration Registry key. After you have restored the database file, you should change the default of 0 conflict-detection attempts (from the Advanced tab of Server properties in the DHCP MMC console) to a non-zero value (5 is the maximum).

Another option is to use the NETSH command-line utility to back up and restore configuration of the DHCP server database. NETSH's functionality is provided through a number of helper DLLs, each dealing with a particular type of Windows networking component. NETSH allows you to dump the configuration of the DHCP server (including all superscopes, scopes, exclusion ranges, and reservations) into a text file that later can be used to restore. Note, however, that NETSH does not back up information about existing leases, which are stored in the DHCP database.

To create the DHCP configuration dump file, execute the following command, where *IPAddressOrName* is the IP address or name of your DHCP server (note that this command can be executed remotely):

```
NETSH DHCP SERVER IPAddressOrName DUMP > C:\DHCPCfg.txt
```

To restore the DHCP server configuration settings using the same file, run this command:

```
NETSH EXEC C:\DHCPCfg.txt
```

*—Marcin Policht*

## Change a Network Adapter's IP Info

#42    Changing TCP/IP settings via the GUI is tedious at best. It's accomplished more easily with a little VB scripting magic.

Changing a machine's TCP/IP settings from the GUI usually involves a number of steps. This becomes tedious if you have to do it often—for example, if the machine is part of a testbed network where you test different deployment scenarios. Using the VBScript in this hack, you can quickly and frequently modify the network adapter information on a computer.

### The Code

To use this script, type it into Notepad (with Word Wrap turned off) and save it with a *.vbs* extension as *ChangeIP.vbs*:

```
Option Explicit

Dim NetworkAdapter, AdapterConfiguration 'Objects
Dim IPAddress, SubnetMask, Gateway, DNS 'String Arrays
Dim RetVal 'Integers

For Each NetworkAdapter In
GetObject("winmgmts:").InstancesOf("Win32_NetworkAdapter")
If NetworkAdapter.AdapterType = "Ethernet 802.3" Then
For Each AdapterConfiguration In GetObject("winmgmts:").InstancesOf("Win32_
NetworkAdapterConfiguration")
If UCase(AdapterConfiguration.ServiceName) = UCase(NetworkAdapter.
ServiceName) Then
IPAddress = Array("192.168.0.10")
SubnetMask = Array("255.255.255.0")
Gateway = Array("192.168.0.1")
DNS = Array("35.8.2.41")

RetVal = AdapterConfiguration.EnableStatic(IPAddress, SubnetMask)
If Not RetVal = 0 Then
WScript.Echo "Failure assigning IP/Subnetmask."
End If
RetVal = AdapterConfiguration.SetGateways(Gateway)
If Not RetVal = 0 Then
WScript.Echo "Failure assigning Gateway."
End If
RetVal = AdapterConfiguration.SetDnsServerSearchOrder(DNS)
If Not RetVal = 0 Then
WScript.Echo "Failure assinging DNS search order."
End If
End If
Next
End If
Next
```

## Running the Hack

To run this hack, modify the IP information in the following lines, as required by your environment:

```
IPAddress = Array("192.168.0.10")
SubnetMask = Array("255.255.255.0")
Gateway = Array("192.168.0.1")
DNS = Array("35.8.2.41")
```

For example, to change the IP address of a machine to 172.16.44.3 with subnet mask 255.255.0.0 and default gateway 172.16.44.1, replace those lines with these:

```
IPAddress = Array("172.16.44.3")
SubnetMask = Array("255.255.0.0")
Gateway = Array("172.16.44.1")
```

Also, note this statement:

```
If NetworkAdapter.AdapterType = "Ethernet 802.3" Then
```

This is where the script checks the AdapterType, which in this script is listed as "Ethernet 802.3". You should modify this line if you have a different networking environment.

Once these changes have been made to the script, create a shortcut to the script and double-click on the shortcut to run the script.

*—Rod Trent*

# HACK #43  Change from Static IP to DHCP

Reconfiguring a network from static IP addressing to DHCP is a chore no system administrator wants to do, but now there's help.

Companies grow over time, and their networks have to grow along with them. This means that the static IP addressing that was used when the network was small will no longer practical once the systems number more than a few dozen. Unfortunately, changing machines from static to dynamic addressing usually means visiting each machine, logging on as a local administrator, and clicking through numerous properties sheets to reconfigure TCP/IP settings for network adapters.

However, there's an easier way. The VBScript in this hack uses Registry writes to change the TCP/IP settings on a machine from static IP to DHCP.

## The Code

Type the script into Notepad (with Word Wrap disabled) and save it with a
*.vbs* extension as *Static2DHCP.vbs*:

```
'All variables declared
Option Explicit

Dim oWSHShell
Dim sNIC, sMan
Dim iCount

Set oWSHShell = WScript.CreateObject("WScript.Shell")

' Set the DCHP service to autostart
oWSHShell.RegWrite "HKLM\SYSTEM\CurrentControlSet\Services\DHCP\Start", 2

' Get Network card
On Error Resume Next
iCount = 1
Do
sNIC = oWSHShell.RegRead("HKLM\SOFTWARE\Microsoft\Windows NT\ " & _
"CurrentVersion\NetworkCards\" & iCount & "\ServiceName")
sMan = oWSHShell.RegRead("HKLM\SOFTWARE\Microsoft\Windows NT\ " & _
"CurrentVersion\NetworkCards\" & iCount & "\Manufacturer")
' Skip the Async and NDIS services
If sMan <> "Microsoft" And Err.Number = 0 Then
Call SetNIC
End If
iCount = iCount + 1
Loop Until Err.Number <> 0

' Clear the error
Err.Clear

' End of Script



Sub SetNIC
Dim iTest
' Set the NIC service to use DHCP
sNIC = "HKLM\SYSTEM\CurrentControlSet\Services\" & sNIC &"\Parameters\TCPIP\"
iTest = oWSHShell.RegRead(sNIC & "EnableDHCP")
If iTest = 0 Then
oWSHShell.RegWrite sNIC & "EnableDHCP", 1, "REG_DWORD"
oWSHShell.RegWrite sNIC & "IPAddress", "0.0.0.0", "REG_MULTI_SZ"
oWSHShell.RegWrite sNIC & "SubnetMask", "0.0.0.0", "REG_MULTI_SZ"
End If
End Sub
```

## Running the Hack

To run this hack, call the *Static2DHCP.vbs* script from a logon script and use Group Policy to assign this logon script to users' machines. When a user next logs on to his machine, the machine's TCP/IP settings will be changed from static to dynamic addressing. To lease an address from the DHCP server, the user's machine needs to be rebooted, so you could also send out a message asking all users to reboot their machines using the method in "Put a Logoff Icon on the Desktop" [Hack #35] or some other approach. If you like, the logon script could also be combined with the SU utility from the Windows 2000 Server Resource Kit to perform a hands-off migration from static to dynamic addressing.

*—Rod Trent*

# HACK #44 Release and Renew IP Addresses

Using this handy script, you can release and renew a dynamically assigned IP address with a click of the mouse—well, two clicks, actually.

Troubleshooting DHCP lease problems is frustrating when it involves users' desktop machines, because help desk personnel have to explain to users how to open a command prompt, use the ipconfig command, and interpret the output. It would be nice if there were a way to release and renew a machine's IP address without having to go through such *techie* steps.

Well, it turns out there is such a way; just use this handy VBScript to release and renew IP addresses assigned through DHCP.

## The Code

Type the script into Notepad (with Word Wrap disabled) and save it with a *.vbs* extension as *ReleaseRenew.vbs*:

```
On Error Resume Next
Dim AdapterConfig
Dim RetVal
Set AdapterConfig = GetObject("winmgmts:Win32_NetworkAdapterConfiguration")

'WMI release IP Address for all installed network adapters
RetVal = AdapterConfig.ReleaseDHCPLeaseAll

'if retval = 1 then display success. If 0 then failure
If RetVal = 1 Then
MsgBox "IP Address Release was successful."
Else
MsgBox "DHCP Release failed!"
End If
```

```
'WMI renew ip for all network adapters
RetVal = AdapterConfig.RenewDHCPLeaseAll

'if retval = 1 then display success. If 0 then failure
If RetVal = 1 Then
MsgBox "IP Address Renew was successful."
Else
MsgBox "DHCP Renew failed!"
End If

Set AdapterConfig = Nothing
```

## Running the Hack

Copy the script to users' machines and create a shortcut to the script on their desktops. Then, when a user has IP address problems and can't talk to the network, tell her to double-click on the shortcut to release and renew her address, and see if that fixes things. If not, escalate to the next level of troubleshooting!

*—Rod Trent*

## HACK #45 Use netsh to Change Configuration Settings

You can use the Windows 2000 Netshell (netsh) command to do some amazing things, including switching your machine between two different network configurations.

If you move your machines around a lot, you know the pain of having to reconfigure their network settings so they can continue to talk on the network. This sort of thing is common in a testbed environment where you are building and testing different network-deployment scenarios prior to rolling out the real thing. You might also have to reconfigure network settings for your computers if you have a routed network with several subnets in one building and frequently move machines from one subnet to another—a common scenario in a physics lab or similar academic environment. Otherwise, if you have a laptop that you need to use at work, at home, and at the sites of several clients, being able to save and reload network configurations would be a real timesaver.

There are a few utilities on the market that allow you to quickly switch between different network configurations. NetSwitcher (*http://www. netswitcher.com*) is one effective tool. But did you know you can do the same thing using the Windows 2000 Netshell (netsh) command?

## Using netsh

Here's how it works. First, you dump your network settings to a text file through the command line, as follows:

```
netsh -c interface dump > NetworkSettings.txt
```

This command stores your current network settings in a text file named *NetworkSettings.txt*. Now, let's say you have to reconfigure your machine's network settings to repurpose the machine or move it to a different part of the network. Then, later, if you need to restore your machine's original network settings, you can simply type the following command and load back in the previously dumped settings:

```
netsh -f NetworkSettings.txt
```

Note that the destination filename is not important, so you can effectively create multiple configuration files. You can create and name one for each network configuration you need. For example, you can use *Work.txt* for the office, *Home.txt* for your home configuration, and something like *Client.txt* to hold the values for a network you are temporarily visiting.

*—Rod Trent*

## Remove Orphaned Network Cards

Moving a network adapter card to a new PCI slot in Windows 2000/XP can sometimes cause unexpected results.

If you swap out a network interface card (NIC) or move it into a different PCI slot but neglect to run the PnP Hardware Removal wizard or use Device Manager to do so, you might end up with an orphaned NIC. When you perform your hardware change with the card, power up the system, and log into Windows 2000/XP, the hardware wizard might display a message telling you that it detected a change. When you go to configure the network card's TCP/IP settings and try to save them, it will say "Hey, those settings are associated with this network card. Are you sure you want to use them for this one?" Then you'll realize the error you made. So, how do you remove the configuration settings for that orphaned NIC?

To remove your orphaned NIC, you first need to know the Registry keys associated with it. This is the first such key:

```
HKLM\Software\Microsoft\WindowsNT\CurrentVersion\NetworkCards
```

You might see one or more subkeys numerically incremented. Selecting the subkey shows you two values:

Description

> This contains the displayed description of the network card.

ServiceName

> This is the GUID of the network card that is referenced in the Services section of HKLM where the TCP/IP configuration information is maintained, and also under the Enum\PCI section where the configuration parameters of the network card are maintained.

This is another important key:

> HKLM\System\CurrentControlSet\Services\{GUID}

Within this key, the Parameters\Tcpip subkey contains the TCP/IP configuration settings for the network card, including the DHCP server IP address, the lease information (if you're using DHCP), the subnet mask, and so on.

Here is the third key:

> HKLM\System\CurrentControlSet\Services\{ServiceName of Network Card}

This key represents certain driver parameters related to error control, path to the driver file, and so on. The Enum subkey also points to the PnP Instance ID of the device, if you want a shortcut to where in the HKLM\System\Enum section of the Registry the device is maintained.

This is the fourth key:

> HKLM\System\CurrentControlSet\Control\Network\{GUID}

This key stores all information related to devices that serve as communications media to transmit/receive data between devices, such as network cards, infrared ports, and so on. It also contains configuration information for the key Microsoft Network services, such as File & Printer Sharing, QoS, and so on. Each device/adapter has a GUID subkey under this section of the Registry, where you can find the information related to that device. For the network cards, find the appropriate GUID and under this fourth key is the Connection subkey that maintains information related to PnP and the name of the connection (as you see when you go to Start → Settings → Network & Dialup Connections). The PnpInstanceID value is what we are interested in, because it points to a section of the Registry that maintains configuration information for Plug and Play devices.

Finally, this is the last key you need to know about:

> HKLM\Enum\PCI\{PnPInstanceID}

This key and its subkeys maintain information specific to the card, such as the PCI Bus it is installed in, driver information, and so forth.

Once you find all this information, you can delete those keys related to the card that was once there in the system. Then, you will no longer have to worry about issues of conflicting TCP/IP information between the old card and the new one or orphaned information that may or may not cause conflicts later on.

Use this hack at your own risk—making any changes in the Registry could have dire consequences. Make a backup first and get comfortable with what you are modifying/removing before proceeding with the recommended steps in this hack.

*—Matt Goedtel*

## HACK #47 Implement Windows 2000 Network Load Balancing

If you need network load balancing software on your network, why not try the NLB component that comes with Windows 2000 Advanced Server?

Installing Windows Network Load Balancing (NLB) is often a terrific idea. Most network load balancing hardware devices today cost over $20,000. Thus, if your web application or content site is not necessarily going to support traffic as heavy as *http://www.msn.com*, NLB is a great choice.

However, this mighty piece of web-balancing code from Microsoft has a few implementation gotchas that can crop up at any minute. Let's quickly review the basics, which most you probably already know. You can run NLB only on Windows 2000 Advanced Server, Windows 2000 Datacenter Server, or any edition of Windows Server 2003. NLB also has a role in Microsoft Application Center, but the concept is the same.

The following tips provide successful techniques to use with NLB.

### Two NIC Environment

Plan on a two-NIC environment. For instance, identify a private network for Windows network activity, such as domain-level functions, file sharing, or name resolution. Identify the second NIC as the public- or client-facing connection. While NLB supports both unicast and multicast routing, using two NICS lets you avoid the complexities of using multicast mode. However, if you do want to use multicast mode with NLB, then either use a VLAN for all NLB NIC connections (which prevents saturating your Layer 2 network switches) or use a hub (that's right, a nonswitched hub) for all NLB NICs and allow the hub to make one connection to the Layer 2 switch front-ending your web farm. For security reasons, ensure also that the NLB NIC is stripped of all services, such as File and Print Sharing and the Microsoft network client.

However, if you want to go home from work early, don't even try to run NLB on one NIC using multicast mode. The underlying technical challenge for Layer 2 switches and NLB is that the NLB-based NICs create a dummy MAC address and provide it to the MAC address table of the switch to which they are connected. NLB has to receive all traffic addresses to the NLB cluster for the software algorithm in use to make a decision on which node to send the traffic to. Some Layer 2 switches get confused at the same MAC address coming through different ports, and this can create the dreaded broadcast storm.

## Sample Environment

The scenario shown in Figure 4-3 illustrates Microsoft Network Load Balancing in use in a standard Microsoft n-tier highly available Internet configuration. The three front-end IIS web servers (the dark shaded area in Figure 4-3) all are running Windows 2000 Advanced Server and illustrate the redundancy and load balancing archived with an NLB solution. Each web server has its own internal or primary IP address of the form 10.0.0.x, which is a nonroutable address for security and management purposes, while the clustered or shared IP addresses are of the form 192.168.18.x. The firewall in front of the web farm is configured to perform a network translation of the actual hosted web site's DNS name and IP address to the listening IP address 192.168.18.158 of NLB. In this case, equal load balancing is used, such that each web server will carry 33% of the load so that NLB will load-balance traffic based on an equal distribution of the incoming traffic. If one server goes down, the load will be distributed to the remaining two servers.

Other Microsoft high-availability technologies can also be seen in this example—for example, the use of a SQL Server cluster (the light-shaded area in Figure 4-3) providing backend database services for this solution. This illustrates the relationship between Microsoft Clustering Services (MSCS) and Microsoft Network Load Balancing (NLB): generally, they secure different tiers of highly available Microsoft solutions. In this case, NLB is used for the web tier, while clustering is used for the database tier.

These tips and the corresponding scenario should save you considerable time when implementing NLB web clusters using Windows 2000/2003. The main thing to remember, though, is to never fall for the one NIC multicast option when using Microsoft Network Load Balancing.

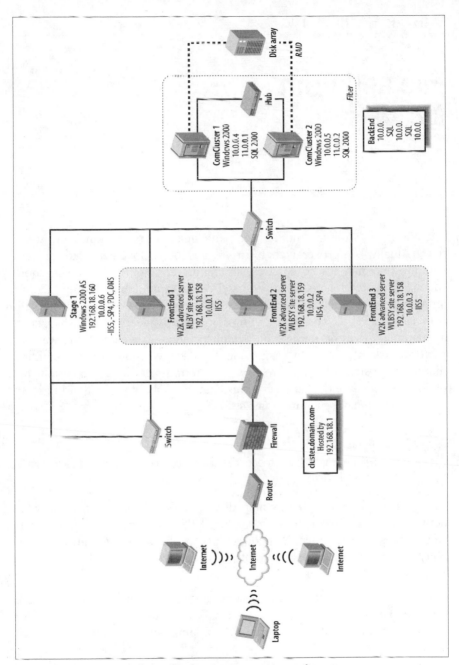

*Figure 4-3. Using Network Load Balancing in an n-tier configuration*

# CHAPTER FIVE

# File and Print

## Hacks 48–53

File and print is the traditional bread and butter of networking, and while it's gradually being overtaken by more advanced document-management solutions, not may companies are planning on retiring their file servers soon. Managing shared folders and printers also makes up a major component of an administrator's daily routine, and a high proportion of calls to the help desk as well. So it's worth examining some new ways to do old tasks, such as mapping drives or configuring default printers, as well as some ways to perform tasks that are not easy using standard Windows tools, including mapping the structure of a directory or determining who has a certain file open on the network. That's what this chapter is about—doing old tasks in new ways and making complex tasks simple.

### HACK #48 Map Network Drives

This quick way to map a network drive can replace the traditional approach of using batch files.

Using VBScript, you can easily map drive letters to shared folders on your network. This approach allows you to use VBScript to map and unmap network drives—for example, in logon scripts. It also allows you greater flexibility in customizing scripts to perform actions across a network and doesn't require the net use command to work.

Basically, the script creates the Network scripting object and then uses the MapNetworkDrive method to assign a drive letter to a network share. I've included examples of code for both mapping and unmapping network drives.

## The Code

First, here's the code for mapping a network drive:

```
Dim net
Set net = CreateObject("WScript.Network")
net.MapNetworkDrive "Z:", "\\server\share"
```

And here's code for unmapping a network drive:

```
Dim WshNetwork
Set WshNetwork = WScript.CreateObject("WScript.Network")
WshNetwork.RemoveNetworkDrive "Z:"
```

## Running the Hack

To use the first snippet of code, type it into Notepad (with Word Wrap disabled) and save it with a *.vbs* extension— for example, as *map.vbs*. Then modify this line to specify the drive letter and share you want to map:

```
net.MapNetworkDrive "Z:", "\\server\share"
```

For example, to map the drive letter K: to the *Sysback* share on a file server with an IP address of 172.16.11.230, change the line to:

```
net.MapNetworkDrive "K:", "\\172.16.11.230\Sysback"
```

Then, run the script either by creating a shortcut to it and double-clicking on the shortcut, by opening a command prompt and typing cscript.exe map.vbs, or by calling it from a batch file using a line like this (where *path* is the absolute path to where the script is located):

```
cscript //nologo path\map.vbs
```

To unmap this drive, type the second code snippet into Notepad, save it as *unmap.vbs*, and change this line:

```
WshNetwork.RemoveNetworkDrive "Z:"
```

to this:

```
WshNetwork.RemoveNetworkDrive "K:"
```

Then, run the script using any of the methods described previously.

*—Rod Trent*

# Determine Who Has A Particular File Open on the Network

Using the Hyena utility, quickly find out which user on your network has a particular file open.

One of the biggest problems for system administrators is dealing with help-desk or user requests that ask you to see who has a particular document open on the network. This can be most effectively completed using a utility called Hyena from SystemTools.com (*http://www.systemtools.com*). With this utility, you can even disconnect the user who has the open file or send her a message asking her to close the file in question.

Here's a quick walkthrough on how to use the product, so you can see how easy it is to use. Start Hyena and begin by selecting the server name where the file is stored. Expand the + sign and the Shares leaf, and select the share you want to examine. Then, drill through the directories until you find the subdirectory you want, such as SqlDev in Figure 5-1.

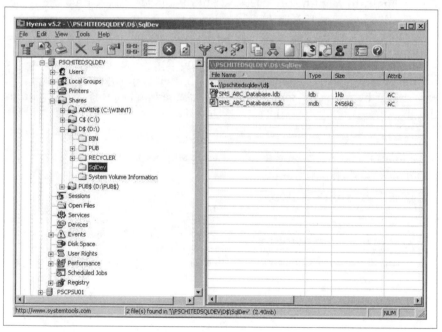

*Figure 5-1. Finding open files in Hyena*

Now, select the file you want (*SMS_ABC_Database.mdb* in our example) in the right pane to see who has it open. Right-click it, and from the context menu select More Functions and then Open By (Figure 5-2).

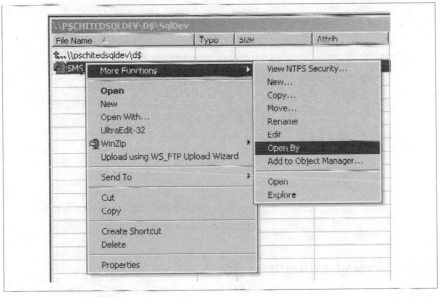

*Figure 5-2. Selecting an open file*

Now, in the menu to the right, you will see who the user is by examining the
User Name column, as shown in Figure 5-3.

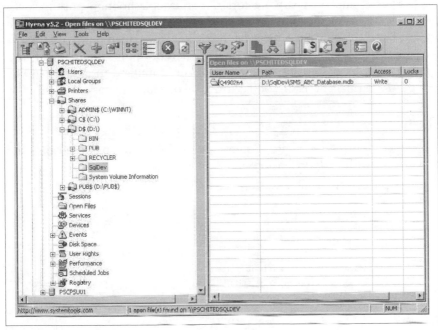

*Figure 5-3. Viewing who has the file open*

Now it is just a matter of either sending the user a message or, if he is unavailable, disconnecting him, by right-clicking on the file and choosing the appropriate menu option (Figure 5-4). If you opt for the latter, keep in mind that the file will be closed without giving the user the opportunity to make any final changes.

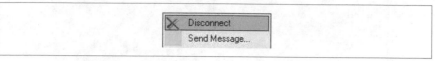

*Figure 5-4. Disconnecting the user*

You can download a free, 30-day, fully functional, evaluation copy of this great tool from *http://systemtools.com/hyena/download_frame.htm*. Enjoy!

—*Don Hite*

# Display a Directory Tree

HACK
#50    Using some simple coding, you can display a complete map of a directory structure from a command prompt.

The Explorer interface makes it easy to browse directories on a Windows machine, but it doesn't provide a simple method to document the structure of directories and their subdirectories. For troubleshooting purposes, it's helpful to know the directory structure on file servers where users store their work. This VBScript simplifies the process of documenting a directory's structure by allowing you to view such structure from the command line. Alternatively, by redirecting the output of the command to a text file, you can print a permanent record of the structure of your directories.

## The Code

Type the following code into Notepad (with Word Wrap turned off) and save the file with a *.vbs* extension as *vbtree.vbs*:

```
' Show simple directory tree

Option Explicit
Dim sArg, oFSO
Set oFSO = CreateObject("Scripting.FileSystemObject")

' Get folder (default is current directory)
If Wscript.Arguments.Count > 0 Then
sArg = Wscript.Arguments(0)
Else
sArg = "."
End If
sArg = oFSO.GetAbsolutePathName(sArg)
```

```
' Process entire tree (if valid folder)
If oFSO.FolderExists(sArg) Then
Wscript.Echo "Folder tree for:", sArg
ShowTree "", oFSO.GetFolder(sArg)
End If

Set oFSO = Nothing
Wscript.Quit(0)


Sub ShowTree(sIndent, oFolder)
Dim oSubFolder, ix
ix = 1
For Each oSubFolder In oFolder.SubFolders
Wscript.Echo sIndent & "+--" & oSubFolder.Name
If ix <> oFolder.SubFolders.Count Then
ShowTree sIndent & "| ", oSubFolder
Else
ShowTree sIndent & " ", oSubFolder
End If
ix = ix + 1
Next
End Sub
```

## Running the Hack

The script is hardcoded by design to display the structure of the current
directory. Place the script into to directory whose structure you want to display, such as *C:\data*. Then, open a command prompt, change the current
directory to *C:\data*, and type cscript vbtree.vbs to display the tree of subdirectories under the current directory (Figure 5-5). Alternatively, you can
type cscript vbtree.vbs > tree.txt to redirect the output of the script to a
text file for documentation purposes.

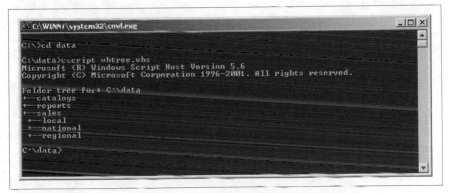

*Figure 5-5. Displaying the tree of subdirectories under C:\data*

Make sure you have the latest scripting engines on the workstation from which you run this script. You can download current scripting engines from the Microsoft Scripting home page (*http://msdn.microsoft.com/scripting/*).

—*Rod Trent*

## HACK #51    Automate Printer Management

Here are a couple nifty ways to manage printers from the command line instead of via the GUI.

Managing printer mappings tends to be complicated task, especially in larger environments. Increased level of difficulty results from the fact that, in such situations, printers are shared (rather than used by individual users). Shared printer devices are typically network-attached (i.e., they either have internal network cards or are connected to external hardware-based print servers). This differs from a home/small office setup, where printing devices connect to individual workstations via parallel, USB, or infrared port.

The way printer software is installed also varies by connection. Local printers are either autodetected (in Windows 2000 and XP) or installed via the Add Printer wizard. In the case of network-attached devices, printers are first installed with the Add Printer wizard on a network server. Next, users connect to these printers (either by double-clicking on the printers' icons in My Network Places/Network Neighborhood or by running the Add Printer wizard), which triggers automatic download of printer drivers and their configuration on the local workstations. The printer mappings are stored as part of a user's profile.

Since the process of connecting to network printers is straightforward, you can leave this task to users. This is a viable solution, as long as printers are easy to find (e.g., by implementing a naming convention that clearly identifies the printer's location). This, however, is not always the case.

### CON2PRT

If you want to be able to manage printer mappings easily, you can use the CON2PRT command, which has been available since the release of the Zero Administration Kit for Windows NT 4.0. CON2PRT allows you to map network printers from the command line and is extremely easy to use. It works with Windows NT 4.0, 2000, and XP and can easily be included in a login script. Its only limitation is the fact that it cannot be used to force the installation of the locally attached printer, but this, fortunately, is rarely needed (since, with Windows 2000 and XP, local printers are usually autodetected).

The CON2PRT command offers three functions:

CON2PRT /f

Deletes all existing printer mappings

CON2PRT /c

Creates a new printer mapping

CON2PRT /cd

Creates a new printer mapping and sets it as the default

For example, to set a default printer to the printer LJ4000_PS_01 on the server SERVER01, you would type in the following:

```
CON2PRT /cd \\SERVER01\LJ4000_PS_01
```

You can find the complete syntax of CON2PRT by typing the standard /? switch at the command prompt, and download *CON2PRT.EXE* (along with the rest of the Zero Administration Kit for Windows) from *http://www. microsoft.com/ntworkstation/downloads/Recommended/Featured/NTZAK.asp.*

## RUNDLL32

While CON2PRT is easy to use, its capabilities are limited to removing all printer mappings and creating new ones (including setting the default printer). Though it seems that this might be all you need when dealing with printers, Windows offers much wider range of functionality.

As you probably know, most of the features used by Windows in the traditional 32-bit Windows environment are implemented in the form of Dynamic Link Libraries (DLLs, files with the extension *.dll*). As the name indicates, DLLs are collections (libraries) of functions that can be used whenever they are needed (dynamically) by any process operating within Windows. Unfortunately, access to functions included in the DLL files, in general, is restricted primarily to programmers. However, there are exceptions to this rule. For example, you can take advantage of certain specifically designed DLLs by running the RUNDLL32 command that is included in every 32-bit version of Windows. Keep in mind, though, that the number of functions available with RUNDLL32 is fairly small (for example, it does not include any of the Win32 API calls exported from the system DLLs).

Printer-management functions used by RUNDLL32 are stored in the *printui.dll* file. To find out the collection of functions included in this file, you can run the following from the command prompt or Start -> Run box:

```
rundll32 printui.dll,PrintUIEntry /?
```

This will display a long list of options available to you. In general, you use the following syntax of commands (where options and commandfile parameters vary):

```
rundll32 printui.dll,PrintUIEntry options commandfile
```

Here are just few of many possible uses of this command:

*Delete a local printer (called* HP LaserJet 5)

```
rundll32 printui.dll,PrintUIEntry /dl /n "HP LaserJet 5"
```

*Delete the local printer on the remote computer (called* RemotePC01)

```
rundll32 printui.dll,PrintUIEntry /dl  /n  "HP  LaserJet  5"  /c\\
RemotePC1
```

*Delete a network printer*

```
rundll32 printui.dll,PrintUIEntry /dn /n "\\SERVERNAME\PRINTERNAME"
```

*Add a network printer*

```
rundll32 printui.dll,PrintUIEntry /in /n "\\SERVERNAME\PRINTERNAME"
```

*Set a printer as the default*

```
rundll32 printui.dll,PrintUIEntry /y /n "\\SERVERNAME\PRINTERNAME"
```

—*Marcin Policht*

## HACK #52  Set the Default Printer Based on Location

Using a combination of Group Policy and logon scripts, you can easily assign different default printers to different users.

At the college, where I work, we use mandatory profiles for students, who log into Windows XP machines in three different computer labs in a Windows 2000 Active Directory environment. Each lab has its own networked printer, which should be used by students working in that lab. But the profile can have only one default printer set, which obviously wouldn't work, since students in two labs would default to a printer that wasn't in their room.

### The Code

Here is the quick and dirty VBScript that solves the problem:

```
set net = CreateObject("WScript.Network")
workstation=net.computername
location=left(workstation,2)
printername=""
select case location
  case "L1"  printername="L1 LaserJet"
  case "L2"  printername="L2 LaserJet"
  case "L3"  printername="L3 LaserJet"
```

```
End Select
if printername<>"" then net.SetDefaultPrinter(printername)
set net = Nothing
```

## Running the Hack

The script looks at the first two characters of the computer name (this specifies which lab the computer is located in) and then sets the default printer accordingly. If the student is logging on to a computer that's not in one of the labs, the default printer isn't changed. If you name printers differently in your own environment, you might have to customize the script further as needed.

We run this script in our own environment by specifying it as a logon script using Group Policy (so legacy Windows 98 machines ignore it), because all our labs have Windows XP anyway. All our machines also have the necessary drivers installed and configured, and the printers have the same names, so we just have to change the default printer.

*—Peter Rysavy*

## Add Printers Based on Name of Computer

Here's a logon script you can use to solve a complicated problem in printer management: performing a logon task based on the name of the computer being logged into.

In various forums, I have noticed questions regarding how to perform tasks at logon based on the name of the computer that the user is logging into. In my environment (a small community college), we thought we could have fewer servers and reduce network traffic by configuring all our computers to use TCP/IP printing. This worked out pretty well for a while, but we discovered a few drawbacks of using TCP/IP printing. For example, there is no control over excessive printing and it is not possible to track costs back to a user. Also, it is difficult to update systems when printers get replaced

We soon split our thinking and were able to switch 99% of our student computers to print through a few servers. To assist us with our print-management needs, we purchased Print Manager Plus (*http://www. printmanagerplus.com*). Print Manager Plus has many benefits for my environment. We are an educational institution that has a number of open-use areas where students and the public can use our computers. We do not track printing costs back to users, and we were experiencing a rising cost of print supplies due to misuse of our printers. The implementation of Print

Manager Plus allowed us to put controls in place that limit abuse in the following ways:

- The user is able to print only 8 pages at a time. If the user's document is 10 pages long, he must print pages 1–8, then 9–10.
- There is a limit on the file size of the print job. The user is unable to print a document that is larger than 15MB when it arrives at the server.

Print Manager Plus has the ability to inform the user when he exceeds the defined limits. I have customized the messages sent from Print Manager Plus to the user so that they present him with options on how to print the document in question.

Server-based printers, however, created a few headaches of their own. In particular, any room is pretty much fair game for us to use when we provide training to not only our students, but also our faculty and staff. We needed a way to set the right printer on any given computer for any user who logs on. Also, we wanted to use one logon script for all users in any domain.

We also had a Windows 2000 Terminal Server available but had not made good use of it until recently. The original thinking was to install a bunch of printers on it and trust users to select the appropriate printer before hitting the print button. We soon had calls asking, "What are all these documents coming out of my printer?"

Anyway, I thought about this awhile and decided that the best approach would be to add the printers based on the name of the computer. We have a standard naming convention in use that made this task possible.

This hack contains the code that I came up with. The code should be pretty readable by itself, but I'll spend some time briefly discussing some of its more major parts.

## The Code

To get the code for the script, I suggest downloading the *Logon.vbs* file from the O'Reilly web site (*http://www.oreilly.com/catalog/winsvrhks/*), because it's too long to type from scratch. This version of the script was tested on Windows 2000 Service Pack 2 running Internet Explorer 6 Service Pack 1 with Microsoft Windows Script v5.6. It was also tested on Windows XP Professional participating in a small Active Directory domain.

I have had a variation of this script in production for a long time now with great success. But, as always, either the differences in your environment or something I missed in editing the script for this hack might cause things behave unexpectedly.

Depending on your environment, the code requires:

- A recent version of Internet Explorer (*http://www.microsoft.com/ windows/ie/default.asp*).
- Windows Script 5.6 for Windows 98/ME/NT (*http://www.microsoft.com/ downloads/details.aspx?FamilyID=0a8a18f6-249c-4a72-bfcf-fc6af26dc390*)
- Windows Script for 2000/XP (*http://www.microsoft.com/downloads/ details.aspx?FamilyID=c717d943-7e4b-4622-86eb-95a22b832caa*)
- Active Directory Client Extensions for Windows 9x, ME or NT4 (*http:// www.microsoft.com/windows2000/techinfo/howitworks/activedirectory/ adsilinks.asp*).

For more information on using Internet Explorer for status messages, see "Using an IE Window to Display Progress" (*http://www.myitforum.com/ articles/11/view.asp?id=3489*), "VBScript Forms (Part 1): Using Internet Explorer for Data Input/Output Forms" (*http://www.myitforum.com/articles/ 11/view.asp?id=4390*), and "Using IE to Browse for Files" (*http://www. myitforum.com/articles/11/view.asp?id=4229*).

**Perform initial tasks.** This section sets up the basics of the script. In this script, I also call a few subroutines/functions (listed further in later sections) that either gather information or perform my required tasks. I like using subroutines and functions, because it makes my code reusable or easily stored in a code library for future coding endeavors. This section accomplishes the following major tasks:

- Call a subroutine that gathers basic system information
- Exit the script if user is logged on locally to the server
- Call subroutines to gather group memberships

The script also performs other tasks, as discussed in comments throughout the code.

```
' File:      Logon.vbs
' Updated:   April 2003
' Version:   2.1
' Author:    Dan Thomson, myITforum.com columnist
'            I can be contacted at dethomson@hotmail.com
'
' Usage:
'            This script can be directly assigned as a logon script for
'            Windows 2000 or greater clients. For older systems, this
'            script will need to be called from a logon batch file.
'
' Input:
```

```
'
' Requirements:
'          Win 9x, ME or NT 4:
'          - Active Directory Client Extensions
'            http://www.microsoft.com/windows2000/techinfo/howitworks/
'            activedirectory/adsilinks.asp
'          - Windows Script
'            http://msdn.microsoft.com/library/default.asp?url=/downloads
'            /list/webdev.asp
'          - A recent version of Internet Explorer
'
' Notes:
'          Tested on Windows 2000 Professional running Windows Script v5.6
'          and participating in an AD domain
'
'''''''''''''''''''''''''''''''''''''''''''''''''''''''''''''''''''''''''''


On Error Resume Next

'''''''''''''''''''''''''''''''''''''''''''''''''''''''''''''''''''''''''''
' Define Variables and Constants
'''''''''''''''''''''''''''''''''''''''''''''''''''''''''''''''''''''''''''

Dim objFileSys
Dim objIntExplorer
Dim objWshNetwork
Dim objWshShell
Dim strDomain            'Domain of the user
Dim strHomePage          'Homepage to be set for user
Dim strLogonPath         'Path to location from where the script is running
Dim strOSProdType        'OS Product type (WinNT, LanmanNT, ServerNT)
Dim strWorkstation       'Local Computer Name
Dim strUserGroups        'List of groups the user is a meber of
Dim intCounter           'General counter

Const UseNTServer = 0    'Sets whether this script runs when logging on
locally
                         'to Windows Servers.
                         'Values are: 1 (Yes) OR 0 (No)

'Initialize common scripting objects
Set objFileSys    = CreateObject( "Scripting.FileSystemObject" )
Set objWshNetwork = CreateObject( "WScript.Network" )
Set objWshShell   = CreateObject( "WScript.Shell" )

'Pause script until user is fully logged on (applies only to Win 9x or ME)
'This will timeout after 10 seconds
strUser = ""
intCounter = 0
Do
  strUserID = objWshNetwork.Username
  intCounter = intCounter + 1
  Wscript.Sleep 500
```

```
Loop Until strUserID <> "" OR intCounter > 20

'Check for error getting username
If strUserID = "" Then
   objWshShell.Popup "Logon script failed - Contact the Helpdesk @ x 345", , _
      "Logon script", 48
   Call Cleanup
End If

'Setup IE for use as a status message window
Call SetupIE

'Display welcome message
Call UserPrompt ("Welcome " & strUserID)

'Add horizontal line as a 'break'
objIntExplorer.Document.WriteLn("<hr style=""width:100%""></hr>")

'Gather some basic system info
Call GetSystemInfo

If IsTerminalServerSession <> True Then
   'Exit if we are logging on locally to a server and the
   'script is set to NOT run on servers
   IF UseNTServer = 0 AND (strOSProdType = "LanmanNT" OR strOSProdType =
"ServerNT") Then
      objWshShell.Popup "Windows Server - Exiting Logon Script!", 10, _
      "Logon to " & strDomain, 16
      Call CleanUp
   End if
End If

'Get group memberships
strUserGroups = ""
Call GetLocalGroupMembership
Call GetGlobalGroupMembership

''''''''''''''''''''''''''''''''''''''''''''''''''''''''''''''''''''''''''''''''
'
' Map drives, add shared printers and set default homepage
''''''''''''''''''''''''''''''''''''''''''''''''''''''''''''''''''''''''''''''''
```

**Determining workstation settings.** This section determines which settings should be applied to the workstation, based on the name of the workstation. Our environment has a nice naming convention: the building, room number, and station number are identified in the name. For example, the name Blg4Rm105-03 identifies a computer as being station 3, located in building 4, room 105. To determine which mappings get assigned to a computer, all I have to do is base my criteria on everything on the left of the dash (-).

''''''''''''''''''''''''''''''''''''''''''''''''''''''''''''''''''''''''''''''''

```
'
' Part A
' This section performs actions based on computer name
'
..........................................................................

  'The left side of the computer name contains building and room information
  If Instr( 1, strWorkstation, "-", 1) > 0 Then
    strWorkstation = _
      Left( strWorkstation, ( Instr( 1, strWorkstation, "-", 1)))
  End If

  Select Case UCase( strWorkstation )

    Case "BLD1RM101-"
      Call MapDrive ("U:", "MyShareSvr1", "MyShare1")
      Call AddPrinter ("Mydomain2", "MyPrtSvr2", "Bld1Rm101-HP4050")
      objWshNetwork.SetDefaultPrinter "\\MyPrtSvr2\Bld1Rm101-HP4050"
      strHomePage = "http://www.chesapeake.edu/academic_info/ " & _
        "acad_computing.asp"
    Case "BLD1RM202-"
      Call MapDrive ("U:", "MyShareSvr2", "MyShare2")
      Call AddPrinter ("Mydomain1", "MyPrtSvr1", "Bld1Rm202-HP4000")
      objWshNetwork.SetDefaultPrinter "\\MyPrtSvr1\Bld1Rm202-HP4000"
      strHomePage = "http://www.chesapeake.edu/library/default.asp"
    Case "BLD3RM104-"
      'This room uses TCP/IP printing instead of a print server.
      'Only set homepage
      strHomePage = "http://www.chesapeake.edu/writing/wchome.htm"
    Case Else

  End Select
..........................................................................
```

**Adding mappings based on group membership.** Adding mappings based upon the computer name is cool. However, there will always be a need to perform tasks based on specific group membership. This section takes care of such tasks.

```
..........................................................................
'
' Part B
' This section performs actions based on group membership
'
..........................................................................

If InGroup( "ShareForStaff" ) Then
  Call MapDrive ("X:", "StaffSvr1", "StaffShare1")
  strHomePage = "http://www.chesapeake.edu/generalinfo/cambridge.asp"
End If

If InGroup( "ShareForStudents" ) Then
```

```
   Call MapDrive ("Y:", "StudentSvr1", "StudentShare1")
   strHomePage = "http://www.chesapeake.edu"
End If

'''''''''''''''''''''''''''''''''''''''''''''''''''''''''''''''''''''''''''''''
' End section
'''''''''''''''''''''''''''''''''''''''''''''''''''''''''''''''''''''''''''''''
```

**Setting the IE home page and final message**. This section sets the IE home page (if specified), starts *SMSls.bat*, and posts a final message to the user. The script tests to determine if the user is a member of the Domain Admins or DoNotInstallSMS groups. If the user is a member of either of these groups, *SMSls.bat* is skipped. This is helpful if you want to get in quick to do a small task or to keep SMS off some of your more persnickety users' computers.

```
'''''''''''''''''''''''''''''''''''''''''''''''''''''''''''''''''''''''''''''''
'Set default homepage
If strHomePage <> "" Then
  Err.Clear
  objWshShell.RegWrite _
    "HKCU\Software\Microsoft\Internet Explorer\Main\Start Page", strHomePage
  If Err = 0 Then Call UserPrompt ("Set Internet home page to " &
strHomePage)
End If

'Start SMSls.bat
'Do not run if a member of the Domain Administrators
'or in the global group DoNotInstallSMS
If InGroup("Domain Admins") OR InGroup("DoNotInstallSMS") Then
  Call UserPrompt ("Skipping SMSLS.BAT")
Else
  objWshShell.Run "%COMSPEC% /c " & strLogonPath & "\smsls.bat", 0, False
End If

'Add horizontal line as a 'break'
objIntExplorer.Document.WriteLn("<hr style=""width:100%""></hr>")

'Inform user that logon process is done
Call UserPrompt ("Finished network logon processes")

'Wait 10 seconds
Wscript.Sleep (10000)

'Close Internet Explorer
objIntExplorer.Quit()

Call Cleanup
'''''''''''''''''''''''''''''''''''''''''''''''''''''''''''''''''''''''''''''''
```

That's the end of the first major section of the script. The following subsections list and explain the various subroutines and functions.

**Connecting to a shared network printer.** The following routine is where the printer mapping occurs. It first verifies that the share is accessible and creates the mapping. If the share is not accessible or is not a valid print share, the user will be prompted with an error message that lets her know she should call the help desk.

```
''''''''''''''''''''''''''''''''''''''''''''''''''''''''''''''''''''''''''''''''
'
' Sub:       AddPrinter
'
' Purpose:  Connect to shared network printer
'
' Input:
'
'           strPrtServerDomain  Domain in which print server is a member
'           strPrtServer        Name of print server
'           strPrtShare         Share name of printer
'
' Output:
'
' Usage:
'
'           Call AddPrinter ("Mydomain2", "MyPrtSvr2", "Bld1Rm101-HP4050")
'
''''''''''''''''''''''''''''''''''''''''''''''''''''''''''''''''''''''''''''''''
Private Sub AddPrinter(strPrtServerDomain, strPrtServer, strPrtShare)

  On Error Resume Next

  Dim strPrtPath      'Full path to printer share
  Dim objPrinter      'Object reference to printer
  Dim strMsg          'Message output to user
  Dim blnError        'True / False error condition

  blnError = False

  'Build path to printer share
  strPrtPath = "\\" & strPrtServer & "\" & strPrtShare

  'Test to see if shared printer exists.
  'Proceed if yes, set error condition msg if no.
  Set objPrinter = GetObject _
    ("WinNT://" & strPrtServerDomain & "/" & strPrtServer & "/" & _
    strPrtShare)
  If IsObject( objPrinter ) AND _
  (objPrinter.Name <> "" AND objPrinter.Class = "PrintQueue") Then

     'Different mapping techniques depending on OS version
     If objWshShell.ExpandEnvironmentStrings( "%OS%" ) = "Windows_NT" Then
       Err.Clear
       'Map printer
       objWshNetwork.AddWindowsPrinterConnection strPrtPath
     Else
       'Mapping printers for Win9x & ME is a pain and unreliable.
     End If
```

```
Else
   blnError = True
End IF

'Check error condition and output appropriate user message
If Err <> 0 OR blnError = True Then
   strMsg = "Unable to connect to network printer. " & vbCrLf & _
            "Please contact the Helpdesk @ ext 345" & vbCrLf & _
            "and ask them to check the " & strPrtServer & " server." & _
            vbCrLf & vbCrLf & _
            "Let them know that you are unable to connect to the '" _
            & strPrtShare & "' printer"
   objWshShell.Popup strMsg,, "Logon Error !", 48
Else
   Call UserPrompt ("Successfully added printer connection to " & _
   strPrtPath)
End If

Set objPrinter = Nothing

End Sub
```

**Mapping a drive to a shared folder.** This routine is where the drive mapping
occurs. It first removes any preexisting drive mapping that might be using
the designated drive letter. Then, it verifies that the share is accessible and
creates the mapping. If the share is not accessible, the user will be prompted
with an error message that lets him know he should call the help desk.

```
'
' Sub:      MapDrive
'
' Purpose:  Map a drive to a shared folder
'
' Input:
'           strDrive    Drive letter to which share is mapped
'           strServer   Name of server that hosts the share
'           strShare    Share name
'
' Output:
'
' Usage:
'           Call MapDrive ("X:", "StaffSvr1", "StaffShare1")
'

Private Sub MapDrive( strDrive, strServer, strShare )

   On Error Resume Next

   Dim strPath      'Full path to printer share
   Dim blnError     'True / False error condition
```

```
blnError = False

'Disconnect Drive if drive letter is already mapped.
'This assures everyone has the same drive mappings

If objFileSys.DriveExists(strDrive) = True Then
  objWshNetwork.RemoveNetworkDrive strDrive, , True
End If

'Build path to share
strPath = "\\" & strServer & "\" & strShare

'Test to see if share exists. Proceed if yes, set error condition if no.
If objFileSys.DriveExists(strPath) = True Then
  Err.Clear
  objWshNetwork.MapNetworkDrive strDrive, strPath
Else
  blnError = True
End If

'Check error condition and output appropriate user message
If Err.Number <> 0 OR blnError = True Then
  'Display message box informing user that the connection failed
  strMsg = "Unable to connect to network share. " & vbCrLf & _
           "Please contact the Helpdesk @ ext 345 and ask them " & _
           "to check the " & strServer & " server." & vbCrLf & _
           "Let them know that you are unable to connect to the " & _
           "'" & strPath & "' share"
  objWshShell.Popup strMsg,, "Logon Error !", 48
Else
  Call UserPrompt ("Successfully added mapped drive connection to " &
strPath)
  End If
End Sub
```

**Gathering local group memberships.** This routine collects information about any local groups to which the user might belong. The names of these groups get placed into the strUserGroups variable for future reference.

```
'
' Sub:      GetLocalGroupMembership
'
' Purpose:  Gather all local groups to which the current user belongs
'
' Input:
'
' Output:   Local group names are added to strUserGroups
'
' Usage:    Call GetLocalGroupMembership
'
```

```
Private Sub GetLocalGroupMembership

    On Error Resume Next

    Dim colGroups    'Collection of groups on the local system
    Dim objGroup     'Object reference to individual groups
    Dim objUser      'Object reference to individual group member

    'Verify system is not Windows 9x or ME
    If objWshShell.ExpandEnvironmentStrings( "%OS%" ) = "Windows_NT" Then
        'Connect to local system
        Set colGroups = GetObject( "WinNT://" & strWorkstation )
        colGroups.Filter = Array( "group" )
        'Process each group
        For Each objGroup In colGroups
            'Process each user in group
            For Each objUser in objGroup.Members
                'Check if current user belongs to group being processed
                If LCase( objUser.Name ) = LCase( strUserID ) Then
                    'Add group name to list
                    strUserGroups = strUserGroups & objGroup.Name & ","
                End If
            Next
        Next
        Set colGroups = Nothing
    End If

End Sub
```

**Gathering global group memberships.** This routine is similar to the previous one, except it collects information about any global (rather than local) groups to which the user might belong. The names of the groups also get placed into the strUserGroups variable for future reference. Since some users might still be running Windows NT domains, I use the WinNT syntax instead of LDAP to perform the query, for cross-platform interoperability. This way is a little easier anyway.

```
'
' Sub:      GetGlobalGroupMembership
'
' Purpose:  Gather all global groups the current user belongs to
'
' Input:
'
' Output:   Global group names are added to strUserGroups
'
' Usage:    Call GetGlobalGroupMembership
'
```

```
' Notes:     Use WinNT connection method to be backwards
'            compatible with NT 4 domains
'
'''''''''''''''''''''''''''''''''''''''''''''''''''''''''''''''''''''''''''
Private Sub GetGlobalGroupMembership

  On Error Resume Next

  Dim objNameSpace
  Dim objUser

  Const ADS_READONLY_SERVER = 4

  Set objNameSpace = GetObject( "WinNT:" )
  'Use the OpenDSObject method with the ADS_READONLY_SERVER
  'value to grab the "closest" domain controller

  'Connect to user object in the domain
  Set objUser = objNameSpace.OpenDSObject( _
    "WinNT://" & strDomain & "/" & strUserID, "", "", ADS_READONLY_SERVER)
  'Process each group
  For Each objGroup In objUser.Groups
    'Add group name to list
    strUserGroups = strUserGroups & objGroup.Name & ","
  Next
  Set objNameSpace = Nothing

End Sub
'''''''''''''''''''''''''''''''''''''''''''''''''''''''''''''''''''''''''''
```

**Determining if user belongs to a specified group.** This simple routine searches the list of group names that is contained in the strUserGroups variable for the specified group and returns True if the group is found.

```
'''''''''''''''''''''''''''''''''''''''''''''''''''''''''''''''''''''''''''
'
' Function: InGroup
'
' Purpose:  Determine if user belongs to specified group
'
' Input:    Name of group to test for membership
'
' Output:   True or False
'
' Usage:    If InGroup("Domain Admins") Then <do something>
'
' Requirements:
'           strUserGroups must have been previously populated via
'           GetLocalGroupMembership and/or GetGlobalGroupMembership
'
'''''''''''''''''''''''''''''''''''''''''''''''''''''''''''''''''''''''''''
```

```
Private Function InGroup(strGroup)

  On Error Resume Next

  InGroup = False
  'Search strUserGroups for strGroup
  If Instr( 1, lCase( strUserGroups ), lCase( strGroup ), 1) Then InGroup =
True

End Function
```
...............................................................................

**Gathering basic information about the local system.** Here is another routine
that gathers specific information about the local computer, such as the user
domain, workstation name, product type, and the path to the location from
which the script is running.

...............................................................................
```
'
' Sub:       GetSystemInfo
'
' Purpose:   Gather basic information about the local system
'
' Input:
'
' Output:    strDomain, strOSProdType, strWorkstation, strLogonPath
'
' Usage:     Call GetSystemInfo
'
```
...............................................................................
```
Private Sub GetSystemInfo

  On Error Resume Next

  'Get domain name
  If objWshShell.ExpandEnvironmentStrings( "%OS%" ) = "Windows_NT" Then
    strDomain = objWshNetwork.UserDomain
  Else
    strDomain = objWshShell.RegRead( "HKLM\System\CurrentControlSet\" & _
                "Services\MSNP32\NetWorkProvider\AuthenticatingAgent" )
  End If

  'Get Product Type from Registry (WinNT, LanmanNT, ServerNT)
  strOSProdType = objWshShell.RegRead( _
    "HKLM\System\CurrentControlSet\Control\ProductOptions\ProductType")

  'Get computer name
  If IsTerminalServerSession = True Then
    'Set strWorkstation to the real name and not the name of the server
    strWorkstation = objWshShell.ExpandEnvironmentStrings( "%CLIENTNAME%" )
  Else
    strWorkstation = objWshNetwork.ComputerName
```

```
      End If

      'Get the path to the location from where the script is running
      strLogonPath = Left( Wscript.ScriptFullName, _
        ( InstrRev( Wscript.ScriptFullName, "\") -1))

   End Sub
```

**Determining if the script is running in a terminal server session.** The   following
routine identifies whether the user is logging on via a Windows terminal session and returns True if this is the case. The determinant test criteria is
whether the workstation has a valid %ClientName% environment variable set.

```
'
' Function: IsTerminalServer
'
' Purpose:  Determine if the script is running in a terminal server session
'
' Input:
'
' Output:
'
'             True if running in a terminal server session
'             False if not running in a terminal server session
' Usage:
'
'             If IsTerminalServerSession = True Then <Do Something>
'

Private Function IsTerminalServerSession

   On Error Resume Next

   Dim strName

   'Detect if this is a terminal server session
   'If it is, set some names to the terminal server client name
   strName = objWshShell.ExpandEnvironmentStrings( "%CLIENTNAME%" )
   If strName <> "%CLIENTNAME%" AND strName <> "" Then _
      IsTerminalServerSession = True

End Function
```

**Setting up IE for use as a status message window.** I like to use Internet Explorer
as a general status message screen for users. This routine gets Internet
Explorer set up and ready for this purpose.

```
'''''''''''''''''''''''''''''''''''''''''''''''''''''''''''''''''''''''''''''''''
'
' Sub:      SetupIE
'
' Purpose:  Set up Internet Explorer for use as a status message window
'
' Input:
'
' Output:
'
' Usage:    Call SetupIE
'
'''''''''''''''''''''''''''''''''''''''''''''''''''''''''''''''''''''''''''''''''
Private Sub SetupIE

  On Error Resume Next

  Dim strTitle    'Title of IE window
  Dim intCount    'Counter used during AppActivate

  strTitle = "Logon script status"

  'Create reference to objIntExplorer
  'This will be used for the user messages. Also set IE display attributes
  Set objIntExplorer = Wscript.CreateObject("InternetExplorer.Application")
  With objIntExplorer
    .Navigate "about:blank"
    .ToolBar   = 0
    .Menubar   = 0
    .StatusBar = 0
    .Width     = 600
    .Height    = 350
    .Left      = 100
    .Top       = 100
  End With


  'Set some formating
  With objIntExplorer.Document
    .WriteLn ("<!doctype html public>")
    .WriteLn   ("<head>")
    .WriteLn    ("<title>" & strTitle & "</title>")
    .WriteLn     ("<style type=""text/css"">")
    .WriteLn      ("body {text-align: left; font family: arial; _
                 font-size: 10pt}")
    .WriteLn     ("</style>")
    .WriteLn    ("</head>")
  End With

  'Wait for IE to finish
  Do While (objIntExplorer.Busy)
    Wscript.Sleep 200
  Loop
```

```
'Show IE
objIntExplorer.Visible = 1

'Make IE the active window
For intCount = 1 To 100
  If objWshShell.AppActivate(strTitle) Then Exit For
  WScript.Sleep 50
Next

End Sub
```

**Using IE as a status message window.** Finally, the last routine is just a little helper for the status message window. There's nothing fancy going on here.

```
'
' Sub:      UserPrompt
'
' Purpose:  Use Internet Explorer as a status message window
'
' Input:    strPrompt
'
' Output:   Output is sent to the open Internet Explorer window
'
' Usage:
'
Private Sub UserPrompt( strPrompt )

  On Error Resume Next

  objIntExplorer.Document.WriteLn (strPrompt & "<br />")

End Sub


'
' Sub:      Cleanup
'
' Purpose:  Release common objects and exit script
'
' Input:
'
' Output:
'
' Usage:    Call Cleanup
'
Sub Cleanup

  On Error Resume Next
```

```
Set objFileSys    = Nothing
Set objWshNetwork = Nothing
Set objWshShell   = Nothing
Set objIntExplorer = Nothing

'Exit script
Wscript.Quit( )

End Sub
```

## Running the Hack

Since I still have a few NT clients on my network, I place a batch file named *logon.bat* in the *NETLOGON* shares on my domain controllers. All users are then assigned this *logon.bat* file as their startup script. This *logon.bat* file verifies that the user is on a supported platform (NT, 2000, or XP) and then kicks in the *logon.vbs* script via a call like this (depending on the path to the script):

```
cscript //nologo %0\..\logon.vbs
```

To keep the user informed of the logon progress, status messages are posted to an Internet Explorer window.

These are the three results of running the logon script:

- The user gets the appropriate printer added.
- The user gets mapped drives added where appropriate.
- The user's homepage is reset (depending on group membership and computer name).

This sample logon script can prove useful for small organizations. However, storing all the mapping information in the script can soon become unwieldy. If you are in a large organization and want to perform tasks at logon based on computer names, it might be best to offload the mapping information to a network database that can be queried via the logon script.

*—Dan Thomson*

# IIS

## Hacks 54–61

Internet Information Services (IIS) is one of the more popular features of Windows server platforms. Whether you're running IIS 5 (Windows 2000 Server) or IIS 6 (Windows Server 2003), the ability to hack the metabase (the place where IIS stores its configuration settings) lets you do things that are impossible to do using the standard GUI tool for managing IIS—namely, Internet Services Manager.

Before you start hacking the metabase, however, you'd better be sure you've backed it up properly and know your way around inside it. Several hacks in this chapter deal with these topics, including how to restore the metabase when you have no working backup. Also included are tips on how to hide the metabase from attackers to make it more secure, how to use scripts to manage different aspects of IIS, and how to allow other HTTP services, such as the Apache web server, to run on Windows and coexist with IIS.

### HACK #54 Back Up the Metabase

There's more than one reason for backing up the metabase, and there are different ways of doing it too.

Instead of storing its configuration settings in the Windows Registry, like most other services store their configuration settings, IIS stores most of its settings in a file called the *metabase*. On Windows 2000 (IIS 5), the metabase is a binary file named *MetaBase.bin*, found in the *%SystemRoot%\system32\inetsrv* folder. Windows Server 2003 (IIS 6) uses XML as the format for its configuration information, rather than the proprietary binary format used by IIS 5. As a result, there are two metabase files in IIS 6: the metabase proper (*MetaBase.xml*), where configuration settings are stored, and an associated XML schema file (*MBSchema.xml*) that defines the XML syntax of the *MetaBase.xml* file. Because of the differences between these two platforms, we'll have to consider them separately when backing up IIS settings.

## Why Back Up the Metabase?

Many IIS administrators don't realize that there are two reasons for backing up the metabase and each reason requires a different method for doing so. The most obvious reason is to prepare for the eventuality of a disaster. Note that I said *eventuality* instead of *possibility*, because wise system administrators know that it's only a matter of time before something horrid happens. To prepare for such a disaster, you certainly want to back up the metabase on your IIS machines, but having a backup of the metabase alone isn't going to be much help if the hard drive containing your boot volume is toast; the proper functioning of the metabase depends on having access to some encryption keys that are part of the System State on your server. *System State* is a fancy phrase for a collection of important configuration information that lets you recover the predisaster state of your system after a massive failure renders it unbootable. You'll find more information about what's included in a server's System State in "Back Up System State on Remote Machines" [Hack #92] in Chapter 10.

So, here's the point: if you back up the IIS metabase without its associated System State, you won't be able to recover your web server after a disaster. Microsoft doesn't document clearly in either their Windows help files or on their web site that, by default, when you back up the System State information on a Windows 2000 or Windows Server 2003 machine, you also automatically back up the metabase—that is, if you've left your backup settings at their defaults. Let's dig a little deeper.

## Advanced Backup Settings

Hidden away in the Windows Backup utility is a properties box called Advanced Backup Options (Figure 6-1). To access Advanced Backup Options, select the items you want to back up, click Start Backup, and then click Advanced.

When you choose to back up the server's System State, the setting "Automatically backup System Protected files with the System State" is selected by default. This setting actually backs up the entire contents of the *%SystemRoot%* folder and all its subfolders along with the rest of the System State information on the server. Of course, the *inetsrv* directory where the metabase is found is part of this directory hierarchy, so the metabase gets backed up along the way. So, if you want to back up the IIS metabase for comprehensive recovery from a disaster, simply back up the System State using Backup (or its command-line version, ntbackup). Since the "Automatically backup System Protected Files with the System State" checkbox automatically adds several hundred megabytes to the size of your System State

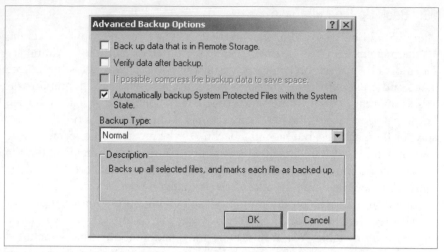

*Figure 6-1. The Advanced Backup Options properties box in the Backup utility*

backup, if you're the kind of person who likes living dangerously and you want to save on tape and speed up your backup, you could deselect this checkbox. Naturally, it's usually best to avoid cutting corners like this and leave the setting checked.

## Quick Backups

Preparing for that eventual disaster isn't the only reason for backing up the metabase. You should also make backup copies of the metabase if you plan on tinkering with it, either using MetaEdit (*metaedit.exe*)—a tool in the Windows 2000 Server Resource Kit, used for editing the IIS 5 metabase—or a text editor such as Notepad, which you can use to edit the XML metabase of IIS 6 directly. The danger here is that indelicately laying hands on the metabase might break something and render your metabase unreadable to IIS, forcing you to restore before your WWW Publishing Service starts again and users can access your web sites. The syntax of the metabase is strict, and any untoward alterations could cause a service to behave unpredictably at best, or just fail altogether at worst. So, before you roll up your sleeves and start fiddling with your metabase, it behooves you to make a quick backup.

You could back up the entire System State on your machine before touching the metabase, but that's overkill. You could use Backup to back up only the *inetsrv* directory on your server, but there are faster and simpler ways.

**IIS 5.** You can back up the metabase from the GUI by using Internet Services Manager, the MMC console used for configuring and managing IIS. Right-click on the node that represents your server and select Backup/Restore

Configuration to open a dialog box of the same name, as shown in Figure 6-2. Click the "Create backup..." button, type a descriptive name for your backup, and click OK. Backups are stored in the *%SystemRoot%\System32\InotSrv\ MetaBack* directory; to be extra careful, you can include this directory in your regular tape backups.

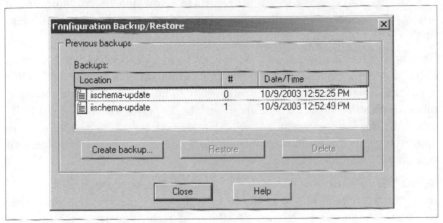

*Figure 6-2. Backing up the metabase*

Restoring the metabase is just as straightforward: select the metabase backup you want to restore and click Restore.

If you're using MetaEdit to editing the IIS 5 metabase, you're in luck; conveniently enough, MetaEdit itself is capable of making quick metabase backups.

Before you start using MetaEdit, however, be sure to download the latest version of the tool from Microsoft's web site. Interestingly, when you search the Microsoft Download Center (*http://www.microsoft.com/ downloads/*) for *metaedit*, you only get Version 2.0 of the tool, which is out of date. To obtain the latest version of the tool (MetaEdit 2.2), see Microsoft Knowledge Base article 232068 (*http://support.microsoft.com/ default.aspx?scid=kb;en-us;232068*), which has a link to the installation package.

Once you download and install the self-extracting file, you have two tools to play with: a Metabase Browser/Editor similar to Registry Editor and a Metabase Consistency Checker designed to ensure the syntax of the metabase remains consistent. Unfortunately, the Consistency Checker isn't too useful, because it won't repair certain types of mistakes you can make with the Browser/Editor, such as entering illegal values for metabase keys. So, just like when you edit the Registry directly, you're on your own and in dangerous territory.

In fact, it's always a good idea to back up the metabase periodically, even if you make changes to your metabase only through the Internet Services Manager GUI. That way, if you make a lot of configuration changes to IIS and discover your web applications acting a mite odd, you can reverse those changes quickly and easily by restoring the metabase from recent backup. In fact, this might be the only way to return to a working IIS configuration if you can't remember all the changes you've made. So, regular metabase backups are a part of good housekeeping on your IIS machines.

Backing up the metabase with MetaEdit is straightforward: simply open MetaEdit (it's installed by default under Administrative Tools) and select Metabase → Backup/Restore from the menu. This opens the same Configuration Backup/Restore dialog box (Figure 6-2) and saves backups in the same *MetaBack* directory as before. GUI- and MetaEdit-made backups are compatible, so you can back up using one way and restore using the other if you prefer.

Remember that these quick backups of the metabase are designed only to recover from a corrupt metabase or to restore the metabase to an earlier working condition; you cannot use them to restore an IIS machine from scratch; use System State for that. Also, note that a metabase backup made on one machine cannot be restored to a different machine, due to the differences in System State information between the machines. There's a workaround for that too, though: export the metabase instead of backing it up. Exporting saves all or part of the metabase in a text file instead of in the proprietary binary format used for metabase backups. Note that exporting the metabase requires you use MetaEdit, because export functionality is not included in Internet Services Manager for IIS 5.

Exporting the metabase is useful if you want to document the contents of your metabase by printing it out. It's also useful for copying web site configurations from one IIS machine to another. For example, if you want to mirror a site on two machines, simply export the metabase keys for the web site and then import the export file into the second machine. But don't forget to copy your site content as well; remember that the metabase contains only IIS configuration information, not the content of your web sites.

IIS 6. Metabase backups are even easier in IIS 6, because the functionality is built right into Internet Services Manager. In fact, in addition to allowing you to back up the metabase manually, IIS 6 also automatically backs up the metabase whenever configuration changes have been made. Let's look at these automatic backups first.

IIS 6 automatically saves time-stamped (versioned) copies of the metabase; these copies are called *history files* and are saved in the *%SystemRoot%\system32\intesrv\history* folder. History files are identified by two numbers: major version and minor version. The major version number is incremented whenever you stop and start IIS using the GUI or net stop iisadmin on the command line, when IIS flushes the in-memory metabase to disk, or when you manually save the IIS configuration to disk. This provides a safety net, so you can recover an earlier configuration if you've made a series of changes and can't remember what they were, let alone how to undo them. When a new major version history file is saved, IIS includes a reference to this file in the *MetaBase.xml* file itself.

Minor versions are somewhat different. IIS increments the minor version number if you have *edit-while-running* enabled and make modifications to the metabase while IIS is running. Edit-while-running is a new feature of IIS 6 that allows you to edit the metabase directly while Iisadmin and other IIS services are still running. Whenever the major version number is incremented, the minor version number is reset to 0.

If you plan to use the new history feature of IIS 6—it's enabled by default—you will probably want to modify the history settings to suit your needs. The default history settings save a maximum of 10 history files before overwriting the oldest file. This might not be enough history if you plan to edit the metabase extensively; you might want to increase this number to 20, 30, or even 100. Make sure you have sufficient disk space for all these files, however; if IIS can't create a new history file due to insufficient disk space, it will automatically shut down without warning or explanation.

To change the maximum number of history files IIS should save, you'll have to modify a metabase setting directly; there's no way to do it from the GUI. The property you need to change is called MaxHistoryFiles and it's located in the <IIsComputer> section (if you're navigating the metabase by its key hierarchy) or the LM location (if you're navigating by location hierarchy) of the XML code. The metabase can be a confusing place; you might take a gander at "Map the Metabase" **[Hack #56]** for guidance.

> After you make changes to the metabase directly, check the history folder for any error files that might have been created. These error files are named in the form *MetaBaseError_versionnumber.xml* and are generated when metabase corruption has occurred after editing. If you see an error file, restore your metabase to the previous history version and try editing it again.

IIS 6 also lets you manually back up the metabase and export portions to a text file, similar to what we did in IIS 5. The main difference is that in IIS 6 export functionality is built directly into the GUI, so you no longer need the old MetaEdit tool for exporting. In fact, you can't use MetaEdit with IIS 6 because of the metabase's format change from binary to XML.

**GUI differences between IIS 5 and IIS 6.** Backing up the metabase from the GUI is done the same way as it was in IIS 5, with a couple of important differences. First, an initial metabase backup is automatically performed once you install IIS on your machine (to reduce the attack surface of your machine, Windows Server 2003 no longer installs IIS by default). This initial backup consists of two backup files: an *.MD0* file that contains a backup of *MetaBase.xml* (the metabase proper) and an *.SC0* file that holds a backup of *MBScehma.xml* (the XML schema that defines the syntax of *MetaBase.xml*). Note that in IIS 5 the schema is included as part of the single *metabase.bin* file, though in MetaEdit the configuration (LM) and schema (Schema) portions of the metabase are displayed as two separate nodes. In other words, every time you back up the metabase in IIS 6, you back up both the configuration file and the schema.

Here's another difference. In IIS 5, using Internet Services Manager, you right-click on the server node and select Backup/Restore Configuration. To do this in IIS 6, however, you right-click on the server node and select All Tasks → Backup/Restore Configuration. This is just one example of the unnecessary, minor changes in Windows Server 2003 that cause frustration for administrators who are used to working with Windows 2000.

You can also now use a password to encrypt metabase backups. An encrypted metabase backup can be restored to a different IIS machine, which gives you a way to clone the IIS configuration of one machine and copy it to another. This was not possible in IIS 5; you could restore a metabase backup only to the same machine and only if you hadn't rebuilt the machine onto new hardware after a disaster. This is one of many good reasons to upgrade your web servers to Windows Server 2003, even if you choose to keep your domain controllers running Windows 2000. Just don't forget the password you use to encrypt your metabase or you won't be able to restore from the saved backup.

Finally, IIS 6 also includes some scripts that can be used to back up and restore the metabase from the command line. For more information about these scripts and what they can and cannot do, see "IIS Administration Scripts" [Hack #59].

# Restore the Metabase

While it's simple to restore the metabase from a backup, what if you have no
backup or can't open the GUI? Use this hack.

In "Back Up the Metabase" [Hack #54], we explored several ways of backing up
the metabase, including backing up the machine's System State information
using the Backup utility, saving the configuration in Internet Services Manager with MetaEdit (a downloadable tool for IIS 5), and using the history
feature of IIS 6.

Restoring the metabase from backup is equally straightforward. If you are
recovering your machine from a disaster, the metabase is restored as part of
the System State information you previously backed up, assuming you
didn't change the default option of including System Protected Files in your
backup. Alternately, if you're restoring the metabase on a working machine
to recover a previous good IIS configuration, simply select the backup in the
Configuration Backup/Restore dialog box and click Restore. Then, follow
the prompts and wait as IIS stops, rebuilds, and restarts. Restoring the IIS 6
metabase from a history file is done in the same way: just select a history file
in the Configuration Backup/Restore dialog box and click Restore.

Notice that the dialog box (refer back to Figure 6-2) displays both metabase
backups stored in *%SystemRoot%\System32\inetsrv\MetaBack* and history
files stored in *%SystemRoot%\System32\inetsrv\History* in one combined list.
You can tell the difference between a history file and a backup file in this list
by looking at the filenames: all history files are named *Automatic Backup*
and are distinguished in the GUI only by their timestamp, while backup files
you create are named whatever you decide to call them.

It all seems so simple, but what if your metabase becomes corrupt and you
need to restore it from backup? If you can start Internet Services Manager,
you can use the Configuration Backup/Restore dialog box as described earlier. But if the metabase is corrupted beyond the ability of IIS to repair it,
Internet Services Manager might not even start, and then you're stuck. What
do you do?

You could restore the entire System State of your machine from backup
media. Unfortunately, that might have unpleasant side effects, especially if
you're running IIS on a domain controller. For example, all those users and
groups you created since the last backup will suddenly be gone (unless you
have another domain controller to replicate the information). There might
also be changes to the Registry that will be rolled back, and these changes
might be harder to troubleshoot.

But there's a better way.

## Manually Restoring a Backup in IIS 5

If you can't open Internet Services Manager, try replacing the metabase with its most recent backup.

First, stop all IIS services by typing net stop iisadmin /y at the command prompt (or use iisreset /stop if you prefer). Then, find the *metabase.bin* file in *%Systemroot%\System32\inetsrv* and rename it *metabase.bad* (keep it in case you need it later). Copy your backup file (it probably has the extension .MD0) from *%Systemroot%\System32\inetsrv\MetaBack* to *%Systemroot%\System32\inetsrv* and rename it *metabase.bin*. Now, restart the computer. You should once again have a working IIS configuration and be able to start Internet Services Manager.

By the by, instead of rebooting your machine, you can try to restart IIS services by typing iisreset /start from the command line. But in my experience, it's better to reboot your machine, because IIS is sometimes a little flakey after a restore like this.

**Restoring without metabase backups.** What if you don't have any metabase backups in the *inetsrv\MetaBack* folder? Perhaps you deleted them all or you never created any in the first place. Hopefully, you do have a recent backup of your system drive—on tape, perhaps? Use the Backup utility to restore the *inetsrv* folder from backup to a new location (*C:\inetsrv2*, for example) and repeat the previous process by copying *C:\inetsrv2\metabase.bin* over *%Systemroot%\System32\inetsrv\metabase.bin*. Be sure to stop the IIS services as before, and reboot the machine when you've finished.

**Restoring without a backup on tape.** But what if there are no metabase backups in your *MetaBack* folder and you don't even have a working backup on tape?

Here's a hack you can try that just might work: look in the *inetsrv* folder on your machine for files named *metabase.bak* or *metabase.bin.bak*. If you find one, you're in luck; this is a temporary metabase backup created by IIS when it has problems updating the metabase due to corruption. Normally, this temporary file is deleted once a successful metabase update is performed, but if your metabase corruption was caused by some interruption in the update process (a server glitch or hiccup), IIS might not yet have gotten around to deleting the temp file and you can use it to restore your configuration. Simply stop the services, rename *metabase.bin* to *metabase.bad*, rename *metabase.bak* to *metabase.bin*, and reboot the machine.

**Reinstalling IIS.** In the worst case scenario, you have no tape backup, nothing in the *MetaBack* directory, and no temporary *.bak* file in *inetsrv*. What do you do? Use Add/Remove Programs in the Control Panel to first uninstall IIS and then reinstall it. After you uninstall it, you should also check the *%Systemroot%\System32\inetsrv* folder (which is not deleted by the uninstall process) for a file named *metabase.bin*. If you find one, delete it before reinstalling IIS.

Moral of the story? Sometimes a reinstall is the only way to recover.

## Manually Restoring a Backup in IIS 6

Remember that the metabase in IIS 6 is structured differently [Hack #54]; it consists of two files, *MetaBase.xml* and *MBSchema.xml*, instead of the single *metabase.bin* file used by IIS 5. Fortunately, you normally have to restore only the *MetaBase.xml* file, because it's highly unlikely that you would have made changes to the schema. The procedures to follow are identical to those described in the previous section, except you replace *metabase.bin* with *MetaBase.xml* in each step where *metabase.bin* occurs. I've also found that restarting IIS by using `iisreset /start` seems to work fine and you don't have to reboot. IIS in Windows Server 2003 does seem more robust than IIS in Windows 2000.

## See Also

"IIS Administration Scripts" [Hack #59]

## Map the Metabase

**HACK #56**

Here are some helpful maps to help you navigate the complexities of the metabase.

While basic IIS configuration can be done using Internet Services Manager, sometimes you need to roll up your sleeves and look under the hood. Under IIS's hood you'll find the metabase, the key repository of IIS configuration information. The metabase contains hundreds of settings, from how a web server performs to the format used for logging visits to sites. Both Windows 2000 and Windows Server 2003 let you edit the metabase directly, but the tools you use are different because the format of the metabase is different in each platform [Hack #54].

Before you start mucking about in your metabase, you need to know your way around, because its structure is quite complex. The goal of this hack is to give you a bird's-eye view of how the metabase is organized, so you can find things more quickly and avoid making mistakes that could confuse your server.

Surprisingly enough, you won't find this information anywhere on Microsoft's web site, even though it is crucial to
metabase exploration.

Once you know the lay of the land, you can start hacking the metabase **[Hack #57]** with a certain level of confidence.

## Logical Structure

The logical structure is the easiest to consider first, because it's much the same for both IIS 5 and IIS 6. The important thing to keep in mind is that the metabase hierarchy reflects the way you manage IIS web sites, directories, and files using Internet Services Manger. For example, when you want to log visits to a site on your server, you can use Internet Services Manager to enable the Log Visits setting at the site level (for all web content on your site), at the virtual-directory level (for content stored in a single virtual directory), or at the page level (for monitoring traffic to individual pages). Most configuration settings can also be configured globally for the entire IIS machine. As a result, when you are navigating the properties sheets of Internet Services Manager, you'll see the following hierarchical progression: Server → Site → Directory → File.

The logical structure of the metabase is organized similarly and uses a location attribute to identify where a setting lies within the hierarchy. The top of this hierarchy is called LM, which stands for *Local Machine* (i.e., the server itself). Each metabase key then has a location attribute that identifies where the key resides. As a simple example, the Path key located at LM/W3SVC/1/ROOT contains the string value *C:\Inetpub\wwwroot* and identifies the location of the content for the Default Web Site. Figure 6-3 shows where this key is located in the IIS 5 metabase using MetaEdit, the tool used for editing the metabase on that platform. Note that the metabase is organized hierarchically, using keys in a fashion similar to the way the Windows Registry is displayed in RegEdit.

To understand the location LM/W3SVC/1/ROOT, let's break it down: LM is the local machine itself, W3SVC means we're looking at web sites (not FTP, SMTP, or NNTP), 1 is the site ID for the Default Web Site, and ROOT contains configuration settings (keys) that apply to all virtual directories and files within the web site. The site ID is a number generated for each web site on the server to uniquely identify the site internally.

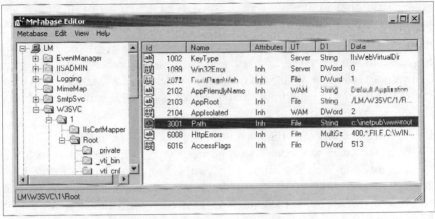

*Figure 6-3. Path key for Default Web Site in the IIS 5 metabase*

**Location map for IIS 5.** Now, here is the big picture of how the IIS 5 metabase is logically organized, omitting some of the deeper levels:

```
LM
LM/IISADMIN
LM/IISADMIN/EXTENSIONS
LM/IISADMIN/PROPERTYREGISTRATION
LM/Logging
LM/Logging/Custom Logging
LM/Logging/Microsoft IIS Log File Format
LM/Logging/NCSA Common Log File Format
LM/Logging/ODBC Logging
LM/Logging/W3C Extended Log File Format
LM/MimeMap
LM/W3SVC
LM/W3SVC/1
LM/W3SVC/1/Filters
LM/W3SVC/1/IIsCertMapper
LM/W3SVC/1/ROOT
LM/W3SVC/2
LM/W3SVC/2/filters
LM/W3SVC/2/root
LM/W3SVC/Filters
LM/W3SVC/Info
```

Not so complicated after all, is it? The main locations under LM are pretty self-explanatory. For example, IISADMIN contains configuration settings for the IISAdmin service, Logging defines the settings for the different logging formats supported by IIS, and MimeMap has a copy of the MIME mappings that define how IIS responds to client requests for files with particular extensions. Everything under W3SVC relates to the World Wide Web Publishing Services on the machine, which you can see is hosting two web sites: the Default Web Site (site ID 1) and a custom web site (site ID 2). If your server is running additional services, such as FTP, you'll also find locations for those within the hierarchy.

Of course, before you can successfully hack the metabase, you need to know how to find the site ID for a given web site and vice versa. In IIS 6, this is easily done. Select the Web Sites node in Internet Services Manager and look under the Identifier column in the pane on the right. This displays the site ID for each web site running on the server.

Finding the site ID under IIS 5 is a little trickier. If you want to find the site ID for a particular site, open its properties sheet in Internet Services Manager, choose the Web Site tab, and click the Properties button in the Logging section at the bottom. If you have W3C Extended Log File Format configured (the default), then the site ID is embedded in the name of the folder in which your IIS log files are saved. In our example, these folders are *%SystemRoot%\System32\LogFiles\W3SVC1* for the Default Web Site and *%SystemRoot%\System32\LogFiles\W3SVC2* for the custom web site. Figure 6-4 shows the Extended Logging Properties dialogue box for the custom web site.

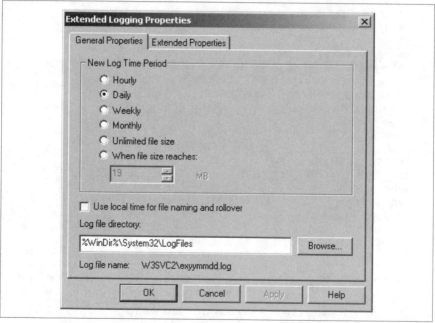

*Figure 6-4. Finding the site ID for a web site in IIS 5*

Of course, if you have dozens of web sites running on your machine, this is a rather slow approach. As a workaround you can use *findweb.vbs*, one of the sample administrator scripts included in the *Inetpub\AdminSamples* folder on IIS 5. Drop to a command prompt and type cscript findweb.vbs *sitename*, where *sitename* is the descriptive name of your site in Internet Services Manager. Be sure to use quotes if there are spaces in the site name. The output of the script will include the web site number—another name for the site ID. For more information about using scripts to administer IIS, see "IIS Administration Scripts" **[Hack #59]**.

What about the reverse? Given a site ID within the metabase, how do you find the descriptive name of the web site as displayed in Internet Services Manager? One way is to use MetaEdit to view the contents of the ServerComment key in the location LM\W3SVC\\*n*, where *n* is the site ID for the web site. The data value for this key is the descriptive name of the site in Internet Services Manager.

**Location map for IIS 6.** IIS 6 is logically organized similarly to IIS 5, but with a few differences:

```
.
/
/LM
/LM/IISADMIN
/LM/IISADMIN/EXTENSIONS
/LM/IISADMIN/PROPERTYREGISTRATION
/LM/Logging
/LM/Logging/Custom Logging
/LM/Logging/Microsoft IIS Log File Format
/LM/Logging/NCSA Common Log File Format
/LM/Logging/ODBC Logging
/LM/Logging/W3C Extended Log File Format
/LM/MimeMap
/LM/W3SVC
/LM/W3SVC/1
/LM/W3SVC/1/Filters
/LM/W3SVC/1/IIsCertMapper
/LM/W3SVC/1/ROOT
/LM/W3SVC/388907640
/LM/W3SVC/388907640/filters
/LM/W3SVC/388907640/root
/LM/W3SVC/AppPools
/LM/W3SVC/AppPools/DefaultAppPool
/LM/W3SVC/Filters
/LM/W3SVC/Info
```

Here, we see that LM is the third level instead of the root. The root level (.) contains keys for versioning (timestamp and change number) and history major version number **[Hack #54]**. The next level (/) contains an AdminACL key used for protecting the metabase against unauthorized modification. Beyond that, everything under LM is pretty much the same as in IIS 5, with the obvious exception of /LM/W3SVC/AppPools and locations beneath it, which contain information about application pools when IIS 6 is running in worker process isolation mode.

Another thing to notice is that the site ID for the custom web site is 388097640 instead of 2. While IIS 5 assigns site IDs to new web sites serially (1, 2, and so on), IIS 6 assigns what looks like a random number as a web site's site ID. Actually, it's not random at all; it's a pseudorandom number derived from scrambling the descriptive name of the web site. So, if you have two web servers, each with a custom site named *My Company Site*, they'll both be assigned the same site ID in IIS 6. The reason for doing it this way is to ensure that web farms with multiple IIS machines that host copies of sites have identical site IDs for mirrored sites. If you prefer, you can disable this feature via the Registry Editor; simply add a new REG_DWORD value to the HKLM\SOFTWARE\Microsoft\InetMgr\Parameters key, give the new value the name IncrementalSiteIDCreation, and assign it a value of 1. Restart IIS to jog the change into effect. This might be useful in a service provider environment, for example, if you have several IIS machines that host thousands of web sites and you don't want to worry about having two users create sites with the same descriptive name.

Finally, be aware that while the basic logical structure of the metabase is almost identical in IIS 5 and IIS 6, there are many new metabase keys in IIS 6 that have no counterpart in IIS 5. Also, some IIS 5 keys have been retired or renamed in IIS 6. A full discussion of these items is obviously beyond the scope of this book; thankfully, I have another for you which does discuss this stuff at length: *IIS 6 Administration* (Osborne/McGraw-Hill).

## Physical Structure

On IIS 5, the physical structure of the metabase is hidden within the proprietary format of the binary *metabase.bin* file, so you need to know only the logical structure (location of keys) to find your way around the metabase using MetaEdit. Things are different in IIS 6, however, because here the metabase is a plain text file (*MetaBase.xml*) that is formatted in XML and adheres to strict constraints laid down by the schema (*MBSchema.xml*). In the XML syntax for the metabase, the location of a key is given by its location attribute within the XML tag for the key. For example, the Path key previously discussed for the Default Web Site in IIS 5 looks like this in the IIS 6 metabase:

```
<IIsWebVirtualDir Location = "/LM/W3SVC/1/ROOT"
    Path = "c:\inetpub\wwwroot"
  >
</IIsWebVirtualDir>
```

If you know a little XML, you can see that IIsWebVirtualDir is an element whose attributes include Location and Path, contained within a pair of opening and closing tags. To be accurate, IIsWebVirtualDir is itself a property called KeyType, and I've left out some other attributes to make the basic structure clear. Anyway, by editing this section of the *MetaBase.xml* file directly, using a text editor such as Notepad, you can easily change the default path for the home directory of the Default Web Site.

**XML map for IIS 6.** So, now let's see the big picture of what the IIS 6 metabase looks like in terms of XML tags instead of location. This is important to know, because while the location map described earlier really defines the hierarchical structure of metabase keys, the actual physical metabase file is formatted in XML and that's what you have to look at when you edit it. Anyway, here's the XML for an IIS 6 machine configured with two web sites (keys that can be repeated are indicated with ellipses):

```xml
<?xml version ="1.0"?>
<configuration xmlns="urn:microsoft-catalog:XML_Metabase_V54_0">
    <MBProperty>
        IIS_Global
        IIS_ROOT
        IIsComputer
        IIsConfigObject...
        IIsLogModules
        IIsCustomLogModule...
        IIsLogModule...
        IIsMimeMap
        IIsWebService
        IIsWebServer
        IIsFilters
        IIsCertMapper
        IIsWebVirtualDir
        IIsWebServer
        IIsFilters
        IIsWebVirtualDir
        IIsApplicationPools
        IIsApplicationPool
        IIsFilters
        IIsFilter
        IisCompressionScheme...
        IIsCompressionSchemes
        IIsWebInfo
        IIsConfigObject
        IIsWebServer
        IIsWebVirtualDir
        IIsWebServer
        IIsWebVirtualDir
    </MBProperty>
</configuration>
```

As you can see from the duplicate sections beginning with IIsWebServer, two web sites are running on this machine. If you examine the details of these sections, you'll find they have identical KeyType attributes but different Location attributes. Also, note that unlike the location map, which accurately reflects the hierarchical structure of metabase keys, the XML map shows that the *MetaBase.xml* file is almost flat, with all KeyType attributes nested equally within <MBProperty> tags, which themselves are nested within global <configuration> tags.

Of course, the metabase can get much more complicated if you have additional web sites, directories, and services installed. But now that you know the basic lay of the land, you should be able to find your way about. Just don't forget to back up the metabase before you start hacking away at it!

## Metabase Hacks
### #57
Here are 10 things you might want to change with IIS, but you can do them only by editing the metabase.

These are a few of my favorite IIS metabase hacks. You can find lots more information—too much, perhaps—in the IIS SDK's IIS Metabase Properties Reference on MSDN (*http://msdn.microsoft.com/library/en-us/iisref/htm/ reference.asp*). Most of the information there is pretty dry stuff—lists of different settings that provide little insight into what might be useful to tweak—which is why I want to start you off with a few interesting hacks to inspire you. Still, it is a good idea to get familiar with how to read the Reference, because it details the allowable values for each property in the metabase.

Except where stated otherwise, all of the following hacks work on both IIS 5 and IIS 6, though the effect in some cases might differ depending on the rest of your IIS configuration; I try to make note of such differences when appropriate. Also, most of these properties require IIS to be restarted before they take effect—something that's usually a good idea anyway whenever you edit the metabase manually. Even on IIS 6, which lets you edit the metabase while IIS services are running, it's often a good idea to use the iisreset command to stop and start IIS after making metabase changes and see if there is any effect.

### ServerListenBacklog

Sometimes, IIS cracks under the weight of too many client requests, even though it still has lots of memory and CPU cycles to work with. Typically, clients start getting "Server too Busy" errors and have to click Refresh several times before they are able to see any content. At the server end, this

# A Warning Before Hacking the Metabase

Before you start hacking the metabase, remember that editing the metabase (like editing the Registry) shouldn't be done lightly; the preferred method is to configure IIS using the Internet Services Manager GUI tool. Unfortunately, a number of useful metabase settings are inaccessible from the GUI and you have to dig right into the metabase to change them.

Also, before you edit the metabase make sure you back it up. That way, if you make a mistake and break IIS, you can restore the metabase from backup and get IIS working again. We looked at ways you can back up the metabase [Hack #54] earlier in this chapter, but it's also a good idea to make a copy of the metabase and edit the copy instead of editing the metabase itself. Then, when you've made your changes, you can stop IIS, rename *metabase.bin* to *metabase.old*, rename your copy of the metabase from whatever you called it to *metabase.bin*, and restart IIS. Should something go wrong, your original metabase is still there in the form of *metabase.old* and can be used to restore IIS to the configuration it had previously. That may sound like overkill, but you can never be too careful when it comes to manually editing critical configuration files. You should at least follow that procedure with IIS 5 (Windows 2000). With IIS 6 (Windows Server 2003), you can probably get by without following this approach, because the history feature saves a copy of the metabase every time you make a configuration change to it. You decide, though. Like most things in IT, it's a tradeoff, and in this case, the tradeoff is between convenience and safety. Making backups of backups is not convenient, but it might help prevent you from burning your fingers.

Also remember that MetaEdit (the downloadable tool for editing the IIS 5 metabase) doesn't check your modifications to ensure that the values you entered are within the allowable range for the properties you edit. Editing the IIS 6 metabase using Notepad or some other text editor is even more dangerous, because you could even assign a string value to a metabase property that should be numeric. So, before you change any metabase property manually, check the Reference to see which range of values is allowed.

might happen on only one IP address, and any others might behave as they should. With a packet-sniffing tool such as the Microsoft Systems Management Server's Network Monitor, you'll see TCP connections resetting almost as soon as they are established. The problem is that the application layer of the TCP/IP stack has run out of resources. To increase the resources available for this layer, you can edit two metabase properties: ServerListenBacklog and MaxEndPointConnections (we will discuss the latter in the next section).

The ServerListenBacklog property determines the maximum number of outstanding TCP socket connections that can be queued. By default, this property is set in the metabase schema and depends on how the Performance Tuning setting is configured on the Performance tab of your web server's properties sheet in the GUI. Specifically, ServerListenBacklog has defaults of 5, 40, or 100, depending on whether you tune the GUI to expect fewer than 10,000 hits per day, less than 100,000 hits per day, or more than 100,000 hits per day. You can override the schema defaults for this property by adding a ServerListenBacklog key at the web site's level (/LM/W3SVC) or at the level of an individual web site, such as the Default Web Site (/LM/W3SVC/1); assign the ServerListenBacklog key any value from 5 to 1000 (on IIS 5) or 500 (on IIS 6). More pending connections are queued as you increase the value for this key, but IIS will consume more memory resources. Experiment to find the best performance for your hardware.

## MaxEndPointConnections

Another property you can tweak to improve performance under heavy load is MaxEndPointConnections, which indicates the maximum number of TCP sockets in a LISTENING state that can be allowed for a single IP address, network interface, or TCP port. By default, this property has the value 100 on IIS 5 and is also set in the schema, but you can add a key to set it at the /LM/W3SCV level or the /LM/W3SVC/n level, where n is the site ID of the web site that contains the application. To get better performance under heavy load, try increasing this setting to 500 or even higher and evaluate the result from the client standpoint. On IIS 5, MaxEndPointConnections works in conjunction with ServerListenBacklog and IIS uses the property with the lower value by default. On IIS 6, however, MaxEndPointConnections is set to 4294967295 in the schema, which means unlimited connections and is usually best left as is.

## AspThreadGateEnabled

Thread gating is a feature of IIS that is turned off by default, but if you turn it on, IIS dynamically adjusts the number of concurrent threads, depending on the load. If threads become blocked (for example, when an ASP application on IIS has to wait for a back-end SQL database to respond), then IIS starts more threads to handle client requests. If processor usage hits the wall, IIS begins decommissioning threads to reduce the amount of context switching going on. The lower- and upper-level CPU usages that start or kill threads are determined by two other metabase properties: AspThreadGateLoadLow and AspThreadGateLoadHigh. By default, these properties have values of 50 and 80 (percent), respectively, but you can change them to see if it improves performance.

I've sometimes found that changing AspThreadGateEnabled from off (0) to on (1) can improve performance somewhat for web servers that host mainly static content. For servers that host ASP applications, use the Performance console first to check if ASP requests are becoming excessively queued. If so, try changing AspThreadGateEnabled to 1 and use Performance again to see if things improve.

This key is already present in the metabase at the /LM/W3SCV level, but you can also set it at the /LM/W3SVC/n level by creating the appropriate key. Note that this particular metabase property applies only to IIS 5, not IIS 6.

## AspProcessorThreadMax

The AspProcessorThreadMax property determines the maximum number of worker threads IIS allows for handling ASP requests. The default value is 25 (threads per processor), and if you multiply the number of processors on your machine by the value of AspProcessorThreadMax, the product represents the maximum number of threads that can service a single ASP application—regardless of how you have tweaked the previously described AspThreadGateLoadHigh property. In some cases, you might want to try increasing this value—for example, when ASP requests are being blocked by slow response from a back-end database. In other cases, decreasing it to 15 or even 5 might improve performance by better utilizing available processor resources, especially under relatively light loads. Basically, just play with it and see what happens. This property is defined at the /LM/W3SCV level, but you can also set it at the /LM/W3SVC/n level.

## AspAllowSessionState

The AspAllowSessionState property enables session state persistence for ASP applications and is set to 1 (on) by default. One way you can often improve ASP performance is to change this property to 0 (off) and then recode your applications to explicitly override session state persistence for pages that use session objects. Simply add the following statement to the top of each ASP page as needed:

```
<% @EnableSessionState=False %>
```

This property is defined at the /LM/W3SCV level, but you can also set it at the /LM/W3SVC/n level.

## AspBufferingOn

Big improvements in ASP performance can often be achieved by turning ASP buffering on using the AspBufferingOn property. This is because ASP buffering lets IIS collect the output of an ASP application in a buffer before flushing it to the client. Fortunately, this property is set to 1 (on) in IIS, provided you're working with a clean installation of Windows 2000 or Windows Server 2003. If you previously upgraded your web server from Windows NT 4.0, however, this property is set to 0 (off) and should generally be changed to 1, at least on all your production servers. However, while turning this property on increases ASP response times overall, from a user perspective it might actually seem to make sites less responsive. This is because instead of feeding the output of the ASP page to the user slowly, bit by bit, the entire output has to be generated and cached before any of it can be returned to the user. So, you'll have to play with this and see what how it feels from a client perspective, but in most cases it's best left turned on. You can also recode your ASP applications to make more use of the Response. Flush method to improve the performance from the user's point of view. This property is defined at the /LM/W3SCV level, but you can also set it at the /LM/W3SVC/n level.

## AspQueueConnectionTestTime

Ever tried to access a page that wouldn't load, so you kept refreshing impatiently? On the older IIS 4 platform, this had the unpleasant result of filling up the ASP request queue with multiple requests from the same user for the same page, which was quite annoying. Fortunately, in IIS 5 the AspQueueConnectionTestTime metabase property was added to foil this kind of unintentional denial-of-service attack on your web server. The default value for this key is 3 (seconds), but you can tweak it depending on how your ASP application is designed. For example, if you have an application in which the user usually just clicks through a number of pages without needing to fill in or read anything, you could add this key to the /LM/W3SVC/n level for that site and lower its value to 2 or even 1. That way, IIS will check more frequently to make sure the client is still connected before responding to another connection request from the same client. This property is defined at the /LM/W3SCV level, but you can also set it at the /LM/W3SVC/n level.

## AspScriptFileCacheSize

The AspScriptFileCacheSize property determines how many precompiled script files or templates are cached in memory by IIS, in case they need to be reused. The default value for this setting is 250 (in IIS 5) or 500 (in IIS 6), but this can be increased to 1000 or more if needed. You can also set it to -1 (on IIS 5) or 4294967295 (on IIS 6) to allow unlimited caching of scripts. Unlimited caching is probably not a good idea unless you have unlimited RAM on your motherboard, but you definitely might consider increasing this setting to 1000 or higher if your server is running applications that have many different ASP pages. This property is defined at the /LM/W3SCV level, but you can also set it at the /LM/W3SVC/*n* level.

## CacheISAPI

The CacheISAPI property determines whether IIS caches ISAPI extensions (such as *asp.dll*) in memory or unloads them whenever they're no longer used. This is set to 1 (on) and should be left that way on production servers, unless you want your applications to run like molasses. However, if you need to debug a custom ISAPI extension you've written, set CacheISAPI to 0 (off); otherwise, you'll end up testing previous versions of your extension instead of testing the current one. This property is defined at the /LM/W3SCV level, but you can also set it at the /LM/W3SVC/*n* level.

## ID 36907

I'll end this list of hacks with something a little bit different. Until now, we've looked only at metabase properties for IIS proper. However, some other Microsoft products also use IIS; one of the most notable is Exchange 2000 Server. Every metabase property is uniquely identified by an internal ID number. For example, the CacheISAPI property has ID number 6034, which can easily be seen using MetaEdit (see Figure 6-5).

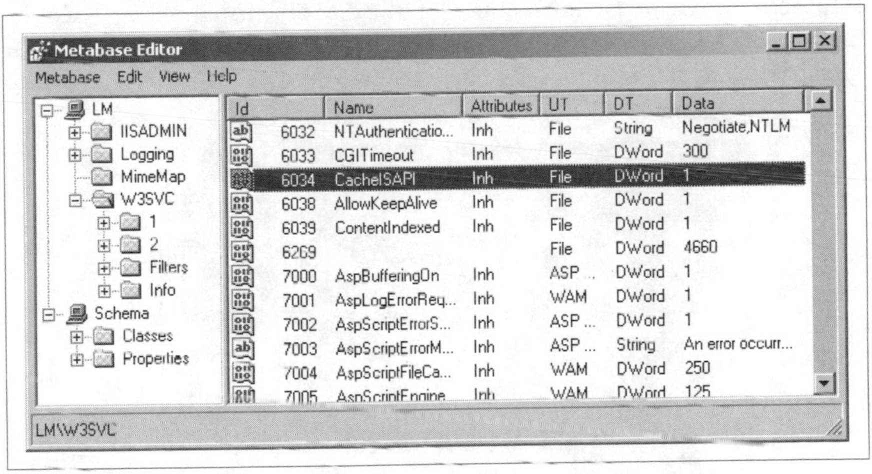

*Figure 6-5. Viewing the CacheISAPI property in MetaEdit*

It's a little-known fact that these ID numbers are grouped into different ranges that depend on the IIS function to which they apply (IIS, ASP, or FrontPage) or the Microsoft server product to which they belong (such as Exchange Server or Application Center). Table 6-1 details the association between metabase Ids and their associated functions or products.

*Table 6-1. Metabase property ID ranges*

| ID range | Function/Product |
|---|---|
| 1–32767 | IIS |
| 28672–32767 | ASP (subset) |
| 32768–36863 | FrontPage Server Extensions |
| 36864–40959 | Exchange Server: SMTP |
| 40960–45055 | Exchange Server: POP3 |
| 45056–49151 | Exchange Server: NNTP |
| 49152–53247 | Exchange Server: IMAP4 |
| 53248–57343 | MSCS |
| 57344–61439 | Application Center |

Metabase property 36907 falls within the range of Exchange's SMTP Service and can be used to change the default SMTP banner with which Exchange responds to incoming client connections. Changing the property's banner from its default—ESMTP MAIL Service, Version: 5.0.2195.1600 (or something similar)—is a useful security measure, because it hides Exchange from unauthorized Telnet connection attempts issued by attackers who are trying to footprint your system.

To change the banner for property 36907, open MetaEdit and find /LM/ Smtpsvc/*n*, where *n* is the number of the SMTP virtual server used by Exchange. Then, select Edit → New → String from the menu to open the Edit Metabase Data dialog box (shown in Figure 6-6).

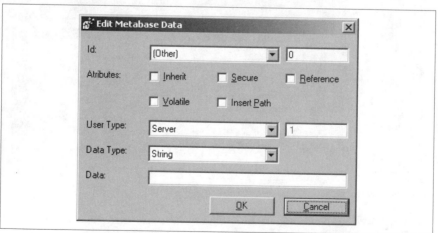

*Figure 6-6. Adding a new property to the metabase based on its internal ID number*

Since the Id drop-down box lists only standard IIS metabase properties, you have to add this property using its ID number instead. Leave the list box set to (Other) and type 36907 in the box beside it. Then, in the Data text box, type the banner you want the SMTP Service to display to clients—perhaps something like "Stop trying to footprint my server!" Finally, stop and restart the SMTP Service on your machine. Now, when a Telnet client tries to connect on port 25, he'll get the message you specified. Of course, you might not want to use that particular message; it might only annoy the attacker and make her even more determined to crack your system!

By the way, you can do the same thing with your POP3 connection and disconnection strings (IDs 41661 and 41662, respectively) and your IMAP4 connection and disconnection strings (IDs 49884 and 49885, respectively). Be sure to restart these services once you modify their metabase settings.

## HACK #58 Hide the Metabase

Protect the metabase on your critical web servers by hiding its name and location from attackers.

Good security begins with pretty obvious things, such as renaming the default administrator account and assigning it a strong password. The same is true for the metabase, the database used by IIS to store its configuration information. In Windows 2000, the metabase file is *metabase.bin* and is located in the *%SystemRoot%\System32\inetsrv* directory. By changing both the name and location of the metabase, you can hide it from malicious hackers, making it harder for them to corrupt the configuration of your web servers.

Changing the name of the metabase first involves stopping the IIS Admin Service. This can be done either from the GUI, by using Internet Services Manager (right-click on the server node and select Restart IIS), or by typing net stop iisadmin /y at the command line. Once IIS is stopped, make a copy of *metabase.bin* before you proceed, just in case something goes wrong, and store this copy offline on a network share or floppy. Then, move *metabase.bin* to a new folder on your server, making sure the NTFS permissions on the folder include Full Control for the built-in SYSTEM identity and the built-in Administrators local group on the machine. IIS requires these permissions to load the metabase into memory and modify its contents when you change your IIS configuration, and you, as administrator, require these permissions to access the metabase later, if necessary. Rename the *metabase.bin* file to something different and give it a unique file extension—something like *ab345mn7.pqr*, for example.

Now, open Registry Editor (Start → Run → regedit) and find the HKLM\
SOFTWARE\Microsoft\InetMgr\Parameters key. Add a new value to this key by
right-clicking on Parameters and selecting New → String Value. Type
MetadataFile for the value name and leave the data type as REG_SZ. Double-
click on the value and change the value data to the full path to where
*ab345mn7.pqr* (or whatever you've called it) is located, as shown in
Figure 6-7. Be sure to include the drive letter in your path.

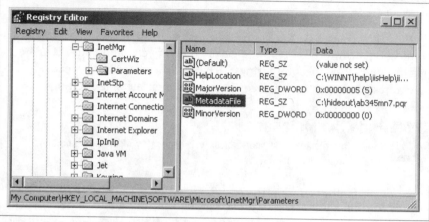

*Figure 6-7. Hiding the name and location of the metabase*

Now, start the IIS services by typing iisreset /start at the command line.
Open Internet Services Manager and verify that you can modify the configuration and save changes successfully. You're metabase is now hidden from
attackers, making your web server more secure.

Open Windows Explorer and find your *%SystemRoot%\System32\inetsrv*
folder again. Surprise! There's a file named *metabase.bin* in this directory
again. For some reason, when you delete or move this file and restart IIS services, Windows automatically creates a new *metabase.bin* file in the *inetsrv*
directory. But if you click on this file, you'll see that it's only 610 bytes in
size; it's not a working metabase. In fact, go ahead and delete this file—you
don't have to stop the IIS Admin Services to do so—and it shouldn't appear
again, even if you restart IIS again.

The metabase is hidden now, but what about backups of the metabase?
"Back Up the Metabase" **[Hack #54]** showed how to back up the metabase in
order to prevent making configuration errors on your IIS machine. If you've
saved the configuration of your IIS machine, copies of your metabase can be
found in *%SystemRoot%\System32\inetsrv\MetaBack*. Unfortunately, there's
no way to change the location where metabase backups are stored, so the

best thing to do might be to copy these backups to a network share and then delete them from the web server itself. That way, there's only one copy of the metabase on your server, one that's hidden and has a different name than *metabase.bin*.

What about IIS 6? Unfortunately, on Windows Server 2003, creating a HKLM\ SOFTWARE\Microsoft\InetMgr\Parameters\MetadataFile Registry key has no effect, so this method doesn't work. But IIS 6 is inherently more secure than IIS 5 for a number of reasons. Because you can encrypt metabase backups to prevent them from being misused, it's probably not that important that you can't hide the metabase on that platform.

## HACK #59    IIS Administration Scripts

Here are some handy scripts that can be used to administer IIS from the command line.

Microsoft does a pretty good job of developing GUI tools for managing most aspects of Windows, but until only a few years ago they were weak on the scripting side. With the advent of Visual Basic Scripting Edition (VBScript) and the Windows Scripting Host (WSH), administering Windows from the command line became a reality. Incorporating Active Directory Services Interface (ADSI) into Windows 2000 and adding a Windows Management Instrumentation (WMI) provider for IIS into Windows Server 2003 has taken Windows scripting even further, and now you can manage just about any aspect of IIS in particular and Windows servers in general remotely from the command line.

Of course, someone still has to write the scripts.

Unfortunately, most administrators who work in the real world of supporting businesses' computing infrastructures have little time for the luxury of learning VBScript and WMI. Learning to write your own scripts to administer Windows is a time-consuming affair, and if you're responsible for managing users, keeping servers running, maintaining security, and preparing for disasters, then time is something that's usually in limited supply.

Fortunately, Microsoft has done some of the work for you by developing some handy scripts that can be used to simplify or automate IIS administration. This is especially true of IIS 6 (Windows Server 2003), but there's also some useful stuff you can use for IIS 5 (Windows 2000).

### IIS 5 Scripts

Windows scripting was still in its infancy when IIS 5 was released, but Microsoft decided to include a few basic scripts with it (along with other sample content) to illustrate the power of what IIS could do. Four pairs of sample scripts are found in *C:\Inetpub\iissamples\sdk\admin*; one script in each pair is written in VBScript and the other is written in JScript, a Javascript (ECMAScript) derivative that's fallen out of favor lately for writing Windows administration scripts. Although these scripts are mainly intended for learning purposes, a couple of them are useful, so I'll briefly summarize what they can do (I'll focus here on the VBScript versions only).

Metabase backups and restores can be performed from the command line by using *metaback.vbs* and *metabackrest.vbs*. These sample scripts require that you use *Cscript.exe*, the command-line version of WSH, to run them. For example, if you want to back up the metabase using *14 Nov 03 Backup* as the name of the backup, just open a command prompt and type the following command:

```
cscript C:\Inetpub\iissamples\sdk\admin\metaback.vbs "14 Nov 03 Backup"
```

A metabase backup with that name will be created in the *%SystemRoot%\ system32\inetsrv\MetaBack* folder with the filename *14 Nov 03 Backup.MD0*. You can even create multiple backups with the same name but different version numbers using the -v switch, like so:

```
cscript C:\Inetpub\iissamples\sdk\admin\metaback.vbs "14 Nov 03 Backup" -v 15
```

This command creates the backup file *14 Nov 03 Backup.MD15*. Versioning is a good way to keep track of minor configuration changes made while tweaking the metabase to improve IIS performance. And running the script repeatedly with the same backup name but without a -v switch will increment the version number of the backup file each time. Of course, like any script, you can also schedule its execution by using the Scheduled Tasks Wizard so that your metabase backups can take place on a regular basis during off hours.

Another script included in *iissamples* is *mkwebsrv.vbs*, which lets you create a new web site from the command-line. Here's an example of how it works:

```
cscript C:\Inetpub\iissamples\sdk\admin\mkwebsrv.vbs C:\data -c "New Site"
-p 80
```

This command creates a new web site named *New Site*, listening on port 80 and having *C:\data* for its home directory. This script is flaky, though, and can create only one new site before errors happen, so I don't advise using it (there's a much better replacement, which we'll discuss in a moment).

The last script is *logenum.vbs*, which can be used to enumerate the different logging modules installed on IIS. This is basically just a sample script to show how ADSI and VBScript can be used to administer IIS. Because it's not very useful, I won't say more about it.

And that's all the scripts in *C:\Inetpub\iissamples\sdk\admin*.

**AdminScripts.** Hidden away in another folder, *C:\Inetpub\AdminScripts*, there are many more scripts you can play with. And I do mean hidden; there's absolutely nothing mentioned in Windows 2000 Help concerning these scripts, and there's almost nothing mentioned on Microsoft's web site. You have to dig around in the Knowledge Base at Microsoft Product Support Services (*http://support.microsoft.com*) to find any information concerning these scripts. That shows the level of commitment Microsoft had to scripting, even as late as Windows 2000, doesn't it?

Anyway, let's see what these scripts can do. Most of them are quite short and simple. First, the *findweb.vbs* script is a useful little utility that can display information about a web site you specify. Here's an example of how it works:

```
cscript C:\Inetpub\AdminScripts\findweb.vbs -w "New Site"
```

Typing this command on my machine displays the IP address, port number, and even the site ID of a web site named *New Site*. Once you know the ID of a site **[Hack #56]**, you can stop, start, pause, or continue that particular web site by using the *stopweb.vbs*, *startweb.vbs*, *pauseweb.vbs*, and *contweb.vbs* scripts. For example, the following command stops the web site that has a site ID of 10—in other words, New Site:

```
cscript C:\Inetpub\AdminScripts\stopweb.vbs -a 10
```

There are also similar scripts, such as *stopftp.vbs*, which can be used to control the status of individual FTP sites. And *stopsrv.vbs* can be used to stop both web and FTP sites in one operation. For example:

```
cscript C:\Inetpub\AdminScripts\stopsrv.vbs -a w3svc/1 msftpsvc/1
```

This command stops both the Default Web Site and Default FTP Site, while leaving both the WWW Publishing Service and FTP Service running. Of course, if you prefer, you can stop these services entirely by using net stop w3svc or net stop msftpsvc.

Then there's *mkw3site.vbs*, which is used to create new web sites. This definitely has more functionality than the sample *mkwebsrv.vbs* script found in the *\iissamples\sdk\admin* folder, and it has options for specifying the site's home directory, friendly name, port number, IP address, host header name, and even the site ID if you desire. For example, the following command creates a web site named *My Site* with a site ID of 101, a home directory of C:\home, and an IP address of 212.44.64.24:

```
cscript C:\Inetpub\AdminScripts\mkw3site.vbs -r C:\home -t "My Site" -i 212.44.64.24 -n 101
```

A similar script, *mkwebdir.vbs*, can be used to create virtual directories within a web site and has similar syntax.

*Chaccess.vbs* is an interesting script that lets you modify the web permissions of a site programmatically. For example, the following command sets the web permissions for New Site (site ID 10) to allow Read and Script permissions but deny Write, Execute, and Directory Browsing:

```
cscript C:\Inetpub\AdminScripts\chaccess.vbs -a w3svc\10\ROOT +read -write
+script -execute -browse
```

Another interesting script is *dispnode.vbs*, which can display a host of information about any node in the metabase you specify. For example:

```
cscript C:\Inetpub\AdminScripts\dispnode.vbs -a IIS://localhost/w3svc
```

This command lists the web permissions, default document, anonymous user account, maximum number of connections, connection timeout, whether logging is enabled, and schema information about the metabase node.

Finally, there's *adsutil.vbs*, the mother of all IIS scripts. This script leverages the Active Directory Services Interface (ADSI) to programmatically manipulate many different aspects of IIS. The power of this little gem is best seen by some examples. You can modify web permissions using a command like this:

```
cscript C:\Inetpub\AdminScripts\adsutil.vbs set w3svc/1/root /accesssource
"true"
```

This command allows Script Source Access on your home directory. The same can be done with other permissions, such as Read, Execute, and so on.

The *adsutil.vbs* script can also be handy if you have to restore the metabase from backup after reinstalling IIS (this works only after reinstalling IIS components, not after reinstalling your operating system). If you reinstall IIS and then use Internet Services Manager to restore a metabase backup, you'll receive an error message saying the restore failed. You can simply ignore the error message and type the following command from a command prompt:

```
cscript.exe C:\InetPub\AdminScripts\adsutil.vbs enum w3svc
```

This retrieves the password for the IWAM_computername account used by IIS (the enum option displays pretty much the whole contents of the metabase, which you have to wade through manually or pipe to grep if you have grep installed). Then, open the properties of the IWAM_computername account in Local Users and Groups in Computer Management and type the password you retrieved for it earlier. Finally, restore the same metabase backup again in Internet Services Manager and the metabase should be restored.

You can do many other neat things using *adsutil.vbs*, such as disabling socket pooling [Hack #60], enabling reverse DNS lookups, enumerating server bindings, configuring IIS to support both NTLM and Kerberos authentication, and modifying just about anything in the metabase you want to play with. For more information on *adsutil.vbs*, you can find a pile of Knowledge Base articles at the Microsoft Product Support Services web site (*http://support.microsoft.com*). You should know, though, that with the advent of IIS 6 on Windows Server 2003, ADSI is now considered on the way out and Windows Management instrumentation (WMI) is all the rage. But that's a story for a different book.

## IIS 6 Scripts

Scripted administration of IIS has really matured on the IIS 6 platform with nine well-designed scripts written in VBScript to play with (no IIS 6 scripts were written in JScript). These scripts are much more functional and less likely to break than the *sample* scripts included with IIS 5. They are found in the *%Systemroot%\system32* directory, which is part of the system path and thus makes using them more convenient. Also, instead of using ADSI, these scripts make use of WMI, a more powerful programmatic approach that can do almost anything on both local and remote servers.

> In the following discussion, I'll leave out the cscript portion of each script command, because by registering *CScript* instead of *WScript* (the GUI version of *CScript*) as your default host for VBScript, you can omit typing cscript at the beginning of each script command.
>
> To register *Cscript* as your default host, either type cscript //H:cscript at a command prompt or simply try to run one of these scripts. You'll be presented with a dialog box that says "Would you like to register CScript as your default host for VBScript?" Click OK. Once you've done this, you don't need to type cscript at the beginning of a script command and you don't need to include the file extension of your script in the command. This definitely makes things more convenient.

**Creating and managing web sites.** First, you can create and manage web sites easily using the *iisweb.vbs* script. The syntax here is similar to *mkw3site.vbs* in IIS 5, but it's easier to use because it needs fewer switches to specify options. For example, to create a web site named *Sales Web* with an IP address of 205.16.45.12 and a home directory of *C:\Sales*, all you have to do is type the following command:

```
iisweb /create C:\Sales "Sales Web" /i 205.16.45.12
```

Other options for the /create switch let you specify a port number, host header name, and whether the web site should be started or stopped once it's created. The command displays output that verifies each setting it configures, including the randomly generated site ID number used by IIS 6 to uniquely identify each web site internally. One limitation of creating web sites with this script is that the home directory must be specified as an absolute path and located on the local IIS machine. This means that if you want to use a network share on another server as a home directory for your site, you'll have to open the site using Internet Services Manager and specify a UNC path to the remote home directory.

What else can you do with *iisweb.vbs*? Well, you can use the /delete switch to delete any web site on your server, including those you created using the Web Site Creation Wizard started from Internet Services Manager. Using the /stop, /pause, and /start switches, you can stop, pause, and restart an individual web site (whether it was created with *iisweb.vbs* or Internet Services Manager) independently of all other sites hosted on the server. You can even stop, pause, or start multiple sites simultaneously by including their names in a single command. Of course, if you want to stop, pause, or start all web sites on your server, using the iisreset command is easier. Finally, the /query switch lets you display a summary of information concerning all web sites running on your machine. By redirecting this summary to a text file, you can quickly document the sites on your server.

Once you've created a new web site, you can add new virtual directories to it by using the *iisvdir.vbs* script. Again, this script can be used to create only local virtual directories (mapped to a physical folder on the IIS machine), not remote virtual directories (mapped to a network share); you can get around this limitation only by using the GUI. But you can also use the /delete switch to delete virtual directories and the /query switch to display all virtual directories within a given web site, including nested virtual directories. The syntax is easy to remember:

```
iisvdir /create "Sales Web" reps C:\SalesPersons
```

This command creates a virtual directory named *reps* within the web site named *Sales Web* and maps this virtual directory to the *C:\SalesPersons* folder on the machine's hard drive.

And guess what? Everything you can do with web sites can also be done with FTP sites by using the *iisftp.vbs* and *iisftpdr.vbs* scripts included with IIS 6.

**Managing the metabase.** What about managing the metabase? In "Back Up the Metabase" [Hack #54], we learned the importance of regular metabase backups, and earlier in this hack we saw how the *metaback.vbs* and *metabackrest.vbs sample* scripts included with IIS 5 provide basic backup and restore functionality. Such functionality is greatly increased in IIS 6 with two new scripts: *iiscnfg.vbs* and *iisback.vbs*.

Backing up and restoring the metabase is done by using the /backup and /restore switches of *iisback.vbs*. These switches include the option of encrypting your backups with a password to make them more secure. For example, the following command creates a backup of *Metabase.xml* and *MBSchema.xml* in the *MetaBack* folder and encrypts the backup with the complex password pa$$w0rD:

```
iisback /backup /b "14 Nov 03" /e pa$$w0rD
```

One nice added feature that the earlier *metaback.vbs* script of IIS 5 lacks is the ability to list all backups from the command line and delete any that are no longer necessary by using the /list and /delete switches, respectively. You can also use the /restore switch to restore the metabase from either a backup file or history file, depending on your needs.

The other script, *iiscnfg.vbs*, is a powerful tool for exporting and importing IIS configuration information. The simplest use of this script is iiscnfg /save, which flushes the current in-memory metabase to disk. This is usually done automatically by IIS shortly after configuration changes are made, but if you're experimenting with configuration changes, you can use this to force IIS to save the metabase immediately and create a new history file as well. Metabase exports take all or a portion of *MetaBase.xml* and save it as an XML file in the directory you specify. For example, the following command takes everything in the metabase about the web site with site ID 1 (usually the Default Web Site) and exports it to the *site1.xml* file in the *C:\stuff* folder:

```
iiscnfg /export /f C:\stuff\site1.xml /sp /LM/W3SVC/1 /inherited
/recursively
```

Here, the /inherited option ensures that any metabase properties inherited at the /LM/W3SVC/1 level from higher levels, such as /LM or /LM/W3SVC, are explicitly written to the export file (since the target import server might not have these properties specified) and the /children option indicates that metabase subkeys should be recursively included in the export file. This is a great feature, because you can use it to export the exact configuration of a web site and then import the configuration (using iiscnfg /import) into another IIS machine to clone a copy of the web site (you still have to copy the site content, though).

You can even clone the entire configuration of your IIS server by using *iiscnfg.vbs* to export the root metabase key (/). There's a caveat, though: exported files of metabase properties that are encrypted can't be imported to other machines. Also, you can't export the metabase schema file (*MBSchema.xml*) by using iiscnfg /export, so if you've made any modifications to the schema, this approach won't work. But most administrators never try to modify the schema anyway, because it's too risky and complicated, so the second limitation isn't really a problem. You can work around the first limitation (encrypted metabase properties); all you need to do is remove or modify any machine-specific settings from the export file before importing it into another IIS server. That means deleting keys that refer to IUSR or IWAM, special built-in accounts used by IIS for authentication purposes; deleting AdminACL settings in the top level (.) of the metabase; deleting keys that specify passwords for remote virtual directories or any other purposes; and modifying any keys that specify paths to content directories not mirrored on the target server. Once you've hacked away and made the necessary changes to your export file, you can import it to another machine and gain an exact clone of your original machine's configuration.

There are also other ways to clone configurations. The iiscnfg /copy command overcomes the limitation of exports by copying both the metabase configuration and the schema files to a remote machine. The command calls the *iisback.vbs* script and removes all machine-specific settings from the metabase, with the exception of content paths. So, if your target machine has a content file structure that is identical to your original machine, you can use iiscnfg /copy to clone IIS in one easy stop.

Why not use iiscnfg /copy all the time instead of using iiscnfg /export /sp /? Though using /export is more complex, it also provides you with greater flexibility. It allows you to make any custom modifications you want to the metabase before you import your configuration to a new machine. For example, the /export switch also includes a /merge option that lets you merge virtual directories to consolidate and simplify a site. You can also use this option to merge good metabase settings over corrupt ones to recover a working metabase after something goes wrong. Anyway, that's just another of those tradeoffs that are common in administering servers: the method that requires more work is more flexible than the rigid, simple approach. Choose the right tool to meet your needs.

**Managing web applications.** Finally, IIS includes two scripts to manage web applications (*iisapp.vbs*) and web service extensions (*iisext.vbs*). The simple *Iisapp.vbs* script lists all web applications running on the server, displays their process identity (PID), and indicates the application pool to which they're assigned.

The *Iisext.vbs* script is more powerful and lets you display all web service extensions running on the server, show the actual executables of these extensions, add new extensions, and enable or disable extensions. For example, iisext /listapp displays Active Server Pages, Server-Side Includes, WebDAV, and any other extensions running on your server;

`iisext` `/listext` does this in shorter form by displaying ASP, SSINC, and WEBDAV; and `iisext` `/listfile` displays the DLLs associated with these extensions, such as *asp.dll*, *ssinc.dll*, and *httpext.dll*. Application pools and web service extensions are new features of IIS 6; for more information on them, see *IIS 6 Administration* (Osborne/McGraw-Hill).

**Running scripts remotely.** Finally, another powerful feature of IIS 6 administration scripts is the ability to run them remotely from a Windows XP workstation or another Windows Server 2003 machine (you can't run them from Windows 2000 because that platform lacks a WMI provider for IIS). All of these scripts support the /u and /p options (to specify credentials that work on the remote machine) and the /s option (to specify the DNS name or IP address of the remote machine).

To create a web site named *Products* with a home directory of *C:\stuff*, IP address 202.44.33.11, and port number 80 on the remote IIS machine named *WEBSRV99*, type the following command at a command prompt on your XP workstation:

```
iisweb /create C:\stuff Products /b 80 /i 202.44.33.11 /s websrv99.mtit.com
/u WEBSRV99\Administrator /p pa$$w0rD
```

Alternatively, telnet into the remote machine (if the Telnet Server services has been enabled on it) and leave out the /s `websrv99.mtit.com` portion of the command. Or, to run the command locally on the remote server, open a Remote Desktop Connection to the remote machine (if Remote Desktop has been enabled on it) and again leave out /s `websrv99.mtit.com`.

Which method is best? Unfortunately, using the /s option sends the credentials over the network in unencrypted form, and Telnet does the same. So, your safest bet is to enable Remote Desktop and use it for remotely managing IIS machines in your server room from your administrator workstation in your office.

## Custom Scripts

If you have a working knowledge of VBScript, ADSI and WMI, you can easily write your own IIS administration scripts to accomplish various tasks. Here are two short but useful scripts to back up and restore the metabase on a remote IIS 5 machine.

First, here's the backup script:

```
Dim IISComputer
Dim Flags
Dim TargetComputer
TargetComputer = "IISComputerName"
```

```
Flags = (MD_BACKUP_SAVE_FIRST Or MD_BACKUP_FORCE_BACKUP)
Set IISComputer = GetObject("IIS://" & TargetComputer)
IISComputer.Backup "MyBackupFile", MD_BACKUP_NEXT_VERSION, Flags
```

To use this script, simply replace the variables *IISComputerName* and *MyBackupFile* with the name of your web server and the full path to the backup file you create. Then, copy and paste the script into Notepad (make sure to have Word Wrap disabled) and save it with a *.vbs* extension. Make sure you have the latest scripting engines on the workstation from which you run this script. You can download the latest scripting engines from the Windows Script home page at MSDN (*http://msdn.microsoft.com/library/ default.asp?url=/nhp/Default.asp?contentid=28001169*).

Here's a similar script for restoring the IIS 5 metabase to a remote machine:

```
Dim IISComputer
Dim TargetComputer
Dim BackupLocation
TargetComputer = "IISComputerName"
BackupLocation = "PathToBackup"
Set IISComputer = GetObject("IIS://" & TargetComputer)
IISComputer.Restore BackupLocation, MD_BACKUP_HIGHEST_VERSION, 0
```

## Where to Find More Scripts

If you're into rolling your own WMI scripts, then more power to you; you have more time on your hands than I do. Busy geeks like me prefer to create our toolkit by collecting prefab stuff from various sources. Here are some places where you can find additional scripts for administering IIS.

The *IIS Resource Kit* (Microsoft Press) was written for IIS 4 (Windows NT) and is a bit out of date. But it still provides a useful introduction to the subject for newbies to Windows scripting. I still use this book from time to time, since IIS 5 is not that much different from IIS 4, but don't use it if you plan to work only with IIS 6, because of the architectural changes and enhancements on that new platform. The CD-ROM included with this book includes a number of useful scripts.

The *IIS 5 Resource Guide*, which is part of the *Windows Server 2003 Resource Kit* from Microsoft Press, also has some information on ADSI scripting, but it's pretty minimal. Most of the book focuses on deployment issues and performance tuning.

Chris Crowe's popular IISFAQ web site [Hack #61] has a pile of useful scripts, many of them written by Chris himself. If you are an administrator who works with IIS, you'd do well to spend a few hours becoming familiar with all the resources on this site.

Finally, there's the *Windows Script Development Center* at MSDN (*http:// msdn.microsoft.com/scripting/*), which has a ton of information on how to get started writing your own WMI scripts, if you have the time and patience to do so.

—*Rod Trent and Mitch Tulloch*

## HACK #60 Run Other Web Servers

Here's how to run another web server, in addition to IIS, on the same machine without conflict over who gets port 80.

Ever have problems when you try to run more than web server on the same machine? Or have you run some other web enabled software together with IIS, only to find that one or both of them break? The problem here is *socket pooling*, a feature of IIS 5 and later that causes IIS to bind to all IP addresses configured on the server, even on a multihomed machine with more than one network card. The funny thing is that socket pooling even binds IIS to IP addresses that aren't yet assigned to any web site on the machine—even if there's no Default Web Site configured to respond to All Unassigned IP addresses by default. This behavior not only prevents other HTTP software from coexisting with IIS, but it can also cause IIS to return errors to clients. A workaround that sometimes works is to set the HTTP port number for the other software to something nonstandard, such as 8099, but that won't work in most cases unless clients using that software also use that port to connect. By default, however, IIS won't let any other application listen on port 80 (the standard HTTP port), even if it's listening on an IP address that is not used by IIS.

### Disabling Socket Pooling in IIS 5

Socket pooling is enabled on IIS 5, by default, but it can be disabled to allow other HTTP-enabled third-party software to run side-by-side with IIS, each responding to requests sent to different IP addresses. There are two ways to do disable socket pooling in IIS 5. First, you can edit the metabase by using the MetaEdit utility **[Hack #54]**. By default, the setting for socket pooling is defined in the metabase schema, but you can use MetaEdit to create a new metabase key called `DisableSocketPooling` in the location `/LM/W3SVC` and assign it the value of true (1). In other words, the default value for `DisableSocketPooling` in the schema is false (0), which means it is false to say socket pooling is enabled. Don't you love those double negatives?

The other way to disable socket pooling is to use the *adsutil.vbs script* included in *C:\Inetpub\adminscripts* [Hack #59]. Type the following command:

```
cscript C:\Inetpub\adminscripts\adsutil.vbs set w3svc/disablesocketpooling
true
```

You should see the response DisableSocketPooling: (BOOLEAN) True. Now, stop IIS services by typing net stop iisadmin /y (which also stops the dependent WWW Publishing Services). Then, restart them by typing net start w3svc (which also starts the parent IIS Admin Service). Socket pooling is now disabled. If you like, you can use MetaEdit to verify that the key has been added.

## Disabling Socket Pooling in IIS 6

The DisableSocketPooling metabase key is also valid in IIS 6 but, interestingly enough, changing it from 0 to 1 doesn't do anything. That's because socket-pooling functionality has been moved from the Winsock HTTP listener used in IIS 5 to the new kernel mode HTTP driver (*http.sys*). As a result, you have to use a nifty little utility called *Httpcfg.exe* to disable it.

This utility is found in the */Support/Tools* folder on your Windows Server 2003 product CD, so begin by inserting this CD and double-clicking on */Support/Tools/SUPTOOLS.MSI* to install these tools on your server. Next, open a command prompt and type httpcfg set iplisten -i *w.x.y.z:n* to add IP address *w.x.y.z* and port number *n* to the IP inclusion list for *http.sys*. This inclusion list specifies which IP addresses *http.sys* listens on and is initially empty by default, which means that IIS listens to *all* IP addresses (not *none*, as you might suspect). However, once you add an IP address and port number (i.e., a socket) to the inclusion list, *http.sys* will now listen only on the specified socket and ignore all others, leaving them available for other applications to listen on. You can add as many sockets to the inclusion list as you choose, and you can display a list of listening sockets at any time by typing httpcfg query iplisten at a command prompt.

Don't forget to restart IIS after modifying the list, because *http.sys* reads this list only on startup. You don't have to restart all IIS services, only the HTTP Service (a subcomponent of the WWW Publishing Services and a service not displayed in the Services console). To restart the HTTP Service, type net stop http /y to stop it and net start w3svc to start it. Note that if you have problems afterwards starting any web sites on your IIS machine, you probably forgot to add their IP addresses to the inclusion list.

## Other Reasons to Disable Socket Pooling

If running third-party HTTP software together with IIS isn't your cup of tea, there are other reasons why you might want to disable socket pooling. The bandwidth-throttling feature of IIS that is configured through Internet Services Manager throttles bandwidth to all web sites running on IIS equally. The same is true of the performance-tuning settings configured through the GUI. If you prefer to configure these settings on a per-site basis, you have to disable socket pooling before it will work. This is not obvious from the GUI, which presents separate throttling and performance options for each site. The fact that these features don't work as advertised has been an open secret among the IIS community for a long time. They work only when socket pooling is disabled, and it's enabled by default.

## IISFAQ

Here's a brief overview of IISFAQ, Chris Crowe's valuable web site that every IIS administrator should know about.

I started the IISFAQ web site (*http://www.IISFAQ.com*) in early 2000 initially as a resource to help me maintain a set of answers to frequently asked questions on the Microsoft IIS newsgroups—specifically, the *microsoft.public. inetserver.iis* newsgroup on *msnews.microsoft.com*. The web site has grown up quickly over the years and is now regarded as one of the major sources of information regarding Internet Information Server on the Web. The web site is not affiliated with Microsoft in any way, but I do have limited access to the Microsoft IIS team though my Microsoft MVP status, which gives me access to some of the best information out there.

On the site you will find more than 50 categories related to IIS, such as:

- Administration
- Configuration
- Installation
- Logging
- Security
- Troubleshooting

There is also a growing repository of articles and links to content around the Web that we think you will find helpful in your search for information on IIS. We try to break down complex problems into helpful, easy-to-read articles that get to the point. Most of the articles include plenty of screen snapshots to help you follow along easily.

The site is kept up-to-date with all the new information that is released regarding IIS on almost a daily basis. The site also specializes in scripts for the management of your web server. There are dozens of scripts written mainly in VBScript, but with the introduction of the .NET Framework we will see more written in C# in the future.

The web site is also the official home to a debugging tool called IISState, which you can use to help diagnose problems—for example, when your web server hangs or causes 100% CPU usage.

There are also discussion forums on the site for those who wish to discuss their issues or to give feedback to others who are having problems.

## My Favorites

Here are a few of my personal favorite articles on the site:

- Backup & Restore of the IIS Metabase: What tools can I use? (*http://www.iisfaq.com/default.aspx?View=A329&P=73*)
- How to Configure ODBC Logging toLlog to a Microsoft Access Database (*http://www.iisfaq.com/default.aspx?View=A151&P=141*)
- Troubleshooting ASP and Microsoft Access Databases (*http://www.iisfaq.com/default.aspx?View=A396&P=160*)

And here are some of my personal favorite scripts on the site:

- A VB script that will archive all the log files for all of the IIS services that are over a specified age, in days (*http://www.iisfaq.com/default.aspx?View=A141&P=109*). This script uses the Microsoft MAKECAB.EXE command to make a *.cab* file. After the CAB file is created, the original log file is deleted if the creation of the CAB file was successful. The CAB file will have the same name as the original log file. You save around 90–95% of disk space.
- A VB script that uses WMI to allow you to create DNS entries on your DNS Server (*http://www.iisfaq.com/default.aspx?View=A319&P=109*).
- A script that enumerates all web sites using C# (*http://www.iisfaq.com/default.aspx?View=A540&P=199*).

I hope you find IISFAQ a useful resource as you work with IIS. Thanks!

*—Chris Crowe*

# CHAPTER SEVEN

# Deployment
## Hacks 62–68

Administering Windows-based networks begins with deployment, and the focus of this chapter is on how to manage the installation (and uninstallation) of Windows 2000/XP/2003 and its individual components. In particular, the first several hacks deal with Remote Installation Services (RIS) and Sysprep, two powerful but complex tools for installing Windows images on large numbers of machines. Other hacks deal with removing unnecessary components manually from the command line, removing components during unattended setup, and creating a network boot disk for unattended installation of Windows. These tips and tools are designed to make the job of deploying Windows easier so that you can get on with the day-to-day job of configuring, maintaining, and troubleshooting systems on your network.

## HACK #62    Get Started with RIS

Remote Installation Services (RIS) is a complex but powerful tool for deploying Windows images. Here's a guide to getting started with it.

In the past, with the many flavors of Windows, there were many ways of configuring and deploying Windows to client machines. Such automated and customized methods included imaging with a tool such as GHOST or scripting with answer files and VBScript or other automation tools to deploy silently and without user intervention. Or, you could make one image on a hard drive and use a hard-drive-cloning device to copy the image to multiple hard disks at once. The technology and methodologies for deploying a customized Windows operating system to client workstations has matured over the years, but not quite to the *plug and play* capability we would all like to see.

As part of Microsoft's change and configuration-management initiative, they developed a service included with Windows 2000 called Remote Installation Service (RIS). RIS supports deploying both automated and customized versions of Windows 2000 and XP Professional to clients that support the PXE/DHCP-based remote technology for remotely installing the operating system on the client computer over the network. The intention that Microsoft was communicating to the corporate technologists when they were developing Windows 2000 was that you could basically plug a new computer into the network, start the computer, authenticate, and the operating system would be installed and configured for the user within a short matter of time.

With a little bit of work, it actually does just that.

Not only can you deploy images of Windows 2000 and XP through RIS, but with a tool developed by 3Com (*http://www.3com.com/en_US/lanworks/index.html*) you also can deploy BIOS updates, other applications, Windows 2000 Server images, and so on. RIS is customizable and flexible; you can modify the Client Installation Wizard to prompt users for information, pass information to setup answer files, and populate environment variables with information. You can deploy disk images with RIS, but I recommend the scripted, silent-installation approach, because it is more customizable. I successfully use RIS in my office to deploy a customized Windows XP Professional image, and it saves me a lot of time.

Think of RIS as a network-based boot disk. The client workstation boots onto the network and obtains an IP address from a DHCP server and the location of the RIS server, RIS verifies the client is a known client, and then the Client Installation Wizard appears. It is similar to using a boot disk with NDIS drivers, a custom menu, and prompts via *autoexec.bat* or some other script called on the disk.

## Requirements for RIS

So, what do you need to get started with RIS? First, you need a PXE-compliant (*PXE* stands for Pre-Boot Execution Environment) network card and system BIOS that supports setting the LAN as a bootup device. Most network cards today—such as ones from Intel, 3Com, SMC, and RealTek— support PXE. For those workstations that are not compliant, you can create a bootable disk with a PXE emulator by using a tool that accompanies RIS. Next, you need a Windows 2000 server that is a member of an Active Directory–enabled domain. Active Directory is required, because it provides client authentication and configuration information for the RIS server and RIS also stores its configuration information within Active Directory. Obviously, you need TCP/IP, because it is the basic networking protocol required for a Windows 2000 network. Finally, you need a Windows 2000–compliant DNS server, so that an RIS server can locate an Active Directory controller, and a DHCP server to assign TCP/IP addresses to clients, allowing them to communicate with a RIS server.

**Hardware requirements.** The hardware requirements for your RIS server are dependent on how many clients will be supported within your environment. How well RIS performs when deploying Windows to clients depends on the hardware configuration of your RIS server—in particular, the disk subsystem, memory, and networking components of your RIS server. Let's consider each of these briefly:

*Disk subsystem*
Storage space for each operating system image you want to deploy must be taken into account, because the size will vary depending on the level of customization, size of images and applications included with each image, and so on. The RIS installation point cannot be on the same volume that the operating system and/or boot files are on. It must be installed on a separate dedicated volume.

*Memory*
In addition to the memory allocated to the operating system, allocate additional memory for the RIS service. Microsoft recommends a minimum of 128 MB for Windows 2000 Server, but I recommend 512 MB for the services and functions this server will be providing, as well as the number of clients it might be supporting.

*Networking components*
A network adapter running at 100 Mbps full duplex is best. If you are supporting a large client base, you might want to have two 10/100 adapters. Solid network connectivity between client and server is important, and you must consider your network topology when planning a RIS implementation.

As with other Microsoft services you provide on your network, proper planning will help you to determine the configuration of your RIS server, how many you may need, and the placement of them. RIS can run on a member server that provides other services on your network; you just need to determine the impact and whether additional hardware is required to support the additional services.

**Services associated with RIS.** RIS relies on three services to provide the capabilities it offers:

*Boot Information Negotiation Layer (BINL)*
The BINL service listens for and answers client DHCP requests (PXE). It also services Client Installation Wizard requests. BINL directs the client to the files needed to start the installation process. This service also checks Active Directory to verify credentials, determine whether a client needs a service, and determines whether to create a new computer account object or reset an existing one on behalf of the client.

*Trivial File Transfer Protocol Daemon (TFTPD)*

An RIS server uses Trivial File Transfer Protocol (TFTP) to download the initial files needed to begin the remote installation process to the client. These files include the Client Installation Wizard and all files needed to start Windows 2000 setup. The first file downloaded to the client using TFTP is *Startrom.com*, a small bootstrap program that displays the Press F12 for Network Service Boot prompt. If F12 is pressed within three seconds, the Client Installation Wizard (OSChooser) is downloaded to begin the remote installation process. When it resides on the server side, this service is called the Trivial File Transfer Protocol Daemon (TFTPD). When it resides on the client, it is simply called TFTP.

*Single Instance Store (SIS) or Groveler*

The SIS services consist of an NTFS filesystem filter and a service that acts on the volume on which the RIS images are kept. SIS services reduce the storage requirements needed to store these images by combining duplicate files.

## Installing RIS

On Windows 2000 Server, go to Start → Settings → Control Panel. Double-click Add/Remove Programs, and then double-click Add/Remove Windows Components. Scroll down, choose Remote Installation Services, and then click Next. Insert the Windows 2000 Server CD-ROM into the CD-ROM drive and click OK. The necessary files are copied to the server. Click Finish to end the wizard. When you are prompted to restart your computer, click Yes. When the server has restarted, log on to the computer with an account that has administrative privilege.

I recommend you always apply the latest service pack for Windows 2000, because it might have fixes or enhancements to RIS. For example, Service Pack 3 includes support for deploying Windows 2000 Server and Windows XP Professional (the original RIS supported deploying Windows 2000 Professional only) and resolves networking issues with RIS clients and installation issues (such as RIS clients hanging during setup). There are also specific hotfixes for RIS, but these are available only if you are experiencing the specific issue and they require a call into Microsoft support to obtain the update.

The directory structure of RIS is flexible; it is designed to support many different languages and hardware platforms. The following directories are created for the RIS service during installation.

*OSChooser*

> This directory contains all of the files needed by the client installation wizard. As noted, the *OSChooser* directory supports many different types of hardware platforms and languages. However, only the x86 platform is supported for RIS in Windows 2000.

*Setup*

> This directory contains the images that have been installed on the RIS server. Notice that the existing operating system images also contain a corresponding *Templates* directory, which contains the SIF file used for unattended installation of the operating system on the client computer. The SIF file also contains the friendly description string and specific image details that are displayed to end users of the client installation wizard and in the Tools tab within the administrative UI. Note that for an image to be displayed in both the administrative UI and the client-installation-wizard UI, it must contain an associated *.sif* file template.

*Tools*

> This directory contains tools that are designed to support deployment through RIS, such as BIOS updates, virus tools, and so on.

To set up RIS after installation, go to the command prompt or Start → Run and type RISETUP.EXE to start the Remote Installation Service Setup Wizard. Follow the instructions on the screen. It will guide you through configuring RIS, and the last step will be to create an image of your Windows 2000 Server/Professional or Windows XP Professional from the CD. I won't get into detail here, because it is a straightforward process, but see Microsoft Knowledge Base article Q298750 (*http://support.microsoft.com/default. aspx?scid=kb;en-us;298750*) for any assistance you might need.

Once you complete the process of configuring RIS, the server must be authorized in Active Directory. This ensures that rogue servers with those services installed (either by accident or intentionally), will not impact or disrupt network operations. Log onto a domain controller in the root domain with Domain Administrator or Enterprise Administrator rights. Go to Start → Programs → Administrative Tools and click on the DHCP snap-in. Right-click DHCP in the upper-left corner of the screen, and then click Manage Authorized Servers. If the RIS server does not appear in the list, click Authorize and enter the IP address of the server.

Once you're finished setting up RIS, you can customize it to the needs of your own networking environment [Hack #63].

—*Matt Goedtel*

**Customize RIS**

**#63** Once you know the basics of setting up RIS, you can customize it for the
needs of your own networking environment.

In "Get Started with RIS" [Hack #62], we looked at how to install and set up
RIS on a Windows 2000–based network. Once RIS is successfully installed
and authorized in Active Directory, you are ready to customize your RIS settings to meet your needs. This might include setting installation restrictions,
defining a computer-naming policy, configuring client response options,
prestaging clients in Active Directory, and permitting clients to install operating system images.

## Configuring RIS

To configure the RIS server to respond to client requests, you need to log
onto one of your domain controllers or install the Administrative Tools
package (*adminpak.msi*) on the member server that is running the Remote
Installation Service. Execute the Users and Computers MMC snap-in, right-
click on the server that is running RIS, and you will see a tab labeled Remote
Install. On this tab, you can enable RIS to respond to client requests (which
is enabled by default) and enable the option to not respond to unknown clients. This ensures that you support only prestaged computer account
objects in your forest as part of your security strategy. If you have multiple
RIS servers as part of a load-balancing strategy and one fails or is unstable,
you can deselect the option to allow it to respond to client requests.

The Advanced Settings button displays a window that allows you to configure additional settings for RIS clients, such as the default computer name
that is generated for each client when a user selects Automatic Setup on the
Client Installation Wizard (CIW) screen. By default, the username of the
user who authenticated in the CIW is used for the computer name, along
with a number. The username can be customized to use different variations,
which you can control by using variables recognized by Active Directory and
the BINL service. For example, `CorpWks%#` = `CorpWks2` uses a number incremented each time a computer account is generated when an image is
deployed/installed via RIS. You can refer to online help or Microsoft Tech-
Net for other variables or variations.

Taking advantage of the Advanced Settings is dependent on the standards
currently implemented in your environment. If you have different standards
per department, site, or domain, you will need to determine if you can leverage this feature. You might need to use a different solution during the build
process. If you are predefining the computer names, which are matched to
the unique GUID of that workstation, then this is a nonissue. In this screen,

you also have the option of specifying the organizational unit (OU) in which the computer accounts are created. By default, they are created in the Computers container.

## Predefining computer accounts in RIS

If you are security-conscious or want to ensure that systems are not arbitrarily imaged from RIS without approval, you should enable the "Do not respond to unknown computers" option on the RIS server. This also allows for greater flexibility, but it requires some up-front work on the administrator's part. Specifically, you can precreate the computer accounts in their respective OUs in Active Directory. Based on the organizational structure of the company and delegation of administration, this will also have some bearing on how you plan your implementation of RIS.

When precreating the computer accounts, you need to select the "This is a managed computer" option and the GUID of that computer is required. For computers that come from one of the leading PC vendors—such as Compaq, HP, or Gateway—the GUID can be found on a sticker adhered to the PC case. If the system does not have that sticker, you can create the GUID by using the MAC address of the network card installed in the PC, or you can boot up the PC and access the BIOS; the GUID might be displayed on the main screen. When using the MAC address of the network card, since the GUID is a 32-byte value, you need to pad the first 20 bytes with zeros; the remaining 12 bytes is the MAC address.

To load-balance your RIS servers manually, when you create the computer account and specify it is a managed computer, you can specify the RIS server to *own* (i.e., support) the client. I don't like this approach, because there is too much overhead management. Also, if the server were to become unavailable, your clients would be unable to obtain any images, updates, or components until that server became available again. Setting up a dynamic load-balancing solution with RIS—by defining one RIS server as the *bridgehead* and all other RIS servers behind it to serve only the images—is a better approach. I have not used any other approach, but I have been looking into how to leverage clustering or other solutions to further bolster the redundancy of RIS.

## Client Installation Wizard

The screens that are presented to the client when he interfaces with RIS are in OSCML format (similar to HTML and modeled after HTML 2.0 format) and have a *.osc* extension. You have great flexibility in how to present those screens to clients, based on your organizational needs and a touch of personalization (e.g., adding your company name to display in the screens). There are also state variables that you can use to make your image installations more dynamic; the values of the response are passed back via BINL to the answer file located in the template folder of the particular image. You can have up to 64 unique variables to use with the CIW. All variables, with the exception of the %LANGUAGE% variable, are set after successful login. As always, make a backup copy before modifying the original file, in case you run into an error or you want to revert back to the original for any reason.

OSChooser and the BINL service use the following variables:

LANGUAGE

The only variable that can be set prior to logon. This variable indicates the language in which the user wants to view the screens. All OSC screens, as well as any ENUM functions the server performs, are pulled from that language. The default value of this variable matches the default language of the server. Refer to the *Multilng.osc* file located in the *RemoteInstall\Oschooser* directory for an example of how to make the server multilingual.

SUBERROR

The server sets this variable internally for any errors it encounters. You can add this variable to an error message screen to diagnose internal failures inside the server.

MACHINEOU

Indicates to the server where the new machine account should be generated.

MACHINENAME

Indicates to the server the name of the new machine.

SERVERNAME

Indicates the name of the server to which OSChooser is connected.

SERVERDOMAIN

Indicates the domain name of the server to which OSChooser is connected.

BOOTFILE

Indicates when a tool is about to be started.

NETBIOSNAME

The NetBIOS name generated (using the DnsHostnameToComputerName( ) call) for the computer on which the image is being installed.

SIFFILE

This variable is local to the server path of the SIF that the user selected to install the OS. It is similar to the following example:

```
X:\RemoteInstall\Setup\English\Images\Win2000.pro\I386\Templates\Ristndrd.sif
```

OPTIONS

This variable is filled with the results of an ENUM action by the server. It contains OSCML and should be placed between a <SELECT> tag and a </SELECT> tag. See the *Tools.osc* file located in the *RemoteInstall\Oschooser\%Language%* directory for an example.

MACHINEDOMAIN

The domain that the new client attempts to join during GUI-mode setup. This might not correspond to the MACHINEOU variable's domain.

SYSPREPPATH

The path to the sources for a Riprep-based image if you use *Riprep.exe* to create your images. For example:

```
X:\RemoteInstall\Setup\English\Images\Win2000.prep\I386
```

INSTALLPATH

The TFTP relative path to the installation image—for example, *Setup\English\Images\Win2000.pro*.

SYSPREPDRIVERS

Indicates the path the server thinks best fits the Riprep-based image. This path is used to find plug and play drivers.

MAC

Sent by OSChooser to indicate the MAC address of the client.

GUID

Sent by OSChooser to indicate the GUID address of the client.

MACHINETYPE

Sent by OSChooser to indicate the type of hardware on which OSChooser is running. For example, on Intel platforms, you would use INTEL = "i386"

USERNAME, *PASSWORD, USERDOMAIN

OSChooser looks for the credentials specified by these three values to process the logon request. *PASSWORD is a short-lived variable that is overwritten as soon as possible on the server and is not accessible to OSC files or SIF files.

TIMEZONE

Set by the server to the server's current time-zone setting. This setting is helpful if you are replicating images to remote servers in different time zones.

## RIS Custom Installation Wizard

Now, let's look at how to customize the RIS Custom Installation Wizard screens and how you can modify them to suit your environment. Here are the default screens that are displayed during the client login and installation process when deploying operating system images to clients using RIS:

*Welcome.osc*
> Displays the welcome screen to the user.

*Login.osc*
> Displays the login screen and requires the user to log into the domain.

*Choice.osc*
> Displays the setup options—Automatic, Custom, Restart, Maintenance, and Tools—to the user. Remote Installation Service (RIS) Group Policy settings control which options appear.

*OSAuto.osc*
> Determines whether a computer account already exists in Active Directory with the same GUID as the computer that is running Client Installation Wizard. If a duplicate is found, *DupAuto.osc* is displayed. If no duplicate is found, then *OSChoice.osc* is displayed.

*DupAuto.osc*
> Displays a message indicating that a duplicate GUID was found in Active Directory and instructs the user to contact the network administrator.

*OSChoice.osc*
> Displays the list of operating system images available to the user who logged onto the RIS server.

*Warning.osc*
> Displays a warning to the user that the hard drive is going to be formatted and all information will be lost.

*Install.osc*
> Displays a summary page to the user.

All these screens are modeled after HTML Version 2.0 specifications and are simple text files with an *.osc* extension, indicating they are in the format of OSChooser Markup Language (OSCML). All of these files are installed in the *RemoteInstall\OSChooser\<language>* folder. The files listed in this hack are only a subset of the total number of *.osc* files stored in this folder. With these files, you customize client login screens in a variety of ways, including changing the text in the title or in the main body and adding additional input fields. You can then use that new information to further tailor the unattended installation of your Windows OS image through RIS. When working with different languages, you will need to modify *Multiling.osc* to list the languages that will be supported by RIS; then, rename *Multiling.osc* to *Welcome.osc*.

There are 24 predefined variables you can use within your own custom screens or answer files. These variables are available only in the *Install.osc* file and in the answer file. Some variables have predefined values, while others do not. To learn more about the predefined variables, see the following URL at Microsoft's web site:

> *http://www.microsoft.com/windows2000/techinfo/reskit/en-us/default.*
> *asp?url=/windows2000/techinfo/reskit/en-us/distrib/dsed_dpl_flwz.asp*

To learn more about configuring your own Custom Installation Wizard screens, see the following Microsoft Windows 2000 Resource Kit article, which breaks down the tags that are supported in OSCML:

> *http://www.microsoft.com/windows2000/techinfo/reskit/en-us/default.*
> *asp?url=/windows2000/techinfo/reskit/en-us/distrib/dsed_dpl_KEMO.asp*

You have a great deal of flexibility when hacking the screens used in RIS; you can even create your own screens to request information for your automated build. Say you want to create a screen to prompt for the local administrator account password, the location of the user's computer, and so on. With the default screens and the reference material provided by Microsoft, you are on your way.

## Deploying Windows Images

Configuring RIS to deploy Windows images is a simple and straightforward task. However, there are limitations to configuring RIS with Windows 2000 and Windows XP images.

You cannot slipstream service packs into the i386 image on an RIS server for Windows 2000 Professional images. To handle this issue, see Microsoft Knowledge Base Article 258868 (*http://support.microsoft.com/default.aspx?scid=kb;en-us;258868*).

When you want to slipstream SP1 into a Windows XP image, you will need to obtain a hotfix from Microsoft, because there are security changes in SP1 for Windows XP. See Microsoft Q Article 327536 (*http://support.microsoft.com/default.aspx?scid=kb;en-us;327536*) to obtain the hotfix.

Beyond those two important items, you might also run across minor compatibility issues with video and network cards.

If you have Service Pack 3 for Windows 2000 installed on your RIS server, you will also be able to support the deployment of Windows 2000 Server.

To add additional images to RIS for deployment, execute *RISSetup.exe*. This executable also accepts two command-line parameters:

-check

> Runs only the server component of RIS setup. It performs a verification of the components of RIS and corrects them.

-add

> Installs a new CD-ROM–based version of Windows XP Professional, Windows 2000 Professional, or Windows 2000 Server.

I recommend you keep handy the deployment guides that complement Windows 2000 or Windows XP and refer to them when you are customizing a build for automated deployment. Also, keep an eye out for any new material posted by Microsoft or the other technical resources on the Web, to help you along the way. Reference material is always a good thing.

Once you've customized RIS for your own environment, you might need to tune it further to make RIS server run effectively [Hack #64].

*—Matt Goedtel*

## HACK #64    Tune RIS

If you can't afford the resources to run a dedicated RIS server for your environment, you can use RIS on a dual-purpose server—as long as you tune it carefully.

Let's talk about fine-tuning RIS if there are other folders on the volume (i.e., other than the OS images used by RIS) and how to handle the restoration of the volume managed by SIS. To do this, we will have to dig deeper into how SIS works.

By storing a only a single copy of data in a folder on the volume, SIS helps reduce the amount of disk space that contains the OS images used by RIS. When SIS Groveler starts, it searches the root of each NTFS volume to see if it contains the SIS folder named *SIS Common Store* and a file called *MaxIndex* within that directory. If the Groveler finds this folder and file and if the SIS filter driver is installed on the system, the Groveler knows to search for and consolidate duplicate files on the volume.

SIS uses the same technology as the Indexing Service, and it is designed to not consume CPU time when the system requires it for other functions. The exception is when disk space drops below a specific value; in this case, the Groveler will increase CPU usage regardless of system activity, to ensure that disk space is not entirely consumed.

To effectively manage duplicate files that it detects when scanning a volume, SIS places the data in the SIS common store and the original files are changed to reparse points with referrals to the `<GUID>.sis` file. When the application tries to access the original file, the filesystem redirects any file I/O to the `<GUID>.sis` file in *SIS Common Store*. For example, if SIS detects the file *net1.ex_* in both the *RIS\SETUP\ENGLISH\IMAGES\WindowsXP. Pro\i386* and *\SETUP\ENGLISH\IMAGES\WindowsXP.Pro.SP1\i386* folders, it places the duplicate file in the SIS common store and the references of those files are changed to reparse points with referrals (or links) to the `<GUID>.sis` file.

Now, let's say you have a dual purpose Windows 2000 Server that is both a file-sharing server and a RIS server. The volume that houses the RIS OS images also has the file shares. When the Groveler service performs its daily ritual, it will scan through all folders on that volume. To improve efficiency of SIS and restore SIS links or reparse points, you can exclude certain directories from the Groveler scan.

To exclude a directory on a single volume, modify the *Grovel.ini* file located in the *SIS Common Store* folder (this folder is hidden by default). First, you will need to modify the NTFS permissions of the folder, because only SYSTEM has full control rights by default. Then, under the [Excluded Paths] section, add the required entry—for example, `Directory 1 Folder = \Folder1`. Note that the value to the left of the equals sign can be of any designation you wish. Now, stop and restart the Single Instance Storage service and you're done.

To exclude a directory on all volumes, open Registry Editor and add an entry to the following key:

    HKLM\Software\Microsoft\Windows NT\CurrentVersion\Groveler\ExcludedPaths

The value can have any name—for example, `Folder 1 Directory REG_SZ \Folder1`. Again, after you've done this, stop and restart the Single Instance Storage service.

In an enterprise environment, you should have a dedicated Windows 2000 server or servers to provide RIS images, depending on how many desktops you are supporting. In a smaller environment, it is reasonable to have a multipurpose server provide RIS, as long as it has the resources to support the additional overhead.

Finally, to restore a volume that is managed by SIS, follow the instructions in KB Article 263027 (*http://support.microsoft.com/default.aspx?scid=kb;en-us;263027*). How you handle a restore depends on the failure you are faced with, such as failed disk drives, controllers, or the like. Follow this article carefully to ensure you are not faced with data corruption because of the linked files managed by SIS!

For more helpful information on using RIS to deploy Windows, see my column at myITforum.com (*http://www.myitforum.com*).

—*Matt Goedtel*

## Customize SysPrep

Using SysPrep to deploy Windows can be a nightmare, unless you find a way to minimize the number of images you have to maintain.

Are you in charge of imaging workstations in your company? Do you have multiple hardware platforms deployed throughout your company? Do you maintain more than five images of those workstations? If you answered "yes" to any of these questions, then this hack might just ease your workload. By using Microsoft's SysPrep utility, system administrators can reduce the number of PC images that are maintained on a daily basis.

Using the approach in this hack, I have moved away from maintaining between 15 and 20 images and now have to update only 2 or 3 images for our entire company. I support nearly a dozen different types of workstation hardware, including several hardware specifications for laptops. SysPrep, while not inherently easy to configure or understand, is well worth the time and energy invested.

### Getting Started

On the lowest platform deployed at your company, install the operating system and leave the administrator account password blank. By leaving the administrator password blank, you prevent passing it in plain text via the *sysprep.inf* file. For our example, we'll use the following credentials:

> Name: Company Name
> Organization: Company Name
> Computer Name: XXXXXX (whatever you want)
> Administrator Password: (blank)

Create an administrative equivalent account called *Test* with a password:

> UserID: Test (or whatever else you want to use)
> Password: test! (or whatever)

Now, decide on the Network Options. Check the radio button that reads "Users must enter a user name and password to use the computer" or "Leave the machine connected to the WORKGROUP." Once the operating system is installed, build a new image from scratch by using the Test account. This image should include the latest operating service pack and security patches, in addition to all software that is to be included in the base image. So that you don't have to rely on hindsight, it is recommended that you upload this base image before applying the SysPrep files. That way, if something goes wrong with the SysPrep process, you still have a valid image and won't have to reinstall all the software again. Make sure to keep this uploaded base image separate from all other SysPrep-generated images. Naming the image *NoSysPrep* might be a good naming convention.

Now, create a folder called *C:\SysPrep* on the base-image machine. Copy the following files to the newly created folder:

*Sysprep.exe*
Prepares the hard drive on the master computer for duplication

*Setupcl.exe*
Regenerates new SIDs for the computers

*Pnpids.exe*
Helps you identify common names for supported Plug and Play devices

*Msdpnp.txt*
Contains inf settings for supported devices

*Sysprep.inf*
The answer file to be used for applying an unattended image to a machine

Now, copy all drivers, for all hardware platforms, to *C:\SysPrep\Drivers* from wherever they reside (whether on a CD-ROM or a network drive). This directory structure will be used when you modify the *sysprep.inf* file. Note that it is important to download the latest drivers for every type of hardware platform in your company. If hard-drive space is not an issue, it might be a good idea to place all device drivers in separate folders for each unique hardware platform in your company.

Once all the drivers are copied locally, log out of the Test account and log on as administrator. (The password should still be blank at this point.) Delete the Test Profile by right-clicking on My Computer and selecting Properties. Then, from the User Profiles tab, highlight the Test Account and press the Delete key. Next, delete the Test account by right-clicking on My Computer, selecting Manage, expanding Local Users and Groups, highlighting Test Account, and pressing the Delete key.

Run Disk Cleanup (Start → Programs → Accessories → System Tools → Disk Cleanup). Then, remove the following two entries from the Registry to keep the base image tidy:

```
HKLM\Microsoft\Windows\CurrentVersion\RecentDocs
HKLM\Microsoft\Windows\CurrentVersion\ RunMRU
```

Change the administrator password from blank to something appropriate to the security needs of your environment. Then, from the command prompt, run the following command:

```
C:\SysPrep\sysprep.exe -pnp
```

By running the sysprep.exe utility, the PC will be powered down once you click OK. This might take several minutes to complete. The -pnp parameter here indicates *Plug and Play*.

Now, upload new image and name it *SysImage* to prevent overwriting the original image. Upon reboot, the SysPrep wizard will run, finding all drivers for each particular hardware device in the system.

## Understanding the SysPrep.inf

The key to making SysPrep work on multiple hardware platforms lies in customizing the *SysPrep.inf* file and the command used to invoke the *sysprep. exe* utility. This following sections explain each section of the *SysPrep.inf* file. The following code is taken directly from the *sysprep.inf* file included with the utility, along with my explanations.

**SysPrepMassStorage.** The key to the *SysPrep.inf* file lies within the SysPrepMassStorage section:

```
[SysPrepMassStorage]
Primary_IDE_Channel=%windir%\inf\mshdc.inf
Secondary_IDE_Channel=%windir%\inf\mshdc.inf
```

These two strings tell the operating system where to look for the IDE drivers. When you run a full-blown Setup from any Windows setup disk, Setup goes out and looks for the default IDE drivers for the primary and secondary IDE controllers before the GUI phase of Setup begins. After it finds the default drivers, it continues with whatever task it needs to perform. After all the files have been copied over and the setup is completed, it will either keep the default IDE drivers or look for a more updated one from the path provided in the *SysPrep.inf* answer file. It rarely prompts for an updated driver, unless you have another IDE controller installed (i.e., in addition to the primary and secondary controllers).

Note that %windir% is the environment variable used to describe the location of the Windows files. For Windows NT/2000 operating systems, the Windows files are located in *C:\Winnt*. For Windows 9x/XP operating systems, Windows files are located in *C:\Windows*. By using this environment variable, the *SysPrep.inf* file can be used for nearly all operating systems without additional coding.

The *Mshdc.inf* file references the Microsoft Hard Drive Controller *.inf* file.

```
PCMCIA\*PNP0600=%systemroot%\inf\mshdc.inf
*PNP0600=%systemroot%\inf\mshdc.inf
PCMCIA\KME-KXLC005-A99E=%systemroot%\inf\mshdc.inf
PCMCIA\_-NinjaATA--3768=%systemroot%\inf\mshdc.inf
PCMCIA\FUJITSU-IDE-PC_CARD-DDF2=%systemroot%\inf\mshdc.inf
*AZT0502=%systemroot%\inf\mshdc.inf
PCI\VEN_10B9&DEV_5215=%systemroot%\inf\mshdc.inf
PCI\VEN_10B9&DEV_5219=%systemroot%\inf\mshdc.inf
PCI\VEN_10B9&DEV_5229=%systemroot%\inf\mshdc.inf
PCI\VEN_1097&DEV_0038=%systemroot%\inf\mshdc.inf
PCI\VEN_1095&DEV_0640=%systemroot%\inf\mshdc.inf
PCI\VEN_1095&DEV_0646=%systemroot%\inf\mshdc.inf
PCI\VEN_0E11&DEV_AF33=%systemroot%\inf\mshdc.inf
PCI\VEN_8086&DEV_1222=%systemroot%\inf\mshdc.inf
PCI\VEN_8086&DEV_1230=%systemroot%\inf\mshdc.inf
PCI\VEN_8086&DEV_7010=%systemroot%\inf\mshdc.inf
PCI\VEN_8086&DEV_7111=%systemroot%\inf\mshdc.inf
PCI\VEN_8086&DEV_2411=%systemroot%\inf\mshdc.inf
PCI\VEN_8086&DEV_2421=%systemroot%\inf\mshdc.inf
PCI\VEN_8086&DEV_7199=%systemroot%\inf\mshdc.inf
PCI\VEN_1042&DEV_1000=%systemroot%\inf\mshdc.inf
PCI\VEN_1039&DEV_0601=%systemroot%\inf\mshdc.inf
PCI\VEN_1039&DEV_5513=%systemroot%\inf\mshdc.inf
PCI\VEN_10AD&DEV_0001=%systemroot%\inf\mshdc.inf
PCI\VEN_10AD&DEV_0150=%systemroot%\inf\mshdc.inf
PCI\VEN_105A&DEV_4D33=%systemroot%\inf\mshdc.inf
PCI\VEN_10AD&DEV_0571=%systemroot%\inf\mshdc.inf
```

Referring back to the `SysPrepMassStorage` section of *Sysprep.inf*, the two strings below the primary/secondary controllers (not shown) are unique IDE drivers for your own specific hardware. If you have a unique IDE controller and would like to use drivers other than the MS defaults, you can add them to this section.

You must be very careful when adding a line in the `SysPrepMassStorage` section of the *.inf* file. By using only the downloaded drivers, instead of the Microsoft default drivers, you might get an error message stating that there is an invalid disk. If you are running a different IDE driver, you might want to run the driver setup at the end of the SysPrep process. This can be accomplished by placing the setup string in the `RunOnce` section of the *SysPrep.inf* answer file. This should then update the IDE controller to the driver that you prefer to use, in addition to creating a stable SysPrep run.

Another thing to consider is an already-configured IDE controller that is a part of your base image. You might lose the updated IDE driver, because the SysPrep setup-wizard parameter pnp (Plug and Play) will overwrite your pre-configured driver. There is a way around this SysPrep feature: omit the pnp parameter when you run sysprep.exe. Omitting the pnp parameter when you run SysPrep runs only a portion of PnP process and not the full PnP feature.

While this might prevent the loss of a preconfigured IDE driver on your workstation image, you should use caution when you choose not to run the full pnp parameter. Running the full pnp parameter as a part of the SysPrep process will indeed allow one image to locate and install a variety of unsupported hardware configurations. If the default Microsoft IDE driver or the specific IDE driver is not detected, then SysPrep will not run correctly.

**Unattended.** The following lines in the Unattended section mean that the whole SysPrep setup will not stop or pause for anything. Note that you can document the *SysPrep.inf* file by using a semicolon as a comment marker, as shown here above the actual command:

```
[Unattended]
; the following optional line means setup won't pause for anything,
including errors
UnattendedMode = FullUnattended
```

The following lines skip the license agreement and any other prompts dealing with licensing:

```
OemSkipEula = Yes
OemPreinstall = No
```

The following line tells SysPrep the folder location for hardware-specific drivers that are not included with the operating system:

```
OemPnPDriversPath = sysprep\Drivers\1\NIC;sysprep\Drivers\1\Sound\
W2k;sysprep\Drivers\1\Sound;sysprep\Drivers\1\video;sysprep\Drivers\6\
NIC;sysprep\Drivers\7\NIC;sysprep\Drivers\7\Video;sysprep\Drivers\8\
NIC;sysprep\Drivers\8\Sound;sysprep\Drivers\8\Video;sysprep|Drivers\Evo\
3cOXNic;sysprep\Drivers\Evo\IntelNic;sysprep\Drivers\Evo\Nvidia;sysprep\
Drivers\Evo\Sound;sysprep\Drivers\Evo\Sound\Smaxwdm\W2k;sysprep\Vli8\
Keyboard;sysprep\Vli8\NIC;sysprep\VLi8\Sound;sysprep\Vli8\Video
```

Typically, you should copy all drivers into a *C:\Drivers* folder and separate them on a machine-by-machine basis. To keep this line from becoming unmanageable, abbreviate hardware-specific folders and document them accordingly. In this particular instance, the 6 represents hardware running at 600 Mhz, 7 represents 733 Mhz, 8 represents 866 Mhz, and so on. Use any method that fits your environment.

If the image you created has all the drivers for all the different hardware, then the OEMPNPDRIVERSPATH is not needed. However, I recommend you reference all drivers, just in case the manufacturer makes any hardware changes. You do have to copy all the drivers into the *SysPrep* folder. The space is lost for the image but will be reclaimed after SysPrep finishes, because the image automatically deletes itself. Just make sure that the drivers you need are inside the *SysPrep* folder.

**GuiUnattended.** In the GuiUnattended section, the asterisk beside AdminPassword means the local administrator password is blank:

```
[GuiUnattended]
AdminPassword=*
OEMSkipRegional=1
TimeZone=20
OemSkipWelcome=1
```

By having a configured local administrator password on your image, this SysPrep answer file will not null out the password, keeping the password the same. This creates good security by not passing the administrator password via the *SysPrep.inf* file.

**UserData.** The UserData section is pretty self-explanatory:

```
[UserData]
FullName="YourCompanyNameGoesHere"
OrgName="YourCompanyNameGoesHere"
ComputerName=xxxxxx
Productid=License info goes here
```

**Display.** By configuring the screen settings in the Display section, you can prevent the screen from coming up to the far-right or far-left side of the monitor. The display will be centered. These settings can be configured to suit your company's needs:

```
[Display]
ConfigureAtLogon=0
BitsPerPel=16
XResolution=1024
YResolution=768
VRefresh=75
AutoConfirm=1
```

The BitsPerPel section references the color. Make sure to check the hardware compatibility with a hardware refresh rate (VRefresh). A refresh rate of 75 should work for most hardware, but sometimes 65 is a better option. The AutoConfirm setting is enabled so that confirmation is already set, thus preventing a change back to the default setting.

**Identification.** The Identification section configures a PC to join a specific workgroup:

```
[Identification]
JoinWorkgroup=WORKGROUP
```

The workgroup name can be almost anything. If you want to have the PC automatically join a domain, other command lines are needed.

**Networking.** The Networking section tells SysPrep to use the default network settings, including Client for Microsoft Networks, File and Printer Sharing, and TCP/IP (DHCP):

```
[Networking]
InstallDefaultComponents=Yes
```

Within this section you can also add additional protocols, clients, services, static IP, and other networking options.

The only issue I have encountered, when running sysprep.exe with the -pnp switch (which causes SysPrep to perform a full device enumeration using Plug and Play), is that my company's preconfigured DNS settings are overwritten because the network card is redetected during the SysPrep process. A possible solution to this issue is to add a line in the RunOnce section of the *SysPrep.inf* file that will automate reconfiguring those DNS entries.

**GuiRunOnce.** Finally, by adding the following line to the GuiRunOnce section of the *SysPrep.inf* file, a script is run from the local machine:

```
[GuiRunOnce]
Command0=C:\temp\Scriptfile
```

The script file can perform a wide variety of commands. Be sure the file exists on the machine before you reference the command in the SysPrep answer file.

Now you know how to customize the *SysPrep.inf* file for your environment! For more helpful information on using SysPrep, see my column at myITforum.com (*http://www.myitforum.com*).

*—Janis Keim*

### H A C K    Remove Windows Components from the
### #66    Command Line

Here's a handy utility you can use from the command line to remove Windows components and protected files.

When asked to remove simple game files from a company's workstations, I replied quickly that it would not be a problem. After all, how tough could it be to delete four executables and their shortcuts? Well, on Windows 2000/XP machines, it can be a little difficult. When you try to delete the files, the OS will see that those files are missing and will replace them (or restrict you from deleting them). Why the files *sol.exe*, *freecell.exe*, and so on are considered critical system files is beyond me, but in order to get rid of them you will need to use the *sysocmgr.exe* utility.

The *sysocmgr.exe* tool is used to add or remove windows components. This utility takes advantage of an *answer.txt* file that can be scripted and pushed via Systems Management Server (SMS) and other methods. For the purposes of this hack, we will use the *answer.txt* to remove four famous games from the computer. In our case, the *answer.txt* file will look something like this:

```
[Components]
solitaire = off
freecell - off
pinball = off
minesweeper = off
```

The utility will parse only the [Components] and [NetOptionalComponents] sections of the file, so you can easily wrap it in with other answer files or inf files.

## Running the Hack

The command line for the utility has several switches, but these are the most important ones for our example:

/i

The location of the inf for *sysocmgr.exe*. This is different than the answer file and is normally in the *System32* directory.

/q

Runs the utility in quiet mode to suppress prompts.

/r

Suppresses a reboot (if required).

/u

Specifies the location of the answer (unattended) file.

/w

Prompts the user to reboot instead of rebooting automatically (if required).

Putting it all together, our command line to remove the games components on Windows 2000/XP machines looks like this:

```
sysocmgr /i:c:\winnt\inf\sysoc.inf /u:c:\UnattendSetup\answer.txt /q
```

Removing these four games does not require a reboot, so we didn't bother to put in the any of the reboot switches.

Hopefully, this will prove useful in your environment; but, as always, test first.

—*Donnie Taylor*

# Unattended Installation of Windows Components

Here's a simple way you can add or remove system components when deploying Windows 2000 and later.

If you're responsible for administering a large number of computers, you appreciate methods of automating common administrative tasks. A need to add or remove individual system components might result from a change in corporate policy, discovery of security vulnerability, or simply a newly emerged business need. Using sneakernet for such tasks might take considerable amount of time.

Fortunately, Microsoft provides a way to accomplish this task in an unattended way. Windows 2000 and XP contain the *SYSOCMGR.EXE* file in the *%systemroot%\system32* folder. When executed, this command-line utility analyzes the content of two files: *sysoc.inf* (the existing configuration file, located in *%systemroot%\inf* folder) and a specially formatted text file (which you can give an arbitrary name) that contains a listing of components to be added or removed.

The *sysoc.inf* file is used by Windows when running the Add/Remove Programs applet in the Control Panel. It's format is typical of standard *.inf* files: it is divided into several sections, each starting with a name enclosed in square brackets. The [Components] section consists of multiple lines, one per component. Each line starts with the component name, followed by references to *.dll* and *.inf* files used during installation or uninstallation. Hide entry determines whether the component appears in Add/Remove Programs applet.

The second text file (which you need to create) can have an arbitrarily chosen name; for example, *c:\comp.txt* will do nicely. This file can be created using Notepad and should contain the [Components] section, followed by one or more lines of the following format:

```
Component_Name = On/Off
```

Here, On is used for installation and Off is used for uninstallation. For example, to remove Windows Messenger and add Faxing, the file should contain the following lines:

```
[Components]
Msmsgs=Off
Fax=On
```

You can also install optional networking components by including the line Netoc=On and the additional section [NetOptionalComponents]. This section

would contain lines that refer to different networking components, such as
SimpTcp or wins, like so:

```
SimpTcp=1
wins=1
```

A value of 1 causes installation and 0 causes uninstallation. The names of the
components are the same as the ones used during unattended installation of
the operating system, which are documented in the *Unattended.doc* file on
the Windows installation CD in the *Support\Tools* folder.

### Running the Hack

Once you've created your *Comp.txt* file, you can now use *sysocmgr.exe* in
unattended installation mode to add or remove Windows components. Simply
ply run the following command:

```
SYSOCMGR.EXE /i:%windir%\inf\sysoc.inf /u:c:\comp.txt
```

Note that this approach will not work with the COM+, Distributed Transaction Coordinator, Microsoft Fax, and Windows Media Player services,
because these components are not removable.

*—Marcin Policht*

### HACK #68 Easily Create a Network Boot Disk

One of the headaches of deploying Windows is creating network boot disks.
Here's a speedy solution.

Creating a network boot disk is not very difficult, but it always seems to take
longer than it should. The Instant Network Boot Disk from Qual-IT
removes the hassle.

The Instant Network Boot Disk works with most network cards. It quickly
provides network access, and it includes filesystem tools and other network
utilities. The tool provides full support for Windows 9x, NT, 2000, and XP
platforms and includes multinational keyboard support, advanced memory
configuration, and a debug mode for troubleshooting drivers that refuse to
load. The disk loads completely into RAM for ultra-fast performance and
includes support for static IP addresses or DHCP and built-in PCMCIA support for some PCMCIA drivers. It also includes PING- and IPCONFIG-
compatible utilities and lets you preconfigure your network adapter settings.

To use the tool, first go to the Qual-IT web site at *http://www.qualit-uk.com*
and click the Tools menu option. Find the latest version of Instant Network
Boot Disk and download it to your machine. To create a network boot disk,
you need a blank floppy and the appropriate driver for your network card.

The steps for creating a boot disk are simple. First, run the tool to create a generic boot disk and then copy your NIC driver to the disk. If space is an issue, delete the included drivers to make room for new ones you need. Now, reboot from the disk and select the "CONFIGURE THIS DISK" option when it appears. Provide the required setup information—for example, the hostname, the IP address or using DHCP, your NIC card, and so on. Now, save your settings and reboot.

Detailed configuration and troubleshooting information is included on the disk in the *readme.txt* file. I've found this utility to be a real time- and headache-saver. Add it to your list of tools today!

—*Patrick Sklodowski*

# CHAPTER EIGHT

# Security
## Hacks 69–78

Probably no aspect of the system administrator's job is more important these days than security, and this is especially so with systems running Windows. The ever-increasing threats of viruses, worms, Trojans, and other exploits means administrators have to spend time and energy learning how to protect their company's networks against the wiles of malicious hackers on the Internet.

This chapter looks at some of the ways you can protect your network from these threats, and includes topics like best practices in virus protection, protecting Administrator accounts, securing backups, protecting domain controllers, and finding machines with automatic logon enabled. A security FAQ and a review of security tools you can download from Microsoft's web site round of this chapter and help you build an arsenal of best practices and tools that can help keep your network secure. For additional security hacks on the topic of deploying and managing security fixes on your network, see Chapter 9.

## HACK #69 Fundamentals of a Virus-Free Network

Here are some fundamentals you need to pay attention to if you want to keep your network free of viruses.

This hack details some of the fundamentals of having a virus-free network, which I have identified through trial, error, and observation in the almost three years of working in the dual role of SMS/Virus Protection Administrator for my employer. As a result, we've had zero network downtime due to virus infection since January of 2000 until now (December 2003).

## Awareness

The first fundamental is *awareness*. Simply put: you can't protect your network against a threat if you don't know the threat exists. Administrators need to keep up-to-date on viruses, current virus trends, and application and operating-system security vulnerabilities. How aware an administrator is about these subjects is very important, because it effects all the decisions that an administrator will make to protect a network from viruses.

There are several ways to gain awareness if network threats. For information on viruses and virus trends, the web sites of antivirus software vendors are the best place to start (I will discuss antivirus software shortly). All of those companies have some kind of virus-information section on their web sites.

I recommend checking the web site that corresponds with the antivirus software that your company uses several times a day (every couple of hours is even better). Virus writers are getting smarter and more devious everyday, and another virus like Nimda or Blaster could spread across the globe in a matter of hours or even minutes if given the right conditions. The more often you check, the better chance you have of getting a heads up on the next virus that goes worldwide.

Since antivirus vendors partly rate the threat level of a virus on how many samples of a virus have been submitted to them by their customers, it is also a good idea to check more than one web site for virus information. I recommend checking out two or three, just to keep an eye on things.

Here are a few good antivirus web sites:

Symantec (*http://securityresponse.symantec.com*)
Network Associates (*http://vil.nai.com/vil/newly-discovered-viruses.asp*)
Trend Micro (*http://www.trendmicro.com/vinfo*)
Computer Associates (*http://www3.ca.com/virusinfo*)
F-Secure (*http://www3.ca.com/virusinfo*)

I usually concentrate on Symantec, Network Associates, and Trend Micro's web sites. According to the latest ICSA Labs 2002 Virus Prevalence Survey (*http://www.icsalabs.com/2002avpsurvey/index.shtml*), these three companies make up about 89% of the global antivirus software market share. If a new worldwide virus outbreak happens, one of these three companies is probably going to be the first to have information on it.

Microsoft has also recently started an Antivirus Information web site (*http://www.microsoft.com/security/antivirus/*) to provide one place for information on viruses that involve security vulnerabilities in their software or operating systems. This is also an excellent source of information for using Microsoft products to help you keep viruses from infecting your network. Microsoft also has a Knowledge Base article that lists other antivirus software vendors (*http://support.microsoft.com/default.aspx?scid=kb;en-us;Q49500*).

For application and operating-system security vulnerabilities, I recommend signing up for the NTBugtraq mailing list (*http://www.ntbugtraq.com*). If a security vulnerability comes out, you can usually read it on this list before you will see it anywhere else. Other good web sites include SecurityFocus (*http://www.securityfocus.com*), CERT Coordination Center (*http://www.cert.org*), and TruSecure's ICSA Labs (*http://www.icsalabs.com*).

I also recommend signing up for Microsoft's Security Notification Service (*http://www.microsoft.com/technet/security/bulletin/notify.asp*), which will notify you via email each time a security vulnerability from Microsoft is announced and will provide information if there is a fix.

The complexities of viruses are increasing every day, as the Nimda and Blaster viruses have taught us all. The vulnerabilities that Nimda used to propagate were several months old when that virus went worldwide. The Blaster virus taught us this lesson again as it spread globally less than a month after the vulnerabilities it used were announced. If more administrators had been aware of those vulnerabilities, then Nimda and Blaster would not have had as big an impact as they did. The lesson to learn here is this: to win the war against viruses, awareness is the first weapon that you should have in your arsenal.

## Antivirus Software

The second fundamental for a virus-free network is *antivirus software*. Now this might seem pretty obvious; anyone who has worked in the Information Technology game long enough knows that antivirus software is essential, especially with viruses increasing in sophistication everyday. However, which features to look for in corporate antivirus software might not be quite so obvious.

The following list of features are things I have identified in my experience to be most helpful in enterprise antivirus software:

*Certification*
> Look for a product that has been certified for use with the operating systems you are using. ICSA Labs (*http://www.icsalabs.com*) is a good place to look.

*Easy to update*
> One of the most important things to look for is antivirus software that makes it easy to update virus definitions. Antivirus software that

requires updates to be deployed with third-party software distribution or any other means that are separate from the antivirus software's own processes can lead to logistical problems when deploying the updates, depending on the size of the network environment and the method of deployment. Antivirus software with some kind of built-in update process is much more desirable. Also, antivirus software that has updates that require user intervention or a reboot to install can lead to similar logistical problems. A built-in, automated, and silent update delivery system will yield much better results and ensure that the software is updated properly.

*Frequency of updates*

When checking out antivirus software, take a look at the company's web site to see how often they provide updates and how they handle virus definition files in emergencies. Make sure that their policy meets the needs of your environment.

*Centralized configuration*

Antivirus software that has the ability to configure all the clients on your network from one centralized console is a lot easier to manage and helps ensure that configuration is consistent.

*Real-time background scanning*

Antivirus software that has the ability to scan files in the background, without user intervention, is essential in today's virus environment. Being able to configure which files the software scans in the background is also important.

*Heuristic capability*

Antivirus software that has the ability to detect virus-like behavior in a file's operation could help identify new viruses and new variants of already-discovered viruses.

*Remote scanning capability*

If you have a virus incident on your hands, the ability to initiate a scan remotely on one workstation or server, and the entire network if necessary, could be what keeps your network from getting damaged due to a virus infection.

*Alerting capability*

With the speed that viruses spread these days, it is essential to have antivirus software that is able to send alerts when a computer virus is found. Without this functionality, you could have viruses hitting every workstation and server on your network and you wouldn't know about it.

*Support for mobile computers*
> Not many businesses today can survive with out laptops. If at all possible, look for software that is able to handle updating computers that are constantly mobile.

*Reporting capability*
> If you work for anyone that has *Manager* in her title, then you are going to have to produce some kind of report on virus activity at one time or another. Help yourself out by looking for antivirus software that can create those reports for you.

This list is by no means exclusive. Some of the things I have listed here might not be important to you at all, and I might not have included things that you consider important. The list of essential features depends on the networking environment you are working in and the operating systems that you have to support. Hopefully, this list will lead you in the right direction if you are considering your own needs for antivirus software.

## Interception

The third fundamental of a virus-free network is *interception*. Simply put: a user can't execute a virus if the virus isn't there.

In the current environment of viruses, things can change quickly. Since a large percentage of viruses in the wild propagate through email these days, a new virus can spread worldwide in a few hours under the right conditions. Depending on the virus, sometimes it takes antivirus software companies several hours to come up with virus-definition files that can contain a new worldwide threat. The best way to protect your network from new virus threats like this is to block all incoming instances of the file types that are known to propagate viruses from reaching your corporate email system.

Now, some would tell you just to block certain files or certain subject lines in emails, because the thought of blocking too much email would cause too many problems. Back when the Loveletter virus came out, this might have been a viable option. Now it is not. The sophistication of viruses has increased, and now just about everything a virus generates is random. (A good example is the W32.Klez.H@mm virus; see *http://securityresponse. symantec.com/avcenter/venc/data/w32.klez.h@mm.html.*) The only common thread you can use is the file types that viruses themselves use.

Are legitimate files going to stopped by using this method? Yes, they will. However, the rewards greatly outweigh the minor inconvenience that this method might cause your user base. In the almost three years I worked in my previous job, we stopped over 7,300 viruses. From that number, I would say that over 90% of the viruses that we stopped were volatile email attachments. On several occasions, using this method protected us from worldwide virus threats before antivirus vendors were able to provide new virus-definition files.

With all of this in mind, the next thing to think about is which file types need to be blocked. A good place to start is the files that are restricted from being accessed after the Outlook 98/2000 E-Mail Security Update (*http://office. microsoft.com/assistance/preview.aspx?AssetID=HA010550011033&CTT=6*) has been installed (this is functionality is embedded into Office XP):

*.ade*
:   Microsoft Access project extension

*.adp*
:   Microsoft Access project

*.bas*
:   Visual Basic class module

*.bat*
:   Batch file

*.chm*
:   Compiled HTML Help file

*.cmd*
:   Windows NT command script

*.com*
:   MS-DOS application

*.cpl*
:   Control Panel extension

*.crt*
:   Security certificate

*.ext*
:   Application

*.hlp*
:   Windows Help file

*.hta*
:   HTML applications

*.inf*
:   Setup information file

*.ins*
:   Internet communication settings

*.isp*
:   Internet communication settings

*.js*
: JScript file

*.jse*
: JScript encoded script file

*.lnk*
: Shortcut

*.mdb*
: Microsoft Access application

*.mde*
: Microsoft Access MDE database

*.msc*
: Microsoft common console document

*.msi*
: Windows Installer package

*.msp*
: Windows Installer patch

*.mst*
: Visual test source file

*.pcd*
: Photo CD image

*.pif*
: Shortcut to MS-DOS program

*.reg*
: Registration entries

*.scr*
: Screen saver

*.sct*
: Windows Script Component

*.shs*
: Shell Scrap object

*.url*
: Internet shortcut

*.vb*
: VBScript file

*.vbe*
: VBScript encoded script file

*.vbs*
: VBScript script file

*.wsc*
> Windows script component

*.wsf*
> Windows script file

*.wsh*
> Windows Scripting Host settings file

At my organization, we use a large part of this list, in addition to other files we feel could pose a potential threat in the future due to their nature. For example, we also restrict the following files:

*.ocx*
> Active X control

*.swf*
> Shockwave Flash object

*.wmv*
> Windows Media audio/video file

The way in which this policy is implemented depends on the configuration of your network and which security measures that you currently use. For an additional perspective on which file types to block, see the following section.

Blocking potentially unsafe email attachments is by no means the only security measure that you should take to protect your network from viruses. However, if you add this protection to what I have outlined here, you will have strong groundwork that could protect you from the next virus threat. Be sure to check out my column at myITforum.com (*http://www.myitforum.com*) for more tips on keeping your network virus-free.

## Interception Redux

Here's another perspective (mine, Brian Rogers) on how to keep your network free of viruses by configuring your antivirus software to block certain file types.

I'd like to share my own recommendations for file types that should be blocked to keep your network free of viruses. I posted this list to the AntiVirus discussion forum at myITforum.com (*http://www.myitforum.com*) awhile back. I compiled my list from various web sites and added a few of my own:

*.bas*
> Microsoft Visual Basic class module

*.bat*
> Batch file

*.cab*
  Cabinet installation file

*.chm*
  Compiled HTML help file

*.cmd*
  Microsoft Windows NT command script

*.com*
  Microsoft MS-DOS program

*.cpl*
  Control Panel extension

*.crt*
  Security certificate

*.exe*
  Program

*.hlp*
  Help file

*.hta*
  HTML program

*.inf*
  Setup Information

*.ins*
  Internet Naming Service

*.isp*
  Internet Communication settings

*.js*
  JScript file

*.jse*
  Jscript Encoded Script file

*.lnk*
  Shortcut

*.mde*
  Microsoft Access MDE database

*.msc*
  Microsoft Common Console document

*.msi*
  Microsoft Windows Installer package

*.msp*
  Microsoft Windows Installer patch

*.mst*
> Microsoft Visual Test source files

*.pcd*
> Photo CD image, Microsoft Visual compiled script

*.pif*
> Shortcut to MS-DOS program

*.reg*
> Registration entries

*.scr*
> Screen saver

*.sct*
> Windows Script component

*.shs*
> Shell Scrap object

*.shb*
> Shell Scrap object

*.url*
> Internet shortcut

*.vb*
> VBScript file

*.vbe*
> VBScript Encoded script file

*.vbs*
> VBScript file

*.wsc*
> Windows Script Component

*.wsf*
> Windows Script file

*.wsh*
> Windows Script Host Settings file

Ever since we blocked attachments with these extensions, we haven't had a single virus infection via email.

*—Chris Mosby and Brian Rogers*

## Antivirus FAQ

Rod Trent of myITforum.com, shares his answers to some frequently asked questions on the subject of virus protection.

As CEO of myITforum.com (*http://www.myitforum.com*) and author of several white papers on security topics, I frequently get questions on protecting Microsoft platforms from viruses, worms, and other threats. Here's a short selection of some questions and my answers. By the way, you can find lots of additional information about protecting your networks at myITforum.com.

## Is It Real or a Hoax?

Q:  *How can you tell whether a virus threat is real or just a hoax?*

A:  Keep the following links handy the next time a user sends you an email saying that one of their AOL buddies alerted them to a new and threatening virus. These links should be your first line of defense when a new virus is reported in the wild:

CERT Institute (*http://www.cert.org*)
McAfee's Virus Hoaxes (*http://vil.mcafee.com/hoax.asp*)
Symantec's Hoax Page (*http://www.symantec.com/avcenter/hoax.html*)
TrendMicro Hoax Page (*http://www.antivirus.com/vinfo/hoaxes/hoax.asp*)
Sophos' Hoax Page (*http://www.sophos.com/virusinfo/hoaxes/*)
Virus Busters (*http://www.itd.umich.edu/virusbusters/*)
Virus Myths (*http://www.stiller.com/myths.htm*)
Hoax Warnings (*http://www.europe.datafellows.com/news/hoax.htm*)

## Disabling Antivirus Programs Is Not Enough

Q:  *How can I disable my antivirus software temporarily when I need to troubleshoot some problem on my system?*

A:  Occasionally, you might be forced to disable antivirus software temporarily to troubleshoot problems with applications, printing, or the OS itself. On Windows 2000 computers, just shutting down the virus engine service is not enough to disable it temporarily. You also have to disable the device drivers associated with the antivirus software.

Here's how to temporarily disable popular antivirus products on Windows 2000. Right-click on My Computer and select Properties. Click the Hardware tab and click the Device Manager button. Click the View menu and click Show Hidden Devices. Now, expand Non-Plug and Play Drivers to find the Antivirus drivers on your system. Right-click on the correct driver and click Disable.

Table 8-1 identifies the names of the device drivers that correspond with products from popular antivirus software vendors. Note, however, that the device drivers for each application can change, so be sure to verify these device drivers at the appropriate vendors' web sites.

*Table 8-1. Device drivers for antivirus software products*

| Vendor | Device drivers |
| --- | --- |
| Symantec | *symevent.sys* |
| McAfee | *NaiFiltr* and *NaiFsRec* |
| Norton | *NAVAP*, *NAVENG*, and *NAVEX15* |
| Inoculan | *INO_FLPY* and *INO_Fltr* |

## Kernel32.exe Has Encountered a Problem

Q:  *I get an error message saying that Kernel32.exe is encountering a problem. Is that a system glitch or a virus?*

A:  If you receive error messages about *Kernel32.exe* encountering a problem, you need to update your antivirus program, because *Kernel32.exe* is not a Microsoft file (though *Kernel32.DLL* is). So, if you see this error message, quickly update your antivirus program and attempt to fix the virus outbreak on the computer.

This issue can occur if your computer is infected by one of the following viruses: Worm_Badtrans.b, Backdoor.G_Door, Glacier Backdoor, Win32.Badtrans.29020, W32.Badtrans.B@mm, and Win32/PWS.Badtrans.B.Worm.

## Stinger Tool

Q:  *Is there a virus-removal tool that can remove multiple viruses, instead of the single tools offered by vendors?*

A:  On the McAfee help forums, you'll find information on a removal utility called Stinger. This tool is constantly updated to include new removal information for new viruses. You can find more information about Stinger at *http://forums.mcafeehelp.com/viewtopic.php?t=764*, and you can download the tool from *http://vil.nai.com/vil/stinger/*.

—Rod Trent

# HACK
# #71
# Rename the Administrator and Guest Accounts

Renaming the default administrator and guest accounts is a simple but effective step to help secure your machines.

To enhance system security on your Windows server-based network, you should rename the administrator account. You should choose a name that does not identify it as an administrator account, to make it difficult for any unauthorized user to break into the computer or network. One of the account settings in Windows 2000/2003 allows you to enter an account name to rename the administrator and guest accounts automatically using Local Security Policy (for standalone machines in a workgroup) or Group Policy (in an Active Directory environment).

To access local policy settings, click Start → Run, type mmc, and press Enter. Select File → Add/Remove Snap-in. Click the Add button, scroll through the list until you see Group Policy (in Windows 2000) or Group Policy Object Editor (in Windows Server 2003). Click add, then finish (the default is to manage Local Computer). Expand Local Computer Policy, Computer Configuration, Windows Settings, Security Settings, Local Policies, and Security Options. If you like, you can save this console with a familiar name to have this MMC snap-in available for future use. Once you've selected Security Options, you should see a screen similar to Figure 8-1 (if you're running Windows Server 2003 or Windows XP).

In the pane on the right, you can see that the first five options detail policies for Accounts. The last two options in the Accounts section are used to rename the administrator account and rename the guest account. Clicking on "Accounts: Rename administrator account" brings up the screen shown in Figure 8-2. You will see a similar screen if you select the Guest option. Simply type whatever name you want to use and click OK. This automatically renames the administrator or guest accounts.

## Some Considerations

Note that if your machine belongs to a domain, the local policy settings you configure using the previous method might be overwritten by any Group Policy settings defined at the domain, organizational unit (OU), or site level.

Windows 2000 provides only the first two Accounts policy settings and they're named differently than the settings shown in Figure 8-2. The Windows Server 2003 setting named "Accounts: Rename administrator account" is simply named "Rename administrator account" in Windows 2000, and

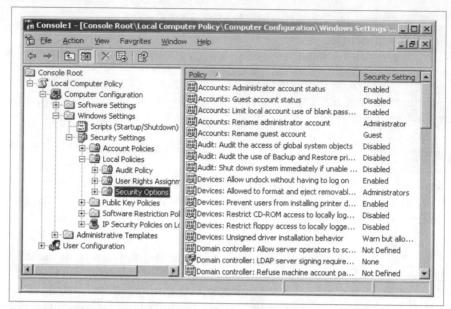

Figure 8-1. Policy settings for the default administrator and guest accounts in Windows Server 2003 and Windows XP

Figure 8-2. Renaming the default Administrator account

likewise with the Guest account policy setting. Windows XP, however, is identical to Windows Server 2003 in this regard.

Finally, as a further security precaution, after you rename the accounts, you might want to add another administrator and guest account (through the User Accounts option). Once you create these accounts, give them a secure password, but give the accounts no rights to anything. Even if the administrator and guest accounts are compromised, the potential intruder will have no rights to do anything to the computer.

—John Gormly

# Get a List of Local Administrators

HACK #72

Local administrators can do anything on their machines. Here's a quick way to determine who has this power.

When an intruder penetrates a network's defenses, the intruder generally tries to elevate the privileges of his account to that of local administrator on the machine. Once the intruder has achieved this, he can do anything he wants to do on the machine.

So, if you think your network defenses have been penetrated, it's a good idea during the triage stage to check which accounts are local administrators on your machines. Using the GUI, this can be done using the Local Users and Groups node in Computer Management, but that is tedious.

A faster way to identify individuals who have local computer administrator rights is to use the following VBScript, which you can customize further as desired.

## The Code

Just open a text editor such as Notepad (make sure you have Word Wrap disabled), type the following code, and save it with a *.vbs* extension as *GetAdmins.vbs*:

```
computername = createobject("wscript.network").computername
set group = getobject("WinNT://" & computername & "/administrators,group")
s = ""
for each account in group.members
s = s & account.name & vbcrlf
next
msgbox s
```

## Running the Hack

Running the hack is simple. Just create a shortcut to it and double-click on the shortcut. A dialog box will display which user accounts are local administrators on the machine, as shown in Figure 8-3. From this list, you can easily detect any unauthorized administrator-level accounts, such as backd00r, that might indicate that the system has been compromised by a malicious hacker.

Make sure you have the latest scripting engines on the workstation from which you run this script. Download the latest scripting engines from the Microsoft Scripting home page (*http://msdn.microsoft.com/library/default. asp?url=/nhp/default.asp?contentid-28001169*). Note also that, when working with the Active Directory Services Interface (ADSI) you must have the same applicable rights you need to use the built-in administrative tools.

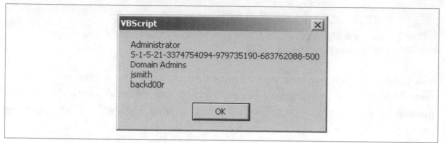

*Figure 8-3. A list of local administrators on a member server*

## Hacking the Hack

The script gets the contents of the local administrators group, but you can easily alter the group information in the script to retrieve the information from any local computer group if you desire. For example, to display members of the Users group just change this line:

```
set group = getobject("WinNT://" & computername & "/administrators,group")
```

to this:

```
set group = getobject("WinNT://" & computername & "/users,group")
```

Then, run the hack again.

*—Rod Trent*

## HACK #73 Find All Computers that Are Running a Service

Use this script to find rogue web servers, misconfigured clients, and other potentially insecure systems on your network.

Querying the status of a service across multiple computers can be an extremely useful tool. You can check for the SMS client service, antivirus services, or even viruses/Trojans that run as a service. Under most interfaces, such as WMI or ADSI, you need to check the status of services with an account that has administrator rights on the machine you are targeting. It turns out that in many organizations there are quite a few PCs on the network that have done a phenomenal job of removing most of the IT department's administrator rights. These unmanaged PCs can be a real risk at times.

One day, I noticed that when you query a remote box with the Windows 2000 services snap-in for the MMC, you do not need administrator rights to check on the services that reside on remote boxes. You simply need an account in a trusted domain with simple user-level rights. On further investigation, it was revealed that what in fact was going on was a direct query to the Service Control Manager (SCM), as opposed to some API call through WMI or ADSI. One of the best free third-party tools that also queries the SCM is Psservice from Sysinternals (*http://www.sysinternals.com*). Although this is strictly a command-line utility, we can tweak it with some parameters and do some fancy parsing to make efficient use of it in a script.

First, the script will search IP addresses by subnet, using a ping response, and find the Windows-based machines by parsing out a NetBIOS call. Then, it will determine if the machine is running a particular service, by querying it with Psservice, and log the results in tab-delimited format. This will retrieve the following data in the log file: IP address, computer name, currently logged-on user, domain or workgroup to which the machine is joined, and the status of the service. The IP address is included even if the node is not pingable and can be treated as a key in most cases. The computer name is resolved with a DNS lookup on the IP address and then, if a NetBIOS name is found, it is switched to that name. Note that this could be blank if both methods fail. The currently logged-on user field should display data if the machine is NetBIOS-compatible and someone is currently logged on. However, if no one is logged on, it will be blank. Note that this logon name could be a domain account or a local account; there is no way to tell. The domain (or workgroup) to which the machine is joined is the domain (or workgroup) associated with the computer account, not the user account.

The status of the service can be any of seven possible values, as shown in Table 8-2.

*Table 8-2. Possible values for server status*

| Status | Description |
| --- | --- |
| UnPingable | The IP address does not respond |
| RUNNING | Service is running |
| STOPPED | Service is stopped |
| PENDING | Service is starting or stopping |
| Blank | Service does not exist |
| Access is Denied | Your account does not have minimal user-level rights to the box |
| The RPC server is unavailable | Computer is running Win9x,Win 3.x, or is a Samba box |

There are several items you will need before the script will run. First, you need the Psservice utility that comes with the Pstools suite from *Sysinternals*. Place the *psservice.exe* utility in the same directory as the script itself. You also need to register the free System Scripting Runtime COM object from *Netal* (*http://www.netal.com/ssr.htm*). To register the COM object,

copy the DLL to your system32 directory and use *regsvr32* to register it.
You'll need to do this for every box you run the script from, but this does
*not* need to be done on the remote machines. By the way, I highly suggest
reading through the documentation on both of these valuable pieces of
software.

## The Code

Type the following script into Notepad (with Word Wrap disabled) and
save as *FindNTService.vbs*. Alternatively, since this is a long one, you're
probably better off downloading the source from *http://www.oreilly.com/
catalog/winsvrhks/*.

```
' Dennis Abbott - speckled_trout@hotmail.com
' you need to register the Scripting System Runtime from www.netal.com in
' your System32 directory on the machine you are running this script from
' first.
' You also need the utility psservice.exe from www.sysinternals.com in
' the same directory as this script and you need a text file with the
' subnets listed with a linefeed after each subnet.
'
' example of subnet listing
'
' 192.168.0.0
' 192.168.1.0
' 34.54.78.0
'
' You can view the script in action by opening the log file with a
' realtime log file viewer such as SMS Trace from Mircosoft.
'
'On Error Resume Next
Option Explicit
Dim Title  'used for dialog boxes as well as the log file name
Dim PathToScript  'path to the directory that the script is running from
Dim PathToLogFile  'full path including filename of the log file
Dim WshShell  'shell object
Dim WshNet  'network object
Dim WshFso  'file system object
Dim WshSysEnv  'environment variable object
Dim ScriptNet  'System Scripting Runtime object from www.netal.com
Dim ComSpec  'path to cmd.exe
Dim DataFile  'file containing machine names
Dim LogFile  'log file for stats
Dim CompName  'name of the current remote target computer
Dim User  'user logged on to remote computer
Dim Domain  'domain that the remote computer is joined to
Dim IP  'IP address of remote computer
Dim CurLine  'used when parsing text files
Dim NbtFile  'file parsed for NetBIOS information
Dim SubnetFileName  'file containing subnets to be searched
Dim I  'counter
```

```
Dim SysFolder   'the system folder
Dim TimeOut   'timeout in milliseconds for ping
Dim Go   'gives user option to quit
Dim ServiceToCheck 'name of the service to look for--NOT THE DISPLAY NAME
Dim EditSubnets   'give user option of editing subnet file
Dim File   'File object
Dim Subnet   'current subnet being searched
Dim Service   'Status of the service
Dim ServFile   'file parsed for the service information

Set WshShell = CreateObject("WScript.Shell")
Set WshFso = CreateObject("Scripting.FileSystemObject")
Set WshNet = CreateObject("WScript.Network")
Set ScriptNet = CreateObject("SScripting.IPNetwork")

SysFolder = WshFso.GetSpecialFolder(1)
PathToScript = Left(WScript.ScriptFullName, & _
(Len(WScript.ScriptFullName) - (Len(WScript.ScriptName) + 1)))
Title = "FindNTService"
Set WshSysEnv = WshShell.Environment("SYSTEM")
ComSpec = WshSysEnv("COMSPEC")
Timeout = 125

'collect input
Go = MsgBox("This utility will search the network by subnet to find " & _
"all machines running a particular service." & vbcrlf & _
"To do this you must supply a text file with the subnets and the name of " & _
"the service." & vbcrlf & vbcrlf & "Do you wish to continue?",vbyesno,Title)
Select Case Go
  Case VbYes
  Case VbNo Wscript.Quit(0)
End Select
If WshFso.FileExists(PathToScript & "\psservice.exe") <> True Then
  MsgBox "The PSSERVICE utility does not exist....GOODBYE" & vbcrlf & _
  "You can get PSSERVICE from www.sysinternals.com",vbok + vbcritical, _
  Title Wscript.Quit(0)
End If
If WshFso.FileExists(SysFolder & "\sscrrun.dll") <> True Then
  MsgBox "The sscrrun.dll does not exist....GOODBYE" & vbcrlf & "You can get
sscrrun.dll from www.netal.com",vbok + vbcritical, Title
  Wscript.Quit(0)
End If
ServiceToCheck = InputBox("enter the service name(not display name) that " & _
"you want to search for.",Title,"w3svc")
If ServiceToCheck = "" Then
  MsgBox "you did not enter a service name....GOODBYE",vbok + vbcritical,
Title
  Wscript.Quit(0)
End If
SubnetFileName = InputBox("enter the path to the file that contains " & _
"the subnets.",Title,PathToScript & "\subnets.txt")
If WshFso.FileExists(SubnetFileName) <> True Then
```

```
    MsgBox "The subnet file does not exist....GOODBYE", _
    vbok + vbcritical, Title
    Wscript.Quit(0)
 End If
 EditSubnets = MsgBox("Do you want to edit the subnets file?",vbyesno,Title)
 Select Case EditSubnets
    Case vbyes WshShell.Run "notepad " & SubnetFileName,1,True
    Case vbno
 End Select

 PathToLogFile = PathToScript & "\" & Title & "_" & Month(Now) & "_" &
 Day(Now) & "_" & Year(Now) & "-" & Hour(Now) & "_" &  Minute(Now) & ".log"
 Set LogFile = WshFso.CreateTextFile(PathToLogFile)
 Set File = WshFso.GetFile(SubnetFileName)
 Set DataFile = File.OpenAsTextStream(1,0)
 LogFile.WriteLine "IPaddress" & vbtab & "ComputerName" & vbtab & _
 "LoginName" & vbtab & "Domain" & vbtab & "Status"
 Do  While Not DataFile.AtEndOfStream
    Subnet = DataFile.ReadLine
    LogFile.WriteLine subnet & vbtab & vbtab & vbtab & vbtab & _
    "beginning subnet " & Now
    Discover(subnet)

 Loop
 MsgBox Title & " script is done.  The log file is located here." & _
 vbcrlf & PathToLogFile

 Function Discover(boundary)
    Subnet = Left(boundary,InstrRev(boundary,"."))
    For i = 1 to 254
        IP = subnet & i
        CompName = Null
        User = Null
        Domain = Null
        Curline = Null
        Service = Null
        If ScriptNet.Ping(ip,,,Timeout) <> 0 Then
            LogFile.WriteLine IP & vbtab & vbtab & vbtab & vbtab _
            & "UnPingableClient"
        Else
            CompName = ScriptNet.DNSlookup(IP)
            If InStr(CompName,".") <> 0 Then
                CompName = Left(CompName,InStr(CompName,".")-1)
            End If
            Call GetNBTstat(IP,User,Domain)
                        Call GetService(IP, Service)
            Call WriteToLog(IP,CompName,User,Domain,Service)
        End If
    Next
 End Function

 Function GetNBTstat(IP,User,Domain)
```

```
WshShell.Run ComSpec & " /c nbtstat -a " & IP & " >" & PathToScript & _
"\nbt.txt",6,True
Set NbtFile = WshFso.OpenTextFile(PathToScript & "\nbt.txt", 1, True)
Do While NbtFile.AtEndOfStream <> True
     CurLine = NbtFile.ReadLine
     If InStr(CurLine,"---") <> 0 Then
          CurLine = NbtFile.ReadLine
          CompName = Trim(Left(CurLine,InStr(CurLine,"<")-1))
     End If
     If InStr(CurLine,"<03>") <> 0 Then
          If Trim(Left(CurLine,InStr(CurLine,"<03>")-1)) <> _
          UCase(CompName) and Trim(Left(CurLine,InStr(CurLine,"<03>")-1)) <> _
          UCase(CompName) & "$" Then
               User = Trim(Left(CurLine,InStr(CurLine,"<03>")-1))
          End If
     End If
     If InStr(CurLine,"<1E>") <> 0 Then
          If Trim(Left(CurLine,InStr(CurLine,"<1E>")-1)) <> _
          UCase(CompName) and Trim(Left(CurLine,InStr(CurLine,"<1E>")-1)) <> _
          UCase(CompName) & "$" Then
               Domain = Trim(Left(CurLine,InStr(CurLine,"<1E>")-1))
          End If
     End If
Loop
     NbtFile.Close
End Function

Function GetService(IP,Service)
  If CompName <> "" and User <> "" or Domain <> "" Then
     WshShell.Run ComSpec & " /c " & PathToScript & "\psservice  \\" _
     & IP & " query " & Chr(34) & ServiceToCheck & Chr(34) & " >" _
     & PathToScript & "\service.txt",6,True
     Set ServFile = WshFso.OpenTextFile(PathToScript _
     & "\service.txt", 1, True)
     Do While ServFile.AtEndOfStream <> True
          CurLine = ServFile.ReadLine
          If InStr(CurLine,"STATE") <> 0 Then
               Service = Trim(Right(CurLine,InStr(CurLine," ")-1))
          End If
          If InStr(CurLine,"RPC") <> 0 Then
               Service = CurLine
          End If
          If InStr(CurLine,"Access") <> 0 Then
               Service = CurLine
          End If
          If InStr(CurLine,"function") <> 0 Then
               Service = CurLine
          End If
          If InStr(CurLine,"Unable") <> 0 Then
               Service = CurLine
          End If
     Loop
     If InStr(Service,vbcr) <> 0 Then
```

```
                    Service = Left(Service,InStr(Service,vbcr)-1)
            End If
        End If
End Function

Function WriteToLog(IP,CompName,User,Domain,Service)
    If IP <> "" Then
        LogFile.Write IP
    End If
    LogFile.Write vbtab
    If CompName <> "" Then
        LogFile.Write CompName
    End If
    LogFile.Write vbtab
    If User <> "" Then
        LogFile.Write User
    End If
    LogFile.Write vbtab
    If Domain <> "" Then
        LogFile.Write Domain
    End If
    LogFile.Write vbtab
    If Service <> "" Then
        LogFile.Write Service
    End If
    LogFile.WriteLine
End Function
```

## Running the Hack

First, create a text file that contains the subnets you wish to query. Each subnet should end with .0 and be on its own line in the file. You can name the file *subnets.txt* and save it in the same directory as the script. Now, simply run the script by double-clicking on it; it will prompt you for input. The first input is just an introduction to the script. Clicking No will exit the script altogether.

The next input is the name of the service; this is not the same as the display name, so be careful here. Table 8-3 shows some examples of services for which the display name differs greatly from the service name. This information can help you detect rogue web servers running secretly on your network, client machines whose antivirus software has been disabled, or machines with SMS client software disabled, making them difficult to keep updated with security patches and service packs.

Table 8-3. Display names and corresponding service names

| Display name | Service name |
| --- | --- |
| World Wide Web Publishing Service | w3svc |
| Norton Antivirus Client | Norton Antivirus Server |
| SMS Client Service | clisvc |

The next prompt is the full path to the text file that contains the subnets. At this point, you can enter a different text file if you wish. Lastly, you have the opportunity to modify the subnets file before you begin. The scan will begin either after you click No or after you close Notepad. You will be notified when the script is finished with a pointer to the log file; there is no progress indicator as the script runs. If you need to cancel the script, go into Task Manager and kill the *wscript.exe* process.

I have used this script to find machines on which the SMS Client Service has been disabled. I have also found numerous IIS web servers and their owners. Lastly, this utility does a great job of finding the FLC service, which is better known as the FunLove virus. I get a big kick out of sending directors a list of developer machines that have FunLove on their box, have also disabled SMS, and are not running antivirus software.

*Always* deploy this script in a lab environment first and do your own benchmarking before pinging those 32,000 nodes.

—*Dennis Abbott*

## HACK #74 Grant Administrative Access to a Domain Controller

Here's a hack that will help you secure any domain controllers you have running at a remote site.

Active Directory has introduced many new levels of complexity to server and security management. For example, if you would like to grant a remote site administrator the rights to install software or services on a domain controller, that person would have to be a domain administrator. Granting that person domain administrator rights introduces the possibility of that user creating new accounts with administrative rights. Obviously, this is not an ideal situation.

The following steps show how to grant a user the same level of rights as an administrator of a member server or a workstation on a domain controller, while preventing that user from having rights to Active Directory.

Please note that this hack does not eliminate all possible security risks, and the users who are granted these rights need to be highly trusted

1. Log onto a domain controller with full domain administrator rights. Make sure your Active Directory domain is in native mode.

2. Inside of Active Directory Users and Computers, create a global security group called DCAdmins. Add all users/groups that will need administrative access to the domain controllers to this group.

3. Create another global security group called DenyDCAdmins.

4. Add the DCAdmins group to the DenyDCAdmins group.

5. Inside of Active Directory Users and Computers, right-click on the domain name and choose Properties. Click on the Security tab (if the Security tab is not available, go to the View menu and choose Advanced).

6. Click on Add and choose the DenyDCAdmins group. Once the group has been selected, click on the Deny checkbox next to Full Control in the Permissions area, as shown in Figure 8-4.

Now, all users or groups that are members of the DCAdmins group have full administrative access to all domain controllers but do not have any access to Active Directory.

These users won't even be able to browse Active Directory to apply permissions on shares or files. It is generally a best practice for these users to have two accounts: one for administering the domain controllers and another for day-to-day use.

Overall, this is a great approach to limit security for remote administrators and operations teams that need to be able to make changes on domain controllers. I highly recommend trying this approach before blanketing your Active Directory environment with unnecessary domain administrators.

*—Tim Mintner*

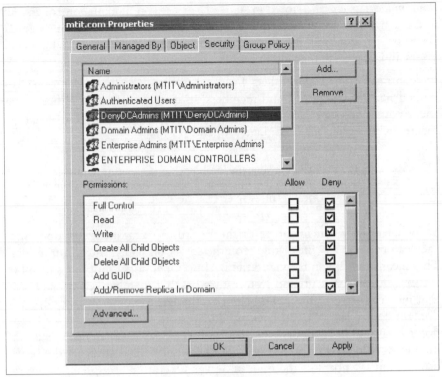

*Figure 8-4. Denying Full Control permission for the DenyDCAdmins global group*

## Secure Backups
### #75
Protect critical business information by restricting who can back up and restore it.

In a small organization, a single administrator might be responsible for backing up and restoring data stored on servers. In a large enterprise, however, it's more likely that administrative responsibilities will be delegated among various groups. Windows 2000 and Windows Server 2003 include special built-in groups for such purposes, but we'll also see how creating custom groups can give you even greater control over who can back up and restore your data.

### Using Backup Operators

There are actually two different Backup Operators groups in Windows 2000 and Windows Server 2003: a local group and a domain local group. What's the difference between local and domain local groups? *Local groups* are defined in the SAM database on a member server or workstation, while *domain local groups* are stored in Active Directory on domain controllers. As a result, member servers and workstations have a built-in local group named Backup Operators, and membership of this group is modified by using Local Users and Groups in the Computer Management console.

By contrast, domain controllers have a built-in domain local group also named Backup Operators, and membership in the group is modified using the Active Directory Users and Groups (ADUC) console (the group is located within the Built-in container for each domain).

In the GUI, the domain local Backup Operators group is actually labeled as "Built-in local" instead of "Built-in domain local." This is an error in the GUI.

So, what exactly can members of the Backup Operators group do? First, they can back up any file or folder on the server on which the group resides. This means that if you belong to the Backup Operators group on a member server, you can back up and restore files on that member server (and *only* that member server). But if you belong to the Backup Operators group on a domain controller, you can back up and restore files on *any* server in the domain. Backup Operators can also perform certain other tasks, such as interactively logging on to the console of the server and shutting the server down. And members of the built-in Server Operators group can do everything Backup Operators can, in addition to being able to create and manage shared folders and printers.

So, who belongs to the Backup Operators group? By default, nobody. The idea is that these users have a powerful ability—to make copies of sensitive business data and restore these copies to another machine—so you should think carefully before you make anyone a member of this group.

How do Backup Operators get these abilities? By the user rights assigned to them. *User rights* indicate authorization or privilege to perform some task and are assigned by using Group Policy (in an Active Directory environment) or Local Security Policy (on standalone servers in a workgroup). In a Group Policy Object (GPO), user rights are found under Computer Configuration → Windows Settings → Security Settings → Local Policies → User Rights Assignment (see Figure 8-5).

By default both the Backup Operators and Administrators built-in groups are assigned the following user rights:

- Back up files and directories
- Restore files and directories

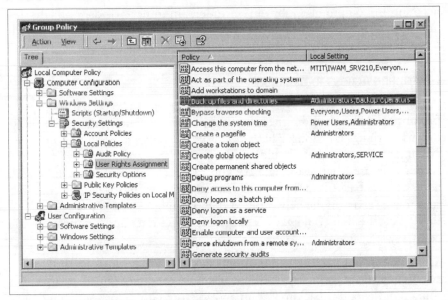

Figure 8-5. User rights displayed in Group Policy

Again, on a domain controller, the Server Operators group also has these rights by default. What's interesting about these two privileges is that they override any NTFS permissions that files and directories might have. Thus, even if the Backup Operators group is explicitly denied Read permission to a folder, members of this group can still back up the folder and its contents. In other words, user rights take precedence over permissions.

Mind you, there is a hack that enables a user to back up files and folders on a machine without assigning them the preceding rights. The trick is to assign them, at a minimum, the following special NTFS permissions on the file or folder:

- Traverse folder/execute file
- List folder/read data
- Read attributes
- Read extended attributes
- Read permissions

You might use this method to grant a user the ability to back up copies of sensitive documents to a local folder on his workstation. By assigning these permissions, users can back up the contents of the folder but can't read the files stored in it. The rational for using this approach, instead of assigning the necessary rights to the user, is that for security reasons you might want to ensure that the user has as few rights as possible, in case the user's account is compromised by an intruder. In other words, though this approach is more complicated, it can help guard against elevation of privilege attacks.

## Restricting Access to Backups

A company's disaster recovery plan often overlooks the fact that those who perform backups shouldn't necessarily be the ones who restore from backups when things go wrong. That's because performing a backup is a routine administrative task that should be done regularly and delegated to some responsible user, but restoring a backup can actually provide the user with access to the backed-up data itself. For example, by restoring a backup job to a rogue server on the network and then running cracking tools locally on the server, the user could gain access to sensitive data and compromise the company's business.

The solution is to ignore the built-in Backup Operators group and create two new security groups instead. For instance, you might name them something mundane, like Backup Group and Restore Group, or something more creative if you prefer. Then, assign the right to "Back up files and directories" to Backup Group and "Restore files and directories" to Restore Group. Don't assign any other rights to these two groups.

Now, assign selected users to each group as desired. Typically, the membership of Backup Group is be more inclusive than Restore Group and should include both junior administrators (who have actual responsibility for day-to-day backups) and senior administrators (who can be there in a pinch if things go wrong). Of course, the junior administrators should not be members of the default Domain Admins group; if they are, they will automatically have the "Restore files and directories" privilege as well.

The Restore Group, however, should have only senior administrators—the most trusted members of your IT department—as members. Whether or not they are all domain administrators is another question; best practice suggests that membership in Domain Admins should be as highly restricted as possible, and potential members of this group should be carefully screened during your company's hiring process. If you think one bad apple spoils the bunch, wait till you see what one corrupt administrator can do to your business!

 If you assign the "Back up files and directories" right to a group and then find that a user who belongs to this group has difficulty backing up one or more volumes, check the disk quota restrictions on those volumes to ensure they aren't restricting the user from accessing those volumes.

Another approach you can use to secure your backups is to take advantage of a setting available on the Backup Job Information dialog box (see Figure 8-6). This dialog box appears after you start the Backup utility, select the volumes or folders you want to back up, and click the Start Backup button. By selecting the checkbox labeled "Allow only the owner and the Administrator access to the backup data," you configure permissions on the backup job so that only the individual who created the backup and the default administrator account can restore the backup.

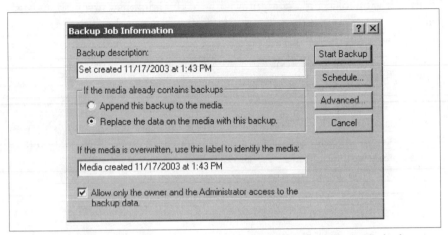

*Figure 8-6. Allowing only the backup owner and administrator to restore the backup*

While this approach is easier than the approach I described earlier, it doesn't provide the same level of security as separating those who can restore data from those who back it up. Also, you can enable this setting only if you are backing up to a new tape or overwriting an old one; if you're appending your backup set to an existing tape, the setting is not available. In other words, the restriction offered by this setting is applied on a tape-by-tape basis, not a job-by-job basis. So, the lesser degree of security offered by this approach, coupled with its lack of flexibility, leads me to suggest you avoid using this setting and instead use the two-group approach I described previously.

# HACK #76 Find Computers with Automatic logon Enabled

> Having automatic logon enabled on a computer can be a security risk. Here's a quick way to find out which machines on your network have automatic logon enabled.

While enabling automatic logon [Hack #4] in Chapter 1 can be useful in certain scenarios, such as a test network, it can also be a security risk, especially if it is enabled on a computer without the administrator's knowledge. Here is a quick and dirty way to locate all machines that have automatic logon enabled in their Registry.

You'll need the following tools:

- The *regfind.exe* utility, which is available from the Windows NT/2000 resource kits.

- A list of machines to search, which can be obtained in many different ways (including an SMS report, server manager, etc.). The list should be a plain text file named *serverlist.txt* in the following format:

```
server1
server2
server3
server4
etc...
```

- A user account that has administrative rights to the Registry on the machines being queried. Typically, a domain administrator account will work just fine.

Create a batch file that will use the provided list and kick off regfind. For this we will use the FOR DOS command (all on one line—text is wrapped here to fit the constraints of the page):

```
for /F %%A in (serverlist.txt) do (regfind.exe -m \\%%A -p "hkey_local_
machine\software\microsoft\windows nt\currentversion\winlogon" -n
"Autoadminlogon" >results.txt)
```

You can see that we are simply parsing the *serverlist.txt* file for each server name, then instructing regfind to locate that Registry key. There are two caveats, though. First, the results can be hard to read while the search is going on. It is recommended that you pipe the results to a text file (the preceding example does this). Second, regfind is case-sensitive. This can make the search a bit longer, but it's still fairly easy. Instead of just a one-line batch file, you simply have a few more (almost identical) lines. A larger sample of the completed batch file looks something like this (again, all on one line—beware of line wrap):

```
for /F %%A in (serverlist.txt) do (c:\work\adminlogon\regfind.exe -m \\%%A
-p "hkey_local_machine\software\microsoft\windows nt\currentversion\
winlogon" -n "Autoadminlogon" >results.txt)
for /F %%A in (serverlist.txt) do (c:\work\adminlogon\regfind.exe -m \\%%A
-p "hkey_local_machine\software\microsoft\windows nt\currentversion\
winlogon" -n "AutoadminLogon" >results.txt)
for /F %%A in (serverlist.txt) do (c:\work\adminlogon\regfind.exe -m \\%%A
-p "hkey_local_machine\software\microsoft\windows nt\currentversion\
winlogon" -n "AutoAdminlogon" >results.txt)
for /F %%A in (serverlist.txt) do (c:\work\adminlogon\regfind.exe -m \\%%A
-p "hkey_local_machine\software\microsoft\windows nt\currentversion\
winlogon" -n "AutoAdminLogon" >results.txt)
for /F %%A in (serverlist.txt) do (c:\work\adminlogon\regfind.exe -m \\%%A
-p "hkey_local_machine\software\microsoft\windows nt\currentversion\
winlogon" -n "autoAdminlogon" >results.txt)
for /F %%A in (serverlist.txt) do (c:\work\adminlogon\regfind.exe -m \\%%A
-p "hkey_local_machine\software\microsoft\windows nt\currentversion\
winlogon" -n "autoadminlogon" >results.txt)
for /F %%A in (serverlist.txt) do (c:\work\adminlogon\regfind.exe -m \\%%A
-p "hkey_local_machine\software\microsoft\windows nt\currentversion\
winlogon" -n "autoAdminLogon" >results.txt)
for /F %%A in (serverlist.txt) do (c:\work\adminlogon\regfind.exe -m \\%%A
-p "hkey_local_machine\software\microsoft\windows nt\currentversion\
winlogon" -n "autoadminLogon" >results.txt)
```

Using this method, you can scan a select list of workstations/servers for this key fairly quickly.

## Hacking the Hack

This procedure can easily be modified to find out other Registry keys as well, simply by changing the key name to search for. Enjoy!

—*Donnie Taylor*

## HACK #77 Security FAQ

Rod Trent, CEO of myITforum.com, shares his answers to common security questions.

At myITforum.com (*http://www.myitforum.com*), we often get questions regarding general network-security issues, and I try to answer them in the form of a Security FAQ. Here's a short selection of the most common questions we receive, along with my responses. You can find more security tips at myITforum.com.

### Steps to Computer Security

Q:   *What can I do to make sure my computer is secure?*

A:   It depends on whether you are a consumer or a business.

---

**Consumers.** Consumers should start by using an Internet firewall on all PCs and laptops. An Internet firewall can help prevent outsiders from getting to your computer through the Internet. If you use Windows XP, enable the built-in firewall feature on that platform. You should also update your computer regularly, either by using the Automatic Updates feature or by regularly visiting the Windows Update web site to download the latest Microsoft security updates. Also, make sure your antivirus software is up-to-date; installing, configuring and maintaining your antivirus software is absolutely essential.

**Businesses.** Businesses should follow a similar but more involved procedure. Start by verifying the configuration of your firewalls for both Internet and intranet. By auditing your firewall configurations, you ensure they comply with your company's security policy. Firewalls are your first line of defense, and best practice requires blocking all ports that are not actually being used by applications on your network. Business should also protect their networks by requiring employees to follow the precautions outlined by Microsoft (*http://www.microsoft.com/protect/*) on both their home PCs and laptops, especially if they use these machines to connect to your enterprise. PCs and laptops that VPN or RAS into your network must be protected by a properly configured firewall.

Businesses must also keep their systems up-to-date with the latest security patches from Microsoft. To do so, subscribe to Microsoft's free security notification service and use Microsoft update services to automatically obtain patches for your network, see "Microsoft Security Tools" [Hack #78] for more information. Finally, business should invest in antivirus software, because such protection is absolutely essential for keeping sensitive business data safe from attackers.

## Vulnerability Types

Q:  *What are the vulnerability types that I need to monitor against?*

A:  A: There are three basic types of vulnerability:

*Administrative vulnerability*
> The failure to observe administrative best practices, such as using a weak password or logging onto an account that has more user rights than the user requires to perform a specific task.

*Product vulnerability*
> A security-related bug in a product that is addressed by a security bulletin/hotfix or a service pack.

*Physical vulnerability*

The failure to provide physical security for a computer. Physical vulnerability can include leaving an unlocked workstation running in an area that is accessible to unauthorized users, leaving a server room unlocked or open, or losing a laptop or leaving it at a customer site.

## Strong Password Policy

Q: *What is the best practice to follow when creating policies for user passwords?*

A: Each company's security-level needs are different, but in general, strong passwords should be at least six characters long, should not contain all or part of the user's account name, and should contains at least three of the four following categories of characters: uppercase letters, lowercase letters, Base 10 digits, and nonalphanumeric symbols found on the keyboard, such as !, @, and #.

## How Microsoft Handles Security

Q: *Is there any documentation on how Microsoft handles security against worms and viruses?*

A: Yes. Microsoft has released a "Security at Microsoft" white paper on how they handle security issues (*http://www.microsoft.com/downloads/ details.aspx?FamilyID=73f1ba8e-a15c-4c05-be87-8d21b1372485*). This paper describes what Microsoft's Corporate Security Group does to prevent malicious or unauthorized use of digital assets at Microsoft. This asset protection takes place through a formal risk-management framework, risk-management processes, and clear organizational roles and responsibilities. The basis of the approach is recognition that risk is an inherent part of any environment and that risk should be proactively managed. The principles and techniques described in Microsoft's white paper can be employed to manage risk at any organization.

## Reporting Security Incidents to Microsoft

Q: *How can I report a security incident or vulnerability to Microsoft?*

A: If you have purchased Microsoft support, you should contact your Technical Account Manager (TAM). You can also use the web form at *https://s.microsoft.com/technet/security/bulletin/alertus.asp* to submit incidents and vulnerabilities.

## Reporting Security Incidents to Government Authorities

Q:   *We've just had a security incident. Who can I call to report it?*

A:   The FBI encourages the public to report any suspected violations of U.S. federal law. Never think that your security incident is insignificant. Your incident might be part of a larger attack or the beginning of a larger attack. You can find your local FBI Field Division information at *http://www.fbi.gov/contact/fo/fo.htm.*

## Getting Government Security Clearance

Q:   *How can you apply for security clearance for a government job?*

A:   In our daily newsletter at myITforum.com (*http://www.myitforum.com/newsletter.asp*), we sometimes post open positions for jobs in the government sector that require special security clearance before applying. Several folks have wondered what it takes to get the security clearance, and a list of good tidbits of information were posted to the myITforum.com Off-Topic list (*http://www.topica.com/lists/myOTforum/*). Here are some additional places you can find information on government security clearance:

> FBI Information Sheet
> *http://www.fbi.gov/clearance/securityclearance.htm*
> Security Clearance for IT Pros
> *http://www.jobcircle.com/career/coach/jf_2002_09.html*
> Security Clearances
> *http://www.taonline.com/securityclearances/*

> —Rod Trent

## Microsoft Security Tools

### #78

Here's a quick guide to various tools from Microsoft to help secure your systems against attack.

This list represents my personal take on the wide variety of security tools currently offered by Microsoft. It includes tools for security assessment, patch management, security scanning, system updating, lockdown, auditing, intrusion detection, virus protection, and system cleaning. There's also a brief list of RFCs that every security professional (including those who work with platforms other than Windows) should become familiar with.

I plan to update this list at myITforum.com (*http://www.myitforum.com*) as new items become available. If you have any suggestions to add to the list, drop me a note at *myITforum@cinci.rr.com.*

## Assessment, Patch Management, and Software Update Services and Tools

The Microsoft Baseline Security Analyzer (MBSA) (*http://www.microsoft. com/technet/security/tools/Tools/mbsahome.asp*) is a popular security tool that scans single systems or multiple systems across a network for common system misconfigurations and missing security updates.

Software Update Services (SUS) (*http://www.microsoft.com/windowsserver system/sus/default.mspx*) simplifies the process of keeping Windows-based systems up-to-date with the latest critical updates. See "Software Update Services FAQ" [Hack #89] in Chapter 9 for tips on using this tool.

QChain (*http://support.microsoft.com/default.aspx?scid=KB;EN-US;296861*) allows administrators to script the installation of several patches without requiring multiple reboots. To use this tool, you create a batch file to update your security configuration with hotfixes. Note that QChain is not required if you are running Windows 2000 Service Pack 3 or later, or more recent versions of Windows, such as XP and 2003.

Finally, the KB 824146 Scanning Tool (*http://support.microsoft.com/default. aspx?scid=kb;en-us;827363*) can be used to identify computers on networks that do not have the 823980 (MS03-026) and the 824146 (MS03-039) security patches installed.

## Automatic Scan and Update Tools for Windows and Office

To keep your operating system up-to-date with patches, use the Windows Update web site (*http://windowsupdate.microsoft.com*), which scans your computer and provides a selection of updates tailored for your operating system, software, and hardware. For updating Microsoft Office products, use the Microsoft Office Product Updates web site (*http://office.microsoft. com/officeupdate/default.aspx*).

## Lockdown, Auditing, and Intrusion Detection Tools

The IIS Web Server Lockdown Wizard (*http://www.microsoft.com/technet/ security/tools/tools/locktool.asp*) works by reducing the attack surface of Internet Information Services and includes URLScan to provide multiple layers of protection against attackers. Note that this tool is designed only for IIS 5 (Windows 2000); because IIS 6 (Windows Server 2003) has this functionality built into it, a download isn't necessary for that platform.

The UrlScan Security Tool (*http://www.microsoft.com/technet/security/tools/ tools/URLScan.asp*) helps prevent potentially harmful HTTP requests from reaching IIS web servers. This tool also is designed mainly for IIS 5, because much (but not all) of the functionality of UrlScan is built into IIS 6.

EventCombMT is available as part of the Security Guide Scripts Download (*http://www.microsoft.com/downloads/details.aspx?FamilyID=9989D151-5C55-4BD3-A9D2-B95A15C73E92*). This multithreaded tool parses event logs from many servers at the same time, which is highly useful for monitoring your event logs for signs of intrusion.

The Cipher Security Tool for Windows 2000 (*http://www.microsoft.com/technet/security/tools/tools/cipher.asp*) permanently overwrites deleted data on hard drives. It's basically a replacement for the cipher command used to manage the Encrypting File System (EFS) from the command line.

## Virus Protection and Cleaner Tools

The Office 2000 Update Service Pack 3 (*http://www.microsoft.com/downloads/details.aspx?FamilyID=5C011C70-47D0-4306-9FA4-8E92D36332FE*) includes the Outlook 2000 SR1 E-mail Security Update (OESU), which prevents users from accessing several potentially dangerous file types when sent as email attachments. It also increases the default security zone settings within Outlook.

The SQL Server 2000 Security Tools (*http://www.microsoft.com/downloads/details.aspx?FamilyId=9552D43B-04EB-4AF9-9E24-6CDE4D933600*) can help you determine whether your computer or environment is vulnerable to the Slammer worm.

## Top Security RFCs

Finally, here are some Request For Comment (RFC) documents that every security professional should become familiar with. These RFCs apply to any enterprise networking environment—pure Microsoft, mixed Windows/Unix, or pure Unix:

*RFC 2196 Site Security Handbook (ftp://ftp.rfc-editor.org/in-notes/rfc2196.txt)*
    Describes how to develop security policies and procedures for sites connected to the Internet

*RFC 2504 Users' Security Handbook (ftp://ftp.rfc-editor.org/in-notes/rfc2504.txt)*
    Similar to the Site Security Handbook, but designed for users.

*RFC 2350 Expectations for Computer Security Incident Response (ftp://ftp.rfc-editor.org/in-notes/rfc2350.txt)*
    Describes expectations for computer security incident response teams.

These RFCs are also worth skimming through:

*RFC2828 Internet Security Glossary (ftp://ftp.rfc-editor.org/in-notes/rfc2828.txt)*
  A glossary of security terms and abbreviations

*RFC 2577 FTP Security Considerations (ftp://ftp.rfc-editor.org/in-notes/rfc2577.txt)*
  A collection of tips on how to implement FTP servers securely

*RFC 3013 Recommended Internet Service Provider Security Services and Procedures (ftp://ftp.rfc-editor.org/in-notes/rfc3013.txt)*
  Describes expectations of security for ISPs

—Rod Trent and Mitch Tulloch

# CHAPTER NINE

# Patch Management
## Hacks 79–89

Patch management is a way of life for system administrators nowadays. With the proliferation of Internet worms and other threats, new patches are being released for Windows platforms on an almost weekly basis. Testing these patches and deploying them on production systems takes time and energy. Occasionally, something goes wrong and a patch designed to correct one problem actually creates another.

The first key to effective patch management is proper business practices: test, deploy, and verify. The second key is proper tools. Windows 2000 Windows Server 2003 come with built-in several tools, while others can be obtained from Microsoft's web site and third-party vendors. The third key is knowledge—knowing how patch-management tools work and how to troubleshoot them when things go wrong. The hacks in this chapter touch on all three keys to effective patch management and help enlarge your understanding and skills in this crucial area of a system administrator's job description.

### HACK #79 Best Practices for Patch Management

By understanding the different kinds of patches and following a simple regime, you can keep your critical systems free from known vulnerabilities.

Patch management is probably the biggest concern of IT departments these days. With new vulnerabilities being discovered almost every week, keeping systems up-to-date with patches is often a full-time job, especially in large enterprises. In addition, the lag time between when a vulnerability is discovered and when a virus or worm appears in the wild is now measured in weeks rather than months. This puts tremendous pressure on vendors to release patches before they've even been fully regression-tested. The result is that sometimes patches fix the problem they're designed to address but break something else unintentionally in the process. Customers often blame vendors in such circumstances but, let's face it, there's a war going on and, like most wars, it's messy.

## Patch Flavors

Before you plan a patch-management strategy, it's important to understand the differences between the various different flavors of patches. Microsoft classifies patches into three basic categories: hotfixes, roll-ups, and service packs.

**Hotfixes.** *Hotfixes* are small patches designed to fix a single problem and are developed either in response to a security advisory or by customer request. Hotfixes are typically issued either to plug security holes, such as buffer overflows, or to fix features that don't behave as intended. Not all patches are created equal; hotfixes that address broken functionality are developed by Quick Fix Engineering (QFE) teams at Microsoft Product Support Services (PSS), whereas those that address security vulnerabilities are identified and developed by the Microsoft Security Resource Center (MSRC).

**Roll-ups.** Occasionally, Microsoft combines several hotfixes together into a single package called a *roll-up*. This is typically done when several security issues have been identified within a short time interval, and its purpose is to simplify the job of installing hotfixes for administrators. Unfortunately, this is not always a good idea. There have been instances in which installing multiple patches broke applications, and the headache then arises: figuring out which patch in the roll-up actually caused the problem.

**Service packs.** At pretty regular intervals, Microsoft combines all hotfixes issued for a platform into a single package called a *service pack*. These service packs are cumulative—for instance, Service Pack 3 includes all hotfixes issued both before and since Service Pack 2 appeared. While service packs undergo more thorough testing than individual hotfixes, there have nevertheless been a few instances in which a service pack caused new problems while solving others.

**MSRC Ratings System.** Hotfixes that address security vulnerabilities are also called *security fixes*, and the MSRC rates these according to a four-point scale from high to low. This is a useful scheme for administrators, because it allows them to decide which fixes should be applied as soon as possible and which can be deferred until later or even ignored. The ratings also refer to the types of vulnerabilities they guard against. An example of a *critical* issue might be a self-propagating Internet worm that can bring servers to their knees and wreak other kinds of havoc, while *important* means that your confidential business information might be at risk of being lost, stolen, or corrupted. *Moderate* means you have a properly configured firewall and are following good security practices, so you won't likely to be affected by this problem, though it's still possible. Finally, *low* means it would take a combination of a genius hacker and a totally negligent system administrator for this exploit to occur (but it's still remotely possible).

## Strategies for Patch Management

My own strategy for effective patch management can be summarized as *Policy*, *Process*, *Persistence* (PPP). Let me unravel this, along with some helpful recommendations from Microsoft.

**Policy.** The first step in developing a patch management strategy is to develop a policy that outlines the who, what, how, when, and why of patching your systems. That takes planning, and with administrators being as busy as they are these days, it's difficult to allocate time for proper planning. Still, planning is essential. My view is that the difference between planning and an ad hoc fix-it-when-it's-broke approach is the difference between peace of mind and success, and constant anxiety and a disaster waiting to happen.

It all boils down to being proactive instead of reactive. *Proactive* management anticipates problems in advance and develops policies to deal with them; *reactive* management adds layer upon layer of hastily thought-up solutions patched together using bits of string and glue. It's easy to see which approach will unravel in the event of a crisis. Once you have a patch-management policy in place (usually it's part of your overall security policy) and a notification arrives of a critical vulnerability in some product, you immediately know who will deal with it, which tools will be used to deploy the patch, whether it needs to be done sooner or later, and so on. For example, a simple element of a patch-management policy might be that critical or important patches should be applied immediately, while moderate or low patches should be submitted to a team member for further study. Another example is proactively scheduling a specific day of the week or month for installing patches (usually weekends, in case something breaks), as opposed to the drop-everything, the-sky-is-falling approach common in a reactive environment. Making a decision tree that addresses these issues ahead of time reduces anxiety and speeds response when the time comes to patch something.

**Process.** The detailed procedure you will use to respond to vulnerabilities and deploy patches should be explicit within your security policy. In this regard, we have some help from Microsoft, which recommends following a six-step process.

## 1. Notification

Information comes to you about a vulnerability, including a patch meant to eliminate it. Notification might be sent via email from the Microsoft Security Notification Service, a pop-up balloon when you're using Automatic Updates, a message displayed in the Software Update Services (SUS) web console, or some other method. It all depends on which tools you use to keep your systems patched and up-to-date (we'll summarize these tools in a moment).

## 2. Assessment

Based on the patch rating and the configuration of your systems, you need to decide which systems need the patch and how quickly they need to be patched to prevent an exploit. Obviously, having an accurate inventory of systems and applications running on your network is essential if you want to keep your network secure against intrusion.

## 3. Obtainment

How you get the patch you need depends on which patch-management tools you choose to deploy. In general, such tools range from completely manual (e.g., visiting the Windows Update web site) to almost entirely automatic (e.g., via Automatic Updates or SUS). Like everything in security, there is a tradeoff: the manual approach is slower, but it gives you more control.

## 4. Testing

Testing should always take place before you apply patches to production systems. Test your patches on a testbed network that simulates your production network. Remember that Microsoft can't test all possible effects of a patch before releasing it, because there are thousands of applications that can run on servers and millions of combinations of applications. So, make sure you test patches before deploying them, especially if you have custom code running on your machines. If you need a way to justify the cost of purchasing duplicate equipment for a testbed network, tell the boss it's like insurance.

## 5. Deployment

Deploy a patch only after you've thoroughly tested it. You are then ready to apply it, but do so carefully. Don't apply it to all your systems at once, just in case your testing process missed something. A good approach is to apply patches one at a time, testing your production servers after each patch is applied to make sure applications still function properly. That's the problem with security roll-ups: by combining several fixes into a single package, the probability of a patch going wrong and breaking something is multiplied. Again, it's a tradeoff: roll-ups speed up patch deployment but give you less control over the result. Fortunately, even a tool like Automatic Updates can be hacked to apply one patch at a time [Hack #86].

*6. Validation*

This final step in the process is often forgotten: making sure that the patch has actually been installed on the targeted systems. Fortunately, there are tools available to scan your network to see whether your systems are properly patched by looking for changes in the server's filesystem and Registry to verify that a patch has been installed properly (see "Beginners Guide to Enterprise Patch Management" [Hack #80])

> As far as notification is concerned, *never* install a patch that is attached to an email message purportedly sent to you by Microsoft. Microsoft doesn't send out patches by email (it sends out notification bulletins only). Such attachments are most likely spam or possibly even viruses, so don't open them!

**Persistence.**  Policies are useless and processes are futile unless you persist in applying them consistently. Network security requires constant vigilance, not just because of the new vulnerabilities and patches that appear almost daily, but also because new tools are constantly being developed to handle the growing problem of keeping systems patched. At the time of this writing, Microsoft's whole patch-management strategy is in a state of flux.

So, we are on the horns of a dilemma. If you assert that Microsoft is responsible for ensuring that Windows systems are patched and up-to-date, then you should agree that Microsoft should have the right to package their products with automatic patching turned-on, so that patches are downloaded and installed automatically whether or not administrators want them. However, most administrators won't agree to this, because they want to maintain control and don't trust Microsoft. In that case, you should agree that the administrators who deploy and configure Windows systems should be considered responsible for keeping them patched properly.

Unfortunately, incidents like the Slammer worm, which propagated using unpatched Microsoft SQL 2000 servers, clearly indicate that not all administrators act responsible when it comes to keeping their systems up-to-date with patches. To be fair, though, poorly patched systems are not always the fault of administrators; sometimes, they are the fault of tight-fisted CEOs who refuse to budget adequate funds for hiring IT staff or procuring patch-management tools and test systems.

The point is that if Microsoft can't control the patching process, then it's pushed back onto the users. And a few irresponsible users can wreak havoc on the systems of responsible ones through the flood of worm traffic they unleash through their unpatched systems. Responsible users then cry out, "Microsoft should stop this from happening!," when perhaps they should be suing the companies that don't keep their systems properly patched.

> I might add another *P* here for *Practice*. Once you've developed your patch-management policy, you should periodically have your staff practice the procedures so that the procedures become second nature. Mind you, with the number of patches coming out of Redmond these days, who needs to practice?

## Patch-Management Tools

Once you have a policy in place and have outlined a detailed process for handling patches, what tools can you use to deploy patches to your systems? Once again, various tradeoffs are involved, including power versus simplicity and risk versus control. Here's a quick summary of what's currently available from Microsoft.

**Windows Update.** The granddaddy of all patch-management tools, Windows Update is a web site (*http://windowsupdate.microsoft.com*) that allows users to scan their computers manually to see which hotfixes, roll-ups, or service packs need to be installed. Windows Update also offers add-ons and enhancements that Microsoft develops for Windows.

The advantage of this approach is that users have complete control over which patches are installed on their system. The disadvantages, however, are numerous. First, your computer must be connected to the Internet, which is where most threats come from. Second, you must have cookies enabled; there goes your privacy, some might say. Third, you must allow ActiveX controls to run, which is another potential source of vulnerability. Finally, you must be a member of the local administrators group when you use Windows Update. This one is serious; in a corporate environment, it means you have to give employees administrative privileges so that they can keep their machines up-to-date.

Clearly, Windows Update is suited only for small offices and home networks as a patch-management solution.

**Automatic Updates.** Starting with Service Pack 3 for Windows 2000, Microsoft includes a feature called Automatic Updates on all subsequent versions of Windows. This feature has some of the security weaknesses of the Windows Update approach—namely, your machines must be connected to the Internet and Internet Explorer must be configured to allow ActiveX controls to run. But on the plus side, Automatic Updates doesn't require that users have administrative privileges, as Windows Update does. The main advantage of Automatic Updates is that it enables systems to download new patches automatically when they become available on the Windows Update web site and install them according to a schedule the administrator can specify. For more information on how this tool works, see "Use Automatic Updates Effectively" **[Hack #86]**.

**Software Update Services (SUS).** The Software Update Services (SUS) tool is available as a free download from Microsoft and takes Automatic Updates several steps further. Instead of requiring each system to be connected to the Internet, SUS downloads and stores patches on one or more SUS servers, where administrators can review them and either approve or decline their installation. Client computers then have their Automatic Updates component configured to point toward the SUS servers instead of the Windows Update web site as the source for their patches. This approach has all the advantages of Automatic Updates, without the disadvantages of requiring every machine to be exposed to the Internet.

**SMS Software Update Services Feature Pack.** At the high end of things is Microsoft Systems Management Server (SMS), a powerful but complex tool for deploying, configuring, and maintaining large numbers of systems. The SUS Feature Pack enables SMS to leverage SUS technology to determine which systems need which patches, push the patches out and install them, and report the results. The Feature Pack gives you more granular control than SUS over which systems receive which patches, lets you build an inventory of installed patches for each system, has better reporting tools, and overcomes SUS's limitation of 15,000 client computers (though, in reality, SUS starts to become unmanageable around 5,000 clients). For further information, see *http://www.microsoft.com/smserver/downloads/20/featurepacks/suspack/*.

**Third-party tools.** Finally, there are a number of third-party patch-management tools available. GFI LANguard Network Security Scanner (N.S.S.) from GFI (*http://www.gfi.com/*) is a good one. In addition to identifying and deploying patches each system needs, N.S.S. can also scan for other vulnerabilities, such as weak password policies and ports that shouldn't be open, and inform you how to harden your systems better. There are also other patch-management systems available from third-party vendors; a quick search on Google will turn up several.

# Beginners Guide to Enterprise Patch Management

Here's another take on managing the patch-management cycle effectively in a large enterprise environment, written by an expert on the subject.

One of the most heated and wildly debated subjects in many organizations today is the subject of desktop security. When large IT organizations have an enterprise product like Systems Management Server (SMS) deployed, security teams usually push to the desktop teams the task of ensuring that the latest security updates released by Microsoft are installed. This means that the responsibility of ensuring that a high percentage of clients in the environment are patched rests on the shoulders of desktop support personnel members or SMS team members. In order to better distribute this responsibility, it's best to understand the functionality that can be extended in the following steps:

1. Identify vulnerable systems
2. Assess the business impact of patching
3. Package patches for distribution
4. Test patches
5. Evaluate successes and failures
6. Finish up

Before we discuss each of these steps in detail, if you are currently looking to evaluate which tools would be best for your organizations patch-management strategies, take a look at these helpful links from Microsoft's two heaviest hitters:

Patch Management Using Microsoft Software Update Services

*http://www.microsoft.com/technet/treeview/default.asp?url=/technet/itsolutions/msm/swdist/pmsusog.asp*

Patch Management Using Microsoft Systems Management Server

*http://www.microsoft.com/technet/treeview/default.asp?url=/technet/itsolutions/msm/swdist/pmsmsog.asp*

## Identifying Vulnerable Systems

SMS stands out from SUS the most in its ability to report on the current client state. In the past, SMS_DEF.MOF updates accomplished this by pulling data from the Registry in HKLM\SOFTWARE\Microsoft\Windows NT\CurrentVersion\HotFix and basing distributions on that data. However, with the advent of the SUS Feature Pack for SMS (SUSFP), this is no longer necessary. A more robust security hotfix and reporting mechanism can now be added to your infrastructure. Installed and missing updates are reported through normal SMS inventory, so collections and queries can be based on of this information. Microsoft also supplies a web-based reporting package with built-in reports to give high-level overviews of an organization's patch state. The job of an IT administrator to manage the environment will be significantly easier if she is able to view which updates are already installed and which are a priority to be deployed.

## Assessing the Business Impact of Patching

The business impact of patching is mostly comprised of developing patch distribution schedules and policies. Each company's needs are different and patch distribution should conform to those specific needs. Many desktop IT divisions let mandates from their security teams determine when and how patches should be deployed; generally, this causes more harm than good. Do your customers have schedules to meet as well? Shipping dates for when the product must be out the door? What if you send a package with 10 critical system updates to 100 workstations? Problems might occur through no fault of your own, no matter how much testing is done prior to deployment. Optimal success is gained by talking to your customer base to determine the best dates for distribution. If a major product order is being shipped on the 15th, you should probably wait until the 20th to send out updates.

What, then, guarantees the least amount of interruption to users, while still ensuring success? Most of the time, this is encapsulated in your company's workstation reboot policy. If most IT administrators had their druthers, every workstation would get restarted on a daily basis or the administrators would be allowed to force system restarts whenever they want to during distributions. But in the real world, especially for engineering or R&D-driven companies, this is not a reality. Even if you are using the SUS Feature Pack (SUSFP) to give your user base the ability to install their updates early, it is still difficult to manage workstations that might not get logged onto for weeks at a time or workstations that run test simulations and cannot get restarted even while a distribution is happening. There is no easy answer to this, and many different internal solutions have been developed by various organizations. If you are faced with this dilemma and are not able to use the built-in tools (such as the SUSFP), the best option is to speak with other members of the IT community in forums, newsgroups, or mailing lists and learn which methods they use to overcome this problem. However, it is crucial to keep two ideas in mind: the impact to your user base and whether the solution still ensures successful installation.

## Packaging Patches for Distribution

If your organization is already using the SMS SUS Feature Pack's patch-installation agent (i.e., the Distribute Software Updates Wizard functionality) for distribution, you can pretty much ignore this section because everything you need is already done for you. Microsoft has developed a common template in the SUSFP that consistently applies patches in a safe fashion, so the SMS administrator no longer needs to perform constant scripting. Most companies using SMS that have not made the transition to SUSFP to distribute patches haven't done so either because their organizations have either specific user-base needs (such as workstations in labs that might go long periods without being looked at) or a scattered hierarchy of sites and multiple administrators that would need to replicate the same settings repeatedly (this scenario introduces an increased possibility for human error, along with other issues).

If you decide to write your own package to suit your company's needs, make sure you perform the following major steps in your code repeatedly for each patch:

1. Determine if the patch is already present by checking for a Registry key's existence, file version, and so on. You'll spend a lot of time reading through Microsoft security bulletins to figure out which data to look for.

2. Detect which operating system your package is running on and install the correct version of that patch for each bulletin.

3. Verify successful installation by again checking for a Registry key's existence, file version, and so on. But this time you will need to code in failure messages (MIFs for SMS) and logging so that you can troubleshoot issues that might arise later.

4. QChain the patches. Many people forget to do this step.

This process is a simplified flow of what needs to be done for a solid patch-distribution package. It might look easy at first glance, but when you are dealing with over 15 hotfixes, the package size can grow quite considerably, and the time the administrator spends coding and working out bugs greatly increases as well. In the past, packages that do just these simple tasks have been known to grow to a few thousand lines of code!

It's easy to see why using the SUSFP Patch Installation agent would make an SMS administrators job easier, since these steps are already done. Proper hotfix command-line switches are really all you need to research.

## Testing Patches

Proper testing procedures should be at the foundation of every software distribution, regardless of weather they are hotfixes. Your company's client base might have any number of different configurations that could effect distribution. I won't discuss package testing in detail here, because entire books can be written on the subject, but I will add a couple of notes.

First, test the patch in its raw installer form from Microsoft to eliminate any chance of causing problems on the system. Next, when testing configurations on workstations that are designated for testing, do the majority of your tests via SMS once you are confident that the package functions correctly. Many problems can be uncovered when distributing via SMS. Because the majority of your enterprise will execute the installation in this method, the majority of your testing should mirror that use.

Also, note that there is *no substitute* for beta testers among your customer base. Not only will you get more feedback if a problem arises, but they are also using the tools that could be affected. Finally, base distributions on testing; don't base testing on distributions

## Evaluating Successes and Failures

Verifying that the client base is up-to-date after distribution might be the most important phase in this entire process. Managing the patch state in your enterprise will never be finished as long as there is person out there who is smarter than the Microsoft developers, which is why companies need to patch in the first place. Unfortunately, many organizations distribute an update and never look at reports to make sure that a high-enough percentage of machines are updated. If your infrastructure is functioning properly, the reporting methods you used earlier to identify vulnerable systems (such as the SUSFP) should show that the patch-installation state is higher after distribution. If this is not the case (if installations are failing but notifications of the failure are not sent back to the IT administrator), you will need to look into either your reporting mechanism or your packaging technique.

## Finishing Up

Thoroughness and attention to detail are the most important aspects to managing a company's patch state. Although there are many delivery machines (such as SMS) that can be used to apply patches to your workstations, the same basic premises should be followed throughout the entire process. Even in this heightened time of hacking, viruses, and worms, a solid patch-management process and attentive IT administration can avoid almost any vulnerability by actively keeping workstations' patch state updated.

Do some research on Microsoft patch release dates and virus/worm release dates. You'll find that in almost every instance a patch has been released far ahead of time. When administrators fail to apply these updates, frantic patching is often required when an attack happens. Do you and your customers a favor: avoid these emergencies by having a stable enterprise patch-management solution in place.

## See Also

Here is a brief list of useful links on different aspects of enterprise patch management:

- Security bulletin email notifications (*http://www.microsoft.com/security/ security_bulletins/decision.asp*)
- White paper on improving patch management (*http://www.microsoft. com/security/whitepapers/patch_management.asp*)
- Security policy, assessment, and vulnerability analysis (*http://www. microsoft.com/technet/treeview/?url=/technet/security/topics/assess/*)
- Choosing a security update management solution (*http://www.microsoft. com/windows2000/windowsupdate/sus/suschoosing.asp*)
- How the SMS Software Update Services Feature Pack works (*http:// www.microsoft.com/smserver/techinfo/administration/20/using/ suspackhowto.asp*)
- Windows patch-management tools (*http://www.nwfusion.com/reviews/ 2003/0303patchrev.html*)
- BigFix (*http://www.bigfix.com/web site/index.html*)
- Shavlik (*http://www.shavlik.com*)

—*Richard Threlkeld*

## Patch-Management FAQ
#81 Rod Trent of myITforum.com shares his answers to some frequently asked questions on the subject of patch management.

As CEO of myITforum.com (*http://www.myitforum.com*) and author of white papers and articles on patch management, I frequently get questions on different technical aspects of deploying patches for Microsoft platforms. Here is a selection of some common questions and my answers. You can find additional entries in the Patch Management FAQ at myITforum.com.

## Downloadable Security Updates

Q: *Can hotfixes be downloaded from Microsoft without using Windows Update or SUS?*

A: You can download the hotfixes via the Windows Update Catalog, Tech-Net/Security Bulletin Search, and the Microsoft Download site.

To download them using the Windows Update Catalog, first add a Windows Update Catalog link to your Windows Update page. This gives you quick access to download updates manually from the Windows Update Catalog. Go to the Windows Update Web site (*http://windowsupdate.microsoft.com*) and click Personalize Windows Update. Then select the checkbox labeled "Display the link to the Windows Update Catalog under See Also" and click the Save Settings button.

To use the Microsoft TechNet/Security Search feature, simply go to *http://www.microsoft.com/technet/security/current.asp*.

Finally, you can download hotfixes from the Microsoft Download Center at *http://www.microsoft.com/downloads/*.

## Article and Bulletin Search

Q: *Where can I search for a specific Microsoft security bulletin?*

A: Use the HotFix & Security Bulletin Service at *http://www.microsoft.com/technet/security/current.asp*.

## Email Notification

Q: *How can I be notified when new security patches are available?*

A: You'll want to sign up for the Microsoft Security Notification Service at *http://www.microsoft.com/technet/security/bulletin/notify.asp*.

## Old Updates

Q: *I went to the original page to download some old updates, but they are no longer available to download. How can I access them?*

A: You can manually download and install them using the Windows Update Catalog. See *http://support.microsoft.com/?kbid=323166* for details.

## Updates for Older Operating Systems

Q:  *I can get updates from the Windows Update web site for Windows XP and Windows 2003. Where can I find updates for earlier operating systems?*

A:  To obtain updates for earlier operating systems, go to of the following links:

- Windows 2000 (*http://www.microsoft.com/windows2000/downloads/*)
- For Windows 98 (*http://www.microsoft.com/windows98/downloads/*)
- Windows 95 (*http://www.microsoft.com/windows95/downloads/*)
- Windows NT 4.0 (*http://www.microsoft.com/windowsnt/downloads/*)

## MBSA Support

Q:  *Is there a support forum specifically for Microsoft Baseline Security Analyzer (MBSA)?*

A:  Yes. Microsoft provides a newsgroup specifically for MBSA. It can be found on the *msnews.microsoft.com* news server in the *microsoft.public. security.baseline_analyzer* newsgroup. You can also access and interact with the newsgroup through the Google MBSA News Group Access interface at *http://groups.google.com/groups?hl=en&lr=&ie=UTF-8&safe=off&group=microsoft.public.security.baseline_analyzer.*

—Rod Trent

# HACK #82   Enumerate Installed Hotfixes

Here's a script you can use to list all hotfixes installed on a machine.

Ever wish you could quickly and easily look at a computer and find out which hotfixes were installed, when they were installed, and by whom? Here is a sample script that shows you how to accomplish this; if you know VBScript and WMI, you can customize it further as necessary. This script will enumerate the installed hotfixes on a computer and display the output in a message box.

The following items will be displayed about each installed patch: the name of the computer on which the hotfix is installed, the description of the hotfix, the hotfix ID, the installation date, and who installed the hotfix.

## The Code

Type the following code into Notepad (with Word Wrap disabled) and save it with a *.vbs* extension as *EnumerateHotfixes.vbs*:

```
strComputer = "."
Set objWMIService = GetObject("winmgmts:" _
& "{impersonationLevel=impersonate}!\\" & strComputer & "\root\cimv2")
Set colQuickFixes = objWMIService.ExecQuery _
("Select * from Win32_QuickFixEngineering")
For Each objQuickFix in colQuickFixes
Wscript.Echo "Computer: " & objQuickFix.CSName & vbCrlf &_
"Description: " & objQuickFix.Description & vbCrlf &_
"Hotfix ID: " & objQuickFix.HotFixID & vbCrlf &_
"Installation Date: " & objQuickFix.InstallDate & vbCrlf &_
"Installed By: " & objQuickFix.InstalledBy & vbCrlf
Next
```

## Running the Hack

Open a command prompt, change to the directory in which the script is located, and type cscript.exe  EnumerateHotfixes.vbs. Figure 9-1 shows sample output from running the script.

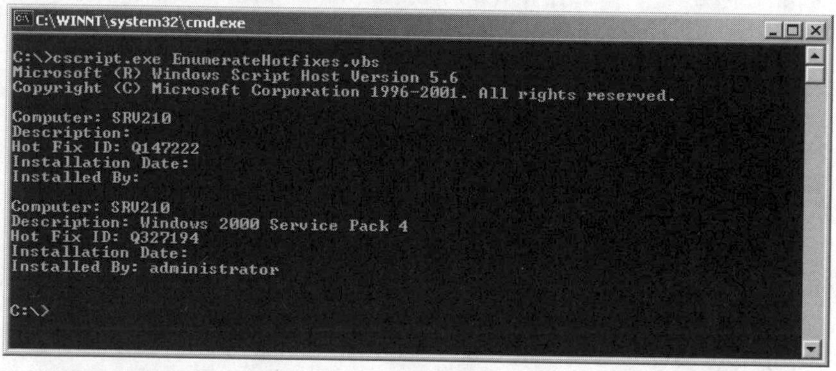

*Figure 9-1. Enumerating hotfixes on a Windows 2000 machine*

To ensure the script works properly, make sure you have the latest scripting engines on the workstation from which you run this script. You can download the latest scripting engines from the Microsoft Scripting home page (*http://msdn.microsoft.com/scripting/*). Also, since the script uses the Active Directory Services Interface (ADSI), you must have the same applicable rights you need to use the built-in administrative tools.

*—Hans Schefske*

### Apply Patches in the Correct Order

**#83** Deploying patches properly can sometimes mean applying them in the right order, as this experience can testify.

There is a specific order you should follow when applying Microsoft security patches. Microsoft's policy (a little understated) is that you need apply patches in the order in which they are released. Understanding Microsoft's naming convention for security patch releases is definitely critical for you to understand patch order. See the article at *http://www.myitforum.com/articles/20/view.asp?id=5891* to understand the security patch naming convention.

What could happen if you patch out of order? Microsoft's patches are released with the assumption you have a patch-management policy in place and that you have applied all patches to date. So, when they develop the next patch, they also assume that the system to which you will apply the latest patch release has the proper file versions.

If you apply the patches out of order, you can effectively overwrite a secure file. For example, say the RPC DCOM worm is patched by using MS03-026. If you have this patch, you will not be affected by the worm. But if you apply MS03-010 *after* you apply MS03-026, a secure DLL will be overwritten with an insecure one, reopening the vulnerability that MS03-026 patches.

Why would someone do this, you might ask? The RPC DCOM worm was something you couldn't get away from. The Department of Homeland Security issued warnings, Microsoft issued warnings, and the warning was blasted all over TV and Internet. This woke up a bunch of system administrators, so they patched with MS03-026. And, since they were patching, they might as well get the other patches they had missed up to that point, applying MS03-010 after the fact.

So, make sure that you are apply your patches in the order in which they are released. If you have some catching up to do, take the extra time to get it right!

—*Rod Trent*

### Windows Update FAQ

**#84** Rod Trent of myITforum.com shares his answers to some frequently asked questions regarding Windows Update.

Windows Update is a simple solution that can be used to keep individual systems up-to-date with patches released by Microsoft. Despite its simplicity, however, not everything about it is obvious and I often get questions about different aspects of how it works. Here is a selection of some of these questions and my answers. For more entries in the Windows Update FAQ, see my column at myITforum.com (*http://www.myitforum.com*).

## Windows Update Information Collection

Q: *I'm worried about privacy. What information does the Windows Update site collect when I access the site?*

A: Windows Update is committed to protecting your privacy. To provide you with the appropriate list of updates, Windows Update must collect a certain amount of configuration information from your computer. None of this configuration information can be used to identify you. This information includes the operating-system version number, Internet Explorer version number, version numbers of other software for which Windows Update provides updates, Plug and Play ID numbers of hardware devices, and Region and Language settings.

The configuration information collected is used *only* to determine the appropriate updates and to generate aggregate statistics. Windows Update does *not* collect your name, address, email address, or any other form of personally identifiable information.

Windows Update also collects the Product ID and Product Key to confirm that you are running a licensed copy of Windows. A licensed copy of Windows ensures that you will receive ongoing updates from Windows Update. The Product ID and Product Key are *not* retained beyond the end of the Windows Update session.

To provide you with the best possible service, Windows Update also tracks and records how many unique machines visit its site and whether the download and installation of specific updates succeeded or failed. In order to do this, the Windows operating system generates a Globally Unique Identifier (GUID) that is stored on your computer to uniquely identify it. The GUID does *not* contain any personally identifiable information and *cannot* be used to identify you. Windows Update records the GUID of the computer that attempted the download, the ID of the item that you attempted to download and install, and the configuration information listed previously.

## Personalizing Critical Updates

Q: *On the Windows Update web site, I'd rather not see certain updates, but the web site won't let me personalize them. Is something wrong?*

A: You cannot use the Personalize button to personalize Critical Updates. If you click Personalize, you will receive a message that states that the Critical Update section cannot be personalized. Sorry!

## Clearing the Secure Sockets Layer

Q: *Windows Update fails when I try to use it. What can I do?*

A: If the Windows Update site fails, one of the steps to fixing the problem is to clear the Secure Sockets Layer. Open Internet Explorer, on the Tools menu, click Internet Options, and then click the Content tab. Then, under Certificates, click Clear SSL State. Click OK when you receive the message that the SSL cache was successfully cleared.

Another thing to check is your firewall configuration; TCP port number 443 (*https*) needs to remain open for access to the Windows Update web site to work. To make sure this port is open, type *https://www.microsoft.com:443* in your web-browser address line and click Go. If you are unable to access the Microsoft web site by using this address, you need to open the port on the company firewall (or personal firewall, depending on your networking environment).

## Removing Items from Your Windows Update List

Q: *How do I remove items from the Product Catalog list?*

A: To personalize your available updates, you can remove items from the Product Catalog list on the Windows Update web site. First, connect to the Windows Update site (*http://windowsupdate.microsoft.com*) and click Product Updates. Then, click Personalize and clear the checkbox next to the items that you do not want to see listed in the Product Catalog. Click Update to save the changes.

## Changing Windows Update Schedule

Q: *I've tried to modify the schedule for updates, but as soon as the computer is rebooted, the settings revert back to the default.*

A: If you try to change the Critical Update Notification settings by using the Task Scheduler and restarting your computer, your changes will not be saved. This behavior occurs because, by design, you cannot modify or disable the Windows Critical Update Notification schedule through the Task Scheduler. Once the computer is rebooted, the Registry or local GPO settings reset the schedule.

## Manually Installing the Windows Update Controls

Q:   *What can I do if the ActiveX controls I downloaded and installed from the Windows Update site become corrupt?*

A:   You might need to install the controls manually. You can do this by downloading, extracting, and installing the controls from the Windows Update web site.

Where you obtain these controls depends on the version of Windows you have. For Windows 98 and ME, download the controls from *http://v4.windowsupdate.microsoft.com/cab/x86/ansi/iuctl.cab*. For Windows 2000, XP, or 2003, download the controls from *http://v4.windowsupdate.microsoft.com/cab/x86/unicode/iuctl.cab*.

After downloading the controls, save the *.cab* file to its own directory. Then, right-click on the *.cab* file and choose to extract the files. You can extract the files to the same directory you created to house the *.cab* file. Finally, right-click the *iuctl.inf* file and click Install.

—*Rod Trent*

### HACK  Obtain Updates via the Windows Update
### #85   Catalog

Whether you use it to download patches or driver updates, the Windows Update Catalog can be your friend.

The Windows Update Catalog provides a comprehensive list of updates that can be distributed over a corporate network. It is a one-stop location for Windows updates, fixes, and enhancements, as well as Designed for Windows Logo device drivers.

To obtain updates from the Windows Update Catalog, first select a category (see Figure 9-2). The Microsoft Windows category has updates and fixes for all Windows operating systems, from Windows 98 to Windows XP and the Windows Server 2003 family. The hardware drivers category provides you with driver updates for many of the devices on your network.

Now, set your search criteria to find the updates you need. Finally, download your selected updates to the location of your choice (e.g., your local hard drive, a server share on your network, or a disk).

Now, let's dig a little deeper into how to use the Catalog effectively.

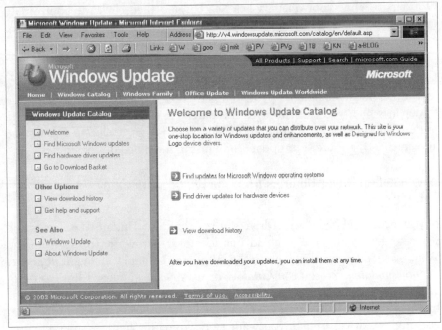

Figure 9-2. Downloading updates using the Windows Update Catalog

## Adding the Windows Update Catalog to Windows Update

One of the ways you can customize Windows Update is to add a link to the
Windows Update Catalog. This gives you quick access to download updates
manually from the Windows Update Catalog. First, go to the Windows
Update web site (*http://windowsupdate.microsoft.com*) and click Personalize
Windows Update. Now, click to select the "Display the link to the Win-
dows Update Catalog under See Also" checkbox. Finally, click Save Set-
tings. You now have a link to the Windows Update Catalog when you visit
Windows Update.

## Downloading Windows Updates from the Windows Update Catalog

To download updates for Windows for managed deployment in your organization, first go to the Windows Update Catalog at *http://v4.
windowsupdate.microsoft.com/catalog/*, or use the custom link you added to
your Windows Update page in the previous section. Then, click "Find
Microsoft Windows updates" or "Find updates for Microsoft Windows
operating systems." Click the appropriate operating system and language for
the update that you want to download, and then click Advanced Search

Options to refine your query. Click Search, and then click the appropriate category for the update you want to download (e.g., Updates and Service Packs) and locate the update. Click Add.

Repeat the previous steps to find and add additional updates to your download basket. Then, click "Go to download basket." In the "Type or browse to the download location of your choice" box, type the full path for the folder in which you want to save the patch, or click Browse to locate the folder. Click Download Now, and then click Accept to accept the license agreement. Distribute your updates and install them on your machines.

## Downloading Driver Updates from the Windows Update Catalog

If you need updated device drivers, the Windows Update Catalog is the place to get them. To download manufacturer hardware drivers from the Windows Update web site, go to the Windows Update Catalog at *http://v4. windowsupdate.microsoft.com/catalog/* or use the personalized link you created previously. Click "Find hardware driver updates" or "Find driver updates for hardware devices." Then, click the appropriate hardware category for the driver update you want to download. Click the manufacturer name, the operating system, the language, and any other items that you want to search for, and then click Search. Locate the driver you want, and then click Add.

Repeat the previous steps to find and add additional driver updates to your download basket and click "Go to download basket." In the Type or "browse to the download location of your choice" box, type the full path for the folder in which you want to save the patch, or click Browse to locate the folder. Click Download Now, and then click Accept to accept the license agreement.

You can now install the downloaded drivers or distribute them to machines that need them on your network.

*—Rod Trent*

## Use Automatic Updates Effectively

**#86**    Automatic Updates is an easy way to ensure that your Windows servers are properly patched against critical vulnerabilities, but there are some nuances to using it effectively.

The other day, a power blackout temporarily knocked out my company's servers. I should have tested the UPS more often, but you know how it is. Anyway, when the power came back on, the servers rebooted. I was sitting at the console of one of them, about to log on, when the server suddenly rebooted itself again. Virus? Disk problem? I stared at the screen, worried for a moment, and then suddenly realized: Automatic Updates! Whew!

Automatic Updates is a patch-management feature that replaces the earlier Critical Update Notification utility that you used to download from Microsoft's web site for Windows 98 or later. Microsoft first made Automatic Updates available for download for Windows 2000 systems running Service Pack 2. Later, when Service Pack 3 was released, Automatic Updates was included as a component of that service pack. Automatic Updates is also included on both the Windows Server 2003 and Windows XP platforms. Automatic updates lets administrators schedule the automatic downloading and installation of critical security updates from Microsoft's Windows Update web site, making it no longer necessary for administrators to use Windows Update to keep their systems patched manually.

## Using Automatic Updates

The way you configure Automatic Updates depends on your platform. On Windows Server 2003 and Windows XP Service Pack 1, use Control Panel → System and select the Automatic Updates tab. On Windows 2000 Service Pack 3 or later, use Control Panel → Automatic Updates.

Whichever platform you use, the configuration options are the same. Figure 9-3 shows the configuration options for Windows Server 2003.

The checkbox lets you enable or disable Automatic Updates on the machine. By default, Automatic Updates is enabled and the second option under Settings is selected. The three Settings options represent different levels of automation.

The first option—"Notify me before downloading any updates and notify me again before installing them on my computer"—is the least automated solution. Windows automatically checks the Windows Update web site for new updates shortly after system startup and every 22 hours thereafter (minus a random offset of up to 5 hours). If new updates are available for download, a notification message appears above the status area at the bottom right of the logged-on user's desktop. However, only administrators can download and install these updates.

If the second option—"Download the updates automatically and notify me when they are ready to be installed"—is selected, Windows automatically checks for new updates according to the scheduled described previously. But this time, if updates are found, they are automatically downloaded in the background. Once downloading is complete, a notification message asks if you want to install them.

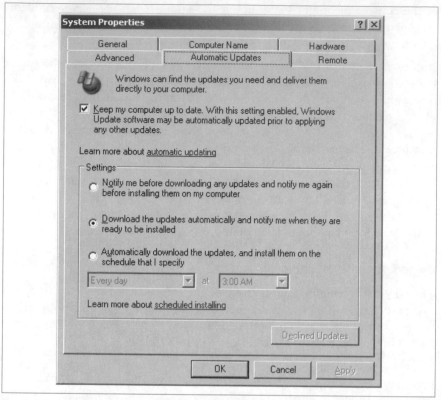

*Figure 9-3. Automatic Updates feature in Windows Server 2003*

The third option—"Automatically download the updates, and install them on the schedule that I specify"—is the most automated solution for keeping your system up-to-date with critical security patches. Windows still checks for new updates according to the previously described schedule, but it then allows you to schedule when downloaded updates should be automatically installed. You can schedule installation of updates every day or once a week at a time of your choosing (the default time, 3:00 a.m., is a good choice, because system and user activity is usually low then).

What actually happens when the scheduled time arrives depends. If a user is logged on at the scheduled installation time, a notification message gives the user five minutes to log off before installation starts. By default, the machine reboots when these five minutes are up, but this behavior can be changed by editing the Registry (we'll see how in a moment). On the other hand, if the user is an administrator, he has the option of declining installation until the next scheduled day and time. If no one is logged on to the machine, the updates are installed automatically and, if necessary, the machine reboots (this is usually the case). Finally, if the machine is down when the scheduled time occurs, installation of updates commences approximately one minute after the machine finishes booting (this time interval can also be changed only by editing the Registry).

If you choose one of the first two methods, a list of available updates is displayed and you can download and/or install only the updates you choose by deselecting the updates you want to decline. If you choose the third option, everything is automatic. Which approach is best? While keeping your systems up-to-date with the latest patches is important, there have been occasions when a patch has broken one feature while fixing another, resulting in systems freezing up or becoming unstable. On critical servers, it's probably best to download updates automatically but not install them until you've had a chance to install them on a test machine to ensure that no system problems or application incompatibilities result. We'll talk about how you can do this in a moment.

There's another reason for not using the fully automated option on critical servers: Microsoft sometimes releases multiple patches at a time, and if you install all of them and the machine becomes unstable, it's hard to trace which patch caused the problem. I suggest that when multiple patches become available and you've tested them, use the following hack to safely install them on your critical servers.

First, click the Automatic Updates notification icon in the status area and click Details to display a list of available updates, as shown in Figure 9-4. Deselect all the patches in the list except the one you want to install first. This will download and/or install only the selected patch (if you're installing updates that have already been downloaded, it will delete all other downloaded updates from your system). Note that the declined patches will not be displayed in future lists generated by Automatic Updates, but by clicking the Declined Updates button (see Figure 9-3 again) you can choose to have Windows notify you again about the updates you declined so you can download/install them later. Once you've installed the first update on your production system and verified it hasn't caused any negative effect, repeat the process to install the second update, third update, and so on.

The main downside of this hack is that your system might require extra reboots. The advantage is that it's safer and helps you pinpoint the source of any problems that arise. For more details on how to keep Windows systems patched and up-to-date, see "Best Practices for Patch Management" [Hack #79].

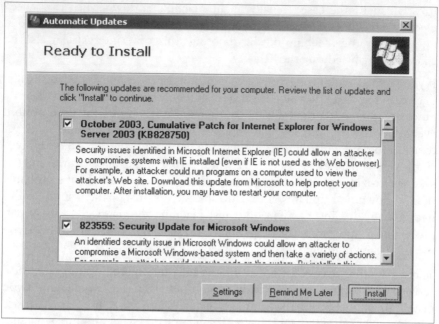

Figure 9-4. List of downloaded updates ready to be installed

 To remove an installed update that's causing problems, go to Control Panel → Add or Remove Programs → Change or Remove Programs and uninstall the offending update.

## Hacking Automatic Updates

While basic configuration of Automatic Updates is done through the GUI, you can tweak it further by hacking the Registry. This approach is useful mainly in a workgroup environment; to learn how to configure Automatic Updates in an Active Directory environment, see "Use Group Policy to Configure Automatic Updates" [Hack #87].

To configure Automatic Updates by hacking the Registry, run *regedit.exe* and find the following key:

    HKLM\Software\Policies\Microsoft\Windows

Under this key, add a subkey named WindowsUpdate, and under that key add a subkey named AU:

    HKLM\Software\Policies\Microsoft\Windows\WindowsUpdate\AU

Then, populate this key the following values and assign them data values as desired (all of them are of type Reg_DWORD). First, the NoAutoUpdate value determines whether Automatic Updates is enabled (0) or disabled (1) on your system. The AUOptions value then determines which of the three scheduling options is used: a value of 2 causes Windows to notify you before downloading updates, a value of 3 automatically downloads updates but notifies you before installing them, and a value of 4 automatically downloads and installs updates without user intervention.

The ScheduledInstallDay value determines the day on which downloaded updates are installed when AUOptions has a data value of 4. A value of 0 for ScheduledInstallDay means that downloaded updates are installed every day, while values 1 through 7 mean that updates are installed once a week on Sunday (1) through Saturday (7), respectively. The ScheduledInstallTime value determines the time on which downloaded updates are installed when AUOptions has a data value of 4. ScheduledInstallTime can have any integral data value from 0 through 23, representing the hours of midnight through 11 p.m., respectively.

The offset time, in minutes, that Automatic Updates waits after the computer restarts before it tries installing overdue updates is determined by RescheduleWaitTime and can range from 1 to 60 (1 is the default). The NoAutoRebootWithLoggedOnUsers value determines whether Automatic Updates is allowed to reboot (0) or prevented from rebooting (1) the machine to complete the installation of updates when a user is currently logged on to the machine. Note that if you set the value of NoAutoRebootWithLoggedOnUsers to 1, Automatic Updates won't be able to check the Windows Update site for new updates until the system is rebooted.

Finally, if UseWUServer is set to 1, the computer will obtain updates from an internal SUS server instead of from the Windows Update web site. Note that this value applies only when Software Update Services (SUS) is being used to deploy critical updates across your network.

Once you've made these Registry modifications, they won't take effect until you reboot your machine. After rebooting, if you try to configure Automatic Updates using the GUI, you'll see that all the options are grayed out, even if you're an administrator. Don't worry, though; just delete the HKLM\Software\Policies\Microsoft\Windows\WindowsUpdate key and its contents, reboot, and you'll again be able to configure Automatic Updates by using the GUI!

# #87 Use Group Policy to Configure Automatic Updates

Use Group Policy to simplify the configuration of Automatic Updates in an Active Directory environment.

Configuring Automatic Updates [Hack #86] is a lot of work if you have to do it separately on every machine on your network. Fortunately, in an Active Directory environment, you can use Group Policy to simplify the job.

First, open an existing Group Policy Object (GPO), such as the Default Domain Policy, or create a new GPO and link it to the appropriate domain, organizational unit (OU) or site. Then, add the *wuau.adm* template to the GPO so that the Group Policy settings for Automatic Updates will be added to your GPO. This is done as follows (note that these steps are unnecessary if you have Windows Server 2003). Begin by expanding Computer Configuration to show Administrative Templates. Then, right-click on Administrative Templates, select Add/Remove Template, click Add, select *wuau.adm* from the list of templates in the *%Windir%\Inf* folder, click Open, and then click Close.

Now, configure the GPO settings for Automatic Updates by expanding Computer Configuration → Administrative Templates → Windows Components and selecting Windows Update in the pane on the left, as shown in Figure 9-5.

Let's dig into what the various settings in Figure 9-5 mean. The first setting, "Configure Automatic Updates," lets you perform basic configuration of Automatic Updates for computers in the domain, OU, or site to which the GPO is linked. The options here are the same as the options available when you manually configure the feature using Control Panel's Automatic Updates utility (Windows 2000) or System utility (Windows Server 2003 and Windows XP); refer to Figure 9-3 for details. The next setting, "Specify intranet Microsoft update service location," applies only if you plan on using Software Update Services (SUS) to deploy updates.

The "Reschedule Automatic Updates schedule installations" option determines the time that Automatic Updates will wait after the computer restarts before installing updates that have already been downloaded and are past the scheduled time for installation. Value ranges from 1 to 60 (values are in minutes); the default is 1 if the setting is not configured and 5 when the policy is enabled. By *disabling* this policy, the installation of overdue updates is deferred until the next scheduled installation day and time.

Finally, "No auto-restart for scheduled Automatic Updates installations" determines whether the logged-on user will be forcibly logged off in order to

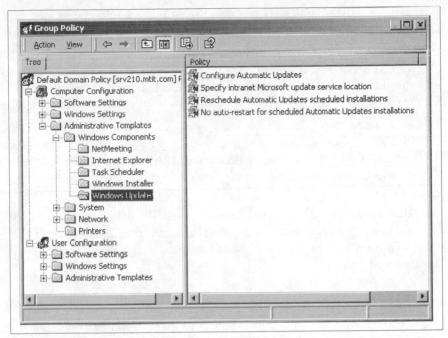

*Figure 9-5. Using Group Policy to configure Automatic Updates*

complete the installation process when a reboot is required. Enabling the policy means that machines will not be forcibly rebooted. While this would seem like a good idea (so users won't lose their work), it does have a downside: Automatic Updates won't be able to check the Windows Update web site for new updates until the machine is rebooted.

Enabling these policy settings will override any configuration of Automatic Updates that was done locally using Control Panel and will prevent you from making such changes locally, even as an administrator (the options in the properties sheet of Figure 9-3 would be grayed out). However, changing these policy settings back to Not Configured will restore the manual settings previously configured for Automatic Updates (though a reboot is required). And while changes made to these policies are automatically applied to client computers every 90 minutes (plus a random offset of up to 30 minutes), you can test the settings immediately by forcing a policy refresh with the command secedit /refreshpolicy machine_policy on Windows 2000 or gpupdate /force on Windows Server 2003.

## Some Recommendations

If you want to configure different Automatic Updates policies for different users or computers, either create multiple GPOs, link each to a different

OU, and place users and computers into these OUs accordingly, or filter the GPO settings to prevent their inheritance by specific users, computers, or groups.

You can also check the Security log in Event Viewer if you want to see whether the machine has been rebooted to install scheduled updates. Look for the following Event IDs:

*Event ID 21*

"Restart Required: To complete the installation of the following updates, the computer must be restarted. Until this computer has been restarted, Windows cannot search for or download new updates."

*Event ID 22*

"Restart Required: To complete the installation of the following updates, the computer will be restarted within five minutes. Until this computer has been restarted, Windows cannot search for or download new updates."

## Digging Deeper

There's another policy that controls how Automatic Updates works, but it's not found under Computer Configuration. Instead, it's found in User Configuration → Administrative Templates → Windows Components → Windows Update → "Remove access to use all Windows Update features."

This policy prevents the currently logged-on user from opening the Windows Update web site in Internet Explorer, in order to manually download and install updates on his machine. Actually, when you open *windowsupdate.microsoft.com*, an "Access Denied" page appears, explaining that a policy is preventing you from using the site. Enabling this policy also has the effect of preventing Automatic Updates from notifying users when new updates are ready to install. In other words, no notification icon will appear in the status area to inform you that updates are ready to install. Finally, even local administrators on the machine are affected by this policy! And domain administrators are affected too!

So, why would you want to use this policy? While it prevents users from visiting Windows Update or interacting with Windows Update, it *doesn't* prevent Automatic Updates from operating if the feature has been configured at the computer level by using the policies discussed in the previous section. This is because this setting is a per-user policy, not a per-machine one, so it affects only users; it doesn't affect configuration done at the machine level.

Enabling this policy might be a good idea, because it prevents users from trying to download and install updates on their own, even if they have administrative privileges.

> While this policy is present on Windows 2000, Microsoft says it works only on Windows XP and Windows Server 2003. But my own experience is that it also works on Windows 2000.

While this policy prevents users from using the Windows Update site, it still leaves the Windows Update icon in the Start menu, tempting users to explore and see what it does. You can remove this icon from the Start menu by enabling another policy: User Configuration → Administrative Templates → Start Menu & Taskbar → "Disable and remove links to Windows Update."

This removes even users' temptation to try to keep their machines up-to-date by themselves. Administrators would do well to use such policies and to explore similar restrictions on user activity provided by Group Policy.

 ## HACK #88  Automatic Updates FAQ

Rod Trent of myITforum.com shares his answers to some frequently asked questions about the Automatic Updates feature of Windows 2000/XP/2003.

As CEO of myITforum.com (*http://www.myitforum.com*), I often get technical questions about Automatic Updates and other Microsoft patch-management tools. Here are a few of the more common questions and my answers. You can find additional tips about using Automatic Updates at myITforum.com.

### Service Still Running After Disabling AutoUpdate

Q: *I've disabled Automatic Updates by going to* AutoUpdate *properties in the Control Panel, double-clicking System Properties, and then clicking the Automatic Updates tab. But the* AutoUpdate *service still runs. Can this be turned off?*

A: AutoUpdate is an always-on service. Disabling this service by accessing the properties disables only the client behavior.

## Disabling Critical Update Notification

**Q:** *How do I disable the Critical Update Notification feature of Automatic Updates?*

**A:** The Critical Update Notification is controlled through the Task Scheduler. If you want to disable the Critical Update notification but keep it installed on the computer, open the Task Scheduler and delete any tasks for Critical Update Notification.

For Windows XP and Windows 2003, scheduled tasks are accessed under Program Files → Accessories → System Tools → Scheduled Tasks. In Windows 2000, however, Task Scheduler is available under Settings → Control Panel → Scheduled Tasks.

## AU Overrides WU

**Q:** *If you use the Windows Update web site on a machine that has Automatic Updates enabled, what is the result?*

**A:** Automatic Updates might try to install updates, even though the Windows Update web site was used. Unfortunately, Automatic Updates is not smart enough to understand when you've decided to use Windows Update instead. When updates are downloaded via Automatic Updates, the download information is stored on the local computer, and this information doesn't change if an update is installed afterward.

Note that Automatic Updates will still display a message that updates are available. This will be fixed in a future version of Automatic Updates, but for now, install the Automatic Updates version of the update, so its installation records are updated correctly. The "you have updates" message will go away once the updates are installed using the Automatic Updates client.

—*Rod Trent*

<sup></sup>**H A C K**
# #89  Software Update Services FAQ

Rod Trent of myITforum.com shares his answers to some frequently asked questions regarding Software Update Services (SUS).

Software Update Services (SUS) is a free patch-management product you can download from Microsoft's web site (*http://www.microsoft.com/windowsserversystem/sus/*). SUS is an excellent solution for keeping small and mid-sized corporate networks up-to-date with patches released by Microsoft. For large enterprise networks, I recommend using Systems Management Server (SMS) as a complete solution.

Here are some common SUS questions and my answers. For more entries from the Software Update Services FAQ, search for "Software Update Services" at myITforum.com (*http://www.myitforum.com*).

## Operating System Support

Q:  *Which operating systems are supported under SUS?*

A:  SUS is supported on the following Microsoft Windows platforms:

> Microsoft Windows 2000 Professional (with SP2 or later)
> Microsoft Windows 2000 Server (with SP2 or later)
> Microsoft Windows 2000 Advanced Server (with SP2 or later)
> Microsoft Windows XP Professional
> Microsoft Windows XP Home Edition
> Microsoft Windows Server 2003

Older versions of Microsoft Windows, including 95, 98, NT, and ME, are not supported by SUS.

## Active Directory Support

Q:  *Is Active Directory required for SUS to work?*

A:  No, it's not required. However, SUS works well with Active Directory.

## Separating Workstations and Servers

Q:  *How can you approve different update lists for workstations and servers?*

A:  If you need different approved lists for workstations and servers, install two different SUS servers in your environment: one specifically for workstations and one just for servers.

## Control Panel Icon

Q:  *My Automatic Updates service is running in Services. But in Control Panel, there is no Automatic Updates icon. I am running Windows XP SP1.*

A:  Windows XP Automatic Updates is not available in the Control Panel. Instead, it has its own tab in My Computer Properties.

## Approving Updates After First Synchronization

**Q:**  *I just installed SUS and downloaded the horde of old updates. How do I handle these? Is there some way to remove them? Or do I need to approve them all?*

**A:**  Go ahead and approve all updates. If the computers already have the specific updates installed, they will ignore them. This allows you to put all old updates into the list of already approved updates so that you can filter them out.

## Downloading and Testing Updates

**Q:**  *I see the downloaded updates in the SUS\Content\Cabs directory, but how can I install a specific update for testing without knowing the Q-number associated with a bulletin?*

**A:**  Instead of spending a lot of time trying to associate a Q-number with the downloaded filename, use SUSAdmin to download the specific update you want. Simply open SUSAdmin by using the URL *http:// SUSServerName/SUSAdmin* and click the Approve Updates link. Locate the update you want to test and click the Details link. When the Details windows displays, click on the filename link. This downloads the update executable to your computer, where you can test the installation.

## Order of Updates

**Q:**  *Do I need to worry about patching out of order through SUS?*

**A:**  The installation is done on the client side (Automatic Updates) and there is no particular order enforced, but it should work correctly in whatever order the installs are done. The functionality of the old *qchain. exe* is built into the current *update.exe* that is used to install patches, and it is supposed to be smart enough to not overwrite newer binaries with older ones.

## Detecting Connection

**Q:**  *How can I tell if my system is connecting to the SUS server?*

**A:**  Check the SUS log file on your system, at *%systemroot%\Windows Update.log*.

## Knowing When the Server Is Synching

Q: *How do I know if my SUS server is synching?*

A: Open Task Manager and switch to the Processes tab. Locate a process called *WUSyncSvc.exe*. If your SUS server is currently synching updates, this process will be loaded and active. Also, the Software Update Services Synchronization Service will be started and running in the list of computer services.

## Cleaning the Updates Directory

Q: *I have uninstalled SUS due to a full hard drive, but the drive remains full. Is there something else I need to delete?*

A: SUS does not remove the synchronized updates during the uninstall. You'll need to remove the files located in the *SUS\Content\Cabs* directory manually.

## Modifying SUS IIS Rights

Q: *I modified the rights for the SUS and SUS\Content\Cabs folders and now clients cannot download updates. What should these rights be set to?*

A: Set anonymous access on the IIS root of the SUS server and give access to the Everyone group.

## Analyzing the SUS Log Files

Q: *Is there a tool/utility that can parse the SUS IIS log file and create any sort of readable report?*

A: There is a standalone SUS Reporting Utility tool you can use. An online version is located at *http://www.susserver.com/Software/SUSreporting/*.

## TimeExpire

Q: *Have you seen the following line in the patchinstall.log file when you send multiple security patches in the same package?*

```
TimeExpire: Sending Command1 message, CurrentTime = (14900746),
StartTime = (14879725)
```

A: This is not an error. It means that the countdown timer expired without the user selecting any option and the system is now taking the default action (reboot, install, or postpone). Entries before or after this line should shed more light as to what was done.

## SUS and Name-Resolution Issues

Q:  *The clients connect OK, and they receive notification that updates are ready to download. I then click the icon to receive a list of updates that are needed. When I click the "Start Download" button, the window disappears and nothing happens. Any ideas?*

A:  This particular issue is because a result of a name-resolution problem. Create an *LMHOST* file entry pointing to the SUS server. Then, the downloads and installations should proceed as expected.

## SUS Feedback

Q:  *Is there an email alias for submitting comments, suggestions, and requests for SUS directly to Microsoft?*

A:  Yes. You can email *cwufdbk@microsoft.com*. You might not receive a direct response, but Microsoft does monitor this mailbox.

*—Rod Trent*

# CHAPTER TEN

# Backup and Recovery
## Hacks 90–100

Backing up systems and configurations for services is your first line of defense against a disaster. Unfortunately, this is often more complicated than it sounds. Restoring an entire system from scratch is usually a complex and time-consuming procedure, and it is usually not necessary when only one component or feature has become corrupted or lost.

This chapter looks at the backup process and examines how to back up specific entities, such as your System State, certificate authority (CA) information, Encrypting File System (EFS) keys, and Distributed File System (DFS) namespace. We also look at how to back up something as simple as an individual file from the command line, to something as complicated as an entire system using the new Automated System Recover (ASR) feature of Windows Server 2003. Also included is a script that can be used to collect disaster recovery files and event logs from remote Windows 2000 servers.

We also map out procedures you can use to recover a failed system, short of restoring everything from backup, navigating through a maze of options (such as Safe Mode, Emergency Repair, Last Known Good Configuration, and the Recovery Console). Finally, we mention a few services you can call on when your worst nightmare happens and you need to recover your business data from a failed disk that has no backup.

## HACK #90 Collect Disaster Recovery Files

Use this handy script to gather emergency repair files and event logs from Windows 2000 servers on your network.

Collecting Emergency Repair (ER) files can be a tedious, time-consuming, and often forgotten task for Windows 2000 administrators. Usually, the lowest man on the totem pole gets this responsibility only after a server goes down, when the easy fix would have been to use the ER diskette but an updated ER diskette was unavailable, leaving the server down for hours. Management then begins searching for a GUI-based product that will collect ER files and simplify everyone's life. Companies like Aelita charge $99 per server to collect ER disks from a remote server and charge $599 per server to collect remote event logs. If you follow this hack, you'll learn how to script the collection of ER files and event logs from remote servers for free.

The script runs an update of the system's Emergency Repair files using *rdisk. exe*, uses the built-in *winmsd.exe* utility to save system information, and uses the following Microsoft Windows NT/2000 Server Resource Kit tools:

*srvinfo.exe*
> To collect more information about the system

*srvcheck.exe*
> To audit shares and security settings

*dumpel.exe*
> To save information from the system's event logs.

After it collects all this information, the script copies it to the repository server. If you schedule the script to run at least once a month, you'll have most of the information you need to restore the system in the event of a failure. In my environment, I run the script every Sunday evening.

When choosing a suitable repository server, make sure the machine has enough hard-drive space to hold all the disaster recovery files. I run this script against 70 servers and use 650 MB of space. An NT 4 server machine will use about 1.5 MB of space on your hard drive, and a Windows 2000 Server will use about 20 MB of space. If you can, run the script on a Windows 2000 machine, because using UNC path names are easier, *srvinfo.exe* will work properly, and the script can be scheduled to run under a different user account.

## The Code

There are four separate files you need for running this hack: *Disaster.bat*, *PassList.bat*, *ReadList.bat*, and *ServerList.txt*. Following is the code for each of them; instructions on how to customize them for your own environment are covered in the next section.

## Disaster.bat.

```
REM ************************
REM Author: David Jaffe
REM Runs Disaster Recovery Commands On Servers.
REM Version 1.1
REM Will Break Out NT 4 Servers From Windows 2000 Servers In Next Version
REM ************************

If "%OS%"=="Windows_NT" goto MAIN
If not"%OS%"=="Windows_NT" goto DOSEXIT

:MAIN
REM This copies ERD files from the target computer to a central repository

net use Q: \\%1\c$
c:\winnt\system32\xcopy.exe q:\winnt\repair\*.* e:\erd\%1\ /q /r /h /y
net use Q: /delete /y

REM Collect Services and Driver details plus more info about the server.
Writes the REM text file to the folder where the scirpt ran from.

winmsd \\%1 /a /f

REM Collects Basic Info about remote target. Writes a text file to the
folder where the scirpt ran from.

srvinfo -ns \\%1 >srvinfo.txt

REM Collects Shares and security settings. Writes a text file to the folder
where the scirpt ran from.

srvcheck \\%1 >shareinfo.txt

REM Collects all event logs and writes text files for each node. Writes the
REM text file to the folder where the scirpt ran from.

dumpel -f eventsys.txt -s \\%1 -l system
dumpel -f eventapp.txt -s \\%1 -l application
dumpel -f eventsec.txt -s \\%1 -l security

REM Copies and deletes all text files found in the folder the script ran
from.

REN serverlist.txt serverlist.doc
copy c:\erdscript\*.txt e:\erd\%1\
DEL  c:\erdscript\*.txt

:DOSEXIT
echo
echo This Program Requires NT 4 Or 2000 Server To Run
echo
```

### ReadList.bat.

```
REM Reads The ServerList.txt And Passes The Names to Passlist.bat

REN serverlist.doc serverlist.txt

for /F %%A in (c:\erdscript\serverlist.txt) do (call c:\erdscript\passlist.
bat %%A)
```

### PassList.bat.

```
REM Runs The Commands Listed In Disaster.bat Incremmentally On Each Machine
Listed In ServerText.txt
c:\erdscript\Disaster.bat %1
```

### ServerList.txt.

```
servernameA
servernameB
servernameC
servernameD
servernameE
and so on.......
```

## Running the Hack

To make the script work in your network, download the files from *http:// www.oreilly.com/catalog/winsvrhks/* (there is also an NT version of the scripts, if you still have NT servers running on your network and want to collect ER information from them as well) into a directory named *ERD-SCRIPT* on the repository server. Then, customize the code in each file as follows for your own networking environment.

**Disaster.bat.** Change all path statements to reflect where you want the disaster recovery files stored. The current script copies everything to e:\erd\ %computername% and locates all executables at c:\erdscript, so you should modify these according to your own environment.

**ReadList.bat.** The lines c:\erdscript\serverlist.txt and call c:\erdscript\ passlist.bat %%A should be changed to reflect the path and folder the files were unzipped to.

**PassList.bat.** The line c:\erdscript\Disaster.bat %1 should be changed to reflect the path and folder the files were unzipped to.

**ServerList.txt.** List all servers from which you want to collect disaster recovery files. Use one machine name per line.

## Conclusion

Using some basic scripting knowledge, you have protected your organization from extended down times and possibly thousands of dollars wasted on a GUI version of this script. Take a look at the following figures to see how you could increase your department's bottom line and take a step forward in your career:

Aelita ERDisk = $99.00
Aelita EventAdmin = $599.00


Total money spent on just 1 server = $698.00
Total money spent on 50 servers = $34,900.00
Total time spent implementing a free script = Half a day

The look on the boss's face when you ask for a raise and then present proof on how much money you just saved the company = priceless!

—*David Jaffe*

# HACK #91  Back Up Individual Files from the Command Line

You can't back up individual files using the ntbackup command, but there's a workaround.

The normal syntax of the ntbackup command in Windows 2000 and Windows Server 2003 lets you select specific folders to back up, but it doesn't let you select specific files. For example, to back up your *C:\data* folder as *D:\backups\031105.bkf* you would type the following at the command line (where /j indicates the descriptive name of the backup job and /f means we're backing up to file instead of to tape):

```
ntbackup backup C:\data /j "Nov 5 2003 backup of Data folder" /f D:\backups\
031105.bkf
```

But what if you want to back up an individual file in the \data folder but not the entire folder? This is easy to do using the GUI version of the Backup tool. Just start the tool, switch to the Backup tab (click Advanced Mode when the wizard starts in Windows Server 2003), expand the C: drive, select the \data folder, and check off the specific files you want to back up.

However, doing this from the command line presents a problem, because the syntax of ntbackup doesn't allow you to specify files. There is, however, a workaround: you can specify the names of the specific files you want to back up in a backup selection (*\*.bks*) file (also called a *script selection file*) and use the @ symbol to specify this file in your ntbackup command, as follows (where *filename*.bks is your backup selection file):

```
ntbackup backup @filename.bks /j "Nov 5 2003 backup of Data folder" /f D:\
backups\031105.bkf
```

The problem is, you can't create a *.bks* file from the command line; you have to do it from the GUI.

## Creating a .bks file

To create a *.bks* file using the Backup utility, you simply create a backup job with the selected files you want to back up and then save the job without actually running it. Then, you can copy the *.bks* file to another location and use ntbackup to back up the files from the command line.

For example, say the folder *C:\data* contains three files—*products.doc*, *sales. doc*, and *reports.doc*—and you want to back up only *products.doc* from the command line. Start the Backup utility (switch from the wizard to advanced mode in Windows Server 2003), expand the folder tree, and check the box beside *products.doc*, as shown in Figure 10-1.

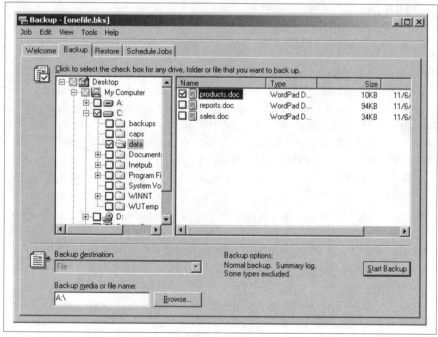

*Figure 10-1. Using Backup to create a backup selection file*

Now, simply select Jobs → Save Selections to create your *.bks* file (specifying a filename like *onefile.bks*), and close the Backup utility. By default, any *.bks* files you create are stored in your user profile in the *C:\Documents and Settings\username\Local Settings\Application Data\Microsoft\Windows NT\ NTBackup\Data* folder. To see this hidden folder in Windows Explorer, select Tools → Folder Options → View → "Show hidden files and folders."

When you open *onefile.bks* using Notepad, it contains one line of text:

```
C:\data\products.doc
```

Now, copy *onefile.bks* to a directory with a shorter path, like *C:\BKS*, since you don't want to have to type *C\Documents and Settings\...\Data* at the command line. Now you can back up the single file *products.doc* from the command line as follows:

```
ntbackup backup @C:\BKS\onefile.bks /j "Nov 5 2003 backup of Data folder" /f
D:\backups\031105.bkf
```

> Make sure you don't forget the @ sign before your *.bks* file; if you do, the backup will fail without warning (a backup-job file will be created, but you won't be able to restore from it). Also, be sure to enter the absolute path for the *.bks* file, because relative paths aren't supported.

## Hacking the .bks file

We've seen how easy it is to back up individual files using ntbackup, by first using the GUI Backup utility to create a *.bks* file. Once you've created such a file, it's easy to hack it using a text editor such as Notepad, because its syntax is easy to understand. In fact, its syntax is so simple you can simply create a *.txt* file containing the right information and then rename it with a *.bks* extension, instead of using Backup to create the *.bks* file first. In other words, it gets even easier!

Anyway, if we start with our existing file, *onefile.bks*, and later decide that we want to back up both the *products.doc* and *sales.doc* files, all we need to do is add a second line to the file, to make it read as follows:

```
C:\data\products.doc
C:\data\sales.doc
```

You can also use your *.bks* file to back up entire folders or volumes by adding their paths to the file, as follows (you should include the backslash at the end of your volume or folder):

```
E:\
F:\budgets\
```

You can also back up the System State information on your server by adding the following line (make sure there is no space between the words System and State):

    SystemState

You can also back up shared folders by specifying their UNC path:

    \\SERVER7\Docs

You can even back up a subfolder within a share (again, note the trailing backslash):

    \\SERVER7\Docs\Latest\

Finally, you can back up a volume or folder and exclude certain files or folders. For example, the following *.bks* file backs up the entire *C:\data* folder with the exception of *products.doc*:

    C:\data\
    C:\data\products.doc /exclude

Creating and customizing *.bks* files this way gives you a lot of flexibility for performing backups from the command line. Unfortunately, neither the ntbackup command nor *.bks* files support the use of wildcards. Perhaps we'll see that support in Longhorn (*http://msdn.microsoft.com/longhorn/*).

## Back Up System State on Remote Machines
### #92

Here's a hack that let's you use the Backup utility to perform a network backup of System State information on remote computers.

The term *System State* is used in Windows 2000 and later to describe various information used to boot, configure, and run the operating system. At a minimum, System State consists of the Registry, boot files, the COM+ class registration database, and any system files running under Windows File Protection. Servers might have additional System State information, depending on their role. For example, on a domain controller, System State also includes the Active Directory directory service database and the contents of the *SYSVOL* directory, but if the domain controller is also a DNS server, then System State includes the DS-integrated DNS zone data as well. And if a server is running IIS, then its System State normally includes the IIS metabase as well [Hack #54].

Backing up System State information is critical for recovery from a disaster, and using the Backup utility, it's easy to back up the System State of the local machine. From the GUI, simply start the utility (Accessories → System Tools → Backup), switch to Advanced Mode if your machine is running Windows Server 2003, switch to the Backup tab, select the checkbox labeled

System State (see Figure 10-2), and configure the remaining backup options as required. The usual practice is also to back up your boot and system volumes when you back up System State, to ensure you have enough information to recover your system after a disaster.

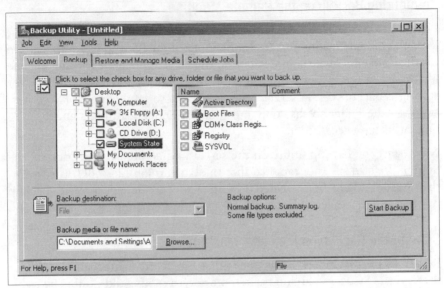

*Figure 10-2. Backing up System State on a domain controller*

Note that the checkboxes for the various components of System State are grayed out in Figure 10-2. This is because System State information is interdependent, so you can't back up or restore parts of it; you can restore the System State in its entirety only. After all, it would be useless to back up the directory service database if you didn't also back up Registry keys associated with the service!

Backing up System State from the command line is even simpler: just include the systemstate option in your ntbackup command. For example, to back up the System State data to file as *D:\backups\101103.bkf* using *10 November 2003* as the name for your backup job, type the following at a command prompt (or include it in a batch file):

```
ntbackup backup systemstate /j "10 November 2003" /f "D:\backups\101103.bkf"
```

The Windows help documentation says that the Backup utility (and its command-line equivalent, ntbackup) can be used only to back up the System State of the local computer. This is unfortunate, because backing up System State is critical for server-recovery purposes. It would be nice if you could back up System State for remote machines over the network, instead of having to do it locally on each server. Fortunately, there's a workaround you can use to accomplish this. It's a two-step process that involves configuring a backup job locally on the remote machine and then configuring a network backup to run from your local server that has the tape drive attached.

## Configuring Backup on the Remote Machine

First, go to the remote server whose System State you want to back up and log on as a domain administrator or member of the Backup Operators group for the domain. Create a new folder on the server and share it using a name like *Sysback*; this folder will be used as a temporary in-transit location for storing a backup of the server's System State, so configure NTFS permissions on the folder so that only members of Domain Admins and Backup Operators have access to it.

Now, start the Backup utility on the server and configure it to back up the System State to file (not tape) so that the backup-job file (*.bkf*) is saved in the *Sysback* share you created earlier. Choose the appropriate backup options and schedule the backup to occur at desired intervals.

## Configuring Backup on the Local Machine

Return to your local server (the one with the tape drive attached) and map a drive to the *Sysback* share on the remote server. You could do this by right-clicking on My Computer and selecting Map Network Drive, or you could do it from the command line using the net use command, whichever you prefer.

Now, start Backup on the local machine and configure it to include the mapped drive as part of your backup job. The mapped drive will be displayed in the Backup utility with a checkbox beside it; just select the checkbox to back it up. Finish configuring backup options and schedule your job to run at desired intervals. Now, when the backup job runs on the local machine, it will back up the System State of the remote machine as desired, provided you coordinate your schedules so that the backup job runs first on the remote machine.

Of course, you can also use ntbackup to configure your backup jobs from the command line, if desired. And if Terminal Services (*Remote Desktop* in Windows Server 2003) is running on the remote server, you could configure the remote job without actually having to walk over to where the remote machine resides.

## Evaluating This Approach

You may or may not want to use this approach to back up the System State of your remote servers. Local backups (using a tape drive attached to each server) certainly cost more in terms of hardware and are more work to administer, but they don't have the single point-of-failure problem that network backups (using a centralized backup server with attached tape drive) might experience. And while network backups can generate considerable network traffic, by scheduling backups to take place during off hours or by using a dedicated second LAN, you can minimize this issue. Like most decisions administrators have to make concerning their networks, it's a tradeoff.

By the way, this hack also shows that you can use the Backup utility to back up the Registry on remote computers—something else Windows help says you can't do!

## Back Up and Restore a Certificate Authority

Backing up your local Certificate Authority is essential, because it forms the foundation for public key cryptography (PKI) for your organization.

If you're thinking of using IPSec in an enterprise environment to encrypt virtual private network (VPN) communications for your remote users, or if you're considering securing email communications in your enterprise by encrypting messages and signing them digitally, then chances are you've thought of deploying your own local Certificate Authority (CA) by using the Certificate Services component of Windows 2000 and Windows Server 2003. The advantage of doing this using Certificate Services, instead of letting a public third-party organization issue and manage it, is that it costs nothing; you can issue, manage, renew, and revoke digital certificates for users throughout your enterprise for free. However, the hidden cost of doing this is that you need to know what you're doing. In particular, what if something goes wrong with the server that functions as your root CA? Proper backups are the key, but knowing how to restore in different situations is even more important.

At the heart of your certificate system is the root CA, which authorizes and validates all digital certificates issued by your enterprise. A small or mid-sized company will typically have only one CA, which functions as root CA and issues certificates for all users and systems on your network. A large enterprise might find this single-CA solution doesn't scale well enough and as a result might choose to deploy a hierarchy of CAs, with a single root CA at the top and one or more subordinate CAs underneath. In a CA hierarchy, the job of the root CA is simpler: to issue certificates for subordinate CAs, which then issue other certificates directly to users. In either case, the key to holding the whole situation together is your root CA. If it goes missing or becomes corrupt, then all the certificates issued by the hierarchy become invalid, because they can't be validated back to the root. So, protecting your root CA is protecting the heart of your network's whole system of encrypted communication and certificate-based authentication system.

## Backing Up a CA

The simplest way to back up your root CA is the most straightforward: simply use the Backup utility (System Tools → Accessories) and select the option to back up the System State of the machine. This will back up everything on the machine that is critical for restoring it, in case a disaster occurs and your root CA server is toast. Then, when you rebuild your server and restore the System State information from tape, your new server will now be the root CA for your enterprise and all the certificates that were previously issued by your old machine will still be valid.

To be safe, Microsoft generally recommends that you restore your root CA on a machine with hardware that is identical to your old machine. But the critical issue here is that your disk layout must be similar to the layout of the old machine, especially if you stored your certificate database and log files in a nonstandard location (by default, they are located in the *%SystemRoot%\ system32\CertLog* folder, but you can change this location when you install Certificate Services). You also have to make sure your new server has the same name as the old machine, because the name of a CA can't be changed after Certificate Services is installed. The name can no longer be changed, because the name of the machine is included within the root CA's own certificate, so changing its name would cause the whole certification-validation process to fail (for a similar reason, you can't change the domain membership of a CA either).

However, System State backups are useful only for recovering from a complete failure of your server, and other things might go wrong with your root CA, such as corruption of the certificate database or certificate log files, some unknown problem that prevents the Certificate Service from starting and requires you to reinstall this service, or the need to move your root CA to a different machine on your network (something you might not have considered). The reason for the last issue is that administrators sometimes don't consider the fact that a root CA is designed to last for years or, more likely, for decades. Once you've deployed a public key infrastructure (PKI) within your organization and started issuing certificates to users for encrypted messaging and secure communication, users become dependent on the transparency of the whole process from their own point of view. The last thing you want to do is build a nice, functional PKI system for your network and have to tear it all down someday and build another, all because you have to change which server hosts the role of root CA.

To prepare for the eventuality of recovering a corrupted root CA (which is still a functioning server, however) or moving the root CA role to another server, you need to perform a different kind of backup, one that backs up only what's essential for the machine to function in that role. Fortunately, Microsoft has made this easy by providing a Certification Authority Backup Wizard. Let's see how this wizard works and what it does.

## Certification Authority Backup Wizard

The Certification Authority Backup Wizard facilitates backing up key data found on your root CA, including the server's own digital certificate (called a *CA certificate*), its private key (used for generating digital signatures and decrypting encrypted information), the database and associated log files containing certificates previously issued by the server, and the queue of certificate requests still pending to be processed by the machine. This information is sufficient to restore your root CA if something is corrupted and the Certificate Service won't work. As we'll soon see, however, there's one additional piece of information you need to restore this data to a different machine.

To start the Certification Authority Backup Wizard, open the Certification Authority console under Administrative Tools. Then, right-click on the node that represents your root CA (or the subordinate CA you want to back up in a distributed enterprise scenario) and select All Tasks → Backup CA to start the wizard. The main screen of the wizard offers several choices, as shown in Figure 10-3.

The first time you back up your CA using this method, be sure to at least select the option to back up the private key and CA certificate for your CA. This will ensure that you can at least restore your CA in the event of an emergency, though if you do only this you will still have to reissue certificates to users. Therefore, in addition to backing up the private key and CA certificate, it's a good idea to also include in your backup the issued certificate log and pending certificate request queue for your server, which contains information about all certificates already issued by your CA and any requests from clients still pending. When you choose this option in the Certification Authority Backup Wizard screen (shown in Figure 10-3), you also have the option to perform an incremental backup of your CA, which makes a backup of only those changes to the certificate database since your last full backup.

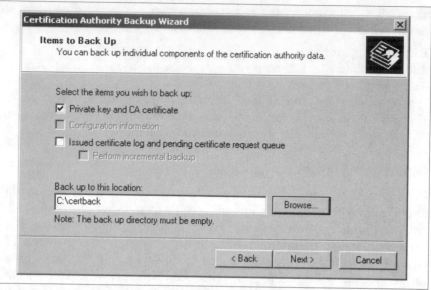

*Figure 10-3. Backing up key data for a CA*

This is trickier than it looks, so let's look deeper at the results of the backup process. If you choose only the first option, to back up the private key and CA certificate, and specify a folder such as *C:\certback* as the target for your backup, the result of the backup will be a file named *CA_Name.p12*, where *CA_ Name* is the name you specified for your CA when you installed the Certificate Service on the machine and the *.p12* file extension means the file uses standard PKCS #12 cryptographic syntax. Since you are required to specify a password later in the wizard, this backup file is itself secured by being password-protected. Best practice here is to choose a complex, difficult password to protect your backup, but make sure you don't forget the password; otherwise, you won't be able to restore your root CA later.

If you choose the other option, to back up the issued certificate log and pending certificate request queue, a subfolder named *Database* will be created in your *certback* folder. Inside this *Database* folder, copies of the certificate database files and certificate database log files for your CA will be created. The log files are basically transaction files that record changes made and pending to the database.

Now, let's say you backed up everything—private key, CA certificate, certificate log, and queue—on Monday, but on Thursday you processed a lot of certificate requests from users and now need to update the backup. There are two ways you could do this. First, you could simply back up everything again to a new (empty) folder and then discard your old backup—nice and simple. The other way (the way recommended by Microsoft) is to make an incremental backup of your certificate log and queue, but if you try to save your incremental backup in the *certback* folder, you get an error saying that you can make backups only to an empty folder. In this case, you might then create a subfolder under *certback*—perhaps a folder such as *certback\ 17Nov03*, which indicates the date you made your incremental backup— and then back up to this folder instead of *certback*. The result will be to create another folder named *DataBase*, this one located at *certback\17Nov03\ DataBase*. Within this folder, you'll find transaction logs but no database. Then, the following week, you can perform an incremental backup to a new folder named *certback\24Nov03*, and so on.

Now, should you ever need to restore your CA from backup, you have to restore the full backup first, followed by all your incremental backups, in order. That's a lot of work. See why you might want to just perform a full backup every time instead?

By the way, if you're wondering about the grayed-out "Configuration information" option in Figure 10-3, that option is used only for backing up a standalone CA (i.e., a CA installed on a standalone server in a workgroup environment). If you're working in an Active Directory environment (which is more likely), then the configuration information for your CA is stored in Active Directory and therefore doesn't need to be backed up separately like this. The nice thing in Windows Server 2003 is that this option is not even visible in the wizard when you're backing up an enterprise CA (i.e., a CA installed on a domain controller or member server in an Active Directory environment).

## Restoring a CA to a Working Server

If your root CA becomes corrupt or your Certificate Services fails to start but your server is otherwise working fine, you can use your previously created backup to restore the private key, root CA, certificate database, and transaction logs to their most recent working state. Just start the Certification Authority console in Administrative Tools, right-click on the root CA node, and select Restore CA to open the Certification Authority Restore Wizard, which is basically a mirror image of the Backup Wizard. If Certificate Services are running, they will be stopped temporarily to continue the restore. Select which components you want to restore, browse to locate the *.p12* backup file created earlier, and enter your password to begin the restore process. Once the restore is finished, Certificate Services will restart and you should have a working CA again for your organization.

What if it still doesn't work? In that case, you might have a corrupt metabase. Internet Information Services (IIS) is a supporting component for the CA web enrollment portion of Certificate Services, and if the IIS metabase becomes corrupt, your CA won't be able to process CA enrollment requests. The solution, once you've restored the CA, is to restore the metabase as well [Hack #54]. Once the metabase has been restored, you should be able to load the Certificate Services web pages and process certificate requests again.

If your root CA still doesn't work, your only solution might be to rebuild the machine from scratch and restore System State from tape backup media. This is a time-consuming process, but if your server is running Windows Server 2003, you might be able to speed the process by using the new Automated System Recovery [Hack #98] feature of that platform.

## Restoring a CA to a Different Server

While root CAs are intended to last decades for large organizations, the actual hardware platforms they run on become obsolete in time spans much shorter than the projected lifetime of the CA. As a result, you might someday find yourself wanting to move the role of root CA from an old machine to a more powerful new one. Leaving aside the problem of upgrading the operating system itself (who knows what version of Windows we'll be running ten years from now?), let's see now how to move the root CA role from one server to another, a process usually called *upgrading your CA*.

First, make a full backup of the private key, CA certificate, certificate database, and transaction logs by using the wizard-based method described earlier in this hack. The result of the backup process is a password-protected file named *CA_Name.p12* that contains the root CA's own certificate and private key, plus a *Database* folder that contains the database files and transaction logs. Then, back up the following Registry key on your old root CA:

```
HKLM\SYSTEM\CurrentControlSet\Services\CertSvc\Configuration\CA_Name
```

This key contains critical information about how Certificate Services are configured on your machine, and you will need this key to move your CA role to a different machine. Make sure you also make a note of the location where the certificate database and log files are located on your server. By default, they are both in the *%SystemRoot%\system32\CertLog* folder, but you might have placed them on a separate drive for increased performance when you installed Certificate Services on your old machine.

Next, you need to prepare your new server to host the role of root CA for your organization. Take the server off the network and rename it with the same name as the old root CA. This step is essential, because the name of the server is included in all certificates issued by the CA. So, in order for previously issued certificates to be validated, the new root CA must have the same name as the old one. While Windows Server 2003 now supports a process that lets you rename your domains and domain controllers, it's obviously simplest if you use a member server for your root CA, because member servers are easier to rename than domain controllers. Copy the *CA_Name.p12* file and *Database* folder from your old machine to a temporary folder somewhere on your new machine, and have the Registry key exported from the old machine ready for import as well.

Now, begin installing Certificate Services on your machine by using Add/Remove Windows Components (Control Panel → Add/Remove Programs). When prompted to specify which kind of CA you want to install (enterprise or standalone, root or subordinate), select "Advanced options" (Windows Server 2003 replaces "Advanced options" with "Use custom settings to generate the key pair and CA certificate instead," but everything else is similar) and click Next to display the Public and Private Key Pair screen of the Windows Components Wizard, as shown in Figure 10-4.

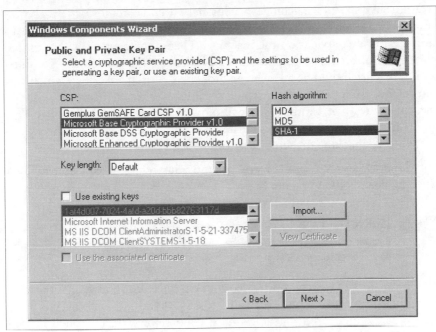

*Figure 10-4. Importing the backed up information from your old root CA*

Click the Import button, browse to locate the *CA_Name.p12* backup file on your server, and enter the password you specified when you backed up your old CA. Complete the remaining steps of the wizard, being sure to specify the same path for the certificate database and log files that you were using on your old CA. Then, restore your database and log files from backup discussed in the previous section. Finally, restore the Registry key you backed up on the old CA to your new CA.

Restart Certificate Services, and you should now have a working root CA running on new hardware that will last you five years? Three years? Who knows, the way hardware platforms are advancing these days. Just be sure to test your new root CA thoroughly in all its aspects (e.g., processing certificate requests, validating certificates, and renewing and revoking certificates) before finally decommissioning your old root CA!

## Decommissioning the Old CA

If you still want to use your old server for some other purpose on your network (as opposed to discarding it in the big blue bin behind your building), then you still have to do two things. First, you have to remove Certificate Services from it. But before you do this you need to remove the CA certificate and private key themselves, because you don't want them kicking around on some old machine on your network. To remove these cryptographic items, open a command prompt and type `certutil -shutdown` to stop Certificate Services on the machine. Then, type `certutil -key` to display a list of all cryptographic keys installed on the machine. Contained within this list should be a key named for the CA itself (*CA_Name*), which you can remove from the server by typing `certutil -delkey` *CA_Name* (enclose *CA_Name* in quotes if it contains spaces). Now you can use Add/Remove Programs in the Control Panel to uninstall Certificate Services, allowing you to use your old machine for some other purpose on your network.

But don't forget this second step: rename your server so it won't conflict with the new root CA on your network!

### HACK #94    Back Up EFS

Backing up EFS recovery keys is essential if you want to be able to recover encrypted documents after a disaster.

The Encrypting File System (EFS) lets you encrypt files so that unauthorized individuals can't read them. Normally, this is a good thing, because it helps secure data stored on a machine's hard drive. However, this hack is concerned with what happens when something goes wrong—for example, if a user's machine becomes toast, taking their EFS private key and certificate to Never-Never Land.

The key to being able to recover encrypted files when something goes wrong is having a designated recovery agent already in place. Then, if you lose your

EFS private key, the recovery agent can decrypt your encrypted files in an emergency. Every time you encrypt a file, EFS generates a unique File Encryption Key (FEK) that it uses to encrypt only that file. In other words, each encrypted file has its own unique FEK. In addition, the FEK is itself encrypted by using your own EFS public key and incorporated into the header of the file. Later, if you want to read the encrypted file, EFS automatically uses your EFS private key to decrypt the FEK for the file and then uses the FEK to decrypt the file itself. The FEK is thus used for both encrypting and decrypting the file (a process known as *symmetric encryption*), while your EFS public/private key pair is used for encrypting and decrypting the FEK (known as *asymmetric encryption*). This combination of symmetric (or *secret-key*) encryption and asymmetric (*public-key*) encryption is the basis of how EFS works.

But what happens if you lose your EFS private key? This might happen if your machine has two drives: a system drive (C:) and a data drive (D:), where encrypted files are stored. By default, your EFS keys are stored on your system drive, so if C: becomes corrupted, then the encrypted files on D: will be inaccessible, right? That's where the recovery agent comes in. Each time you encrypt a file, the FEK is encrypted with both your own EFS public key and the EFS public key of the recovery agent. That means that the recovery agent can always decrypt the FEK by using its EFS private key and thus decrypt the file when something goes wrong and your own private key is lost or corrupt.

What are these recovery agents? By default, on standalone Windows 2000 machines, the built-in local administrator account is designated as a recovery agent, so you can always log on as administrator and decrypt any encrypted files stored on the machine. You can add other users as recovery agents by using the Local Security Policy console, which you can open by using Start → Run → secpol.msc. Then, expand Security Settings → Public Key Policies → Encrypted Data Recovery Agents, right-click on that node, and select Add to start the Add Recovery Agent Wizard. Any user accounts that already have X.509v3 certificates on the machine can then be added as recovery agents.

On standalone Windows Server 2003 machines, the built-in administrator account is not a designated recovery agent. In fact, there are no default recovery agents in Windows Server 2003 in a workgroup environment. You must designate an account for this role.

In a domain environment, things are a little different. The built-in domain administrator account is the default recovery agent for all machines in the domain, and you can specify additional recovery agents by using Group Policy. Open the Group Policy Object (GPO) for the domain, OU, or site in which the intended recovery agent account resides, and navigate to Computer Configuration → Windows Settings → Security Settings → Public Key Policies → Encrypted Data Recovery Agents. Right-click on this node and select Add to start the same Add Recovery Agent Wizard as before, but this time browse the directory to locate the account you want to add.

Once Group Policy refreshes, your new recovery agent will be able to decrypt files encrypted by other users, but only if the users encrypt the file after the new recovery agent was designated. This is because files encrypted previously have no information about this new recovery agent in their headers and therefore can't be decrypted yet by the new recovery agent. Fortunately, if the user who encrypted a file simply opens and then closes the file, this alone is sufficient for EFS to add the new recovery agent to the encrypted file's header. The moral of the story is that you should think before you implement EFS, and designate recovery agents before you allow users to start encrypting files. Otherwise, you might find yourself sending out an unusual email to everyone saying, "Please open and then close all files you have encrypted on your machines" or something similar.

## Backing Up Encrypted Data and EFS Keys

Backing up files that have been encrypted using EFS is easy: simply use the Backup utility to back them up like any other files you would back up. What's really important is that you also back up the EFS certificate and public/private key pair for each user who stores data on the machine. Since EFS is implemented on a per-user basis, this means you have to back up this information for each user individually. However, this information is stored in the user profile for each user, which means that simply by backing up user profiles you also back up their EFS certificate and keys. More specifically, a user's EFS private key is stored in the \Application Data\Microsoft\ Crypto\RSA subfolder within that user's profile, while the user's EFS public key certificate and public key are stored in the \Application Data\Microsoft\ SystemCertificates\My Certificates\My folder under the subfolders \Certificates and \Keys.

You can back up users' EFS certificates and key pairs as part of your regular backup program and, if you have roaming user profiles configured, you can do this centrally from the file server where such profiles are stored. If you don't have roaming profiles implemented and users store important documents on their own machines, it might be necessary to have users back up their own profiles locally by using Backup to back up to file instead of tape. Unfortunately, this guards against profile corruption only, and it might not help if a disk failure causes the backed-up profile to be lost as well. A better alternative is to have users export their EFS certificate and private key to a floppy and have them store it somewhere safe. That way, if their system drive crashes, they can still decrypt information on their data drive by importing their previously exported EFS certificate and private key.

The steps to export a user's EFS certificate and private key are fortunately quite straightforward and can be done easily by any user. Simply open Internet Explorer, select Tools → Internet Options, switch to the Content tab, click the Certificates button, and select the Personal tab, as shown in Figure 10-5.

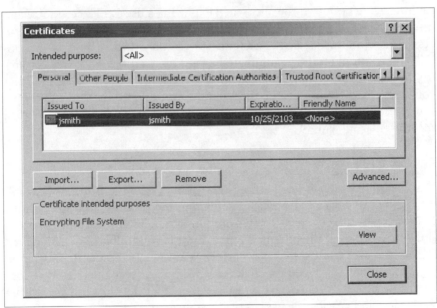

*Figure 10-5. Exporting the EFS certificate and private key for user jsmith*

Then, select the certificate you want to export (the correct certificate will display "Encrypting File System" beneath "Certificate intended purposes," near the bottom of the properties page) and click Export to begin the Certificate Export Wizard. Choose the option to include the user's private key in the export (the public key is automatically included in the certificate), specify a password to protect your export file, and choose a name and destination for your export file. As mentioned previously, users will typically export their EFS keys to a floppy, but you could burn them to a CD or even store them on a secure network share if you prefer. The important thing is, wherever you export this information, keep it safe so that no one except the user and trusted administrators can access it. Anyone who gets their hands on the export file and cracks the password can use it to decrypt any encrypted files they have access to.

The result of this export process will be a *.pfx file (called a *Personal Information Exchange file*), located in the target folder or media. Then, if the user's EFS keys later become corrupted and the need arises to reinstall these keys, this can be done either by repeating the previous process (but clicking Import instead of Export in Figure 10-5) or more simply by double-clicking on the .pfx file itself to start the Certificate Import Wizard. This wizard is smart enough to figure out that the EFS certificate and private key stored in the .pfx file should be imported into the user's personal certificate store.

An interesting option to consider when exporting a user's EFS certificate and private key is to delete the user's private key from his profile during the process. This option is labeled "Delete the private key if the export is successful" and is found on the penultimate page of the Certificate Export Wizard. If you choose this option, you'll be able to encrypt files by using EFS, but you won't be able to decrypt them unless you supply the private key on some medium—something that might be an option to consider in a high security environment.

## Restoring EFS Keys

If a user's EFS private key becomes corrupted or lost and the user hasn't backed up the key to a floppy as described in the previous section, then it's time for the recovery agent to step in. On a standalone machine, you can simply log on using the built-in administrator account, locate the encrypted folders the user can no longer access in Windows Explorer, right-click on each folder, select Properties, click Advanced, and clear the "Encrypt contents to secure data" checkbox for each folder. This decrypts the files within the folders and enables the user to read them again.

In a domain environment, you typically don't want to log on to a user's machine as a domain administrator and see a local user profile being created for your account as a result. Instead, simply instruct the user to use the Backup utility to back up to file any encrypted volumes or folders on her machine. The resulting backup file (*.bkf file) processes files it backs up as a data stream and preserves their encrypted status. Then, have the user copy her .bkf file to a network share where you as domain administrator can access the backup file, restore it to another folder, decrypt any files the user needs, and copy these files to the share where the user can access them.

While this is the most common solution, there's another approach that's worth considering: unite the user with his EFS keys again. Even if the user hasn't previously exported his keys to a floppy for safekeeping, chances are, in a domain environment, that you make regular backups of user's profiles (assuming roaming profiles are enabled). By simply restoring a user's profile from backup you restore his EFS certificate and keys, allowing him to read his encrypted files again. Then, tell him politely but firmly to immediately export his certificate and keys to a floppy, because you don't want to have to go through this again!

If EFS is being used to encrypt files on a file server where multiple users store their files, then this process can be complicated if you've designated different recovery agents for different groups of users. In particular, you might need to determine which recovery agents are designated for any encrypted files that users can no longer access. To do this, you can use the efsinfo command-line utility included in the Windows 2000 Server Resource Kit. This handy little utility can tell you who originally encrypted a file and who the designated recovery agents for the file are. Just type efsinfo /r /u filename, where filename includes the path to the encrypted file. Once you know any recovery agent for the file, you can proceed to decrypt it as shown previously.

What if the individual who can't access her encrypted files is your boss and she needs access to her files immediately? Export your own EFS certificate and private key to floppy as a domain administrator or other recovery agent, walk the floppy over to your boss's office, insert the floppy into her machine, import the certificate and private key, and decrypt her files. Then, delete the certificate and key from her machine. When she tries to encrypt a file again, a new EFS certificate and private key will automatically be generated. Smile, because you've acted like Superman, and send her an email later asking for a raise.

But what if your own EFS certificate and private key as domain administrator or recovery agent is lost or corrupt?

## Backing Up Recovery Agent Keys

Obviously, it's a good idea for administrators and other recovery agents to also make backup copies of their own EFS certificates and private keys. Otherwise, a point of failure exists in this whole recovery process and users' encrypted files could be lost forever and unrecoverable.

If you're operating in a workgroup environment, recall that the built-in local administrator account is the default recovery agent in Windows 2000. This means you have to back up the EFS certificate and private key of the administrator account, so log on to the machine using this account and use Start → Run → secpol to open Local Security Policy as before. Select the Encrypted Data Recovery Agents node under Public Key Policies in the left pane, right-click the EFS certificate in the right pane, and select All Tasks → Export to start the Certificate Export Wizard. Choose the option to export the private key as well, specify a password to protect the export file, and specify a name and destination for exporting the information—typically, some form of removable media, such as a floppy. Keep that floppy safe.

In a domain environment, the built-in domain administrator account is the default recovery agent and the EFS certificate and private key are located on the first domain controller in the domain (the one that created the domain when you ran dcpromo on it). Log onto this machine using that account, use Start → Run → dompol.msc to open the Domain Security Policy, select Encrypted Data Recovery Agents in the left pane, right-click the EFS certificate in the right pane, again select All Tasks → Export to start the Certificate Export Wizard, and proceed as before. If you are not given the option to export the private key, you might not be logged onto the right domain controller, so change machines and try again.

Another method for exporting certificates and keys is to use the Certificates snap-in. Open a blank MMC console, add this snap-in while logged on as administrator, expand Certificates - Current User → Personal → Certificates, and find the certificate you want to back up by looking under the Intended Purposes column, as shown in Figure 10-6. The power of this approach is that you can also use it to back up and restore other sorts of certificates and keys, including EFS keys.

Now that you've backed up your recovery agent's EFS certificate and keys, you're ready for the worst—unless your dog eats your floppy!

## Work with Shadow Copies

**#95**   Shadow copies are a new feature of Windows Server 2003 that lets you save point-in-time copies of your files—an excellent complement (but not a replacement) for your regular backup plan.

Windows Server 2003 includes a new feature called the Volume Shadow Copy Service (VSS) that can save administrators time when users are concerned. When shadow copies are enabled on an NTFS volume, Windows makes point-in-time shadow copies (or *snapshots*) of files on the volume at predefined intervals. Users can then access these shadow copies to recover accidentally deleted or overwritten files without requiring the administrator to intervene to restore these files from backup media. This feature also allows users to compare current versions of documents with previous

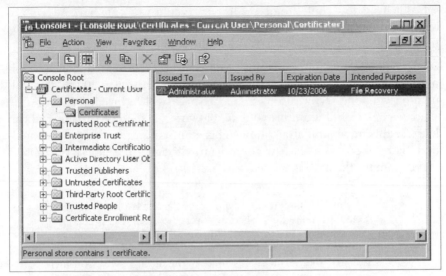

*Figure 10-6. Using the Certificates snap-in to back up a recovery agent key*

versions, to check for differences without requiring that users actually save separate versions of these documents along the way. Either way, administrators are freed from the hassle of responding to users' requests for restoring their files from backups, and any time gained nowadays for the harried network administrator is an asset.

On the other hand, implementing shadow copies on file servers is not a replacement for a regular backup program, because shadow copies are stored on disk in the same way the original files are stored. So, if a disk goes on your file server, it could mean that both the original files and shadow copies might be gone, depending on how you've configured your file server. Also, shadow copies are read-only copies and can't be edited directly. In fact, a shadow copy of a file isn't really a file at all; it's a block-by-block record of changes that were made to the file since the last shadow copy was made. So, to protect your business from data loss, be sure to combine shadow copies with regular tape backups using the Windows Backup utility or some third-party product.

## Implementing Shadow Copies

Like most successful IT initiatives, implementing shadow copies starts with good planning. Disk space considerations are a good place to start, since shadow copies require a minimum of 100 MB of free space for each volume on which you enable them. That minimum can also grow quickly, depending on how actively users modify their files and how aggressively you've scheduled shadow copies to occur. In fact, even if you only have a few kilo-bytes of files on your file server, the first time a shadow copy of a volume is made, it takes up the full 100 MB space allocated to this feature.

By default, the maximum amount of disk space used for shadowing a volume is 10% of the size of that volume. So, if you shadow a 20 GB data volume on your file server, up to 2 GB of space will be needed to store the shadow copies of files on this volume. However, if the need arises, you can increase this maximum at any time. This is important, because if the maximum is reached, then shadow copies start dropping the oldest versions to make room for the new.

If this 10% limit reminds you of the default settings for Recycle Bin, you're right. Shadow copies are designed to function as a kind of network-enabled recycle bin for your users. In other words, if you enable shadow copies on a volume, any shared folders on the volume automatically save point-in-time versions of documents in these shares. Actually, it would be nice if the Recycle Bin automatically did that locally as well. (Perhaps in Longhorn?)

One planning option to consider seriously is to store shadow copies on a different volume than the one where users' data files reside, preferably on a different physical drive as well. That way, you can plan separate disk-space needs for original files and their copies. However, many administrators don't realize that if you discover later that your shadow volume is insufficient and you want to move the shadow copies to a different volume, doing so causes you to lose all shadow copies of user files. Backing up the shadow volume in this case and restoring it to the new volume won't work, because VSS can't be configured manually to find its copies in a moved location. To work around this problem, you can store your shadow copies on a dynamic volume, which you can extend later by adding free disk space on the same drive or another drive.

Also remember that shadow copies are enabled on a per-volume basis. So, when you enable this feature on a data volume, all shared folders on that volume will have shadow copies created for files within them. This is an important issue that is usually not considered in the planning stage. In fact, this issue should actually be considered before you even set up your file server in the first place. In other words, to implement shadow copies effectively, you need to ensure that shared folders on your file server are grouped together appropriately onto separate volumes, according to the level of user activity for those shares. Group together shares within which users frequently modify files according to how often they modify them: high-activity shares on one volume, medium activity on another, low activity on a third. This will help you plan separate shadow-copy schedules for each volume: frequent copies for high-activity volumes and infrequent copies for low-activity volumes. If you are planning on upgrading your Windows 2000 file servers to Windows Server 2003, consider reorganizing the volumes and shares on your servers as part of the upgrade process.

Configuring shadow copies is basically a three-step process: configure it on the server, configure it on the client, and educate users how to use it. The last step is often forgotten from the IT perspective, because it's not strictly in the "techie" realm of things, but it's just as important as the other two steps. For increased security, shadow copies are disabled on all NTFS volumes until you enable them on the server. If you're logged on locally, the easiest way to enable shadow copies is to right-click on any volume, select Properties, switch to the Shadow Copies tab, select the volume on which you want to enable shadow copies, and click Enable (see Figure 10-7).

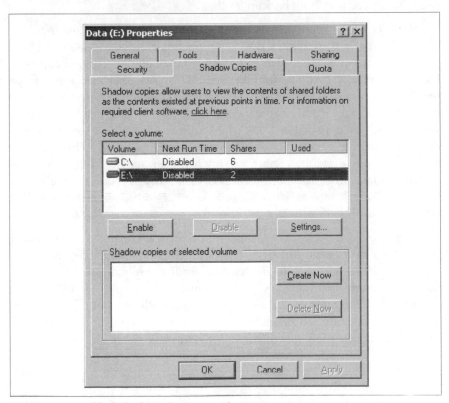

Figure 10-7. Enabling shadow copies on a volume

Actually, before you enable this feature on a volume, it's a good idea to first review the default settings for shadow copies by clicking on the Settings button shown in Figure 10-7. The default settings store the shadow copies on the same volume as the one you are enabling, use up to 10% of the volume to store copies, and make new shadow copies of files every weekday (Monday through Friday) at 7 a.m. and noon. The rationale behind the schedule is to save copies before users arrive at work (when they open their files) and around lunchtime (when they are halfway through their workday).

You can create almost any schedule you want for when shadow copies should occur, but avoid scheduling it to occur too often (e.g., once an hour), due to the excessive load it will place on your server. When planning your schedule, also remember that shadow copies will save a maximum of 64 different versions of a file before deleting older versions to make room for new versions. So, if you leave the default twice-a-day schedule in place, users will be able to restore a version up to 32 days old. Anything older than that you'll have to restore from backup for them.

Be sure to clearly communicate to users your schedule of when shadow copies will be made so that they don't rely on this feature excessively. Users should still consider themselves responsible for making versioned copies of files they work on and should view shadow copies only as a tool of last resort—just in case they accidentally delete a file or overwrite it—rather than something they'll use to save versions of their work. As administrator, you can also force a shadow copy to occur at any time; just select the volume and click the Create Now button shown in Figure 10-7. This can be a useful feature if there are certain times when user activity is high, such as year-end finalization of budgets. Instead of modifying your schedule, you could manually create an extra shadow copy or two during the days just before the deadline.

You might be wondering *where* shadow copies are stored on a volume. If you create a new 5,000 MB data volume E:, enable shadow copies on the volume, and click Create Now to generate shadow copies immediately (even though there are not files yet on your volume), then, when you select the E: drive in My Computer, you should see around 4,900 MB of free space. In other words, shadow copies immediately use the minimum 100 MB allocated to it the first time they operate. But your drive is still empty when you open it in Windows Explorer. If you use Tools → Folder Options → View to show hidden files and unhide hidden system files, you'll see a folder named System Volume Information that has System and Hidden attributes enabled; that's where your shadow copies are all stored. This volume is accessible only to the built-in system account on your server, not to administrators.

Once you've reviewed and modified the shadow-copy settings for a volume and enabled shadow copies on that volume, your server begins to save shadow copies of all files stored on the volume. That includes *all* files, not just ones in shared folders on the volume. In other words, even if you modify a file locally on the volume and the file is stored in a folder that isn't shared, a shadow copy will still be created for that file. That way, if you later decide to share the folder for others to access, a history of versions of files in the folder will be displayed.

In a network environment, where it's not convenient to log on locally to your file server, you can still enable shadow copies by using Computer Management. Just open Computer Management on your administrator workstation, connect to the remote file server, right-click on the Shared Folders node, and select All Tasks → Configure Shadow Copies.

> This works only from workstations running Windows XP Professional with Service Pack 1 and the Windows Server 2003 Administration Tools Pack or, alternatively, from another machine that is running Windows Server 2003.

Once shadow copies are enabled on the server, they still have to be enabled on the users' client computers. By default, only Windows Server 2003 has shadow-copy functionality built right into it; all previous versions of Windows require that special client software be installed on them before users can use this feature to access previous versions of files. If your desktop computers are running Windows XP Professional (the desktop operating system that most closely integrates with Windows Server 2003 on the back end), you can install shadow client software on them easily. Just share the *%Systemroot%\System32\clients\twclient\x86* folder on your server, and then instruct users to connect to this share and double-click on *twcli32.msi* to run the Windows Installer File. Alternatively, you could use the software-installation feature of Group Policy to deploy this feature automatically to all desktop machines in an organizational unit, domain, or site. You could even email the installer file to your users, along with instructions on how to install and use it.

If your desktops are running Windows 2000 Professional (with Service Pack 3 or later) or Windows 98 Second Edition (SE), you need to download a different shadow-software client from the Microsoft Windows Download Center (*http://www.microsoft.com/downloads/*) and deploy it by using one of the methods described previously (you also have to install the same client software on the server). If your desktops are running Windows NT 4.0 Workstation or Windows Millennium Edition (ME), then you're out of luck.

## Using Shadow Copies

Let's say you've enabled shadow copies on volume *E:* on a Windows Server 2003 file server, and this volume is used to store users' files in a series of shares named *Budgets*, *Projects*, and so on. How can a user access previous versions of her files in these shares, and what actions can she perform on them? Say a user uses Start → Run → \\*servername*\budgets, where *servername* is the name of the file server where the Budgets share is located. This will open a window on the user's desktop, displaying all files stored in that share.

Users can right-click on a particular file in that share, select Properties, and switch to the Previous Versions tab shown in Figure 10-8. If this tab is missing, then the user's computer doesn't have the shadow-copy client software installed.

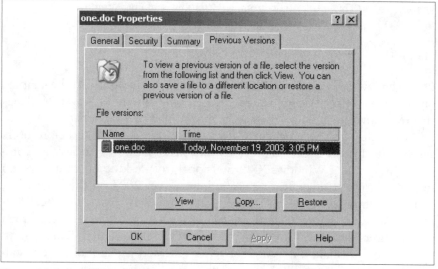

*Figure 10-8. Accessing previous versions of a file using shadow copy client software*

All previous point-in-time versions of the selected file are displayed in this tab (if no previous versions are displayed, the file hasn't been modified since it was created). The View, Copy, and Restore buttons enable the user to perform different tasks with these versions. For example, to view the contents of a previous version, click View. This is helpful when you're not sure which previous version is the one in which you wrote that lovely paragraph but later deleted in a fit of writer's despair. Once you've found the previous version of the file you want, you could save it to your My Documents folder and give it a descriptive name.

Alternatively, if you already know which version you're interested in (such as the most recent previous version) you could click Copy to copy that version to a different location. If you're really confident, you could click Restore to overwrite the current version of the file (the one you're working with as a user) with the previous version specified.

If you're not even sure which file had that wonderful paragraph you wrote, but you know it's in the Budgets share, you could right-click on an empty area within the open share window, select Properties, and switch to the Previous Versions tab of the share itself. This displays all previous shadow copies made of that share and lets you view previous versions of individual files within the share, copy a previous version of all files in the share to another location, or roll back all files in the share to the specified previous version.

The bottom line is, when educating users on how to use shadow copies, tell them to ignore the Restore button and always use View and Copy instead. One user carelessly restoring an entire shared folder to its previous version could result in lost work and its accompanying frustration for other users who have access to the same share. Of course, if users work only with their own files but store them in the same share, this might not be an issue, depending on how NTFS permissions are configured on the shared folder. But if users have collaborative access to a document, problems can result when using shadow copies. Of course, such problems can result even without shadow copies functionality.

Here's something else to consider that is often forgotten: NTFS permissions change differently, depending on whether you copy a file or move it. So, in the case of shadow copies, if you restore a previous version of a file, it overwrites the original file in its original location but maintains the same NTFS permissions as the original file. But if you copy a previous version of a file to a different location on your drive, the copy inherits the permissions of the folder you copy it to.

## Traps

In addition to poor planning and scheduling, resulting in insufficient disk space, there are a few other things you need to watch out for when implementing shadow copies. The first thing has to do with the block-based mechanism by which the VSS makes copies of changes made to files. If the filesystem cluster size is smaller than this block size, some of your shadow copies might disappear when you defragment your volume using the built-in Disk Defragmenter node in Computer Management. To prevent this from happening, always ensure that volumes on which shadow copies are stored have cluster sizes of 16 KB or greater. By default, on Windows Server 2003, any volumes larger than 2 GB will have a cluster size of only 4 KB, which is insufficient.

To solve this problem, when you format the volume, specify an allocation unit size of 16 KB instead using either Disk Management or the /a switch with the format command. On large volumes, you could use even higher cluster sizes of 32 or 64 KB. But if the volume will be used to store many small files, this can result in much wasted space on your drive. So, 16 KB is probably the optimal solution in most cases.

If you upgraded your server from Windows NT 4.0 Server and the volume was converted from FAT to NTFS by using the convert command, you're out of luck. Because convert always uses an allocation unit size of 512 bytes to optimally align with FAT filesystem boundaries, don't use a converted volume for storing shadow copies on a server. However, if your machine was previously running Windows 2000 Server, you might be in luck, because that platform allowed you to format FAT volumes with larger cluster sizes.

Here are some other things to watch for:

- Don't enable shadow copies on a volume that has mount points on it. A *mount point* (or *mounted drive*) is a special volume that is attached to an empty folder on an NTFS volume. In other words, a mount point named *Data* could be attached to the folder *E:\Stuff* if volume E: is formatted using NTFS. In Windows Explorer, *Data* would appear just like any other volume, and mount points would therefore provide a way to get around the 26-letter limit for naming volumes using drive letters. The problem is that mount points are not included when shadowed copies are made for a volume, which means that files stored in these mounted drives will not have previous versions accessible to users. Also, if you share a mount point that's located on a volume that has shadow copies enabled, users won't be able to access previous versions of files in the folder attached to the mount point. So, it's best to avoid mount points entirely on shadowed volumes.

- Avoid using shadow copies on dual-boot configurations, where Windows Server 2003 and some earlier operating system such as Windows NT 4.0 Server are installed on the same machine. Corruption of shadow copies has been known to occur in such scenarios.

- Best practice is usually to enable shadow copies on any volume where data files are stored, because the enhanced Backup utility included with Windows Server 2003 can back up open files on a volume on which shadow copies are enabled. That means that if users leave files open on their machines at night, the files can still be backed up instead of being

locked and prevented from being backed up as in previous versions of
Windows Backup. In this kind of scenario, it might be a good idea to
schedule additional shadow copies to occur an hour or so before
Backup is scheduled to run. You can also turn backing up of shadowed
volumes on and off using the /SNAP switch in ntbackup, the command-
line version of the Backup utility.

- Don't enable shadow copies on a system or boot volume, because there
  have been reports of excessive generation of shadow copies. This causes
  poor system performance, especially on domain controllers where the
  contents of Active Directory is frequently updated. Programs that create
  many temporary files on these volumes can also cause shadow copies to
  grow quickly and fill up your volume if you give them enough room to
  do so, and a system volume that fills up is one that blue-screens.

- If you accidentally delete any of the default hidden administrative shares
  on your server, you won't be able to enable shadow copies on any volumes on your machine. Fortunately, Microsoft has a workaround in
  such circumstances. Search the Knowledge Base on Microsoft Product
  Support Services (PSS) at *http://support.microsoft.com* for information
  on how to restore default administrative shares.

- Finally, before you delete a volume that has shadow copies enabled on
  it, disable shadow copies on the volume. If you don't, your event log
  might fill up with ID 7001 error messages, which can be annoying.

## HACK #96 Back Up and Clear the Event Logs

Here's a nifty script you can use to back up and clear the Event logs on your
servers.

Managing Event logs is an essential part of a system administrator's job.
These logs are useful for a number of reasons, including troubleshooting system problems, verifying that services are functioning properly, and detect-
ing possible intrusion attempts. While Event Viewer can be used to save and
clear these logs, it can be handier to use a script you can run manually (by
double-clicking on a desktop shortcut) or automatically at different times
(by adding a task to the Scheduled Tasks folder).

This hack provides a script to do just that. This VBScript will back up your
Windows Event Logs and then clear the information contained within them.

## The Code

Type the following script into Notepad (make sure to have Word Wrap disabled), and save it with a *.vbs* extension as *archivelogs.vbs*:

```
Option Explicit
On Error Resume Next
Dim numThreshold
Dim strMachine
Dim strArchivePath
Dim strMoniker
Dim refWMI
Dim colEventLogs
Dim refEventLog

If WScript.Arguments.Count < 2 Then
WScript.Echo _
"Usage: archivelogs.vbs <machine> <archive_path> [threshold]"
WScript.Quit
End If

If WScript.Arguments.Count = 2 Then
numThreshold = 0
Else
numThreshold = WScript.Arguments(2)
If Not IsNumeric(numThreshold) Then
WScript.Echo "The third parameter must be a number!"
WScript.Quit
End If

If numThreshold < 0 OR numThreshold > 100 Then
WScript.Echo "The third parameter must be in the range 0-100"
WScript.Quit
End If
End If

strMachine = WScript.Arguments(0)
strArchivePath = WScript.Arguments(1)

strMoniker = "winMgmts:{(Backup,Security)}!\\" & strMachine
Set refWMI = GetObject(strMoniker)
If Err <> 0 Then
WScript.Echo "Could not connect to the WMI service."
WScript.Quit
End If

Set colEventLogs = refWMI.InstancesOf("Win32_NTEventLogFile")
If Err <> 0 Then
WScript.Echo "Could not retrieve Event Log objects"
WScript.Quit
End If

For Each refEventLog In colEventLogs
```

```
'if shouldAct( ) returns non-zero attempt to back up
If shouldAct(refEventLog.FileSize,refEventLog.MaxFileSize) <> 0 Then
If refEventLog.ClearEventLog( _
makeFileName(refEventLog.LogfileName)) = 0 Then
WScript.Echo refEventLog.LogfileName & _
" archived successfully"
Else
WScript.Echo refEventLog.LogfileName & _
" could not be archived"
End If
Else
WScript.Echo refEventLog.LogfileName & _
" has not exceeded the backup level"
End If
Next
Set refEventLog = Nothing
Set colEventLogs = Nothing
Set refWMI = Nothing

Function shouldAct(numCurSize, numMaxSize)
If (numCurSize/numMaxSize)*100 > numThreshold Then
shouldAct = 1
Else
shouldAct = 0
End If
End Function

Function makeFileName(strLogname)
makeFileName = strArchivePath & "\" & _
strMachine & "-" & strLogname & "-" & _
Year(Now) & Month(Now) & Day(Now) & ".evt"
End Function
```

## Running the Hack

To run the script, use *Cscript.exe*, the command-line script engine of the Windows Script Host (WSH). The script uses the following command-line syntax:

```
archivelogs.vbs machine archive_path [threshold]
```

In this syntax, machine is the name of the server, archive_path is the path to where you want to save the backup, and threshold is an optional parameter that checks to see the size (in MB) of the logs.

> If the logs are above the threshold value you specify, the script will back them up. Otherwise, it will skip them.

The following example shows how to run the script and provides typical output when the script is executed against a domain controller. The archive directory *C:\Log Files* must first be created on the machine on which you run the script.

```
C:\>cscript.exe archivelogs.vbs srv210 "C:\Log Archive"
Microsoft (R) Windows Script Host Version 5.6
Copyright (C) Microsoft Corporation 1996-2001. All rights reserved.

Security archived successfully
System archived successfully
Directory Service archived successfully
DNS Server archived successfully
File Replication Service archived successfully
Application archived successfully

C:\>
```

The result of running the script is a set of files in *C:\Log Files* of the form *srv210-Application-20031217.evt*, *srv210-Security-20031217.evt*, and so on. Note that each archive file is named according to the server, event log, and current date.

If you plan on using the Backup utility instead to back up the Event log files on your Windows 2000 servers, it might surprise you to know that being part of the Backup Operators group will not allow you to back up or restore these Event log files; this right is available to only local or domain administrators!

—*Rod Trent*

### H A C K   Back Up the DFS Namespace
### #97
If you've implemented the Distributed File System (DSF) on your network, you need to back up your DFS namespace regularly.

The Distributed File System (DFS) is a feature of Windows 2000 Server and Windows Server 2003 that lets you create a single logical tree of shared folders that are physically located on different file servers on your network. This makes it easier for administrators to manage shared folders, and it also helps users find shared resources, since the resources appear from the user's point of view as a single hierarchical set of folders on a single machine. As a result, to locate a particular shared folder on the network, users don't have to know the actual file server on which the folder resides; they just have to connect to the DFS tree and browse until they find the folder they require. Then, if the user has the appropriate permissions to access the folder, he can do whatever he needs to do with the files stored within it.

A collection of shared resources arranged in a logical hierarchy like this is called a *DFS namespace*. This namespace begins with the DFS root, which forms the bottom of the DFS tree. The branches of the tree are called *DFS links* and they map to shared folders on different file servers across your network. Windows 2000 Server machines can host only one DFS root (hence, only one namespace), but the Enterprise Edition of Windows Server 2003 supports multiple DFS roots on a single machine.

If you're using DFS, it's important that you back up your DFS configuration for your Windows 2000 domain. Unfortunately, many disaster-recovery products on the market that support Windows 2000 do not have a native add-in to support the backup and restoration of the DFS namespace.

Fortunately, Microsoft has included in Windows 2000 two command-line-based tools (DFScmd and DFSUtil) to facilitate such a need. While the functionality in these tools is also provided in the GUI by the DFS snap-in for the MMC, using the command-line tools gives you the added flexibility of using them to create a script that you can execute via Task Scheduler to automate the backup process if your DFS topology changes often.

## DFScmd

The first command-line utility, DFScmd, allows you to back up the DFS namespace to a text file that can be accessed later to restore the namespace if necessary. Here's the syntax to perform a backup:

```
DFScmd /view \\DFSName\DFSShare /BATCH >> "path\filename.bat"
```

For example, if you have a domain-based DFS namespace for the domain *Consoto.net*, with a DFS root named *DFSRoot*, then your backup syntax would look like this:

```
DFScmd /view \\Consoto.net\DFSRoot /BATCH >> C:\Temp\dfsbackup.bat
```

Here's an example of what is saved in this batch file:

```
REM BATCH RESTORE SCRIPT
REM dfscmd /map "\\consoto.net\DFSRoot" "\\servera.consoto.net\DFSRoot" "DFS
Root for Consoto.Net members."
dfscmd /map "\\consoto.net\DFSRoot\Departments\Finance" "\\serverb.consoto.
net\finance$" "Finance Department."
dfscmd /map "\\consoto.net\DFSRoot\Departments\ISS" "\\serverb.consoto.net\
dept_1ss$" "Information Systems Department."
dfscmd /map "\\consoto.net\DFSRoot\Domain Support\IIS Published Sites" "\\
serverc.consoto.net\inetpub$" "IIS Web Sites published for Internet/Intranet
Access."
The command completed successfully.
```

To restore the DFS volume structure (namespace) from the server it was originally hosted on to a new file server in the domain, perform the following steps. Start Distributed File System from Administrative Tools and on the Action menu click New DFS Root. Click Next and then choose the proper type of DFS root for your domain. Select the server that will host the DFS root and then click Next. Select the share that will become the DFS Root Share and then click Next. Finally, insert a comment, click Next, and then click Finish. The new DFS root is now available.

Now, run the batch file created earlier to restore the DFS volume structure. When the batch file has completed execution, verify that the namespace has been properly created. In our example, the DFS namespace should now appear in the Distributed File System Administrator like this:

```
DFSRoot
    Departments
        Finance
        ISS
    Domain Support
        IIS Published Sites
```

## DFSUtil

The second command-line utility, DFSUtil, allows you to query and perform troubleshooting of the DFS metadata with domain-based DFS implementations. *DFS metadata* is configuration information of DFS that is stored in the Active Directory–based Partition Knowledge Table. The functionality of the command-line-based DFSUtil parallels the functionality of the Distributed File System MMC snap-in.

While DFScmd is a built-in operating system command, DFSUtil can be found on your Windows 2000/2003 product CD under the *Support\Tools* directory in the *SUPPORT.CAB* file. If you plan on using these utilities, I recommend you download the latest *SUPPORT.CAB* file from Microsoft's web site at *http://www.microsoft.com/downloads/* if you are running Windows 2000 Service Pack 2 or later. The service packs include updated versions of *DFSUtil.exe* that resolve issues encountered with the original version found on your Windows 2000 Server CD.

*—Matt Goedtel*

## Recover with Automated System Recovery

#98    Automated System Recovery (ASR) is a new feature of Windows Server 2003 that makes recovering from a disaster a whole lot easier.

Rebuilding a server after a disaster is generally not a trivial task. The process usually involves reinstalling Windows from scratch, reconfiguring disk partitions to the exact configuration they had before the failure, and then restoring the system volumes, boot volumes, and all your data volumes. The process is not especially complicated, but it takes a considerable amount of time to do it right, usually with significant involvement of the administrator along the way.

With Windows Server 2003, however, things have suddenly gotten much easier. Automated System Recovery (ASR), a new feature included in the Backup utility, greatly simplifies the process of recovering a server that won't boot because of severe problems with the system/boot volume, such as Registry corruption. By automating the process of restoring a failed server, ASR saves you time and reduces the chances for making mistakes. ASR is an essential part of the Recovery Roadmap [Hack #99] for troubleshooting problems that might happen to Windows servers, and this hack leads you through the process step by step. I'll also clarify how best to use this feature and how to resolve problems that can arise.

## ASR Backup

The simplest way to back up your system with ASR is to use the Backup or Restore Wizard that starts by default when you select Accessories → System Tools → Backup. Simply start the wizard, select "Back up files and settings," and choose the option to back up "All information on this computer." Then, specify the remaining backup job parameters as usual. The result is that all information on your hard drives is backed up, including the boot, system, and data volumes. Later, should a disaster occur, you can restore your system by using the ASR restore process to the exact configuration it had earlier.

The backup is done by using shadow copies [Hack #95] to ensure that any open files on the system and boot volumes are properly backed up. Note, however, that this applies mainly to the system and boot volumes, which are critical for successful ASR backup. While shadow copies are also used to back up data volumes, these shadow copies are deleted afterward unless you've specifically enabled shadow copies on these volumes to help protect users' work from accidental loss or damage.

An alternative method for performing ASR backup is to start Backup and switch to Advanced Mode. Then, under the Welcome tab (Figure 10-9), select the Automated System Recovery Wizard button. This wizard lets you back up only information on your system and boot volumes that is critical to restore your system; it does not back up any data volumes, which are usually best left for your regular backup program to handle anyway.

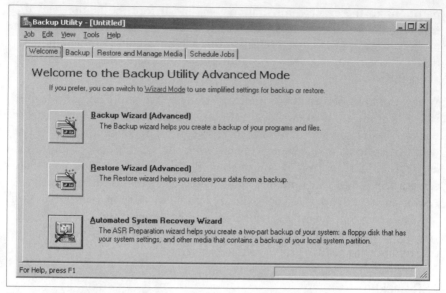

*Figure 10-9. Starting the Automated System Recovery Wizard*

During the ASR backup process, you're asked to insert a blank, formatted floppy to create a system recovery disk (commonly called an *ASR floppy*). This floppy is critical to the ASR restore process, so it's worth digging a little deeper into how it's used. The ASR backup process saves two files onto your floppy: the ASR state file (*asr.sif*), which contains information about the disk signatures and configuration of disk volumes on your machine, and *asrpnp.sif*, which contains information about different Plug and Play devices on your system. These two files are critical for the recovery of your system, because they connect the underlying hardware configuration with the operating system above it. As we'll see in a moment, you need to insert this floppy at the beginning of the ASR restore, in order to rebuild the disk subsystem and hardware configuration of your system before restoring the contents of the system and boot volumes.

What if you have no floppy disk drive on your machine? Fortunately, you can still use ASR to back up your system, but its a bit of a workaround. During the ASR backup process copies of these *asr.sif* and *asrpnp.sif* files are also saved in the *%SystemRoot%\Repair* folder on your server. So, when you receive a prompt at the end of the backup process to insert a floppy, simply ignore the prompt and instead copy *asr.sif* and *asrpnp.sif* from *Repair* to a network share on another server (one that has a floppy disk drive installed). Then, copy the files from the share on that server to a blank floppy you insert into its drive, and you now have a working ASR floppy for your backup. Then, go buy a USB external floppy drive, because you'll need it if you ever have to rebuild your original server from the backup set you created. In other words, you can perform ASR backup without a floppy, but you cannot perform an ASR restore without one.

What if you lose your ASR floppy? Well, the procedure just described will work in this case too. Just insert a new blank, formatted floppy into your server and copy *asr.sif* and *asrpnp.sif* from the *Repair* directory to the floppy Note that these files must be located in the root folder on the floppy for the restore process to work, so use a separate floppy for each ASR backup; don't try to combine several ASR backups in different folders on one floppy.

However, since the *Repair* directory is located on the boot volume of the system itself, if your system volume is toast, then so is your *Repair* directory and the files within it. So, what if you've lost your ASR floppy and the *Repair* directory is gone with your hard drive? There's still a workaround that can save your bacon: use the Backup utility on a different machine to open the backup catalog for the ASR backup set you want to restore, expand the *%SystemRoot%\Repair* directory on the boot volume, select *asr.sif* and *asrpnp.sif* as the files you want to restore, insert a blank floppy, and restore these two files to the root of the floppy. Presto! You now have a recovered ASR floppy you can use to initiate a restore.

## ASR Restore

The ASR restore process in a nutshell is as follows: first, the disk configurations are restored; then, your system and boot volumes are formatted; and, finally, a bare-bones version of Windows is installed that starts Backup and rebuilds your system and boot volumes from your ASR backup set stored on tape media.

> Note that *your system and boot volumes are formatted*. Clearly, using the ASR restore process should be considered a last-ditch effort, to be used only when everything else fails. See "Recovery Roadmap" [Hack #99] for information on how to choose between the various recovery options for Windows servers.

**Using ASR restore.** Let's look at a restore in more detail. First, make sure you have your ASR floppy, tape backup media, and original installation files for Windows Server 2003 (i.e., the product CD). If you have any mass storage controllers on your server that require an updated driver to replace the one on the product CD, be sure to have this handy as well.

Also—and this might be important—be sure to back up any data files or folders located on your system or boot volumes. Since ASR reformats these volumes, anything other than the Windows operating system files that are located on these volumes might be lost. Mind you, best practice is to never store data files on these volumes—you should store them on separate volumes instead—so if you've been following this practice you have nothing to worry about, right? Note that I said *might* be lost, not *will* be lost. While Windows documentation says that non–operating system files stored on system/boot volumes won't be restored by ASR, my own experience is that they are restored sometimes and other times not. So, just to be safe, back up these volumes separately using normal backup procedures so you can later restore any missing data files.

Now, insert your product CD and boot from your CD-ROM drive (press the appropriate key to do this if required). Press F6 when prompted if you have an updated device driver for your mass storage device. Then, press F2 when text-mode setup prompts you to perform ASR restore, and insert the ASR floppy when asked to do so. The recovery process will rebuild the disk signatures and partition table, reformat the system/boot volumes, copy installation files, and begin installing Windows. A short while into the installation of Windows, the Automated System Recovery Wizard screen will ask you to specify the location of the tape backup media where your ASR backup is located. Once you specify this, the recovery process continues and it's considerably faster than the Windows installation process itself, which is nice. Be sure not to interrupt this process; otherwise, you'll have an incomplete and nonfunctional server. Once the restore process is finished, the logon screen appears and you're done.

That is, you're done unless your system was totally fried and you have to rebuild it from scratch—in which case, you have to complete the procedure by restoring any data volumes on your server from your regular backup sets.

Here's one more thing that's helpful, but not documented. Running the ASR restore process also creates a *setup.log* file that identifies the system and boot volumes, checksums for kernel files, the directory where Windows is installed, and the device drivers loaded during setup. A copy of this file is placed in *%SystemRoot%\Repair* and also another one is placed on the ASR floppy itself, which is handy for verifying the details of the restore process. Print that log and keep a record of it for troubleshooting purposes later.

**Hacking the restore.** If your original machine is *really* toast, you can use ASR to restore to a different machine. However, to do this, you must ensure that the hardware on your new system is identical to your original (toasted) system, with the exception of the video card, network card, and hard disks, which can be different brands or types. Concerning hard disks, however, make sure the number of hard drives in your new system is equal to or greater than the number of hard drives on the old system, and also make sure that the storage capacity of each drive is the same or larger than drives on your old system.

If you're using ASR to restore a failed server to another system with hardware that does differ significantly from the old one, there's a workaround: you can hack the *asr.sif* file to make the ASR restore process install additional device drivers (or any other kinds of files) that might be needed by the text-mode setup process to install Windows successfully and complete the recovery.

The *asr.sif* file is a text file with different sections, identified by brackets:

```
[VERSION]
Signature="$Windows NT$"
ASR-Version="1.0"

[SYSTEMS]
1="SRV230","x86","5.2","C:\WINDOWS",1,0x00020112,"360 0 -60 0-10-0-5 2:00:
00.0 0-4-0-1 2:00:00.0","Central Standard Time","Central Daylight Time"

[BUSES]
1=1,3

[DISKS.MBR]
1=1,1,1,0xdbe3dbe3,512,63,255,16514064
```

By adding an additional [InstallFiles] section, you can specify additional files that need to be copied to the machine during text-mode setup. For example, adding the following section will cause the driver file *MyDriver.sys* to be copied from the root of the floppy disk that has the volume label My Drivers to the *%SystemRoot%\System32\Drivers* folder on the machine:

```
[InstallFiles]
1=1,"My Drivers","Floppy","%SystemRoot%\System32\Drivers\MyDriver.sys","My
Company Name",0x00000001
```

During text-mode setup, a prompt will ask you to insert the floppy disk that has the driver file for My Company Name, and the 0x00000001 flag indicates that this prompt will always appear. Other flags can also be used, including 0x00000006, which indicates that ASR recovery can't proceed unless you load the specified driver file; 0x00000010, which indicates that any existing copy of *MyDriver.sys* should be overwritten by the new file; and 0x00000020, which prompts before overwriting an existing version of the file.

Using this hack, you can customize the ASR restore process to make it successful, even if there are some hardware differences between the original machine and the new one.

## Using ASR

Finally, many administrators don't understood *when* to use ASR to back up the system and when they should just use regular backups. You should back up your system anytime you change your hardware or operating system configuration. Examples of such changes might include upgrading to a new version of the operating system, installing service packs or hotfixes, adding new disk storage or changing the partition layout of your volumes, switching from basic to dynamic storage, installing a new Windows component or service, installing and configuring a third-party application, installing new hardware or upgrading device drivers, and so on.

Doesn't this sound suspiciously like the instructions for creating the old Emergency Repair Disk (ERD) on Windows NT/2000? Yes, though ASR is a far more powerful feature than the ERD. since it backs up the System State and Registry on your machine, it does include similar functionality to the ERD, including saving a copy of your Registry hives in the *Repair* folder. But while the ERD could be used only to replace corrupt or missing system files or Registry hives, ASR is a complete system-recovery feature that does everything the ERD did and more—automatically.

You don't need to use ASR for backup when your system is tuned and running perfectly and only user data files are being created, modified, or deleted on your server. If you've properly partitioned your system so that all user data files are on data volumes separate from the boot and system volumes, then you can simply back up these data volumes on a daily basis to ensure nothing is lost in the case of a disaster. But if you change your basic operating system or underlying hardware in an significant way, use Backup to create a new ASR backup set so that you can recover your system to its current state, should massive failure occur.

## Recovery Roadmap

#99   When it comes to troubleshooting startup problems, finding the right tool for the job is the key.

Would you try to crack a walnut with a bulldozer? Or pry open a door with a toothpick? Every tool has its purpose, and using the right tool for the job gets the job done quick and easy. The same is true concerning the maze of troubleshooting options available for restoring Windows 2000 and Windows Server 2003 systems that fail on startup. Safe Mode, Last Known Good Configuration, Emergency Repair Disk, Recovery Console, Automated System Recovery, Windows Startup Disk—which should you use and in which situations? This hack helps you get your toolbox in order by answering that question.

## Windows 2000

I'll start with Windows 2000 and then highlight differences in troubleshooting issues on the newer Windows Server 2003 platform. Obviously, we won't be able to cover every possible scenario or even the intricate details of specific situations, but if you follow the procedures outlined in this hack, you should be able to get started and figure the rest out yourself, with the help of various Knowledge Base articles on Microsoft Product Support Services (*http://support.microsoft.com*).

To make things crystal clear, here's the big picture, right from the start:

1. If the system won't boot, boot with the Last Known Good Configuration.

2. If that fails or isn't an option, try booting into Safe Mode or one of its variants.

3. If that fails or isn't an option, try using the Recovery Console together with a Windows Startup Disk to repair your machine.

4. If that fails or isn't an option, try the Emergency Repair Process to repair your machine.

5. If that fails, you'll probably have to completely rebuild your machine from tape backup media.

There are exceptions to this procedure, based on possible knowledge you have of what might be wrong with your machine, and we'll talk about that later. But first, let's unpack these steps one at a time.

**Last Known Good Configuration.** When you press F8 during the startup process (or when you see the "Please select the operating system to start" message, if you have the Recovery Console installed), the Windows Advanced Options Menu is displayed. One of the options on this menu is Last Known Good Configuration, which uses the Registry settings that Windows used for its last successful logon. Every time you boot Windows and log on successfully, this information is updated in the Registry and becomes your next version of Last Known Good Configuration. This applies only to normal mode; logging on to Safe Mode successfully does not update your Last Known Good Configuration settings.

Digging a little deeper, when you use Last Known Good Configuration, Windows restores the HKLM\SYSTEM\CurrentControlSet Registry settings from a previous set of settings, such as ControlSet001 or ControlSet002. In addition, Last Known Good Configuration also rolls back the device drivers used by your system to those that loaded during your last successful logon. However, Last Know Good Configuration cannot be used to restore missing or corrupt operating-system files.

When should you use Last Known Good Configuration to recover your system? Choosing this option overwrites any Registry changes or device-driver configuration changes you made during your last successful logon session and restores your system to the previous logon session's configuration. In other words, you lose any configuration changes made and any updated drivers installed since the last successful logon to your system. As a result, you should use this tool only if you think that some configuration change you recently made or a device driver you updated might be causing your system to fail upon startup. Typically, a problem like this will cause a STOP error (blue screen) of some sort, and the message on the screen might give you a clue about which driver or service might be causing the failure.

So, the moral of the story is, if you change something, reboot, and your system won't start, try Last Known Good Configuration to restore your system.

**Safe Mode.** If you think your problem isn't due to a recent misconfiguration error on your part and you haven't updated any device drivers lately, then try Safe Mode if your system won't start. Safe Mode lets you start your system using a minimal set of device drivers and services. This allows you to get to a logon screen and start using Windows to look for what might be wrong. Safe Mode can also be accessed by using the Advanced Options menu by pressing F8. There are three versions you can use: Safe Mode, Safe Mode with Networking, and Safe Mode with Command Prompt.

I suggest you always try Safe Mode with Networking, because might may need to access your Windows installation files on a network distribution point to repair your server—for example, by extracting driver files from a .cab file. If Safe Mode with Networking fails, try Safe Mode; if that works, then something might be wrong with your network card or networking subsystem settings. If that fails, try Safe Mode with Command Prompt so that you can at least get to the Windows command-line troubleshooting tools to look for what's wrong with your system.

You can log on to Safe Mode by using either a domain administrator account or the local administrator account. On a domain controller, the local administrator account is the only local account present on the machine and is stored in a minimal version of the SAM database found on member servers and workstations. This is also the account used to run the Recovery Console, and it uses the password you specified when you first installed Windows (unless it's been changed).

When should you use Safe Mode and its variants? Usually, you might try this if you recently installed new hardware or software on your machine, not necessarily during the most recent logon session. Once you're logged on in Safe Mode, you can start disabling hardware devices one at a time until you find exactly which device is causing the problem. Or, if the issue is software-related, you can try to reconfigure or even uninstall different applications to isolate the problem and then see if you can reboot in Normal Mode.

Some of the Windows tools you might use in Safe Mode to try to determine the cause of startup failure include Event Viewer, System Information (Start → Run → msinfo32), Device Manager, and so on. Also, successfully booting into any version of Safe Mode creates a log file named *Ntbtlog.txt* (found in *%SystemRoot%*) that describes the services started and the drivers loaded during startup. By examining this list, you might be able to determine which failed service or missing/corrupt driver is preventing Windows from starting, and then you can use the GUI tools to fix your problem.

**Recovery Console.** The Recovery Console is a command-line interface that you can start either by selecting it from the Boot Loader menu (if you've previously installed the Recovery Console on your server) or directly from the product CD. You must log onto the Recovery Console using the local administrator account on your machine, even if it's a domain controller. Recovery Console provides you with a minimal version of Windows that lets you run various commands to perform tasks such as copying and replacing system files, enabling or disabling problem services, repairing a boot sector, or even reformatting your drive.

Best practice is to install the Recovery Console on your machine before you need it. That way, you won't be running around looking for your product CD when a disaster occurs and you can't start your system. To install the Recovery Console on a machine, insert the product CD, open a command prompt, change to the *I386* folder on the CD, and type winnt32 /cmdcons. If you haven't installed the Console and need to run it directly from the CD, insert the CD and select the Repair option.

**Windows Startup Disk.** Sometimes, Windows won't boot because the boot sector is damaged on your system volume or a virus has infected your master boot record. A Windows Startup Disk can be extremely handy in such circumstances. The name of the disk is a bit of a misnomer, because you can't start Windows from the disk itself. Rather, the disk can be used in conjunction with the Recovery Console to repair certain kinds of problems that might arise.

But first, here's how to create one of these disks so that you'll have it ready when you need it. Stick a blank floppy disk into your machine and double-click on My Computer. Right-click on your *A:* drive and select Format. Check the option for Quick Format and click Start to format your disk. Now, double-click on the *C:* drive to open it in My Computer, select Tools → Folder

Options, and on the View tab clear the checkbox labeled "Hide protected operating system files." Drag and drop the *boot.ini*, *ntldr*, and *ntdetect.com* files from the root of the C: drive to your floppy, and include the *Bootsect.dos* and *Ntbootdd.sys* files if these are also present. Open a command prompt window and type attrib -h -s -r a:\*.* to set the attributes properly for the files on your floppy. Eject the floppy and label it *Windows Startup Disk* or something similar. Finally, hide your protected system files again in My Computer so that you don't accidentally try to delete any of them.

Now, if your system won't start because of a damaged master boot record, a corrupt boot sector, or missing or corrupt system files such as *Ntldr* or *Ntdetect.com*, you can start the system by using the Recovery Console (from the product CD if necessary), insert your Windows Startup Disk, and copy the files you need from the floppy to your C: drive. Then, you can run other Recovery Console commands to repair the boot sector (using the fixboot command), repair the master boot record (using the fixmbr command), and so on, until you have a working system that will start.

**Emergency Repair Process.** The only other thing you can usually try (short of reinstalling Windows from scratch) is the Emergency Repair Process. This feature of Windows 2000 is basically a holdover from Windows NT. The Emergency Repair Disk (ERD) itself isn't as useful (since a floppy can't contain the whole Windows 2000 Registry) as the other actions that are performed by Windows when you create this disk. In particular, when you create an ERD by starting the Backup utility and selecting Tools → Create an Emergency Repair Disk, be sure to select the "Also backup the Registry to the repair directory" option, which backs up all your Registry hives to the *%SystemRoot%\ Repair* folder. Then, when you need to repair the Registry or replace missing or damaged files on your machine, you can press *L* when the startup process asks you for your ERD floppy. Doing so will ignore the floppy and use the information in the *Repair* directory instead. Of course, if your boot volume is badly damaged, your *Repair* folder might be corrupt or missing, in which case you will likely have to reinstall Windows from scratch anyway.

The repair process finds the *boot.ini* file, reads the ARC paths to the operating system, and then attempts to load the *%systemroot%\System32\Config\ Software* Registry hive. If the *boot.ini* file is corrupt or missing or if the Software hive is corrupt, the repair fails (unless you actually do have an ERD handy, in which case the repair process can gain access to a working copy of the *Setup.log* file for your machine). Hopefully, you updated your EFD the last time you reconfigured your machine or installed new hardware on it to keep it current.

## Windows Server 2003

Things are pretty much the same in Windows Server 2003, except for one major difference: the ERD of Windows 2000 has been replaced by the new Automated System Recovery (ASR) feature of Windows Server 2003 [Hack #98]. This new ASR feature is a powerful tool of last resort for restoring your system when everything else fails. ASR includes the functionality of ERD and much, much more and can really save your bacon in an emergency when your server won't start and everything else (Last Known Good Configuration, Safe Mode, Recovery Console) fails.

## Right Tool for the Job

Finally, here's a list of the proper tools to use when any of these common issues prevent your system from starting:

*A configuration change made during the last logon session*
Try Last Known Good Configuration and reconfigure accordingly.

*A device driver updated during the last logon session*
Try Last Known Good Configuration and try a different driver.

*Server misconfiguration*
Try Safe Mode and reconfigure accordingly.

*A newly installed device*
Try Safe Mode and disable, reconfigure, or uninstall the device.

*A newly installed application*
Try Safe Mode and uninstall the application.

*A newly installed hotfix or service pack*
Try Safe Mode and uninstall the hotfix or service pack.

*A problem service that prevents Windows from starting*
Try using the Recovery Console to reconfigure or disable the service.

*A corrupted boot sector or master boot sector*
Try using the Recovery Console and repairing the problem.

*A missing or corrupt system file*
Try using the Recovery Console and copying the file from a Windows Startup Disk or from the installation files on CD or a distribution point.

*Registry corruption*
Try using the Emergency Repair Process to restore the Registry or restore the System State from tape backup media using Safe Mode.

*Massive corruption or loss of system files or the Registry*
Try the Automated System Recovery (ASR) feature of Windows Server 2003 if you previously created an ASR backup set; otherwise, rebuild your server from scratch by reinstalling Windows.

## Data Recovery of Last Resort

**#100** When the hard drive crashes on your server and your tape backup turns out to be a dud, who you gonna call? Use this hack.

You have critical data on your server and your hard drive crashes. And you haven't made a backup recently. What do you do? I know, not making regular backups is irresponsible, but these things happen. Or perhaps you have a RAID 5 unit and the unimaginable happens: two drives fail simultaneously. And Friday's backup tape is unreadable, because you haven't cleaned the tape drive for over a year. Another example of being irresponsible, but let's lay aside the blame until we fix the problem, okay? So, what do you do?

You need a data recovery company—fast. I know seasoned administrators who have been in this unfortunate situation, and here's a list of companies they've recommended to me that you can try if this ever happens to you:

*Ontrack*

A popular data-recovery service provider that offers various levels of services, including in-house, remote, and do-it-yourself. They also have a partner program that offers discounts based on referrals and resale. They have worldwide locations in the US, Europe, and Tokyo. Their web site is *http://www.ontrack.com*.

*DriveSavers*

An industry leader in data recovery that offers free estimates. They also have a terrific list of tips on their site (*http://www.drivesavers.com*), explaining how to anticipate and prevent drive problems before they occur.

*ActionFront*

An ISO 9001:2000 Certified company with data recovery labs in Atlanta, Santa Clara, and Toronto. On their web site (*http://www.actionfront.com*), you'll find a free 22-page Data Emergency Guide you can download, and it's definitely worth a read.

These are only a few of the many data recovery services out there, but they come highly recommended by competent IT professionals I know personally, so I pass them on to you. However, you should know that data recovery usually isn't cheap, so clean that tape drive regularly if you don't want to break your IT budget!

By the way, if you've ever had to use a data-recovery service yourself and would like to recommend them, feel free to post a comment on this book's web page (*http://www.oreilly.com/catalog/winsvrhks/*).

# Index

## A

account information searches, Active
    Directory, 95–96
account management, Active Directory
    users, 91–93
accounts
    Active Directory, listing
        disabled, 93–94
    administrator, renaming, 239
    guest, renaming, 239
    inactive, retrieving, 62–65
    no expiration, 93
    users, preventing local, 108–109
ActionFront, data recovery, 348
Active Directory, 62
    accounts, listing disabled, 93–94
    contact information,
        storing/displaying, 77–84
    DC (Domain Controller), checking
        existence, 77
    domains
        list all computers, 76
        listing, 76
    information display, 75–77
    OUs
        control delegation, 70–72
        creating automatically, 65
        creation automation, 65–68
        object modification, 69–70
        sending information to HTML
            page, 72–75
    site assigned, viewing, 76

    trust relationships, listing, 77
    users
        account expiration, 93
        account information
            searches, 95–96
        account management, 91–93
        disabling domain account, 92
        name change, 91
        Windows 2000, unlocking domain
            account, 92
        Windows XP icon restore, 85–87
ADM files, 34
administrator
    account renaming, security, 239
    domain controller access, 249–250
    local, listing, 241
AdminScripts folder, 191
ADSI (Active Directory Services
    Interface), xx
adsutil.vbs administrative script, 192
ADUC (Active Directory Users and
    Computers) console, 88
aging, DDNS, 115–120
antivirus software, 229
archivelogs.vbs code, 332
AspAllowSessionState property,
    metabase hacks, 183
AspBufferingOn property, metabase
    hacks, 183
AspProcessorThreadMax property,
    metabase hacks, 183
AspQueueConnectionTestTime
    property, metabase hacks, 184

We'd like to hear your suggestions for improving our indexes. Send email to *index@oreilly.com*.

AspScriptFileCacheSize property, metabase hacks, 184
AspThreadGateEnabled property, metabase hacks, 182
ASR (Automated System Recover) backups and, 336–342
assessment tools, security, 261
attribution for use of code examples, xxv
auditing tools, security, 261
automatic logon
    after booting, 10–13
    configuration
        manual, 10
        script method, 11
    Sysinternals, 13
Automatic Updates, 284–289
    FAQ, 293
    Group Policy and, 290
    patches and, 269
awareness, security and, 228

**B**

Backup Operators, 251
    Server Operators and, 253
Backup utility
    bks files, 304
    CAs, 310
backups
    access restriction, 254
    ASR and, 299, 337
    CA, 299
    CAs, 309–316
    command line, individual files, 303–306
    configuration
        local computers, 308
        remote computers, 308
    DFS namespace, 299, 334–336
    DHCP databases, 126
    EFS keys, 316–322
    ER files, collecting, 299–303
    Event logs, 331–334
    last resorts, 348
    metabase (IIS), 164–170
        quick backups, 166
    Recovery Agent keys, 321
    recovery file collection, 299–303
    security, 251–255

shadow copies, 322–331
System State, 299
    remote computers, 306–309
bks files, 304
boot disk, creating for network, 225
boot up, automatic log on, 10–13
businesses, security FAQ, 258

**C**

CacheISAPI property, metabase hacks, 185
CAs (certificate authorities)
    backups, 299, 309–316
    decommissioning, 316
    restores, 309–316
certification, anti-virus software, 229
Certification Authority Backup Wizard, 311
Chaccess.vbs administrative script, 192
ChangeIP.vbs code, 128
ChangeWINS.vbs code, 125
CheckMembership.vbs, 104
Cipher Security Tool for Windows 2000, 262
CIW (Client Installation Wizard), RIS and, 208
CIW (Client Installation Wizards), RIS and, 209–213
code examples in this book, use of, xxv
code listings
    archivelogs.vbs, 332
    ChangeIP.vbs, 128
    ChangeWINS.vbs, 125
    CheckMembership.vbs, 104
    CreateOU.wsf, 66
    CreateUserHomeDirectory.vbs, 106
    DelegateOU.vbs, 71
    DeleteOldComputers.vbs, 64
    DisabledAccounts.vbs, 93
    Disaster.bat, 300
    EnumerateHotfixes.vbs, 278
    ExportAdUsers.vbs, 79
    FindUser.vbs, 89
    GetAccountInfo.vbs, 95
    GetAdmins.vbs, 241
    GroupMember.vbs, 100
    LogoffIcon.vbs, 109
    ModifyUsersOU.vbs, 102
    ModifyUsers.vbs, 69

OU2HTML.vbs, 73
PassList.bat, 300
PWDNeverExpired.vbs, 97
ReadList.bat, 300
ReleaseRenew.vbs, 131
ServerList.txt, 300
Static2DHCP.vbs, 130
vbtree.vbs, 142
command line
    backup individual files, 303–306
    printer management, 144
    Registry keys find and replace, 9
    Run As, 3
    Windows component
        removal, 222–223
commands, executing on each computer
        in domain, 27–30
computer accounts, retrieving
        inactive, 62
computer name, printer management
        and, 147–163
computers
    automatic logon enabled
        finding, 256
    finding, security, 242–249
    listing all on domain, Active
        Directory, 76
CON2PRT command, 144
configuration
    anti-virus software, 230
    backups
        local computers, 308
        remote computers, 308
    logon, automatic, 10
    networks, changing with Netsh, 132
    remote computers, displaying, 43–56
    RIS, 208–209
configurations, 299
consumers, security FAQ, 258
contact information, storing/displaying
        in Active Directory, 77–84
CreateOU.wsf code, 66
CreateUserHomeDirectory.vbs
        code, 106
CSV files
    group membership and, 99–101
    password expiration, 97

**D**

Data Replicator, 57
databases
    DHCP
        backups, 126
        recovering, 127
    WINS, recreating damaged, 123
DC (Domain Controller), checking
        existence of, 77
DDNS (Dynamic DNS)
    aging, 115–120
    scavenging, 115–120
default printers, setting based on
        location, 146
DelegateOU.vbs code, 71
delegating, OU control, 70–72
DeleteOldComputers.vbs code, 64
DesktopChecker, 43–56
DFS (Distributed File System),
        namespace backups, 299,
        334–336
DFScmd utility, 335
DFSUtil, 336
DHCP (Dynamic Host Configuration
        Protocol), 111
    databases
        backups, 126
        recovering, 127
    scavenging and, 116
    servers
        availability, 126
        redundant, installing, 126
    static IP, changing from, 129
directory trees, displaying, 142
disabled accounts, listing in Active
        Directory, 93–94
DisabledAccounts.vbs code, 93
disabling EFS, 37–39
Disaster.bat code, 300
DNS (Domain Name System), 111
    error messages, 121
    newsgroups, 122
    troubleshooting, 120–123
domain controllers, admin
        access, 249–250
domains
    account disabling, Active
        Directory, 92
    Active Directory
        list all computers, 76

domains (*continued*)
    listing, 76
    computers, executing command on
        each, 27–30
    users, searching for, 88–90
downloading
    scripting engine, xx
    scripts, xx
drag and drop to Run menu, 7
drive mapping
    logon script information, 103–106
    network drives, 138
    renaming, 26
    shared folders, 155
DriveSavers, data recovery, 348

**E**

EFS (Encrypted File System)
    backups, 316–322
    disabling, 37–39
    keys
        backups, 299, 318
        restores, 320
encryption
    data backups, 318
    EFS, disabling, 37–39
enterprise patch management, 271
EnumerateHotfixes.vbs code, 278
environment variables
    adding, 31–34
    removing, 31–34
    retrieving, 31–34
ER (Emergency Repair)
    files
        collecting, 299–303
        winmsd.exe utility and, 300
    rdisk.exe and, 300
error messages, DNS, 121
Event logs
    backups, 331–334
    clearing, 331–334
    information script, 39–41
EventCombMT tools, 262
example code from this book, use
    of, xxv
executables, Run As and, 4
expiration
    passwords, checking for
        non-expired, 97–99
    user accounts, 93

ExportAdUsers.vbs code, 79
extending Group Policy, 34–37

**F**

FAQs
    Automatic Updates, 293
    patch management, 275–277
    security, 256–263
    Windows Update, 279–282
file types blocked, security, 232
files
    ADM, 34
    EFS, disabling, 38
    usage monitoring, 140
find and replace in command line,
        Registry keys, 9
FindUser.vbs code, 89
folders
    AdminScripts, 191
    EFS, disabling, 38
    shared, drive mapping, 155

**G**

GetAccountInfo.vbs code, 95
GetAdmins.vbs code, 241
government security clearance, 260
GPO (Group Policy Object), 34
group membership
    enumerating to CSV file, 99–101
    logon script information, 103–106
Group Policy
    ADM files, 34
    Automatic Updates and, 290
    extending, 34–37
GroupMember.vbs code, 100
guest account, renaming, 239
GUI
    IIS and, 170
    Run As and, 2

**H**

hiding/showing metabase, 187–189
HotFix & Security Bulletin Service, 276
hotfixes, 265
    downloadable, 276
    listing installed, 277
HTML, OU display, 72–75
Hyena utility, file use and, 140

# I

icons, logoff on desktop, 109
ID 36907, metabase hacks, 185
IIS 5
   administration scripts, 189
   metabase backups, restoring, 172
   metabase, location map, 175
   socket pooling, disabling, 199
IIS 6
   administrative scripts, 193
   metabase
      backups, 168
      location map, 177
      restoring backups, 173
      XML Map, 179
   socket pooling, disabling, 200
IIS (Internet Information Services)
   administration scripts, 189–199
   introduction, 164
   metabase backup, 164–170
   web servers, running, 199–201
IISFAQ web site, 201
inactive accounts
   retrieving, 62–65
installation
   RIS, 206
   Windows components, 224
Instant Network Boot Disk, 225
interception, security and, 231
intrustion detection tools, 261
IP addresses
   releasing, 131
   renewing, 131
IP (Internet Protocol)
   adapter information, changing, 128
   static, switching to DHCP, 129

# K

KB 824146 Scanning Tool, 261

# L

local accounts, preventing user
      creation, 108–109
local administrators, listing, 241
local machines, backup
      configuration, 308
lockdown tools, security, 261

log on
   automatic
      after booting, 10–13
      finding enabled computers, 256
      manual configuration, 10
      script method, 11
      Sysinternals, 13
   printer management based on
      computer name, 147–163
logical structure of metabase, 174
logoff icons, placing on desktop, 109
LogoffIcon.vbs code, 109
logon scripts
   drive mapping information, 103–106
   membership checking, 103–106
Lost Password Recovery, 57

# M

mapped drives
   logon script information, 103–106
   renaming, 26
mapping drives
   network drives, 138
   shared folders, 155
mapping metabase, 173–180
mappings, group membership and, 152
MaxEndPointConnections property,
      metabase hacks, 182
MBSA (Microsoft Baseline Security
      Analyzer), 261
   support, 277
membership, logon script
      information, 103–106
metabase
   backing up, 164–170
      quick backups, 166
   hacks, 180–187
   hiding, 187–189
   logical structure, 174
   management scripts, 194
   mapping, 173–180
   physical structure, 178
   restoring, 171–173
   Windows Backup utility, 165
MetaEdit, 167
Microsoft
   security and, 259
      reporting, 259
      tools, 260–263

ModifyUsersOU.vbs, 102
ModifyUsers.vbs code, 69
MSRC ratings system, 265
myITforum.com, 58

## N

Netsh
    network configuration, 132
    network configuration settings, 132
network adapters
    IP information, 128
    WINS settings, 124
Network View, 58
networks
    anti-virus software, 229
    boot disk, creating, 225
    configuration, changing with
        Netsh, 132
    drive mapping, 138
    file useage, 140
    NICs, removing orphaned, 133
    printers, connecting to shared, 154
    Run As and, 5
    service managment, remote
        machines, 111–115
    virus-free, 227–236
newsgroups, DNS, 122
NICs (network interface cards)
    orphaned, removing, 133
    two-NIC environment, NLB
        and, 135
NLB (Network Load Balancing),
        implementing, 135
ntbackup, command line and, 303

## O

Ontrack, data recovery, 348
organization of book, xxi
orphaned NICs
    removing, 133
OU2HTML.vbs code, 73
OUs (organizational units), 62
    control delegation, 70–72
    creating, automating, 65–68
    HTML page display, 72–75
    objects, modifying, 69–70
    users
        property modification, 102–103

## P

PassList.bat code, 300
passwords
    expiration, checking for
        non-expired, 97–99
    Lost Password Recovery tool, 57
    policies, 259
    users changing, 91
patch management
    best practices, 264–270
    enterprise patch
        management, 271–275
    FAQ, 275–277
    introduction, 264
    policies, 266
    processes, 266
    tools, 261, 269
    vulnerable systems and, 271
patches
    Automatic Updates, 269, 284–289
    business impact, 272
    distribution, 273
    email notification, 276
    flavors, 265
    hotfixes, 265
        downloadable, 276
    MSRC ratings system, 265
    order of application, 279
    roll-ups, 265
    service packs, 265
    SMS, 270
    SUS, 270
    testing, 274
    Windows Update FAQ, 279–282
permissions for using code
        examples, xxv
permissions, user
        configuration, 106–107
physical structure of metabase, 178
PPP (Policy, Process, Persistence), 266
Print Manager Plus, 147
printers
    computer name and, 147–163
    default, setting based on
        location, 146
    managing automatically, 144
    mappings, group membership
        and, 152
    network, connecting to shared, 154

Printers folder, Run As, 3
processes, finish before
  terminating, 13–21
PWDNeverExpired.vbs, 97

## Q

QChain, 261
quick backups, metabase, 166

## R

rdisk.exe, ER files, 300
ReadList.bat code, 300
recovery
  ASR (Automated System
    Recover), 336–342
  file collection, 299–303
  startup troubleshooting, 342–347
Recovery Agents, key backups, 321
redundant DHCP servers,
  installing, 126
Regfind utility, 9, 256
Registry keys, find and replace in
  command line, 9
ReleaseRenew.vbs code, 131
releasing IP addresses, 131
Remote Assistance, shortcuts to, 42–43
remote computers
  backups
    configuration, 308
    System State, 306–309
  configuration display, 43–56
  network services,
    managing, 111–115
  shut down, 21–26
renaming mapped drives, 26
renewing IP addresses, 131
Restore Groups, 254
restores
  CAs, 309–316
  EFS keys, 320
  metabase, 171–173
RFCs (Request For Comments), 262
RIS (Remote Installation Services), 203
  CIW And, 209–213
  configuration, 208–209
  customizing, 208–214
  installation, 206
  overview, 203–207
  predefining computer accounts, 209

system requirements, 204
tuning, 214–216
Windows images deployment, 213
roll-ups, 265
Run As, 1, 2
  command line, 3
  executables and, 4
  GUI and, 2
  limitations, 3
  network shares and, 5
  Printers folder, 3
  shortcuts, 5
  Task Manager, 5
  Windows Explorer and, 4
Run menu, drag and drop to, 7
RUNDLL32 command, 145

## S

scanning
  anti-virus software, 230
  tools for, 261
scavenging, DDNS, 115–120
scripting engine, downloading, xx
scripts
  automatic logon, 11
  downloading, xx
  event log information, 39–41
  IIS administration, 189–199
  running remotely, 197
  testing, 62
  VB, WMI agents and, xx
Secondary Logon service (see Run As)
Secure Sockets Layer, clearing, 281
security
  administrator
    account renaming, 239
    local, listing, 241
  antivirus FAQ, 237
  assessment tools, 261
  auditing tools, 261
  awareness and, 228
  Backup Operators, 251
  backups, 251–255
  computers, finding, 242–249
  domain controllers, admin
    access, 249–250
  FAQ, 257–260
  file types blocked, 232
  government clearance, 260

security (*continued*)
  guest account, renaming, 239
  interception and, 231
  intrusion detection tools, 261
  lockdown tools, 261
  Microsoft, 259
    reporting, 259
    tools, 260–263
  password policies, 259
  patch management tools, 261
  reporting to government
      authorities, 260
  software update tools, 261
  virus protection
    FAQ, 237, 238
    tools, 262
  virus-free networks, 227–236
  vulnerability, 258
Server Monitor Lite, 57
Server Operators, Backup Operators
    and, 253
ServerListenBacklog property, metabase
    hacks and, 180
ServerList.txt code, 300
service packs, 265
Services node, remote machine
    management, 111–115
shadow copies
  backups and, 322–331
  implementation, 323
  uses, 328
shared folders, drive mapping, 155
shortcuts
  to Remote Assistance, 42–43
  Run As, 5
shut down remote computers, 21–26
SMS (Systems Management Server), 270
socket pooling, 199
  disabling
    IIS 5, 199
    IIS 6, 200
    reasons for, 201
software update tools, security, 261
SQL Server 2000 Security tools, 262
startup, troubleshooting, 342–347
static IPs, DHCP switch, 129
Static2DHCP.vbs code, 130
SUS (Software Update Services), 261
  patches and, 270
Sysinternals, auto log on, 13

SysPrep, Windows deployment
    and, 216–222
system requirements, RIS, 204
System State, backups, 299
  remote computers, 306–309

**T**

Task Manager, Run As and, 5
termination, finish process prior
    to, 13–21
testing scripts, 62
third-party tools, 56
  Data Replicator, 57
  Lost Password Recovery, 57
  myITforum.com, 58
  Network View, 58
  Server Monitor Lite, 57
  VNC (Virtual Network
      Computing), 57
tools
  DNS troubleshooting, 120
  patch management, 269
  third-party, 56
    Data Replicator, 57
    Lost Password Recovery, 57
    myITforum.com, 58
    Network View, 58
    Server Monitor Lite, 57
    VNC, 57
trust relationships, listing in Active
    Directory, 77

**U**

updates
  tools for, 261
UrlScan Security Tool, 261
users
  account information search, Active
      Directory, 95–96
  accounts, no expiration, 93
  Active Directory
    account management, 91–93
    disabling domain account, 92
    name changes, 91
  groups, enumerating membership to
      CSV file, 99–101
  home directory
      configuration, 106–107
  local accounts, preventing
      creation, 108–109

membership, logon script
information, 103–106
OU, properties
modification, 102–103
passwords, changing, 91
permissions, configuring, 106–107
searching for, 88–90

## V

variables
environment
adding, 31–34
removing, 31–34
retrieving, 31–34
vbtree.vbs code, 142
virus protection
FAQ, 237
tools, 262
virus-free networks
anti-virus software, 229
basics, 227–236
file types blocked, 232
interception and, 231
VNC (Virtual Network Computing), 57
VSS (Volume Shadow Copy Service)
backups and, 322–331
implementing copies, 323
shadow copy uses, 328

## W

web applications, administrative
scripts, 196
Web Server Lockdown Wizard, 261
web servers, IIS and, 199
web sites
administrative scripts, 193
DNS troubleshooting tools, 120
IISFAQ, 201
Windows
command line, removing
components, 222–223
deployment, SysPrep and, 216–222
image deployment, RIS and, 213

installing components,
unattended, 224
Windows 2000, locking accounts, 92
Windows 2000/3000, implementing
NLB, 135
Windows Backup utility, metabase, 165
Windows Explorer, Run As and, 4
Windows NT, recreating WINS
databases, 124
Windows Server 2000/3000, recreating
WINS databases, 124
Windows Update
catalog, 282–284
controls, manual install, 282
Critical Updates, personalizing, 281
FAQ, 279–282
information collection, 280
removing items, 281
schedule changes, 281
Secure Sockets Layer and, 281
Windows XP Active Directory icon
restore, 85–87
winmsd.exe utility, ER files and, 300
WINS (Windows Internet Name
Service), 111
databases, recreating damaged, 123
settings, changing for all
adapters, 124
WMI (Windows Management
Instrumentation)
agents, VB scripts and, xx
IIS administration, 189
workstation, printer settings, 151
WSH (Windows Scripting Host), IIS
administration, 189

## X

XML metabase map, IIS 6, 179

# Colophon

Our look is the result of reader comments, our own experimentation, and feedback from distribution channels. Distinctive covers complement our distinctive approach to technical topics, breathing personality and life into potentially dry subjects.

The tool on the cover of *Windows Server Hacks* is a squeegee, which dates back to the Middle Ages when fishermen used a wooden ancestor of this tool called a squilgee to remove fish entrails from the decks of their boats. In *Moby Dick*, author Herman Melville describes this tool known as a nipper, describing them as "leathern" squeegees cut from the tail of a whale. In Melville's story, not only does this precursor to the squeegee clean whale oil from the deck, but "by nameless blandishments, as of magic, allures along with it all impurities."

The modern squeegee was born at the turn of the 20th century, when window washers began using a "Chicago squeegee." This heavy steel contraption used two rubber blades, held into place by 12 screws. While easier to use than implements made of wood and whale tails, it was far from perfect. One window cleaner, Ettore Steccone, set out to improve the squeegee, and in 1936 he patented a device called the New Deal. This squeegee, now called the Ettore, is still in wide use by professional window cleaners today. Though Steccone eventually lost his patent, the light weight and distinctive single slit-cut rubber blade of his tool served as a blueprint for all squeegees that followed.

Philip Dangler was the production editor and proofreader for *Windows Server Hacks*. Brian Sawyer was the copyeditor. Marlowe Shaeffer, Mary Brady, and Darren Kelly provided quality control. Johnna VanHoose Dinse wrote the index.

Hanna Dyer designed the cover of this book, based on a series design by Edie Freedman. The cover image of a squeegee is an original photgraph by Hanna Dyer. Emma Colby produced the cover layout with QuarkXPress 4.1 using Adobe's ITC Garamond and Helvetica Neue fonts.

David Futato designed the interior layout. Andrew Savikas converted this book to FrameMaker 5.5.6 with a format conversion tool created by Erik Ray, Jason McIntosh, Neil Walls, and Mike Sierra that uses Perl and XML technologies. The text font is Linotype Birka; the heading font is Adobe Helvetica Neue Condensed; and the code font is LucasFont's TheSans Mono Condensed. The illustrations that appear in the book were produced by Robert Romano and Jessamyn Read using Macromedia FreeHand 9 and Adobe Photoshop 6. This colophon was written by Philip Dangler.